A SWEDISI.

MW01038914

A Liberal European Nation's Struggle with Racism and Xenophobia, 1990-2000

Dennis Sven Nordin

University Press of America,® Inc.
Lanham · Boulder · New York · Toronto · Oxford

Copyright © 2005 by
University Press of America,® Inc.
4501 Forbes Boulevard
Suite 200
Lanham, Maryland 20706
UPA Acquisitions Department (301) 459-3366

PO Box 317
Oxford
OX2 9RU, UK

Library of Congress Control Number: 2005921028
ISBN 0-7618-3151-7 (paperback : alk. ppr.)

Dedication

A Swedish Dilemma is dedicated to victims everywhere who have not been able to realize their dreams and full potential because of discrimination.

CONTENTS

Tables

Preface

By escaping wars since the Napoleonic Era and moralizing to the world about correct values and courses of action, Sweden has gained an enviable reputation as a nation above many of the problems afflicting other lands. Whether the issue was involvement of the United States in Vietnam or apartheid in South Africa, the result was preaching that would flow from Swedes either about the immorality of warfare or about the evils of discrimination. Since these lessons had come with assertiveness and passion, a global impression developed about a Nordic paradise where every resident had equal opportunities, prosperity, peace, and freedom. To solidify herself as a haven from want and despair, Sweden began accepting refugees after 1945 from oppressive regimes and war zones. As people in need received asylum, word spread of Scandinavian openness and generosity, thereby generating many additional applicants for what the Swedes were willing to offer.

A process begun first on a significant scale with the Hungarian freedom fighters in 1956 would continue without any measurable internal protest or strife until Sweden's industrial expansion slowed and unemployment grew. Resentment caused by mounting competition for resources and jobs terminated quickly whatever fantasies and fascination Swedes might have had in the beginning with ethnic and racial diversity in their once largely homogeneous population. Even at the outset of accepting into the Nordic nation almost everyone with a horror story from his or her homeland, Sweden did not fully integrate her newcomers and provide them with equal opportunities. From the outset there were almost always definitely set limits and barriers which confronted a majority of nonethnic Swedes. No matter their educations, training, and experiences, they suffered a plight as victims and not as beneficiaries of fair and equal treatment. In final analysis nothing in their backgrounds could qualify them to succeed or win in head-to-head competitions with the indigenous citizenry. For meaningful, good-paying jobs, public- and private-sector employers simply did not hire individuals with non-Swedish names and credentials. Outside the job market similar discriminatory experiences would become the rule in housing, politics, education, justice, etc.

A Swedish Dilemma captures the realities of violence and discrimination faced by Sweden's immigrants from 1990 through 2000. During this period a shift by a determined corps of fanatic resisters to Sweden accepting additional refugees and immigrants occurred. In response politicians pandered to the worst offenders and refused to legislate effectively on behalf of the rights of minorities. Moreover the menace of individuals who had struck violently and maliciously at nonethnic Swedes was never taken seriously. Offenders who denied basic human rights and even murderers rarely received penalties from Swedish courts as true reflections of the seriousness of the crimes committed.

The author lived in Sweden during two periods, 1975-78 and 1989-2001, as an immigrant of Swedish emigrant parents. During the first experience employers never considered his credentials equal to any but the most menial tasks, this despite a doctorate from an American university and his ethnic heritage. He then did what many other aliens would do; he started a business based upon ties to his native country. During the second round of living in Sweden, the author did not have problems because of a transfer of sorts of being able to go from America to Sweden with the same employer. Nevertheless it was during the second time in the Scandinavian nation that a changed attitude was observed toward aliens. As a result the author began to ask outsiders about their experiences. Since his Swedish is clearly accented by lazy American vowels, immigrants opened up to him with their tales of woe. This general response spurred an interest to look more formally into the problems faced by minorities in the population of Sweden.

As the first chapter clearly indicates, Sweden's problems are not unique; all across Western Europe newcomers confronted much the same hostility as those who came to Sweden. Hopefully, therefore, this study will initiate work on relations in other countries. It is only through exposure that improvements and progress can occur. Inasmuch as problems are found throughout much of the continent, there were reasons for a focus on Sweden. First there is present there an arrogance of superiority about abilities to handle problems which other nations have had and not resolved. Second firsthand experiences advised the author of inconsistencies found in what Sweden was projecting about herself to the world and what the nation was practicing at home. Third published sources were readily available and understandable to the author.

Certain people deserve credit for their assistance in making this study possible. First of all every person who opened up to the author must receive praise and gratitude. Without their willingness to trust him with their stories of horror and anguish, inspiration for this book would have been missing. Also a word of thanks must go to Professors Roy V. Scott and JohnPeter Horst Grill for reading the manuscript and suggesting improvements. Gratefulness must also go to the two gentlemen who fetched literally thousands of reels of microfilm at the Swedish newspaper library at Lund University and to staff members at the main library on this campus, who secured countless interlibrary loans. For preparing the manuscript for camera-ready condition, John Johnsey at Mississippi State University deserves special mention for doing a painstaking job skillfully. Swedish wife Gun deserves an endurance prize for tolerating continuous complaints about her native country's flaws. Last but certainly not least, the author's parents who had emigrated from Sweden to the United States during the 1920s showed their son how successful immigrants could be, if given the chance, to contribute to a new society and live as comfortably as any middle-class native couple.

Dennis S. Nordin

Mississippi State University, Mississippi State, Mississippi
December 15, 2004

Chapter I

European Diasporas & Swedish Traditions

Europe has a problem engulfing every aspect of the continent's life and challenging experts and lay citizens alike as few matters have done after the Axis Powers' defeat in 1945 and communism's demise in 1991. Sweeping across the continent and covering it in pain and shock from Finland to Portugal and the British Isles to Italy are racism and xenophobia, two negative forces have emerged to pose as twin menaces and a great contemporary challenge. Although they had been sapping Europeans' energy and wits on an increasing scale ever since the Second World War, the spark for the initial signs of open resentment came with an outbreak of civil war in the former Yugoslavia and the corresponding flood of refugees into Western Europe from the Balkans.

All of a sudden people were noticing tremendous growths of minorities in their countries. Recipients first appeared apathetic, watching with no apparent concern as a massive surge of humanity was arriving with strange names and foreign languages in Europe's perceived-to-be homogeneous lands. Quickly, however, native populations' passivity turned into worry and resentment. Almost as soon as the newcomers' costs to taxpayers had become apparent, there were public outcries and expressions of discontent among receiving countries' native populations. If there had been any previous tolerance or empathy for displaced, savaged refugees quartered provisionally in others' homelands, it gave way to economic self-interest and an unwillingness to share resources with strangers. Nations became tribal bastions ravaged by "We-and-They" divisions complete with racial violence, discrimination, legal constraints, hateful political parties and organizations founded on xenophobia, and alien ghettoizations.

Put simply Europeans no longer had any reason to sneer; a smugness and condescension about the United States having contradicted her national ideals with the presence of a downtrodden black minority had lost appropriateness. In a turnabout Americans now held a superior position, assuming a critic's role while confirming in the process what nationalistic rationalizers had responded to Europeans' supercilious criticisms of and advice to the United States about the shamefulness of denying fairness and justice to African Americans. For chauvenistic defenders of American wrongs, a stock reply had been "if you were to have a minority, things would be no different in your country."

In regard to handling minority questions, Sweden—like other European states—was accustomed to being on the giving end of criticisms. During America's great crusade for civil rights and subsequent civil disorder, Swedish television news teams and reporters had literally bivouaced in the United States, waiting for a story to unfold from Alabama, Mississippi, Watts, Detroit, or Harlem. With an undertone of superiority, prime-time specials covered either Southern white resistance to societal change or destructive manifestations of urban despair.[1]

Swedish interest in African Americans is rooted in research begun on the topic in the late 1930s by a Stockholm professor. During the summer of 1937, acting on behalf of fellow trustees of the Carnegie Corporation, Frederick P. Keppel invited Gunnar Myrdal to direct a major study on African Americans. After preliminary correspondence exchanges and then some intense personal discussions in the spring of 1938, there was agreement; Myrdal accepted the challenge to head the project.

Choosing the Swede had followed a desire to find someone "with a fresh mind, uninfluenced by traditional attitudes or by earlier conclusions." Hence the board of trustees had concluded an "import" candidate from a nation without an imperial history would best suit their endeavor. These conditions had led searchers to Switzerland and the Nordic countries and had ended with their selection of Myrdal, a relatively young scholar whose work as a social economist at the University of Stockholm and as a Spelman Fund fellow in the United States had already achieved international recognition. Freeing himself of obligations at home, the Swede set out for the United States at summer's end.

On September 10, 1938, or more than one year after Keppel's first contacts with Myrdal about a proposal, the Swedish professor arrived in the United States anxious to begin the most comprehensive probe ever undertaken of the American minority. To gather impressions and discover firsthand what might lay ahead, the visiting scholar—accompanied by fellow Swede Richard Sterner of the Royal Social Board and hosted by Southerner Jackson Davis—toured the South by automobile. With their "eyes wide open," the three men were on what Myrdal would describe later as "an exploratory journey," gathering impressions but intentionally not collecting data. During the three men's probe of Dixie, they stopped often to inspect educational facilities, commercial enterprises, factories, farms, plantations, churches, and governmental entities. As scholars in search of information, their stops meant, of course, exploiting opportunities to question—"all sorts of people, colored and white"—educators, preachers, sharecroppers, police officers, politicians, journalists, and assembly workers. Myrdal viewed his travel in the South as an epiphany. To Keppel in a memorandum that is included in the preface of *An American Dilemma*, the Swede confessed that without having had his firsthand encounters with people from the South, his study would have lacked "concrete points at which to be fixed."

The Swedish investigator's eyeopening experience of witnessing blacks in the region improved his frame of reference for reviewing bibliographies on African Americans' social, political, educational, and economic status. Once engaged in the more formal side of research as his prelude to soliciting critical feedbacks to proposals and conclusions, Myrdal intermixed his schedule with a combination of library work and solicitations of advice. He conversed and corresponded with experts, trying in the process to learn as much as possible about a minority from American specialists. Satisfied he had found direction for a study, Myrdal—with Carnegie board approval and financial support— assembled a six-member staff to begin full-time research. To fill gaps and provide supplementary expertise and collaboration, the project director relied upon help from several experts. Clearly from the outset of Myrdal's endeavor, there was striving after thoroughness. The guest researcher wanted apparently to look at every phase of the African American existence. As he put it, the goal was "a more complete record than is up to now available of American shortcomings in this field."

As a final product, *An American Dilemma* fulfilled its creator's ambitions as the consummate study on African Americans heretofore published, but as is so commonplace with Nordic scholarship, it reflected the penchant of its region's academicians for excessive organizational breaks. Accordingly the book has eleven parts, 45 chapters, and more than 315 sections. So many divisions and subdivisions distract somewhat from the author's intention of providing a cohesive narrative on American race relations. Myrdal's pigeonholing is only one of several problems with the study. Its lifelessness and stodgy presentation of facts make it difficult to read. By preparing his book in classic Nordic style without any passion and emotion, the Swede showed little interest in providing specific examples of individual African Americans experiencing life under the handicap of second-class citizenship. In other words Myrdal did not use any of human-interest stories that he had heard during his guided travels through the South in 1938. The result is an encyclopedic-like tedium so typical of works by researchers with Myrdal's regional background. At treating a subject, he—like so many Nordic contemporaries and their academic heirs with topics— seemingly had allowed mulish "scientific" detachment overwhelm all other considerations. As a result *An American Dilemma* emerged spiritless and colorless.

For alternative perspectives Myrdal neither consulted black newspapers nor persons. Ignoring without explanation these sources contributed to dullness and one-sidedness. Worse failures than not consulting the African American press and considering personal viewpoints led to distorted optimism about Northern attitudes and an incorrect prediction about future racial bliss in the North. Even more devastating, there was a misreading of the South. As investigators working with Otto Kerner on a report on white-black relations would show a generation later, significant sectional differences on race were nonexistent. Thus the visiting scholar missed a salient point; on almost equal terms and to similar degree, racism was a national phenomenon. By relying exclusively upon leftists and activists, the visitor also missed accommodating views from, for example, Congressman Arthur W. Mitchell, newspapermen John Mitchell and P. B. Young, as well as prominent members of the Tuskegee Machine; their moderation might have balanced Myrdal's overall perspectives. After all these

African American leaders were not as impatient with and unsympathetic toward *all* white Southerners as the minority race's Northern spokespersons.[2]

Weaknesses aside, Myrdal's *An American Dilemma: The Negro Problem and Modern Democracy* has proven itself inspirational and prophetic in ways never envisaged by the Swedish social scientist. Just as he—a European—had been the choice of Americans interested in developing a study on the divisive domestic cancer of racism, there began a corresponding need for an impartial outsider's probe into and documentation of "Old World" racism and xenophobia. Since the model is a book about an American problem by a Swede, it follows logically then that an outsider is best suited to reversing matters with a close examination of Sweden for possible warts and blemishes on her record.[3]

Without a figurative "axe to grind," the author's purposes of *A Swedish Dilemma: A Liberal European Nation's Struggle with Xenophobia and Racism, 1990-2000* are threefold. In the first place there is exploration into prejudice's roots to ascertain how small pockets of hatred and distrust have grown by menacing proportions into a national crisis. Secondly there is probing to see what Sweden has been doing about a seriously disruptive force in her midst. Finally there are judgments about why Swedish measures have been failing along with suggestions from successful American experiences with racial, ethnic, and cultural diversity for conceivably better alternatives.   Behind *A Swedish Dilemma* lies one simple commitment: without compromise or equivocation, its intents are respect and praise for actions and policies aimed at national cohesion in a societal framework that fosters deference to personal rights regardless of race, creed, gender, and ethnic background. For refugee matters the principles established by a United Nations commission in 1951 determine minimally acceptable actions and policies.

To avoid the false impression that xenophobia and racism are exclusive to Sweden, expression about the general negative reactions to minorities allover Europe is provided as a backdrop to the Nordic nation's problems. Logically enough the topic's introduction should begin with examining stereotypes and images. Almost universally—from depictions in political cartoons to those in motion pictures—mental pictures have developed about how residents from different countries appear and behave.   For example mention or imagine Scandinavians, and tall, blue-eyed, fair-complexioned, blond-haired people are in focus. Shy and self-conscious, they almost always appear intimidated by intimacy and emotion. Ingmar Bergman's films have contributed to the images with Erland Josephson and Liv Ullmann matching preconceived mental portraits of Nordic residents. In contrast, imagemakers have depicted French and Italian men as suave and romantic. Meanwhile English counterparts generally emerge as stiff and formal, not at all unlike the character played by John Cleese in *A Fish Named Wanda*.   Moreover a visit to European countries does little to correct misconceptions.   In general, during excursions to foreign nations, tourists see only cities' historic hubs and quaint country villages; most visitors encounter just the kind of people they had expected to see in particular lands. Of generally no interest, on the extreme outskirts of metropolitan areas, immigrant ghetto communities exist but almost anonymously. Not mentioned in visitor guides and excluded from bus tours, hidden enclaves house Europe's minorities.

Four reasons account for European nations' multiethnicity. First of all the minorities responded to organized recruitments and employee searches, filling labor shortages and performing undesirable tasks. In Germany *der gastarbeiter* from Turkey best exemplifies this group. Secondly countries with imperialistic pasts often have gained many residents as reminders of once flourishing colonial eras. France has millions of people with Southeast Asian, North African, and sub-Saharan African heritages; Great Britain has West Indians, Indians, Africans, and Pakistanis; and Indonesians, Surinamese, and Lesser Antilleans populate the Netherlands. Third there are refugees who fled wars and famines. In 1992, for example, two-thirds of exile-seekers or 438,200 individuals sought German asylum. Finally there are immigrants. More than five percent of Belgium's population were arrivals from other European Union states.

To find evidence of all four categories of European "foreigners," just check national soccer and Olympic squads; team members often defy stereotypes of how athletes should look from competing nations. France's World Cup-winning footballers had European, African, and Arabic roots, with Zinedine Zidane, the son of Algerian-immigrant parents, the most celebrated of them all. After success before a largely native French audience, these athletes with multinational roots became national heroes to a million people—including President Jacques Chirac and Prime Minister Lionel Jospin—who feted them at Champs Elysées and who momentarily forgot their heroic sportsmen's origins.

Excepting when glory comes to a European nation because of foreigners' accomplishments, immigrants usually have daily lives filled with hostility, suspicion, and prejudice. Problems for minorities have persisted, defying centuries of immigration. Counter to a popular belief, European countries qualifying in 2000 as immigrant lands witnessed influxes of strangers into them over many centuries. Invading Turks, Tartars, Romany, Jews, Moors, and Vikings had swept into different parts of the continent, settling and leaving their imprints. Royal families' intermarriages sealed alliances and brought the households of different nationalities into power; toiling at the service of nobles and kings were thousands of imported artisans and artists. Less spectacularly for more than a century, newcomers migrated into Europe, seeking basically the same advantages as immigrants expected from the United States, Canada, and Australia.

France provides a good example of how diversity occurred. Her population for example in 1886 included a million foreigners or about 2.5 percent of all residents. North Africans began arriving after 1910 because French chemical plants, steelworks, and automobile factories were recruiting Belgians, Italians, Poles, Armenians, and Moroccans. In 1929 aliens in the Republic represented seven percent of the population. During the next year more outsiders came to France than to the United States. Another surge of industrial recruitees began in the 1960s with the arrivals of North Africans, Yugoslavs, and Portuguese. This wave has been ongoing as immigrants have continued to come in from a once mighty French empire.

A mixed reaction to the history of immigration followed. On the one hand the Revolution of 1789 bequeathed a legendary ideal of a single, homogenous nation, whereby Frenchness had not so much to do with ethnicity as it would to conforming to things French. It meant adhering to France's unwritten code of acceptable behavior for residents, preferring French over other languages and placing French national interests first. These requirements form its theoretical bases and practical adjustments. There are foreigners who have followed these tenets but are still excluded because a counter force prevails to offset the full acceptance of outsiders. It results from what French natives refer to as *francais de souche*. Translated literally, it means people of "real" French stock. For nativists only these people should enjoy full citizenship. According to Mouloud Aounit, a representative of the Movement against Racism and for Friendship between People, "France is afraid of itself because it is a country of immigration, but has never accepted itself as such."

Denial's consequences have been manyfold. In both local and national politics, its effects exist in the extreme right-wing National Front—split into Jean-Marie LePen and Bruno Mégret factions—movement. In control of some municipalities and a brokering force in others, the party through its platform maintains an overriding message: "national preference" in the distributions of welfare, jobs, housing, education, and miscellaneous governmental services should be the right of *francais de souche*. LePen has repeatedly called on authorities to "send home" three million people who, in his judgment, have not met the three mentioned requirements for French residency. With so many aliens in the country, LePen and Mégret express worries about French national identity being at stake. If the majority does not face reality and take immediate action, "tomorrow our country becomes covered in mosques."

A visit to the outskirt of any large French city confirms the presence of multitudes who remain at best on the peripheries and at worst completely outside the mainstreams of traditional French life. Teenagers outwardly defy Frenchification as they listen to rappers like "Nique Ta Mére" (Screw Your Mother) with such nihilistic messages as "We've got nothing to lose, because we've never had a thing" and with dire warnings to ethnic Frenchmen not "to sleep soundly: the *bourgeoisie* should tremble, the rabble is in town." Like her tricolored flag, France has clearly trifurcated, with *une blanche majorité* confronted and challenged by *une beure* (slang for Arab) *minorité* and *une noire minorité*. Visually suburban *banlieue* (slums) bear greater resemblance to South Bronx than to Paris' elegant residential neighborhoods. At skyscraper housing estates bordering French cities, graffiti, paper debris, and broken glass abound along with roaming gangs of youths fighting each other and imperiling peacefulness for other residents. Racial violence has so overtaken immigrant enclaves in Paris' Seine-Saint-Denis area that 300 sport clubs with over 40,000 active members are under Ministry of Athletics orders not to compete with each other.

Socially and authoritatively parents are often separated from their children. Although as an immediate consequence of a 1974 change in French law, male workers from North Africans were finally granted permission to bring spouses and children into France, a common consequence has been the development of serious generational gaps within these families. Torn between their parents' world and the street, immigrant offspring have opted altogether too often for the latter's temptations. During the late 1980s and early 1990s, a generation of French-born descendants of North Africans reached maturity without firsthand knowledge of their parents' homelands. According to Algerian intellectual and French resident Tahar Ben Jelloun, patriarchs' nostalgic desires to return home to Algeria, Morocco, or Tunisia have met firm opposition from their offspring. Jelloun, in an article entitled "The Immigrants' Impossible Return Trip," tells the story of a Moroccan father who took a French pension and returned alone to North Africa, leaving behind a wife and several dependent children. After a marriage to a much younger woman—his privilege under Moroccan law—he erred by returning to his family's home in France in order to collect personal belongings. An argument ensued over his financial responsibilities; it ended with a jilted wife fatally stabbing her estranged husband.

Overall France has had a mixed record with outsiders. On a positive note she has bestowed an everlasting embrace on foreign intellectuals and artists and given them an exalted place in society. There has even been tolerance of eccentric behavior from these special strangers in her midst. Excepting these granted allowances for an elite group, more than fifty percent of the ethnically French population, according to opinion polls, has racist tendencies; the group associates *Maghrebi* neighborhoods with drugs, violence, and petty crime.

As split as the nation appears, French leftists find several hopeful signs for improvement that contradict unfavorable associations with foreigners. First, according to some measures of public opinion, a French majority opposes discrimination despite an otherwise racist judgment about minority peoples. Second National Front popularity seemingly has peaked, and support for its racist platform is in decline. Third and perhaps the best indication of changing French attitudes toward minorities, mixed marriages that pair Christians and Muslims have become commonplace.[4]

Unlike France where difficulties have prevailed because of an unwillingness to accept peoples who have resisted integration into mainline society, racists in Germany and Great Britain have sought removals of visible minorities from their nations because of desires to maintain homogeneity. To frighten away prospective immigrants and intimidate foreigners already in these countries, nativists have used violence. Earlier in the United Kingdom than elsewhere, shaven heads for racist white youths became symbolic of their disdain for blacks, Asians, and punks. Skinheads at first were somewhat apolitical, belonging to no particular party or organization. Leaderless and spontaneous, they roamed in packs, engaging in unprovoked violence. From their prowling after victims, racist gangs spotted and assaulted spiked-hair punks as well as innocent people of color; unprovoked, these attacks occurred in response to unfortunate people being in the wrong place at the wrong time. In addition English hoodlums sought out and terrorized many immigrant shopkeepers.

Although links to hate organizations with fascistic characteristics have existed, especially among football hooligans, many studies by social scientists of skinheads and neo-Nazis have not found English extremist leaders acting as grand strategists with plots of specific acts of violence; these experts explain the phenomenon by either emphasizing youth unemployment or blaming it on harmful effects from the British Empire's decline on the national psyche. A third group of investigators fault Britain's law-enforcement profession's for ignoring and downplaying racism. In an atmosphere where public servants charged with enforcing law, investigating crimes, and protecting individuals have failed to take their duties responsibly if sufferers are nonwhites and in a nation with a legacy of cruel brutality of Third World populations, it should come as no surprise how many English people either have looked indifferently at racist acts or have participated in them.

It all emerged in a judicial police review released February 24, 1999. The publication of the judges' findings followed a lengthy investigation into all the circumstances that had surrounded the death of Stephen Lawrence almost six years earlier. The report was extremely critical of law enforcement's role and its ineptitude at probing for clues. With a better collection of evidence, a court might have been able to convict the racists who had murdered a young black Londoner in 1993. Moved to action by the report's content, Home Secretary Jack Straw ordered "the most far-reaching shake-up of policing for a generation." According to the investigators, police racism had led to "a series of errors, failures and lack of direction and control." The result was a court verdict that freed rather than convicted five suspected murderers. The 365-page summary of hearings chaired by Sir William MacPherson, a retired High Court judge, contained seventy recommendations. A black churchman put these succinctly, noting "the experience of black people over the last 30 years has been that we have been overpoliced and to a large extent underprotected." To correct matters Britain must act against underreported racial crimes and underrepresented minorities in law enforcement and work at establishing trust between nonwhite Britons and police officers. A brief statistical summary revealed the problems' severity. An estimated thirty percent of Metropolitan Londoners belonged to ethnic minorities, but only 3.9 percent of the 26,000 people involved in maintaining civil law and order had alien, non-Anglo-Saxon backgrounds. Results also showed shoddy investigations and a disinterest in protecting everyone's rights.

Regardless of roots and reasons, racial crime has been soaring in English cities. Statistics for London have noted a trend toward more racially motivated unlawfulness. Between April 1, 1999 and March 31, 2000, there were 23,346 reported racial crimes contrasted to 5,876 for the same twelve-month span two years earlier. Although the worst incident in terms of lost lives to a single prejudicial act had occurred in 1981, an arson fire responsible for the deaths of thirteen blacks, later racial attacks—both in quantity and viciousness as noted by the aforementioned Lawrence-murder inquiry—have been generating more interest and prompting greater ramifications. Minorities have become more aware of police prejudice and have been less likely to accept hastily drafted police conclusions. Suspicions and refusals to believe initial police reports at least twice have led to case reopenings. Black musician Michael Menson's sadistic murder in 1997 by a gang which doused him in a flammable fluid and set it alight illustrates just the kind of slipshod police work that has upset minorities and has led to demands for more thorough investigations; as with a similar earlier case involving two blacks in Telford, the police in their first inquiry attributed Menson's death to suicide.

In addition to doubting police trustworthiness more than ever, minorities and their supporters were feeling less secure. For daring to date or marry interracially, even nonwhites who have competed for and brought glory to the crown have become targets for retribution. Ashia Hansen, a leading black English female athlete, went into hiding after a gang of white youths had stabbed her Caucasian boyfriend in Birmingham.

Beside the aforementioned factors for a rising racist-based criminality, nativist concerns about continuing immigrant and refugee inflows into the country have—according to Chair Naz Coker of the Refugee Council—"legitimised racist language" and contributed to callousness. Tory leaders have had a role in it, too; they have rancorously referred to refugees "flooding" into Great Britain as "bogus" asylum-seekers. Whenever refugees entering Great Britain have halted in southeast England because of bureaucracy, Tories "playing the race card" produced consequences at such English Channel ports as Dover. Violence that occurred during the weekend of August 15, 1999, was typical. Stranded strangers became easy prey for knife-wielding local youths who were disgusted that so many hapless newcomers had become lodged down temporarily in their community.[5]

As much as Great Britain has been experiencing problems with racist and nativistic tormentors and maimers of nonwhite residents and aliens, negative acts there have not received anything close to the attention that observers have given to monitoring race-motivated crimes in reunified Germany. After every wave of xenophobia, Federal Republic citizens, as inheritors of the legacy of Nazi deathcamps, have come under close observation after every wave of xenophobism. Beyond Modern Germany's borders, worries and interest have followed neo-Nazi demonstrations and criminal acts.

Analysts have struggled to ascertain if these might represent a revival of just the kind of movement that had produced the deaths of so many million Jews and Roma. With unification of the communist-run East to the democratic West in October 1990, many alarming signs have appeared in the ex-Democratic Republic of Germany. Its high unemployment and envies of the western sector's greater wealth and power released from communist shackles a negative force directed at foreigners. At only two percent—versus the West's ten—Eastern *Länder* aliens have become "a convenient scapegoat for the easterners' fears and feelings of inferiority," nevertheless. A 2000 poll of 16,000

Mecklenburg-West Pomerania teenagers showed a disturbing forty percent of them blaming unemployment on non-Germans and an alarming eighteen percent supporting violence as a remedy. All across Germany the number of hostile acts aimed at refugees and Turkish immigrants became so numerous in the 1990s that they need no documentation. Although youthful skinheads and older allies have belonged to banned neo-Nazi organizations, the responsibilities for literally terrorizing the ex-DDR *Länder* and arousing strong sympathetic followings elsewhere in the country have rested with the younger members.

Resentments have lost their regional character, as a European reporter found after traveling to Bremen's outskirts for a visit to Osterholz, a faceless high-rise apartment community with an immigrant majority. Here, in the midst of a foreigners' enclave, he found walls covered with Nazi graffiti and a bitter German teenager who willingly explained the reasons behind hateful slogans. The symbols and words reflected a declaration "aliens have no right to be here"; the young acquaintenance declared it was his intention "to see that they disappear." In 1991, with an appeal that non-Germans were competing with the native population for jobs, housing, child care, and welfare, the German People's Party or *DVU* (*Deutsche Volkspartei*) simultaneously expressed many Bremen voters' frustrations with Helmut Kohl's governing coalition and with the right-leaning prime minister's leftwing *Bundestag* opponents. In the 1991 elections the extreme rightwing party received significantly more votes locally than it ever had in any earlier contest after the war.

Although most hostility and violence have been directed at nonwhites, refugees, homosexuals, and Turks, Germany's minuscule Jewish population remained a favorite Neo-Nazi target. During 2000 attackers desecrated two Jewish cemeteries, detonated a bomb outside a Jew's house, and injured six Jewish immigrants with exploding shrapnel at a Dusseldorf railway station. Overall racist attacks have been increasing. Police recorded 129 racially motivated crimes—including a Mozambican's death from skinheads' brutal kicks—in June 2000, or 32 more than the previous June. "Yet," warns an *Economist* editorial, "because racist violence in Germany raises such awful ghosts, dealing with it there is all the more necessary." Looked at carefully and compared to similar crimes in other nations, German violence has three noteworthy characteristics that are not especially unique. First of all it has resulted from organizations. Secondly these are neo-Nazi groups with growing memberships and unwavering devotions to Adolf Hitler and Third Reich principles. Finally leaders have used the Internet effectively to inform members of activities and to expand their rolls.[6]

In Europe nativism has by no means been limited to France, Great Britain, and Germany.[7] To varying degrees xenophobia and racism have been prevalent problems throughout the continent. These phenonmena have surfaced differently in each country. After the Iron Curtain's collapse, skinhead gangs have increasingly plagued Central European nations. According to data collected by the Anti-Defamation League, there are approximately 18,000 youths associated with racist movements in Hungary, the Czech Republic,

Poland, and Slovakia. United by the same prejudicial creed that mixes white supremacy, neo-Nazi dogma, and unbridled nationalism as that of their German counterparts, participants have found common enemies to target for violence and intimidation. Since 1991 in the Czech Republic, there have been a reported 1,600 racial attacks, including 21 murders. Killing American Robert Joyce in the town of Hodonin during autumn 1998 has received the most publicity. Despite video evidence that a kicking attack had occurred as retaliation for the victim's intervention on behalf of a gypsy boy whom a group of skinheads had been harassing, police were reluctant to act.

Roma have been especially vulnerable in Central Europe. These possessors of a distinctive culture have represented a large conspicuous minority in each country. In Hungary almost six percent of the population have association with a clannish people known for a nomadic past and violin rhapsodies. *Cigany*, or gypsy in Hungarian (and with spelling variations in other European languages, too), has connoted such negativism that the minority's leadership prefer to be called Roma.[8]

Prejudice, or what might better be called national self-interest governed by xenophobic parameters, has been prevalent in referendum-prone Switzerland, too. Voters there had an opportunity on September 24, 2000, to place a ceiling on immigrants. The question on the ballot was whether the country should limit the number of aliens to eighteen percent. With foreigners accounting for 19.3% of the nation's more than seven-million residents, some Swiss favored imposing a fixed percentage; 64 percent of the electorate disagreed, however. Although the initiative lost decisively, the federal government followed its defeat with a law intended to make immigrating to the country more difficult for non-European Union nationals.[9]

Many kilometers away in Spain, Moroccans have been objects of hate and violence. The Strait of Gibraltar separating the Mediterranean Sea from the Atlantic Ocean is narrow, and daily there are several ferries connecting Tarifa to Tanger. The combination of accessability and good paying jobs—by North African standards—has led to conflicts between Spaniards and Moroccans. A constant influx of laborers into Spain from across the strait has annoyed many native residents. In early February 2000, after the killing of a Spanish woman by a Moroccan man in an El Ejido market, Spaniards responded with a three-day rampage. Referred to as *la guerra*, it was a war against the thousands of North Africans living in the Spanish port of El Ejido. In this city of 55,000 inhabitants, rioters burned shanties that had housed 500 workers. According to Alejandro Fernandez, the murdered woman's fiancee, "When a people rise up, it is because they are tired."

Looked at objectively, both Spanish frustrations with Arab workers and the immigrants' complaints against Spaniards appear understandable. From the hosts' perspective, they have appreciated the work done by foreigners under 30,350 hectares of plastic-covered hothouses where summer temperatures can reach 45 degrees Centigrade, but they have also feared and resented El Ejido's 4,000 North Africans without fixed incomes. As one official put it, "If they

don't work, they can't eat. So they rob, they deal drugs, they cause trouble."
Arabs living in shanties on the city's outskirts or renting one small apartment for
as many as twenty persons have also irritated many Spaniards because the
deplorable living conditions are the result of wages going to Africa and not to
community improvement. Moroccans have complained about racism, claiming
to be unwanted in El Ejido's bars, disliked for looking at local women, and
denied the right to build mosques. Spanish attitudes toward the North African
workers duplicate themselves elsewhere in Europe but with different minorities
in the spotlight.[10]

The hate and prejudice epidemic sweeping Europe has not even exempted
once tolerant Danes and Norwegians. With political equivalents of France's
LePen, Norway and Denmark possess party leaders who use similar nativistic
arguments and demagoguery to stir up their people against minorities. In
Norway Carl I. Hagen has cultivated a dubious distinction. Norwegian opinion
polls during 2000 have shown his populistic message gaining favor with many
voters. Through a spokesperson for the Forward Right Party (*Fremskrittspartier*
or *Frp*), prime-ministerial candidate Hagen has denied charges that he is
ethnocentric and chauvinistic. Speaking of the rightwing party, Chairperson Jan
Petersen has noted its general support of tolerance for immigrants and respect
for national diversity. Inasmuch as Petersen has been reassuring a concerned
citizenry of *Frp* intentions, his remarks have not been altogether effective at
countering another party insider's perspective of Hagen. *Frp* youth section
leader John-Ragnar Aarset referred to the party candidate as Jörg Haider's "little
brother." Given the Austrian populistic rightwinger's open praise for certain
aspects of the Third Reich and his frequent criticism for the number of refugees
and immigrants allowed into Austria, the assessment of Aarset certainly has
brought doubts about Petersen's sincerity and truthfulness about immigrant
questions.[11] No matter who is correct, there have been signs of Norway's lack
of interest in extending civil rights to her minorities. On August 27, 1999, a
court decision officially condoned discriminatory policies. The country's
supreme court upheld on that date a landlord's rights to rent "only to whites"
and to announce "foreigners not wanted."[12]

To the South in neighboring Denmark, Mogens Glistrup—unabashed and
unabated—has been so outspoken against the presence of Muslims that his own
political-party colleagues reported him to the police. Retaliation followed
Glistrup's talk to a national radio audience on September 30, 1999, when he
advised the government to issue an ultimatum to Islam's faithful, giving them a
maximum of three months to leave Denmark. If their departures would not
come voluntarily, Glistrup proposed detaining them until the government could
sell them to the highest bidder.[13]

Although his explusion advice remains on the extreme periphery of Danish
opinion, there are indications of a national frustration with Muslims' refusals to
accommodate themselves to a secular society. These appeared after stores of
Denmark's largest supermarket group, FDB, had imposed a ban against female
employees wearing chador while they worked as cashiers. For prohibiting the

scarves, FDB chair Ebbe Lundgaard received backing from 56 percent of the population, a confirmation of sorts for the opinion of outspoken Pia Kjaersgaard, the leader of the far-right People's Party, who had declared "Islam is pushing its way forward everywhere, at the cost of Danes" who are forced to watch as "our entire cultural foundation is crumbling" because "the government is Islam's willing stooge."[14]

Feeling threatened and unappreciated, masked immigrant demonstrators responded violently the night of November 9, 1999, to news of a Danish-born Turkish citizen's deportation.   Before police could restore order in Copenhagen's Nörrebro district, a rampaging mob set alight automobiles, crushed display windows, and covered buildings and streets with stolen paint from a looted store.   City authorities estimated damages at several million Danish kronor.   As an aftermath several responses followed. Corresponding to Nordic panaceas for most problems—allocations and research—Denmark's Social Democratic-led government thought a combination of study and money could resolve the aliens' complaints.   Deciding January 26, 2000, the immigrant difficulties had resulted from an information gap, parliament earmarked forty-million kronor for two projects.   In the context of globalization and increased migration, the first called upon the nation's researchers to respond within a month with enlightenment about the relationship between the nation's different cultures.   To the country's already top-heavy bureaucracy, the second added another layer, establishing a government-sponsored center for migration studies.

For dealing with outsiders, hardliners Kjaersgaard and Glistrup offered more controversial programs.   The People's Party's leader advised automatic expulsions for three generations of a family if one member commits a crime. Glistrup, Kjaersgaard's counterpart in the Forward Right Party, expressed a renewed admiration for accused Bosnian-Serb war criminals Radovan Karadzic and Ratko Mladic's ethnic cleansing of Muslims by calling for a similar effort in Denmark.   Although neither Kjaersgaard nor Glistrup's parties seldom win as much as ten percent of the Danish popular vote, their ideas about immigrants are not altogether disavowed.   Once known as a tolerant people, Danes have increasingly lost their patience with aliens' demands for living their way and not according to Danish traditions.[15]

With approximately twenty million residents who are either aliens or foreign-born, the fifteen member states of the European Union (EU) in 2000 have found themselves in an ambivalent position of wanting the benefits of immigration but disliking the compromises and challenges immigrants have brought.   There is no better place to look for evidence of duplicity than the Europeans' relationship to their body for continental unity.   In its evolution from a simple coal-and-steel, free-trade body to an instrument for European unity, the Union has not managed to overcome nationalistic loyalties.

In Denmark, for example, the contest between advocates and foes of Danish membership in the European Monetary Union had much more to do with holding onto a national symbol—the Danish kronor—than to the merits and drawbacks of joining.   Predictably the most outspoken politicians against generous immigration and refugee policies were also the most vocal critics of Denmark surrendering any part of her sovereignty. Analysts who studied the referendum's defeat September 28, 2000, immediately interpreted it as a personal victory for Kjaersgaard because of her vociferious clamoring against Danish participation.[16]

As a collective body, the EU has shown timidity in handling refugee and immigration questions. Although the members' citizens have had freedom to move about the Union, working and studying without restrictions, human rights organizations have criticized the organization's general ineptitude and unwillingness either to clarify or expand the 1951 United Nations-sponsored Geneva Convention on Asylum as it pertained to political refugees. If a clear trend has emerged from Strasbourg and Brussels, it has been a move toward tightening requirements for sanctuary. By adopting agreements in the 1980s for a common EU refugee policy and a harmonized policing of borders, the European parliament in effect absolved national politicians of their personal responsibilities for capitulating to nativistic demands. A joint policy also gave European leaders an excuse for restricting further their nations' rules on these subjects.[17]

Immigration restrictions and prejudice against minorities have cost European nations dearly. While three "traditional immigrant" nations had an uninterrupted decade of prosperity, European lands have consistently stagnated. By almost all quantitative measurements, the United States, Canada, and Australia have outperformed "Old World" countries. In terms of per capita, for example, Americans, according to recent figures published in *Fortune*, have approximately $7,000 more purchasing power than Germans, their closest European rival. Moreover the North Americans are more productive and inventive. Whereas 55 percent of all worldwide patents have come from the United States, only fourteen percent resulted from the combined cleverness of German, Dutch, French, Italian, and British minds.[18]

Unsurprisingly there have been logical reasons for these existing gaps. For one thing Europeans are accustomed to looking suspiciously at foreigners, judging them either as problem-causing parasites suckling on generous welfare programs or as criminals breaking laws.[19] Secondly altogether too often for aliens with university degrees, bureaucratic mindsets, ministries of education, prejudice, and such ludicrous excuses as accents have relegated holders of diplomas to subservient jobs below their abilities and experiences. In sharp contrast Sharon Levin of the University of Missouri and Paula Stephan of Georgia State University have found sixty percent of the American-based authors of the most-cited papers in the physical sciences and almost thirty percent of the writers of the most-used life science papers to be foreign born. Of biotechnology firms with initial stock issues in the early 1990s, almost one fourth had either been founded or chaired by people born outside the United States. In California's high-tech industries, according to the Levin-Stephan study, Asians held more than 50,000 positions and contributed seventeen-billion dollars worth of annual revenue to the gross national product.

Americans have not only employed aliens possessing foreign degrees, but they have done a superior job of opening their universities to non-Americans. By surveying enrollment statistics, Professor Corrado Letta of the Luigi Bocconi University in Milan discovered a significant disconnect; in schoolyear 1988-1989, only approximately 35,000 Oriental Asians attended Western European educational institutions, while schools in the United States enrolled almost 150,000. In the sciences and technology many graduate programs in America would fold without the Asian influx.

Moreover, unlike Europeans, Americans were confronting their "dilemma," obtaining in the process some effective results. African American syndicated columnist William Raspberry, writing on racial progress in 1999, offered conditional praise for improvements in the United States. However the journalist would not speculate on how much better his country has become on racial issues than Great Britain.

Just as Americans paid dearly for segregatioin and discrimination, Europeans are losing because of their prejudice against aliens and their opposition to immigration. For example orthodox economists who have studied the effects of the ratio of workers to pensioners have agreed that Europeans must either change their attitudes about accepting more immigrants or find incentives for noticeably increasing their domestic birthrates. With populations aging and too few babies being born to European women, "the choices are stark: abolish retirement or import workers from Bombay," with the latter option a reference to Prime Minister Gerhard Schröder's rejected shock-effect proposal for relieving Germany's shortage through the recruitment of 20,000 Indian software programmers. In the immediate wake of Schröder's suggestion, its nativistic opponents like Christian Democrat Jürgen Rüttgers were rebutting the prime minister with their solution of "*Kinder statt Inder*," or "Offer jobs to our children, not to Indians." Given Europe's generally hostile environment for immigrants and refugees, Croatian author-journalist Slavenka Drakulic's question to landsmen still living as refugees outside their homeland no doubt inspired thoughts by asking "what are you doing here, the war in Bosnia has ended?"[20]

The macroscopic overview of modern Europe wrestling with immigration and minorities sugguests an intriguing question about Sweden. With a history of peaceful neutrality dating to the Napoleonic wars and an almost unbroken record of Social Democratic reforms stretching back to the Great Depression, has the liberal kingdom escaped the ravages of xenophobia and racism so commonplace in other European countries? Has the nation been an oasis? For decades around the world, the Scandinavian nation has been envied and admired. That globally she has a respected reputation for decency can be seen in a story told by a Swedish tourist upon her return from Saudi Arabia. At a beach she had overheard a lifeguard tell a companion where it would be best to live. Hearing Sweden, the friend would learn that "there you do not need to work because the state takes care of you."

Beside a reputation for generous social welfare, there are the spectacular fetes of her most outstanding citizens; these have suggested possibilities in Sweden for liberal, benevolent attitudes toward strangers. The heroism of Raoul Wallenberg rescuing Jews in Hungary from Nazi death camps and the peace efforts of Dag Hammarskjöld intervening in colonial Africa, when coupled with the annual granting of Nobel Peace awards in Stockholm and the country's grants of sanctuary which saved Oliver Tambo and other prominent African National Congress leaders from certain punishment in South Africa could easily lead to speculation that Swedes somehow have deviated from the European bouts of destructive nationalism and prejudice.

Sweden's latest effort at forging a positive public image for herself occurred on January 26, 2000. Stockholm hosted then an international conference on the Holocaust. To determine if these efforts and events had only been isolated acts of kindness and generosity not altogether representative of Swedish public opinion, the full national record must undergo rigorous scrutiny and must pass careful examination.[21]

For a comprehension of Sweden's relationship to foreigners, an excellent beginning would be to eliminate a myth about her past. Contrary to common perceptions, the monarchy has always been both an emigrant and an immigrant nation. English coinmakers were the first recorded newcomers; they appeared at Sigtuna with their craftsmanship around 1000. After the Dominican Order's establishment of a monastery in Västerås in 1244, exchanges transpired with French monks. Meanwhile at the same eastern town, there developed trade with Hanseatic-League cities, Lübeck and Hamburg. As these commercial exchanges increased, Germans began to settle in Västerås, this to manage more effectively the copper and iron shipments from there through Lake Mälaren to ports across the Baltic Sea. Businessmen from Lübeck subsequently became dominant figures in the Swedish economy, overseeing ore extractions by their methods, forging iron, developing business activities in Arboga, Kalmar, Norrköping, Nyköping, Visby, Stockholm, and Örebro, and enriching the language with new words. Resulting as verbal legacies from the Hanseatic commercial activities during the Middle Ages are Swedish words for pay, mayor, trade, buyer, innkeeper, carpenter, and butcher.

During the 1500s and 1600s, at the peak of the Vasa Kingdom's power over the Baltic region, about one-thousand skilled Walloon craftsman emigrated to Sweden from Belgium, settling primarily either in Finspång, Lövsta, or Österbybruk. Then in the first half of the 1700s, Englishman Edward Davies established the first textile factory in Borås, and two Scots opened Jonsered's workshop in Göteborg. In the coming years several other residents from the British Isles followed these pioneers, establishing themselves as the leaders of Swedish industry. However it was a German, Rügen-born Baltzar von Platen, who became the Father of the Göta Canal, the man-made waterway that links Göteborg in the west to Stockholm in the east. This infrastructural miracle completed in 1832 became workable because of a series of 58 locks between Sweden's two largest lakes, Vänern and Vättern, and behind these was

Scotsman Daniel Fraser's design efforts made at a Motala workshop. As with manufacturing and engineering, printing depended upon the immigrant families of Gleerup, Gumpert, and Bonnier; they established themselves as Sweden's leading book publishers.[22]

Until the outbreak of world depression in 1930, Sweden lost more people to emigration than she gained from immigration. For every year thereafter in the Nordic country, population statistics have shown arrivals outpacing departures. A number of challenges were either preceding or complementing the shift. Between 1860 and 1917, Sweden did almost nothing to restrict migration. For prospective newcomers during World War I, the state began requiring them to have passports, visas, and residence permits. It was also then that the *Riksdag*, Sweden's parliament, enacted its first deportation law; it was in response to job competition, alleged security threats from anarchists, socialists, and foreign spies, and influxes of Jews from eastern pogroms. At the same time the government declared roaming vagrants and gypsies *persona non grata*, a status both groups would retain until 1954. The next restriction came in 1931 when the *Riksdag* prohibited "colored peoples" from visiting and settling in Sweden. Prior to the ban, during the 1800s and early 1900s, it was common for touring circuses and carnivals to display native Americans, persons of African heritage, dwarfs, giants, and disfigured individuals as human freaks. Resulting from the new regulations, only two groups could migrate unconditionally into Sweden; they were the descendants of the founders of Swedish settlements in Ukrainia and around Narva in Estonia, who had migrated to these places many centuries earlier.[23]

Prohibitions on the free movements of people into Sweden impacted hardest on Jews. At the beginning of the 1930s, there were approximately 7,000 Jews living in the country. Most were concentrated in Stockholm, Göteborg, and Malmö. A majority were either descendants of buyers who had come from Germanic duchies and the Netherlands or were the relatives of a small group who had left Eastern Europe around 1900. In daily life religion was the only major factor that separated the first Jewish migrants from others in Sweden, but for Jewish latecomers their distinctiveness was general poverty and a clinging to an orthodox faith mixed with Zionist beliefs. Embarrassed by all this, the more liberal-minded Jews who had originally migrated as merchants found themselves in conflict with the Jewish newcomers.

The first major challenge facing both Jewish groups and the *Riksdag* occurred soon after Adolf Hitler's election to the German chancellorship in 1933. Members of Berlin's synagogues then began asking Sweden's Jewish families to accept and care for their children during summer months. From the beginning of the Third Reich to *Kristallnacht*, about 3,000 Jews received permits either to come to or travel through Sweden. Following violent Nazi attacks on Jews and their property the night of November 9, 1938, the targeted minority flooded Sweden with requests for asylum but to no effect. For many reasons their plight as a persecuted people did not move Swedish authorities to offer them refuge *en masse*. Among the most effective opponents, in terms of influence over sanctuary laws and policies, members of the Swedish academic community certainly exercised a decisive role in the decision to reject Jewish migrants. Boisterously proclaiming "Sweden for Swedes" at rallies and then voting against acceptances in university referendums, students and faculties showed adamant opposition to granting sanctuary. Campus demonstrations reflected both fears of competition from Jewish intellectuals as well as pro-Nazi sympathies. By chartering an airplane to Berlin for a private party with Third Reich filmmaker and propagandist Leni Riefenstahl, a group of Lund University students confirmed their sympathies for Hitler's regime. Months later in another despictable act, counterparts studying medicine in Stockholm bitterly reacted against the city medical board applying for work permits on behalf of ten German-Jewish physicians.

As a result of pressures and prevalent anti-Semitism in Sweden, only 500 of the thousands who had applied for sanctuary were able to obtain refuge before the German September 1, 1939, attack of Poland and the *riksdag*'s subsequent declaration of neutrality. For the kingdom impartiality had two interrelated consequences. Policymakers decided continuing trade with Germany should have paramount importance, and nothing should interfere with this commerce or with German-Swedish friendship. In sum expressing concerns for Jewish rights in the Third Reich through diplomatic protests and asylum offers would not occur because Swedes feared such acts might offend *der Führer* and thus upset a profitable outsourcing of his *Kriegsmacht* with Swedish machine components and raw materials. Rather than protest anything, the government in Stockholm cooperated with the Nazi regime by registering foreigners and passing secretly onto Berlin the names of Jews on its alien lists. More than fifty years after the war's end, General Secretary Israel Singer of the Jewish World Congress came to Sweden to demand an investigation into how much Jewish-owned gold and valuables had gone to the kingdom from the Third Reich as payments for traded goods. Embarrassed by Singer's disclosures, Swedish officials agreed to cooperate fully; they ordered an audit of bank archives and a full reimbursement of all stolen Jewish property.[24]

Denying exile to Jews was just one example of how Sweden's willingness to serve as authoritarian Germany's handmaiden. Predating Hitler's rise to power, eugenics fascinated Swedes as much as Germans. Phrenologic experiments begun at Stockholm's Karolinska Institute during the late nineteenth century would continue there and in Uppsala for several decades. As with German efforts, Swedish researchers also directed their work at confirming Teutonic superiority. Alleged evidence came from a large collection of diverse skulls, all individually tagged to indicate ethnic and racial origins. Using so-called craniometers, craniologolists determined cranium-to-torso proportions. Since Sami were Sweden's largest minority, their ancestors' skeletal remains received the closest scrutiny. Although an 1892 fire at Karolinska had destroyed much evidence and data, investigators showed no interest in abandoning craniology and eugenics. To assist in this effort, the Swedish government in 1921 funded

Herman Lundberg to set up Uppsala University's State Institute for Racial Biology.

The professor's work would eventually confirm what many Swedes had long believed about themselves. In Lundberg's distorted but ordered arrangement of human beings, it was possible to rank peoples and races according to their primary activities and accomplishments. Hunters, fishermen, and nomadic peoples—such as Lappland's wandering Sami reindeer herders—were at the bottom of the Uppsalan's scale, whereas scientists ranked first.

Results from Lundberg's work appeared in many publications, generating interest and the founding of organizations dedicated to nativistic causes. From 1923 to 1927, while exiled in Sweden after the failed Munich beer-hall *putsch*, early Hitler disciple Hermann Wilhelm Göring joined a Lundberg-inspired racist group. The Uppsalan's research not only affected thought and justified calls for exclusionary policies, but a number of governmental programs aimed at both "inferior" and "deficient" individuals owed their life existences to his efforts.

In an attempt to "upgrade" the population and "protect" future Swedish generations from wretched women delivering babies, the nation's Social Democratic government adopted a sterilization program in the 1930s; it had support both from social planners like Alva and Gunnar Myrdal and racists. Consequently thousands of women—unaware they were signing away their rights to bear children—entrusted themselves to surgeons who then secretly tied their fallopian tubes or removed their ovaries.

Lundberg's conclusions also rendered Hitler's Aryan doctrines believable and palpable to many Swedes already indoctrinated with anti-Semitism from Lutheran teachings about Jewish responsibility for the crucifixion, August Strindberg's depictions of Jews in *Röda Rummet* (*The Red Room*) and *Det nya Riket* (*The new Kingdom*), Albert Engström's caricatures found in the humor magazine *Strix*, and such popular motion pictures as *Trötte Teodor* (*Tired Theodore*), *Söderkåkar* (*South Side Houses*), *Kära släkten* (*Dear Family*), and *Pettersson & Bendel*. A not so subtle message emerged; in literature, cartoons, and films, Jews—stereotyped with dark eyes and hair and crooked, prominent noses—did not deserve Swedes' trust or sympathy because they were "greedy, unscrupulous, and single-mindedly focused on financial profit." There were also warnings not to indulge in racial mixing because it meant participation in the genetic crime of tainting superior "Swedish blood" with that of an inferior race.

In an atmosphere charged with excessive prejudice against Jews, there was neither astonishment nor repugnance caused by Linköping newspaper *Östgöta Correspondenten*'s reaction to *Kristallnacht*. As it surmised from the horrific events in Nazi Germany, "Experiences from history have shown that Jews have difficulties living together with other peoples . . . [and] have a big responsibility for the development of anti-Semitism in many countries."[25]

Subjected as Swedes had long been to "scientific racism" and prejudical stereotypes and threatened as many had felt from the Soviet experiment's leftist admirers' growing popular influence in Swedish labor and politics, Hitler's twin goals of fighting communism and saving Teutons from "inferior" peoples made sense and attracted a sympathetic following. Included among his admirers were Swedish churchmen who saw fascism as a bulwark against atheistic Marxism. Lund University's New Testament exegetist Hugo Odeberg was one who admitted to appreciating the Nazi regime because special for him with what the National Socialists empowered, there would be less Jewish interfering in Hebrew history studies. Immigration and customs officials considered the red "J" stamped in Jews' passports advantageous because it facilitated excluding them from Sweden as an undesirable minority. According to their twisted logic, keeping out Jews would contain anti-Semitism.

Support also came from Swedish academics, journalists, and agrarian leaders. Among the first group, a long relationship existed between Scandinavian and Teutonic higher education. German universities—with seminars, "scientific" scholarship, and staffs arranged rigidly according to a strict pecking order with special titles and ranks—became the models for Swedish institutions, and German-language fluency was mandatory for success in Swedish academe. As admirers of Germany, several professors in Sweden considered Hitler's elevation of the state an awe-inspiring development that might bring about a German resurgence and recovery of her lost prominence in the world.

Inasmuch as academic circles did praise the Third Reich, not many scholars formed or joined Swedish fascist movements; their memberships and top leaders were drawn from other sources. Organizational activity began in Älvdalen on August 12, 1924, when brothers Birger, Sigurd, and Gunnar Furugård chartered the first of a series of national socialist political parties. They called their creation *Svenska Nationalsocialistiska Frihetsförbundet* or *SNSFF* (The Swedish National Socialist League of Freedom). Soon after its founding, *Nationalsocialisten*, a propaganda organ and newspaper, was reaching individuals interested in learning more about Nazi philosophy. Of the three siblings, Birger was definitely *SNSFF*'s driving force. His interest had begun while completing studies in veterinary medicine at Lund University. Professor Bengt Lidforss had been most influential, directing Birger to read racist magazines, newspapers, and books from Germany and to visit Imperial Russia. From travels there between 1916 and 1918, Furugård had developed an intense hatred of both communism and Jews, the minority because in his mind it had been responsible for the Bolshevik Revolution in 1917. Due to Birger's urging in 1923, his brothers visited Hitler in Germany.[26]

The Furugårds were not alone at organizing a group sympathetic to and supportive of the German nationalist's teachings. Separate from their efforts, Elof Eriksson, a *Skånsk* (a resident of Sweden's southernmost region) agricultural leader, began the weekly publiccation of *Nationen* (the Nation) in 1925. In it the founder railed against Jews, monopolies, wealthy financiers, Bolsheviks, and disarmament. Since Eriksson's agenda dealt only with Swedish issues, its appeal was greater than what the Furugårds were able to generate. In particular nothing upset the agrarian spokesperson more than the Wallenberg and Bonnier dynasties. He accused them of being a secret government, controlling respectively Sweden's finances and culture. Disgusted with the passivity and direction of Swedish politicians, Eriksson organized *Sveriges Fascistiska Kamporganisation* or *SFKO* (The Fascist Fighting Organization of Sweden). In 1929 a joint delegation representing *SNSFF* and *SFKO* went to Nürnberg and participated in a massive Nazi rally. During the Swedes' visit they met Hitler and heard speeches from the German movement's leaders.

Attendees were so impressed with what they had learned, they left with an enthusiastic resolve to unite their two organizations into one for a "New Sweden" under the name *Nysvenska Nationalsocialistiska Förbundet* (The National Socialist League); leadership and the title *"Sveriges führer"* went to Birger Furugård. *SFKO*'s Sven Olof Lindholm as first deputy assumed organizational duties. Final steps in the Nazis' development occurred with the opening of League headquarters in Göteborg and soon thereafter with the publishing of party organ *Vår Kamp* (Our Struggle). Satisfied after almost three years of existence that National Socialism was impressing the Swedish electorate, Furugård and Lindholm decided the 1932 general elections would present an excellent opportunity to offer their party's candidates to the nation. There was some success in certain districts, but it was not enough to give the National Socialists *riksdag* seats.

Meanwhile Swedish movement leaders kept on good terms with their German mentors. Furugård addressed them at a 1933 assembly of Nazis, while Lindholm was attending the event as Hitler's personal guest. Shortly after the two Swedes' return home, Furugård and Lindholm split over socialism. The veterinarian with primarily small businessmen's backing wanted nothing to do with it, whereas Lindholm wanted it integrated into party plans and doctrine. As a result of differences the latter man left, forming *Nationalsocialistiska Arbetarpartiet* (The National Socialist Labor Party). Apparently for allowing a breakup, Furugård lost the top post in the Göteborg-based organization to Colonel Martin Ekström. One of the new leader's first acts was to direct a name change. Hereafter Ekström and his followers belonged to what they now called *Nationalsocialististiska Blocket* (The National Socialist Block).[27]

Hitler assuming control of Germany was a defining moment for his Swedish admirers; their hope at first was for similar success in the Nordic kingdom. Through the outbreak of war in 1939 and the pinnacle of the dictator's power over Europe, his movement inspired Swedes. Then just as quickly after the Third Reich army had stalled at Stalingrad and the Allied forces had opened a beachhead in Normandy, fanatic Swedish believers' dreams of succeeding with a fascist regime at home suffered closure just as it had earlier for a majority of less enthusiastic followers. Even before Germany's major military setbacks, National Socialists in Sweden splintered into many factions over issues and leadership. More importantly there developed considerable disillusionment with Hitler's actions and activities. In particular his armies' invasions of Denmark and Norway along with their occupations drove away many one-time sympathizers. Dissuaded Swedes finally associated the dictator's control with cruelty.

On the other hand for several hundred hardcore believers in National Socialism, there remained a willingness to serve the Führer in his military. No less than 260 of these Swedes belonged to the elite *Waffen SS*, participating in *Korps Steiner*, a special pan-European unit. At least one volunteer guarded prisoners at the Treblinka death camp. Home in Sweden during 1941, another band of Nazi fanatics secretly formed *Bruna Gardet* (the Brown Guard). Its purpose was to aid in an anticipated German invasion of Sweden. This fifth column consisted of an estimated 500 to 700 militiamen, each armed with stolen weapons and devoted to *"Tro, kämpa, segra svenskar!"* (believe, struggle, defeat Swedes).[28]

Sweden's official policy toward the Third Reich was inconsistent. The state church, for example, did not denounce anti-Semitic brutality until long after hearing about the "final solution." In a prayer given November 28, 1943, the Reverend Olle Nystedt of Göteborg's Cathedral Church was almost alone at appealing for a hardened reaction and for warning "If we remain silent, the stones should cry." At responding to a threatened death sentencing of all Jews, the government remained equally noncommittal. In Berlin, for example, after career diplomat Göran von Otter's receipt of details about a plan for mass exterminations, he conveyed the information to Ambassador Arvid Richert. There is no evidence the senior Swedish official ever forwarded von Otter's communique about expected Nazi executions.

Neutral Sweden acted duplicitously both at offering sanctuary during the war and in her dealings with Germany. Although at the war's outset Sweden claimed that noninvolvement in the conflict would prevent her granting exit visas to Jews, it did not keep her from developing an altogether different response to Finnish citizens after the Russian attack on neighboring Finland on November 30, 1939. During the so-called Winter War between Finland and the Soviet Union, Sweden's status did not hinder her from accepting about 70,000 Finnish youngsters. Treated as foster children, young Finns lived with Swedish families for the war's duration. Again—seven months later in June 1940 after the USSR's seizure of Estonia—Swedish neutrality did not interfere with the thousands of refugees fleeing the Baltic nation for Nordic safety.

Neither did Swedish officials seem to see any compromise in their nation's position of granting a fully armed and equipped, Norwegian-based German military division transit rights to cross northern Sweden on a reinforcement mission to Third Reich troops already fighting communist forces in Finland. Yet, inasmuch as allowing Nazi soldiers direct movement from Norway across Sweden into Finland violated all pretenses of neutrality, for disgusting one-sidedness, the action was not nearly as disgraceful as the covert help *Säpo* or the Swedish Security Police gave the Gestapo. Norwegian historian Lars Borgersrud found in Swedish archives evidence of the law-enforcement agency collectively branding as communists the Norsk saboteurs who were operating against German occupiers. Making matters worse, *Säpo* returned to Nazi officials escapees who had sought Swedish refuge from certain inprisoning or death sentencing.

Excepting Wallenberg's heroic rescue of 3,500 Jews in Hungary, there were not many commendable acts committed by Swedish governmental officials on behalf of a people targeted for their "final solution" in 1942. Altogether only approximately 900 Norwegian Jews and 8,000 Danish Jews—including their non-Semitic spouses—reached and received sanctuary in "neutral" Sweden.

Meanwhile near the end of the war and the defeat of Germany eminent, Nazi political parties did poorly in the 1944 national elections, garnering only 0.43% of the Swedish vote. However paltry the percentage, the fact they were still operating legally indicated the *Riksdag*'s unwillingness to ban groups with Third Reich sympathies. Even after Germany's surrender, two active pro-Nazi groups—*Sveriges Nationella Förbund* or *SNF* (Sweden's National Federation) and *Nysvenska Rörelsen* or *NsR* (New Swedish Movement)—remained active, surviving unchallenged by law. Even stranger perhaps, Hitler's more fortunate Swedish volunteer fighters who returned home would never be interrogated, investigated, or indicted to determine if they had been war criminals.[29]

In the immediate postwar period Sweden did take some positive steps, however. For Nazi deathcamp survivors the nation extended itself, welcoming as many as wanted to come and live there. Jerzy Einhorn was among the many thousands who accepted an open invitation between 1945 and 1949 to settle in Scandinavia. Arriving in 1946 at twenty-two years old after having survived a Polish concentration camp, Einhorn studied medicine in Stockholm. Licensed to practice in 1954, this death-camp survivor went on to become a professor of radiology at Karolinska Institute, a researcher of cancer treatments, and an author of books on radiation therapy, endocrinology, and radiobiology. Many other survivors stayed in Sweden just long enough to recover physically before departures for Israel.

At the other end of the spectrum Sweden was equally generous toward displaced peoples from the Baltic region as well as toward some three million Germans driven from their Sudetenland homes by revengeful Czechs at the war's conclusion. Regarding the latter group, although an overwhelming majority of these homeless people chose either one of the German zones or Austria, about 4,000 Sudetens accepted Sweden's offer of residence. Most of these were men in their late twenties with histories of work as technicians and skilled tool-and-die craftsmen. Given how these skilled people were youthful and had vocational experiences, they attracted the attention of technological companies like Asea in Västerås; it alone employed several hundred Sudeten exiles. Overall Sweden's immigration practices were liberal between 1945 and 1954. Although theoretically anyone wanting to migrate to the country still needed a valid visa and a passport, possession of proper identification was more discretionary than mandatory. Persons judged useful to the national economy received approval for residency and work, whether with or without the allegedly necessary documentation.[30]

Sweden's noninvolvement in the world war left her in a position to prosper unprecedentedly during the first two decades after the war, and as her thriving industries expanded to meet demands from a rebuilding Europe, assembly lines and work benches required additional capable workers. As the nation literally advanced during one generation from poverty to wealth, ambitious immigrants arrived—some on their own and others recruited—to work for the highest wages on the continent.

The largest contingent came from Nordic countries, war-ravaged Finland and Sweden's unsettled neighbors, Norway and Denmark. By a regional agreement signed in 1954, citizenship in one of the countries guaranteed the right of free movement to work in any other Nordic nation. As a result sixty percent of the immigration to Sweden between 1950 and 1970 came from neighboring nations. Finns during this period, for example, were arriving at an average annual approximate rate of 9,000, with a first-decade total of almost 80,000 coming to Sweden to find jobs. It should be noted that a significant number of the Finnish migrating multitude had no intention of staying in Sweden. Results were transient existences in a neighboring kingdom and routines of working for high wages, saving as much as possible, and returning home. With Finland's rapid reconstruction and a subsequent development of a viable economy primarily dependent upon exports to the Soviet Union, a once devastated neighbor to the east offered enough incentives to begin holding onto most of her workers.

The returns of growth and prosperity in Norway and Denmark brought them to a stage by 1970 of almost equaling their previously much richer neighbor Sweden in individual median earnings. Restoration factors combined to cause a marked general decline in Nordic emigration. In the 1970s only fifty percent of Sweden's immigrants had originated their migrations in the region. With the Nordic nations accounting for only thirty percent of newcomers to the monarchy the following decade, the trend of declining departures for Sweden continued. Thereafter a pattern of sharply reduced movements of workers from border nations to Sweden accelerated to such degree in the 1990s that for the three kingdoms, a one-time recipient had now become more a source itself of skilled and professional employees in the now more prosperous Danish and Norwegian economies rather than a receiver and an employer.[31]

Obviously from the aforementioned percentages, Nordic nations were not the exclusive providers of workers to Sweden's expanding industry; there were also intensive recruitments elsewhere. In attempts to find good candidates for employment at such Swedish multinational manufacturers as Volvo, Saab-Scania, Asea, and SKF, labor agents went to Yugoslavia, Turkey, Greece, and Italy, screening and soliciting individuals to live and work in Sweden. At the first-named automobile producer's main assembly plant at Torslanda outside Göteborg, for example, aliens once accounted for seventy percent of its blue-collar workers. Although Finns and Yugoslavians easily outnumbered all other nationalities, one examiner of the work force there found fifty-five different lands represented among its assemblers. No matter workers' origins, Volvo greatly benefitted from their employment. Just for a five-year period covering car-model years 1966 through 1970, imported workers allowed production to grow by sixty percent. Without the foreigners such expansion could not have occurred. Beside increased outputs, immigration also had a braking effect on inflation. Had aliens not filled employment vacancies, higher labor and production costs would have followed acute labor shortages.[32]

With industrial prosperity came increased national wealth and public income, and the Social Democratic governments in power during the postwar decades chose to spend the additional tax revenues on a combination of more generous welfare programs, infrastructure improvements, defense, education, housing, and foreign-aid projects. On the surface Swedish grants to struggling Third World nations had little to do with an ongoing employee shortage, but there was synergy in the mix. Through exercising roles as example and lesson giver to the world, Sweden was able to meet her employment needs because of a carefully created image of the nation as a fair and wonderful place to live and work. A foreign policy predicated in part on condemning inhumane brutality wherever it was occurring and on giving refuge to Hungarian freedom fighters in 1956 did much to solidify Sweden's reputation as a neutral nation with a commitment to international morality and human rights. The act of accepting about 15,000 escapees from Iron Curtain totalitarianism appeared to outsiders as Swedish humanitarianism. In fact though a willingness to take Hungarians also meant an intake of intelligent workers. Inasmuch as the 1956 Hungarian experience netted so many benefits, its example would become an integral part of Swedish foreign policy. Thus the pattern of criticizing ruthlessness and granting its victims sanctuary repeated itself many times after 1956 as the following table attests:

SWEDISH REFUGEE ACCEPTANCES, 1960-1989			
Trouble Spot	Problem	Years	No. of Refugees
Greece	Military Junta Rule Attacks Leftists	1967-1974	5,000
Czechoslovakia	Soviet Invasion Crushes Revolt	1968	5,000
Poland	General Oppression & Anti-Semitism	1968--	12,000
Chile	Violent Dictatorship Kills & Jails Leftists	1973--	25,000
Turkey	Oppressive Reaction to Kurds' Civil War	1970s--	18,000
Turkey	Assyrian & Syrian Christians' Rights Lost	1975--	19,000
Lebanon	Palestinians Caught in Civil War & Affected by Israel invasion	1975--	13,000
Vietnam	New Regime's Foes from Chinese Minority	Late 1970s into 80s	9,000
Eritrea	Independence Struggle	1969--	11,000
Iran	Religious Oppression and War with Iraq	1979--	35,000

33

For Finns who had never learned Swedish and other non-Scandinavians, adjusting to Sweden presented problems. First of all there was a language barrier to overcome. Recognizing the value of communication, the largest employers of foreigners often established voluntary study programs. As valuable as these were, they did not assist all newcomers. Moreover pedagogs had concerns about immigrants' children. Fearful in 1966 their parents would begin establishing special ethnic schools just as Jews and Estonians had done, the *Riksdag* responded to these worries by authorizing and funding home-language courses for alien children. To equalize access to Swedish studies for foreign workers, the government made it possible for them to obtain 240 hours of language instruction during regular working hours. Conceived as a program to benefit immigrants, it many times had an opposite effect. Since having alien employees studying instead of working was costly for companies, private firms simply stopped hiring people, whenever possible, who were not fluent in Swedish. Parliament, therefore, rescinded the law in 1986.[34]

The discontinued language program was one of a long series of mistakes in immigrant and refugee policy that the Swedish government would commit. A much more serious problem resulted from its misjudgment of Swedes' general attitudes toward and reactions to persons of diverse backgrounds, religions, customs, mores, and habits because the consequences would cause continuous problems and friction. Behind the social planners' thinking had been a naive hope for assimilation. It had been based upon their unrealistic aspirations and expectations. Their solution to problems had been to overcome obstacles to assimilation by generously committing public resources to outsiders in order to centrifuge their differences literally into a Swedish mass.

Success for the plan was dependent upon an important element that the men and women behind the grandiose programs had assumed would cooperate to make the efforts function smoothly. Svensson—Sweden's equivalent of Jane and John Doe—wanted no part of any scheme intended to place him or her on equal footing with anyone with strange ways. Combining many generations of indoctrination about the superiority of Teutonic "blood" to an insular existence of mistrust and shyness contributed to the infeasibility of expecting average Swedes to embrace a fidelity with total strangers for whom there would be no or little comprehension and tolerance. Having once dominated and controlled both Finland and Norway, Swedish people had condescension of neighboring populations despite many more similarities with them than disparities. For a long time Swedes joked about Finns and Norwegians' incompetencies and their alleged inferiority. With this being so about neighbors who had by and large shared life styles and traditions with Swedes, the thought of assimilating, for example, Turks and Kurds seemed foolhardy and unimaginable. Remarks from an immigrant who had come from Greece in 1969 showed just how well he was understanding the matter after years in Sweden. As he summed up his place in his adopted land, "Swedes view us as animals, not as people, even if we had come here ready, without any cost to Sweden. We took jobs which Swedes did not want."[35]

To survive in an hostile environment, immigrants banded themselves in ethnic enclaves. The government—despite opposite intentions—had inadvertently helped to organize these. It was not unusual for the first wave of recruited workers to be housed in military-type barracks. Near SKF's Göteborg factory, so many workers from Milan, Italy, were living in these makeshift buildings that the area soon had the nickname "Little Milano." As Peppino Masella remembered the experience, he and the other Italians living there had been largely dependent upon their own resources to survive in a foreign country. Nevertheless there had been camaraderie and security and what he described as "the best time" of his life. Recalling from thirty years before an interview with a Swedish reporter, Masella remembered little or no social interaction among the different ethnic groups which constituted SKF's multinational workforce. Each held onto traditions and vacationed in their respective homelands, and to the best of Masella's knowledge, racism did not exist.   Each major nationality maintained clubs and organizations, and nobody was especially concerned with learning perfect Swedish.   On their own these individuals grasped and used as much of the language as they found necessary to communicate and understand basic demands associated with their jobs and leisure.   Moreover the workers suffered neither from deceptions nor identity crises because none of the Italians in Masella's close circle ever considered themselves Swedish.   On the other hand Swedish authorities did not interfere and try to impose new standards on the Italians.   In fact officials broke rules in order to allow a continuation of the Italian custom of having wine with meals, something Swedes could not do because of the limitations imposed upon them by ration cards used for all alcohol purchases at state-run liquor dispensaries.   In sum, according to Masella, nothing tampered with a good life.[36]

Into this bliss entered reformers who had imagined how their planning well conceived programs and projects might improve matters, and successive Social Democratic governments agreed.   Housing came first.   Parliament reacted first to an acute postwar shortage, authorizing and funding the construction of large housing estates on the outskirts of every major city.   The goal was simple; to what emerged throughout Sweden as faceless, dull, concrete-brick-and-mortar apartment complexes flocked thousands of immigrants, such social outcasts as alcoholics, drug addicts, and released felons, retirees on fixed incomes, as well young Swedish families.   All came together with one thing in common—to fill a need for adequate accommodations.

Interactions proved more complex than the reformers had ever foreseen, however.   Swedes so accustomed to quiet and order almost at once became uncomfortable living among clamoring outsiders who were not following such basic rules as keeping stairwells clear of clutter and common laundryrooms clean of lint and split detergent.   Even more upsetting to the ethnic natives, the strangers in their midst were always assembling in groups, speaking loudly, laughing, and generally disturbing the peacefulness that so many Swedes had grown to expect of neighbors.   Consequently stigmas quickly attached to these planned communities and rendered them as unacceptable places for Swedes to live and raise families.   The result was an exodus as soon as other affordable housing could be found elsewhere.   As they departed, their places were taken by immigrant families.

The first twenty years of Rinkeby outside Stockholm illustrate just how ghettoizing progressed in a typical Swedish development built in the late 1960s and early 1970s.   With hoopla and hope, construction began in 1969 on a planners' ideal community that would contain modern apartments, a church, a shopping center, schools, and meeting facilities.   Within twenty years after its completion, Rinkaby had deteriorated into a slum inhabited almost exclusively by immigrants and their children.   Mention the "global village" by name to any Swede anywhere in Sweden after 1990, and the project will conjure up mental pictures of an undesirable place to live or visit.

Like it in Göteborg but on a smaller scale and less well known across the nation, Bergsjön is home to approximately 2,400 people. Most are *invandrare*, originally Swedish for immigrants but by 1990 an almost derisive term that is meant to encompass anyone without ethnic Swedish birth or roots. Pensioners Holger and Irene Josby lived at Bergsjön until it "had become a pure ghetto." Then the uprooted vegetation, breakins, and "disrespect for Swedish ways" made them uncomfortable. Somewhat reluctant to discuss what had been on their minds before a move to a less hostile environment, the retirees had not wanted their criticisms interpreted as racism. By 1990 project communities like Rinkaby and Bergsjön—plus all the negative connotations these places and *invandrare* configured in the Swedish mindset—were already symbolic examples of what could possibly go wrong for both immigrants and refugees during the next decade in a Scandinavian nation that not so many years earlier had been imagined as generous, tolerant, and liberal.[37]

Chapter II

Asylum in Hell

Events that unfolded in little Kimstad during the first half of 1990 would repeat themselves many times—with modifications but with similar results—across Sweden for the next ten years. In a place where headlines are read and not made, an explosion occurred that literally rocked all of Sweden and summoned up feelings not hitherto expressed by otherwise placid Swedes. Before elaborating on the details of what happened here, there is a need to note some facts about the place and its distant relationship to a relatively close, large metropolis. From the hamlet by automobile before reaching a motorway for the final kilometers to neighboring Norrköping, it is first necessary to navigate eight kilometers of crooked, narrow county roadway. Although the village is located only approximately two metric miles southwest of one of Sweden's largest cities, there exists between two places a significant chasm in terms of population and mentality. Norrköping—once known as Sweden's Manchester—is obviously a manufacturing center; its towering smokestacks, trams, and ethnically diverse population transmit an aura of cosmopolitanism.[38] Crossing railroad tracks at the entry into Kimstad, visitors can sense something very different from the neighboring city; they imagine immediately from first impressions that this is a close-knit community where everybody is probably acquainted with everyone and where life remains stationary to the citizenry's contentment. As Kimstad's confrontation with change shows from 1990, such perceptions about the place are more correct than wrong.

To the chagrin of many of Kimstad's residents, who valued their homogeneous environment, news arrived on December 7, 1989, from the Immigration Board or *Siv*[39] of plans to convert an unused convalescent home into a refugee center and to build new residences on the grounds for several hundred aliens. Two months elapsed before someone from the government agency behind the project arrived in the community with specific details. The information session of February 8, 1990, proved eventful. Expecting only to inform local residents of the anticipated development, Jarl Gustavsson found himself in a most uncomfortable position of fending off hostile questions and reactionary comments about aliens. Among other things, Gustavsson heard that "we do not want any *svartskallar* [literally translated black heads, but it is an all-inclusive term with negative connotations for dark-skinned peoples and is a Swedish equivalent of nigger] here!" Claiming "seventy-five percent of all the rapes are done by non-Nordic men," one participant demanded a response to the question, "does the Immigration Board take responsibility for this?" It was bedlam at the community forum. Shouting and interrupting prevented the spokesperson from answering questions or offering explanations. Gustavsson left Kimstad, concluding his agitators must have been outsiders representing a racist organization. He was not alone at attributing the discourteous protests to non-Kimstadians. Politician Rune Rosenqvist, a leading Social Democrat from Norrköping and the head of the building board responsible for all construction permits, also concluded the views expressed had not "shown the true opinions in Kimstad." Nevertheless, by the next morning after a passionate evening, the whole village was buzzing about the announcement and its response.[40]

Initial reactions from project supporters and foes alike were surprise and disbelief, but for opponents of the planned construction their mood would shift quickly to hostility and negativism. Margareta Widell, a local elected official and a member of the Moderate Party (the most conservative of Sweden's seven major political parties), was most critical not only of placing unwanted exiles in her community but also of Sweden's entire refugee policy. In her opinion "we should look carefully at whom we are allowing into Sweden and not like today opening up to whomever calls" because "everyone does not fit in here." Her point was only one of many perspectives offered by Kimstad's foes to having refugees forced on their community. Sheet-metal worker Jan Träff—careful to qualify himself not as a racist but as an impartial individual whose children play with those of Palestinian neighbors—did not believe national resources could cover domestic needs and the expense of accepting thousands of refugees. After all, he complained "we cannot give our elderly the care they should have. The waiting periods for operations only grow longer. There is a shortage of doctors. We must now set a stop to refugees and begin thinking about ourselves." The tinsmith recalled a recent experience of not obtaining communal assistance with a sewer-line connection from his workshop because of insufficient funds. Amazingly, he noted, money was available for linking a proposed refugee complex to the main waste-disposal system.

Questions also arose about the scale of the planned operation in relation to Kimstad's population. One conclusion was the community should accept "refugees in proportion to how many we are," or in another words, "a pair of families." With only a few strangers living among the villagers, surmised one opponent, residents "would not have to be afraid of them clumping together and becoming major risks for [causing] trouble." Critics were also quick to complain about profits from unwanted refugees going to Wibarco, the property developer and landlord. The thought of these irritated townsmen because then a hated project would become a corporation's "quick stroke of fortune making" at the town's expense.

As much as individuals were expressing logical reasons for opposing a sanctuary for displaced persons in Kimstad, something closer to the truth for the real reasons behind strong sentiments against the project was probably found in young people's statements. Due to youthful recklessness and general disregard for consequences, youths' indiscretion and tendency for candor were more than likely truer reflections of what they had heard at home than what their parents willingly admitted to reporters. When teenagers mentioned how "the blacks should be flogged" and boasted about their intention to "knock them down as quickly as we can," the young speakers most likely were only repeating what their elders had expressed. Ironically after the youngsters had spoken to the reporter of hating Turks and wanting to kill them, they began to cross the street to a fast-food emporium for kebab and pizza. In there working behind the counter of the restaurant, the newspaperwoman spotted three Turks. Seeing inconsistency between the young men's statements and their intentions, she could not resist asking two questions. "Are you really thinking of eating the Turks' food? Don't you hate Turks?" Seeing no apparent inconsistencies, one of her respondents clarified himself, offering what he thought would be a distinction. "Yes, but not them there! We know them!"

As much as foes were vociferous and demonstrative, not every resident of Kimstad opposed the refugee center. Since the issue was fraught with so much emotion, the community sharply divided. With enemies of the refugee-center so engulfed in their opposition, tolerating equivocators or supporters became difficult. As one backer noted, her neighbors were glancing downward rather than acknowledging her presence in local stores. Another supporter was less fortunate; his car became a spray-paint target of vandals. For avowing an agreement with the Immigration Board's decision to build in Kimstad, Annelie Lindvall, a local political leader, received hate letters; her critics called her a witch, an ultimate insult rooted deeply in Sweden's pagan past. Undaunted, Lindvall found no basis for further debate on the topic because of the issue's polarizing effect.

Teachers in the community schools found themselves helpless pawns in the debate. Since their centrally administered lesson plans included exercises on racism, there was a risk their teaching might be construed as criticisms of the proposal's foes. In addition the uproar over refugees was a disruptive force in local schools. Students worried about eventual fights between citizens and newcomers, and teachers had the challenge of overcoming pupils' prejudicial attitudes about aliens being "worst people than Swedes."

At confronting local attitudes and engrained racism and xenophobia, Kimstad educators received a boost from the town's only church on Palm Sunday when Vicar Christina Bergstrand-Nilson turned a traditional religious high point into a bold bid at overcoming a majority's opposition to the refugee project. (According to recently announced results of a polling of Kimstad residents, two-thirds of the sample had reacted negatively.) At a service where collections have customarily gone to Lutheran Help, the state church's world assistance program, the minister chose for her sermon a variation of the Golden Rule. She noted for a congregation how "we must be prepared to help people who seek protection and support. We may not turn away the hungry and suffering." As a reenforcement of the lesson for her parishioners, Bergstrand-Nilson introduced Wiwi Samuelsson, *Siv*'s information director. The guest in turn spoke of asylum seekers' ambitions and frailities and of another Swedish community's reversal on the question of accepting refugees. From its initial strong resistance to having a sanctuary, attitudes changed there soon after the refugees' arrivals.[41]

In the midst of all the hoopla over a refugee center in Kimstad, opponents began sensing progress in their efforts at blocking a sanctuary. On April 6, 1990, Wibarco announced a major scaling down of the project, this time from fifteen to ten units and from 200 inhabitants to 150; during the corporation's first discussions with the Immigration Board about a development in Kimstad, 22 residences had represented the number under consideration. *Siv* planners rejected the reduction, claiming it would render the operation too expensive to run efficiently. In terms of minimal personnel requirements and the estimated cost-per-person calculations, a facility domiciling only 150 people would not represent a sound investment of *Siv* resources.

Agreeing a temporary impasse had resulted, representatives from *Siv* and Wibarco agreed to study each other's positions before reconvening in a week. As headstrong as ever about not wanting a center in their town, adversaries of the development did not interpret downsizing as a victory. No doubt Ann-Christin Bobeck expressed the growing pessimism and lack of faith many foes were beginning to have in the democratic process. She speculated about how "it does not matter what we say. The politicians are taking the decision over our heads." In the final analysis her prediction was correct because on April 11, 1990, the building board granted a permit for the construction of nine units. For fiscal reasons *Siv* planner Stefan Kungsmark was against any proposal that would call for opening a center with fewer than 200 people, but in the end he accepted what amounted to a mini-center. It was Rosenqvist's persuasiveness about dominant attitudes in the village that brought about the acceptance of a downsized facility. Thinking an attempt at appeasement would show he had listened to and "been influenced by opinions in Kimstad," the building board head erroneously assumed a less ambitious project would be interpreted by its hardheaded foes as an acceptable compromise.[42]

Rather than placating center foes, the reduction in size emboldened them to concluding more demonstrations would cause a complete abandonment of its development. Convinced they were winning the battle, opposition leaders called for a massive show of continuing community outrage with having any refugees placed in Kimstad. On May 17, 1990, two groups of residents assembled in the village. A small assembly of townspeople were at the local church, praying for spiritual guidance and wisdom in their responses to the challenges of hatred and division, while a much larger gathering estimated at 300 people assembled at a grocery store for a protest march to the local school.

Galvanized by a single goal, these participants showed determination to stop any imposition of unwanted strangers—regardless of their numbers—on them. At the rally Moderate Widell had wanted to speak, but her political party forbade it. As a result Dr. Eva Bergqvist, a physician who resided near the proposed down-sized facility, emerged from her fellow marchers to offer a rousing rebuttal to the government's generous asylum policy, stating in easily understood terms what its consequences have been for Swedes. By choosing to "decide over the people's heads" and allowing in boatloads of human beings from all corners of the world, politicians have allowed the Immigration Board "to expand in a way the tax system does not allow." As her audience shouted its agreement with each consequence, Bergqvist described a "society in crises," citing Swedish munificence's toll. Included were hospital ward and military installation closures, nonreplacements of old textbooks, and deteriorating care and neglect of pensioners. In return for such decline and decay, the doctor concluded, the nation was compensated with people who "stole, . . . destroy fruit, . . . throw garbage, [and drive around in] their good-looking cars."

To explain its position *Siv* had dispatched a representative to Kimstad, but nobody wanted to hear any of the spokesperson's comments or to learn of the agency's plans. No sooner had Kungsmark attempted to address the ruly crowd than it submerged his voice in shouts about him being a "blockhead, traitor, and goddamned oppressor." Quickly aware the shouters of invectives had no intention of allowing him to speak, the unwelcomed guest made way for opposition leader Göran Eldh. In a clear mockery of Kungsmark, the local organizer asked listeners to denounce racism, the Immigration Board, and the refugee center; they responded as cued.[43]

Newspapers captured Kimstad's determination to thwart all efforts at allowing in refugees, and television crews came to the village to obtain film footage of interviews with local citizens who wanted to give reasons for their strong resolves. Since the national population was unaccustomed to fellow Swedes challenging government policies with courage and outspokenness, candid residents of bucolic Kimstad gained near-celebrity status and a response of gratitude and support from throughout the kingdom. For example Träff gained some prominence after an appearance on television during which he had asked how there could be money for "a bunch of refugees when for thirteen years we have not gotten a bicycle path." The tinsmith received 500 letters. Most were supportive, but there was also hate mail. To accusations of racism, he offered denial by replying that a refugee could be "altogether coal black as long as he worked."

Events in a town that refused to surrender to the national government on developing and opening a sanctuary for exiled persons began a dialog on official policies governing immigrants and refugees. Prior to the protests in Kimstad, according to church historian Kenneth Ritzén of Uppsala, citizens withheld their true feelings, and the government succeeded at suppressing and silencing its

critics. Following the example of irate residents of a country town near
Norrköping, people across Sweden felt free to lambast generosity.

Uppsalan Leif Andersson became a firsttime public critic, daring now to
speak openly about abuses. Asking and then answering his own question why
many Africans were crossing the entire European continent to reach Sweden, he
replied it was because of his nation's reputation for "serving everything" to
newcomers. If blame should be assigned for an unfortunate state of affairs,
none should go to the so-called refugees; it was Swedish politicians' fault for
having established a haven with programs that teach aliens about how best to
"exploit the system" and for allowing them to ignore the basic societal rules that
govern such elementary matters as parking. Regarding his nation's future,
Andersson claimed solidarity with many compatriots who were worried about
Sweden's abilities to withstand challenges and costs from people who did not
share Swedes' regard for maintaining "system and order, working hard, and
acquitting themselves generally well." To doubters he suggested they compare
Swedish yards to ones found in the newcomers' homelands. While his fellow
countrymen kept their properties "neat and and well-groomed," those found in
other parts of the world "looked damn nasty." Carefully first hedging how he
was "not a racist **but**" [author's emphasis], Andersson told of a soccer match
played in heavily immigrant-concentrated Tensta, outside Stockholm. After a
referee's call had gone against the home side, "50 relatives went on the pitch,
ready to lynch the official," an incident Andersson could not imagine occurring
with Swedish spectators because of their better understanding of the game. As
much as there were few things Andersson liked about non-ethnic Nordics, he
was willing to concede that "carneval and . . . exotic foods," flamboyance, and
talkative spontaneity while queuing for service were exceptions. Moreover he
found aliens' general demeanor around strangers a pleasant contrast to the
"stiffness and silence" of Swedes.[44]

Although Andersson and many of his countrymen were racists and
xenophobes, their collective concerns about what they saw happening to "their"
Sweden clearly represented a populistic movement. For Svenssons who had
found in the example of Kimstad resisters a cathartic that opened them to
purging pent-up hostilities toward refugees and immigrants, defiance assumed a
much more daring dimension in the early morning hours of May 24, 1990.
Villagers awoke to learn two of fifteen barracks intended to house 175
refugees[45] were now after an arson attack smoldering ashes. With a smell of
smoke hovering in the air and police appearing clueless about responsibility,
local residents filed past the site for personal inspections of damages estimated
at 500,000 kronor.

Reporters on hand for first reactions gathered a range of expressions from
curious townspeople, but in all likelihood only the most sensational responses
were published. They were, nevertheless, representative because of the issue's
polarization of the populace. One visitor's "lone regret [was] the fire had not
taken the rest [of the complex] also." Without making elaboration about whom
or what should be mindful of possible actions if the project were not abandoned,

a companion viewed "this is [as] a warning." For a pipefitter who was laying water and sewer connections to the refugee center and observing the curious crowd, there was a joke about a missed opportunity; "we should have made a good amount if we had taken admissions" to see the charred ruins.

Project supporter and Social Democratic chair of the local governing board Lindvall expressed dismay, hoping only that "the people understand what they have applauded." Despite misgivings with her constituency, she found it "difficult to believe that it is a Kimstad resident who has set the fire." Meanwhile over at Immigration Board headquarters in Norrköping, General Director Christina Rogestam reacted with resolve. Agency plans would go forward, she promised, because "if we withdraw, it gives a clear signal: burn down two barracks and the Immigration Board capitulates." Ever hopeful of people's goodwill and understanding, she believed "once the people [of Kimstad] have contacts with the asylum recipients and learn to know some of them, they will surely develop another point of view."[46]

During the following days Kimstad was under careful scrutiny. Many investigators from Sweden's homogeneous police force were there,[47] searching the area for clues and conducting a door-to-door canvass for information and leads. Although there seemed commitments to finding whomever had set the buildings ablaze, nothing substantial ever resulted from the officers' efforts. If anything were known, townspeople were not telling. After one week of being in a hostile environment without cooperation and with neither data nor suspects, detectives abandoned all direct efforts at solving the puzzle of responsibility.

Arson had one positive consequence, however. Refugee-development supporters were "no longer afraid to say it." Unlike before the fire when "it had been uncontroversial to be with the enemies of immigrants and almost heroic to dare to say all people have the same value," a climate for greater outspokenness unfolded. Now it was foes who were defensive. Träff and Eldh, the project's leading critics, found themselves targets of harrassment. The tinsmith was particularly upset after anonymous telephone callers had labeled him a Nazi. To have this association because of desires for a calm community and concern for his family, he moaned, was "a knife in the back." Eldh had trouble understanding how blame could be placed on him when everybody should be recognizing the real culprits behind Kimstad's problems. Steadfast in his beliefs, he never doubted for a moment that "the big scoundrels in this drama are the politicians." For them he had a prediction about what would happen in Sweden. "The people's judgment will be hard. They can vote, but their voice is not heard. We live in a dictatorship."

Prime Minister Ingvar Carlsson—although not specifically mentioned but likely classified by Eldh as one of the dictators—interpreted the arson as part of a larger plot by "groups trying to build up hatred toward foreigners." Seen as an "escalation," the fire and "this type of violence" did not occur as "a complete surprise" to Sweden's leader; "tendencies have been existing, but this can be an alarm clock. It is time to go to a counterattack." Promising toughness against perpetrators and protection for potential victims, Carlsson noted in a press interview how his political party, the Social Democrats, were already engaged in a campaign to enlighten and inform Swedes about refugees and immigrants. When asked why aliens had been having so much trouble with finding jobs, the prime minister would not speculate more than to say language difficulties accounted for some of their problems.[48]

True to Rogestam's intentions expressed immediately after the fire, the Immigration Board did not surrender to terror, threats, and arson. On June 14, 1990, exactly three weeks after an attempt at intimidation had resulted in fire gutting two barracks, the first refugees came to Kimstad. Two groups—one friendly to their arrival and another hostile—were present for either welcoming or jeering the community's newest residents. Kept at a safe distance from each other by many law-enforcement officers, supporters had permission to interact with Mustafa Ahmed, a Bulgarian Turk and the first alien of twenty-seven who entered a well-protected compound on a sunny June afternoon. Wiping sweat off his forehead, he confessed to having "been afraid to travel here, but today after meeting all these people I have lost all my fear." Almost overwhelmed by friendliness, Ahmed willingly learned Swedish folk dances from Swedes, listened attentively to the singing of their national anthem, and enjoyed their refreshments.

Many dignitaries were on hand to welcome the refugees. Superintendent Per Wass of Älvås—the Kimstad refugee facility's official name—was one of several speakers. Among other things he mentioned how Finns had lived there during World War II, and he did not mince words about the negative reactions of area residents to reopening the center to new sanctuary seekers. On a brighter note Sven Olsson of the advisory board described the establishment of a voluntary network of twenty support families to assist Älvås residents. Vicar Bergstrand-Nilson ended the brief welcoming ceremony with a short homily about how "we can have different understandings of God but He sees us all in the same way."

Her reassuring inclusive remarks were a prelude to fun activities. Soon everyone participated in a traditional Swedish ring dance and, for alien boys and girls' benefit, local children demonstrated a playful activity that included hopping around in a circle to a song entitled "the little frogs." If there were a highlight to a delightful afternoon of understanding and barrier breaking, it would have been a timid eight-year old accompanied by her mother walking slowly to Sukriya—at thirty months, the youngest of the new residents—to present her with a favorite doll. In a response that needed no translation, the little girl showed appreciation for the gift by hugging her generous new friend. Seeing this warm communication without words between two girls of diverse backgrounds, Kimstad parents through translators advised alien counterparts to discard all worries because "we are not dangerous; nobody needs to be afraid of us." One mother was so certain of her Kimstad neighbors' harmlessness that she advised Älvås girls' parents to be unconcerned about their daughters' safety if they should want to venture into town by themselves: "We assure that they can go safely on the streets." Reassuring "none of us will cause trouble," the

Kimstad parent noted how the overall goal of fellow residents from her town would soon be "creating comradeship."[49]

Inasmuch as *Siv* had successfully defended its position by settling refugees in Kimstad, something much larger resulted from the episode. Released from latency, a Swedish will to resist unpopular governmental intrusions and to demonstrate discontent with defiance and bravado emerged. A bucolic community's example of moving from dormancy to activism spread quickly across the nation. Even at the price of being considered racist, Swedes indicated their disapproval and discontent with both the scope and the cost of a national refugee policy. Their thoughts surfaced in letters to newsapers and in other measures of public opinion.[50] According to one scientific poll that broke down opinions regionally, that was released only two days after the first arrivals at Älvås, *Svenska Institutet för Opinionsundersökningar* or *SIFO* (the Swedish Institute for Opinion Investigations) found sixty percent of its sample of the opinion that Sweden was continuing to accept too many asylum seekers. In the Skåne region in Sweden's extreme south, seventy-three percent felt this way, while at the other extreme of opinion, only forty-seven percent of polled Stockholmers agreed. Thirty-five percent there believed entries were at the correct level, and totally unlike anywhere else in the country, fifteen percent in the capital district wanted the government to accept more refugees. In terms of justifiable grounds—if any—for granting sanctuary, sixty-seven percent of the entire sampling accepted political persecution as a legitimate reason, and fifty-one percent thought sufferers from calamities and poverty should qualify. A big majority did not believe desires to reunite with family members, to obtain Swedish medical care, to worship freely, or to work and study in Sweden were bases for residency permits. Regarding preferences—if these were stated—for aliens' nationalities and ethnicities, Swedes objected least of all to immigrants with Nordic, Baltic, and Germanic backgrounds. For these peoples favorable ratings ranged from ninety-two percent for Danes to sixty-three percent for Poles. Concurrently Bulgarian Turks and Iranians, at thirty and thirty-one percents respectively, were seen as the least desirable prospective newcomers. Almost as many Swedes favored as opposed arrivals of Vietnamese, Chileans, and Ethiopians.[51]

If polls and expressions can be believed—and they should be—about Swedish attitudes, Kimstad was important because events there underscored just how out-of-sync the national government officials' policies and actions were with public opinion. Whether it had been due to their exaggerated beliefs in largely mythical Swedish generosity and superiority, which were allowed to express themselves in foreign relations and state-owned media reports as harsh critiques of other nations' faults or had come from the development of Social Democratic pomposity, arrogance, and aloofness, which manifested from the political party's success at concentrating so much power over the last half century, the results were ignorance and disregard of the popular will insofar as the matter of strangers coming into the country.

Unaware of people's genuine worries and concerns about the costs and consequences of offering an unabated refuge in Sweden, politicians erred in two important ways. First of all they either ignored or refused to believe polls. Secondly there were no significant attempts at either explaining or justifying Swedish refugee policy. By abdicating an important responsibility, Carlsson and members of his government permitted a spread of misconceptions and rumors, a problem they could have easily countered with facts and figures. As results of the monarchy's aging population, declining birthrate, and mounting welfare benefits, her economy needed infusions of workers and taxpayers from outside her borders.

Neither Prime Minister Carlsson nor anybody else of some importance and stature in government was explaining such fiscal realities to the nation. One can only speculate about how much silence owed itself to the previously assigned attributes to Social Democrats and how much came from ignorance of basic economics. Then again it might have simply been the politicians' honest attempt at removing refugee matters from public debate, this in order to deny opportunities for their exploitation by potential demagogues. Regardless of the national leadership's motives or reasons, a vacuum resulted that left a majority of the native population distrusting and disrespecting the Swedish government at the time when it was accepting more outsiders into the country despite what amounted to increasing resentment for the ones already in Sweden.[52]

Sparks from the arson attack of Kimstad's refugee barracks nearing completion and occupancy literally and figuratively ignited fires elsewhere. As foes of sanctuaries increasingly became frustrated, a wave of immitations occurred throughout Sweden. As their means of communicating opinions and exasperation, they turned to violence. Attacks with Molotov cocktails, smoke bombs, gasoline-soaked tires, stones, explosives, airgun pellets, shotgun shells, and bullets became almost daily fare on television news and in newspaper articles.

Swedes' discontent with refugees even drew inspiration from resisters to change in the United States. Reminiscent of the segregationists' intimidations from the Second Abolition Crusade between 1955 and 1965, Nordic imitators of the Ku Klux Klan lit fiery crosses and also left behind the scrawled letters KKK as their trademarks of hostility.

Outbreaks occurred at both unfinished and occupied refugee facilities. Some succeeded at disrupting activities by inflicting material damages and by causing bodily injuries. Others failed, excepting, of course, in the sense their misfired attacks had a psychological impact upon alien residents. Although almost twenty refugee camps were targets for violence during a one-month span after Kimstad and most of these attacks occurred after boarders had gone to bed, casualties were scarce. The highest toll was at Motala where a smoke-bomb attack resulted in eleven persons' hospitalization for minor inhalation problems.[53]

Insofar as destructiveness to property and systematic precision, arson at Laholm during the early morning hours of May 26, 1990, had no parallels.

Methodically arsonists used outstretched wire from one barrack to the next to hang gasoline-soaked rags. With all sixteen units so connected, they doused each in a flammable liquid. Being careful not to engulf themselves in flames, the terrorists linked a long gunpowder fuse from an ignition point to the first structure. Once ignited, the fire spread rapidly along the line of buildings. After the chain-reaction fire, only racist graffiti sprayed on cement foundations and one fully furnished building remained; inspectors set damages at 300,000 kronor. Just as with the xenophobic crime at Kimstad two days earlier, solving the Laholm arson evaded police. Since nobody ever claimed responsibility for the fire, words found on cement slabs indicated prejudice as the primary motive; their proclamations advising "No niggers" and "No blacks in Laholm" were clear enough indications of this to all but some local residents who refused to believe anyone from their community could have been behind the act. One elderly gentleman even hypothesized the crime had been a plot by the barracks' owners to collect on insurance.[54]

The violence directed against refugees represented the second part of a double nightmare. Often leaving behind devastated homelands for anticipated peace and opportunities in a nation with a reputation for gentle, liberal-minded people, many Swedish newcomers arrived with personal experiences already deeply scarred by death, rape, torture, bloodshed, and prejudice. Having escaped insidious, destructive wars, these victims quickly realized they had not fled terror after all because of an error in their choice for exile. Instead of an awaited tranquil haven, Sweden seemed another hell to confront. Now these wretched souls, spending their nights away from windows—huddled in fear of incendiary devices entering and setting them and their children alight—often could not sleep restfully because of thoughts about might befall them next in their "sanctuaries." Most likely nobody had warned them in advance of long journeys to expect physical danger and psychological complications from a residence in Scandinavia, but realities of life there proved to be deja vu. At refugee compounds, spotting male residents posted nightly around residences as guards against intruders became a common sight.

Despite the accelerated violence against foreigners in Sweden and many associated unpleasantries with asylum there, information about these problems did not spread to deter future migrants from reaching the country. As a result almost 500,000 hopeful people with expectations of fresh starts and excellent opportunities in an atmosphere of kindness, fairness, and justice arrived at Swedish docks and airports between January 1, 1990 and December 31, 2000. When all living immigrants and refugees are added, nonethnic Swedes account for more than 1,750,000 people or about twenty percent of the Nordic nation's 8,878,828 residents; roughly twenty-five percent of children under eighteen-years old have foreign backgrounds.[55]

To understand how a once largely homogeneous population had turned increasingly heterogeneous so rapidly, one must look at many factors. Crises in global hotspots and poverty pushed individuals from their homelands, and a combination of Swedish policies and a positive reputation pulled disportionate numbers of these people to the Nordic kingdom. The imposition of a despotic theocracy in Iran, Eritrea's war of independence, Iraqi dictatorial abuses, the Palestinian conflict with Israel, minority suppressions in Bulgaria and Turkey, Latin American military juntas' suppressions, Somalian disintegration, and in ex-Yugoslavia ethnic cleansing, civil war, and nationalism combined as causes for mass migrations.

To deal with refugees the United Nations in 1951 enacted guidelines for signatories to follow. Accordingly grants of refugee status should go to every person who lives in fear of persecution because of race, religion, nationality, political opinion, or social-group affiliation. Qualifiers under one of these five categories are known as Convention Refugees. Recipient nations are obliged to grant asylum and abstain from returning applicants to their homelands for as long as they might face danger. In addition to this classification international arrangements provide for Quota Refugees. As the name implies "safe" nations receive specific allocations based upon abilities and capacities to provide new homes for displaced persons. Unlike other exiles who must accept transitional adjustments and pass judgments about their worthiness, quota designees have the right to integrate directly into nations with work permits and permanent residences.

For Vietnamese "boat people"—persons who constituted a major source of Sweden's Quota Refugees—multinational Perstorp Corporation arranged a good start. It did everything after the Asians' arrivals at Malmö, including the bus transport from the city to Perstorp, provision of furnished apartments ready for their occupation, and help from experienced Vietnamese guides on hand to assist with commercial activities, insurance and health matters, and school enrollments. Upon completing orientations, these Southeast Asian newcomers had jobs that awaited them at one of the sponsor's many manufacturing plants.

Extralegally—beyond the UN requirements and the scope of the world body's many conventions—some sovereign states like Sweden chose on their own initiatives to exceed mandated generosity; the Nordic nation extended her refuge philanthropy to a general class of sufferers who are known collectively as "Humanitarian Refugees" as well as to some army deserters and pacifists. In wartime escapees from military service qualified for exile if Sweden looked disfavorably upon the war being fought, one of its participant's objectives, or a nation's involvement. During the Vietnam and Iraq-Iran wars, the monarchy accepted draft dodgers and deserters from these conflicts. Taking these actions became Sweden's way to protest what she was alleging to be illegal American aggression in an internal conflict and a means to criticize what she was judging Iranian ambitions against a weaker neighbor. Moreover the Nordic kingdom took in De Facto Refugees or warfare's civilian victims.

Neutral Sweden kept a generous policy with broadly based eligibility until December 13, 1989. Since rescinding had occurred on Saint Lucia Day, critics began dubbing the revision somewhat sarcastically the Lucia Law because its namesake's canonization had resulted from her charitable work among needy persons. Overdue enactment was really a response to Sweden's need to align her asylum policies to those of other nations. Statistics illustrate the degree of a Swedish magnamimous policy's uncontrollability. During the autumn prior to passage, 6,000 people a month sought sanctuary, or in other words as many applicants as had requested it for all of 1976. Put in another context, monthly numbers for Sweden were equaling annual demands placed on neighboring Denmark and Norway.[56]

Change presented Sweden with two undesirable problems. As evidence from Kimstad, Laholm, and many locations has shown, native Swedes clashed even more over refugee policy, with one side claiming capitulation to nativists and the other demanding even more restrictions and changes. The new law also complicated Sweden's foreign relations, first by her placing cost burdens involved with returns on the transportation companies which had transported people ineligible for Swedish asylum in the Nordic land and second by the monarchy flushing back all the unwanted individuals into dispatching nations.

With Aeroflot the largest air carrier of refugees to Stockholm's Arlanda Airport and Poland the major entrepôt for migrants on their way to Sweden from other nations, both the airline and the sending-off country experienced difficulties with Sweden after the Lucia Law's enactment. The carrier, in its own defense, claimed to have a preboarding routine of checking individuals' documents as a condition to fly, but the procedure proved ineffective because as soon as its planes had become airborne, passengers began shredding their passports and birth certificates, knowing in doing this they were destroying all evidence of middle passages. Under international law an asylum seeker was supposed to seek refuge at the first destination after a homeland departure and not travel to a third nation.

Swedish-Polish relations also deteriorated because of the former nation's accusations about lax border controls leading to illegal migrants being allowed to board boats bound for Ystad, Sweden. Poles countered, complaining about her Nordic neighbor shuffling these people immediately back onto ferries for returns to their country. The impasse ended with Poland improving her border checks and Sweden assisting with care of the several thousand stranded people who had begun to overwhelm such Polish ports as Swinoujscie. As victims of people smugglers, most of these individuals had been wayfarers escorted over mountain passages from Iran and other Middle Eastern troublespots into the United Arab Emirates for eventual circuitous transit to Poland. Having been lured into believing Sweden would be a land of milk and honey, these travelers risked all their resources on opportunities that would never be realized.

Withdrawal of unilateral generosity came as a response to critics who had disliked a policy with its grants of asylum to persons whom advocates of tougher rules had deemed "not real refugees" but rather seekers after Sweden's high living standards. At the time of the *Riksdag*'s concession to hardliners, almost 19,000 persons were already in Sweden, awaiting status judgments. At asylum hearings after the Lucia Law, applicants were forced to show complete evidence of their worthiness as true asylum seekers under the United Nations Convention on Refugees and provide legal documents with accurate data about their personal identities and national origins. If aspirants required assistance in their presentations or in their appeals of deportation orders, legal counsel along with translators were available to advise applicants at no cost. With an average of three hours required in most instances to hear and settle typical asylum cases and insufficient trained personnel to gather information and render verdicts, it is easy to understand why ever-increasing numbers of asylum seekers taxed all available resources.

Effects of "raising the bar" for aliens to clear in order to obtain resident permits were evident only months after the Lucia Law's passage. Prior to the parliamentary tightening in 1989 eighty percent of candidates had received a right to sanctuary, while three quarters into 1990 under the revised legislation, less than fifty percent gained admission into Sweden. No longer generous to a fault, the Nordic kingdom had aligned its policies more closely with those of a great majority of affluent industrialized nations. There remained one problem, however; nobody publicized or circulated news of Swedish toughness among potential migrants. They had no inkling of the nation's foresaking a liberal policy for a much more restrictive set of asylum parameters. As a result the nation continued to be "flooded" with refuge seekers whose presence required lodging and resources until such time as their personal cases could be sorted and judged.[57]

Statistics from the United Nations Refugee Commission note clearly the ineffectiveness of Sweden's tougher policies. Three tables show a pattern of similar consequences but in different factual alignments:

Table Number 1, Permanent Asylum Permits, 1987-1996

NATION	NUMBER
Sweden	*191,310*
Germany	144,310
Great Britain	96,905
France	91,305
Netherlands	88,250
Denmark	50,325
Switzerland	49,015
Norway	48,410
Austria	15,015
Belgium	11,860
Finland	10,250
Spain	5,685
Italy	3,555
Greece	1,360
Portugal	250
Ireland	70

Table Number 2, Permanent Asylum Permits per 100,000 Residents

NATION	NUMBER
Sweden	*2,199*
Norway	1,126
Denmark	968
Switzerland	710
Netherlands	581
Finland	205
Austria	190
Germany	180
Great Britain	168
France	159
Belgium	119
Spain	15
Greece	13
Italy	6
Portugal	3
Ireland	2

Table Number 3, Refugees Granted Permanent Resident Permits, 1992-1996

NATION	Asylum Decisions	No. Allowed to Stay		Pending Cases, 1996
Ireland	156	69	44%	n.a.
Great Britain	212,173	69,805	33%	29,642
Belgium	24,487	6,191	30%	12,421
Portugal	2,107	177	8%	269
Spain	53,355	3,308	6%	4,730
France	154,898	36,084	24%	17,153
Switzerland	108,415	36,536	34%	17,936
Netherlands	210,628	91,202	43%	22,857
Greece	5,340	550	10%	1,635
Italy	12,418	1,217	10%	681
Germany	1,098,642	104,371	9.5%	117,333
Austria	64,571	5,876	9%	6,991
Denmark	45,879	31,756	69%	5,893
Norway	70,183	27,231	39%	1,778
Finland	13,570	6,568	48%	711
Sweden	*158,576*	*63,879*	*40%*	*5,774*

The three tables each contain lessons and consequences about Sweden's refugee policies. From the first and second charts generosity seems an obvious conclusion; it emerges as a result of the Nordic kingdom outpacing all other European nations with its astonishing ten-year record of 191,310 refugees obtaining permanent residency, a figure that worked out to 2,199 recipients for every 100,000 Swedish residents. At 144,310 permit bestowals—or 47,000 fewer than the leading total—the Federal Republic of Germany paled in comparison to the Scandinavians, especially if the ratio of grants to German population is factored into the equation; with more than ten times as many people as Sweden, Germany—with a rate of only 180 asylum grants for every 100,000 inhabitants—showed an obvious reluctance to accept her fair share of refugees-turned-immigrants.

Although everything in the third table is somewhat self-explanatory, there is more to refugee processing than these statistics for the 1992-to-1996 period relate. Insofar as access to legal assistance one question to examine is whether or not people seeking sanctuary in the sixteen countries had the same rights to lawyers. Throughout the refuge-seeking ordeal in Sweden, applicants awaiting decisions on bids to stay could freely consult lawyers on retainer for this purpose by the government. Excepting Switzerland, Finland, Norway, and Denmark, other European nations were not so generous; either they relied upon volunteers working pro bono on cases or they required refugees to pay for their own counsel. The Norwegian government assumed all legal fees, but if there were questions about law, refugees were responsible for finding and contacting attorneys.

Detention represents another aspect of refugee care with varying approaches. Sweden maintained four especially designated lockup centers where in most cases refugees could be held for a maximum of two months. Exceptions could occur if Swedish law enforcement authorities stipulated longer detentions at closed-door hearings; only rarely did Swedish holdings exceed one year, however. Unlike Italy where lockups were nonexistent, all other national standards for detaining refugees resembled Sweden's policies. For the most part when there were specified maximum lockup periods, three months were the norm. Although most countries maintained special facilities for detaining asylum seekers, there were cases of prisons being employed for this purpose. Great Britain—in many respects the nation that handled seekers of sanctuary cruelest—had no time limits, and her jails often served as holding centers. One-year detentions were commonplace in the United Kingdom, and there were instances of detainees spending as much as six years locked up in British cells.[58]

As much as laws seemingly safeguarded a refugee's rights while under Swedish custody and statistics tended to show asylum seekers faring better in the Scandinavian kingdom than elsewhere in Europe, one must consider other indicators and factors before concluding too much prematurely—and possibly incorrectly—in Sweden's favor. As details implied about events during "the long hot summer" in "the land of the midnight sun," anxiety had significance as a negative intangible. Although fearing violence from Swedish extremists persisted at many refugee settlements, another more constant source of fright and uncertainty would have a more universal effect upon petitioners in their struggle for consent to remain in Sweden. Trepidation over future status in many cases compounded every unpleasantry that had followed abandoning homelands for uncertain futures in a strange land with a cold climate as well as an unfathomable language. Begun at processing, doubts could linger and hang over refugees for months and even years without a ruling for either a residence permit or a deportation order from the Alien Review Board.

For large numbers of desperate searchers after peace and safety, even the act of entering Sweden could prove humilitating. From bitter past experiences with authority figures, many new arrivals could not relax during confrontations with uniformed police who generally looked upwardly with suspicious glances during their studious inspections of requested travel documents, this no doubt in their attempts at ascertaining if pictured persons in passports did in fact resemble the individuals now before them. Final judgments about validity and legitimacy had rested with Sweden's border guards until late 1996, when many fundamental responsibilities passed to the Immigration Board. No matter who had charge of making determinations, trauma associated with being subjected to the mercy of authoritarian figures did not easily vanish.

More emotional hurdles to overcome followed the initial clearances of paperwork. For randomly selected entrants, the next ordeals were unpleasant because guards searched their possessions and frisked their bodies. Enduring the latter experience proved especially revolting to Muslim women and rape victims; for these female applicants just the thought of total strangers feeling and probing them for such contraband as drugs and weapons was humiliating, shocking, and embarrassing. Compulsory fingerprinting appeared next on the processing agenda. Done for identity purposes and the prevention of reentries, it customarily occurred as a prelude to complete medical examinations. From doctors' stations applicants reported to nurses for blood tests in order to screen for HIV and AIDS. The precaution followed a 1990 report, a reenforcement of nativistic thinking about the responsibility for a dreaded killer's spread across Sweden; according to its finding five of eight persons then diagnosed with the disease had foreign backgrounds.

As an Iranian man discovered from an unwillingness to sign bureaucratic forms and be fingerprinted, noncooperation at any stage of "inspections" could have dire consequences. For not complying to incomprehensible orders, police beat him so severely that his deep wound required attention at a hospital. An inquiry into the brutal incident resulted in exoneration. Although the beating had come under police-imposed incarceration for "disagreeable demeanor," the Swedish court that examined allegations of brutality by five policemen would judge the victim's injuries suffered from the officers' repeated baton slugs and their knee thrusts to the alien's back "as justifiable uses of force to obtain necessary fingerprints."

Such unfortunate episodes as this were unusual; most individuals did not balk at the expectations laid before them. For not complicating procedures and by demonstrating docility, their fates upon a satisfactory completion of all the aforementioned preliminaries were not at all as unpleasant as what the Iranian had experienced. Instead of equally harsh treatment, most seekers after asylum found themselves simply herded onto buses for movement to special transitory facilities where Immigration Board officials would hold them, pending all test results and bed availabilities at the regular refugee camps dispersed throughout Sweden.[59]

At any stage of processing authorities could determine grounds or reasons for discontinuing interrogations or inspections. As with the hundreds of people who had come by ferry to Ystad from the Middle East via Poland only to be returned quickly from the southern Swedish port to Swinoujscie, other hopeful migrants suffered similar fates. Among them were more than 1,000 Roma who had arrived in spurts during the summer of 1991. Although they had legally qualified as victims of persecution as defined by the United Nations Convention on Refugees in 1951, Sweden did not want them. As with people allover Europe, residents of the Nordic kingdom had prejudices against gypsies. For one young Romany resident who had taken a Swedish name in an attempt at hiding his true identity, there was a summarization of feelings with a rhetorical question. In a plea for understanding his position in Nordic society, he asked, "Can you imagine how it feels to be regarded and treated as shit your entire life?" Hence not only were the ones who had already arrived placed on ships bound for return trips to Poland, but Polish television twice carried an interview with a Swedish embassy spokesperson. The Swede advised gypsies not to bother trying to come to Sweden because immigration authorities would never allow them to stay. In conjunction with a media campaign, two Swedish policemen boarded a Sweden-bound ferry from Poland to relay again the same message to Romany travelers who had ignored or not heard advice about not attempting to obtain Swedish asylum.

Margareta Levenhagen, a Swedish law-enforcement officer based in Malmö and a member of the alien section, claimed positive effects from the information barrage aimed at gypsies who might otherwise have contemplated coming to Sweden with hopes of gaining asylum. According to her, "It had a very positive effect. The police judgment was that several hundred Roma who had thought of traveling to Sweden in order to seek asylum would give up when they received information about the small possibilities that they may stay."

Sweden's lack of keenness about accepting gypsies was matched by an almost equal disdain for welcoming in Russians. With the Soviet Empire's fall mass hysteria swept across the three northernmost Nordic countries. Like her neighbors to the east and west, Sweden was gripped with fears of a great Slavic migration into Scandinavia. To signal clearly and remove all doubts about what would be awaiting unwanted Eastern Europeans, Sweden speedily dispatched homeward most every arriving migrant from the ex-Soviet Union and from many of her former satellite states. A case in point occurred during August 1993, when a contingent of forty-eight Russians entered the kingdom at Holmsund with visums and intentions to pick berries in northern Sweden.

Although for many years migrant workers from poorer nations had harvested both lingonberries and cloudberries from Swedish forests for canneries, these particular pickers did not receive this opportunity. Almost seven years later on March 6, 2000, 108 Russian asylum seekers from Lithuania, Latvia, Georgia, and Azerbaijan failed at pushing their claims of mistreatment as minorities in the newly independent nations which had been carved from ex-Soviet Union republics; officials deported them, too.

World-class hurdler Ludmila Leonova Narzojilenko (Engquist) and the champion cross-country skier, Antonina Ordina, were two famous exceptions, but with them there were Swedish hopes for glory and medals from athleticism and associations with Sweden. These women's cheerful readiness to compete in blue-and-yellow sportswear was enough to compensate for their heritages. After Narzojilenko's gold medal at the 1996 Olympic Games, the foreign track star won the hearts of Swedes by draping their flag over her shoulders before a victory lap around the track; the Russian's victory and response to it gave her a ranking just behind Queen Silvia as Sweden's most popular, admirable alien.[60]

By not welcoming most migrants from behind the fallen Iron Curtain, an opening developed there for the operation of various mafia-run activities that would exasperate Swedish attempts at curtailing two of the most undesirable forms of immigration, people smuggling and white-slave trading. Combatting these directly involved *Siv* and law-enforcement officials. Gangsters dealers who specialized in one or the other kind of human cargo presented Swedish authorities with especially difficult tasks because of Sweden's jagged eastern shoreline that stretches from Haparanda in the north to Ystad in the extreme south and that contains in its archipelago thousands of islands. Even along the west coast moving northward from Ystad beyond Strömstad to the Norwegian border, Sweden's geography presented insurmountable obstacles to patrol and a contrabandist's perfect setting. Often a combination of factors contributed to successful people-smuggling operations. They included an indefensible 1,800-mile expanse—if measured in approximate flight miles without allowance for inlets and islands—of coastal territory, brave but desperate individuals willing to risk everything on gambles of coming to Sweden, unscrupulous, greedy ship captains anxious to cash in their navigational skills for quick profits, and mafia organizers who foresaw golden opportunities from people's woeful plights to tap for personal enrichment. The result was scores of vessels being put at sea, loaded with people and destined for Sweden's outer reaches for a clandestine late-night or early-morning offshore deposit of human cargo.

Whether arriving in rubber dinghies or wading to shore, these strangers slipping into Scandinavia frequently could not survive for very long without detection or shoreline assistance. Usually their captures within a few hours of disembarkations were foregone conclusions because in most cases these people lacked knowledge of the country and its language, had no contacts available to guide them into an underground subeconomy, and did not possess the necessary financial resources to remain free. For a majority of smuggled men and women entering Sweden under the cover of darkness, none of this really seemed to matter, however. Although there were apprehensions and frightful uncertainties, these did not shake confidence in the Nordic nation's ability to fulfill its reputation for generous dealings with human hardship cases.

In the most remote areas of offshore islands or on the mainland, Swedes discovered wretched souls shivering from exposures to wind and water. Wet and cold, they primarily needed dry clothing and warm beverages. Receiving basic requirements preceded interrogations about their harrowing experiences. In most cases stowaways then related somewhat reluctantly traveling in stages after a start somewhere in the Middle East. For large fees agents moved them along to Russia for eventual dispatches to Baltic Sea ports and short voyages across then to Sweden. When asked why they had endured so much to reach another country, their answers usually mixed horrorific homeland experiences with desires for asylum in a nation where they and their children might await better, peaceful futures. Favorable decisions or immediate deportations then followed the questioning.

Verdicts hinged on such factors as the credibility and believability of tellers' stories, the current policy toward illegal entries, probers' attitudes and disposition, and whether or not applicants possessed valid passports, visums, and birth certificates. Since mafia organizers' price for sneaking people into Sweden usually included fake documents, officials—especially mindful as they were of just this possibility—checked paperwork extra thoroughly, therefore. Attempts at using false records generally failed and prompted immediate and irrevocable deportations. Overall being caught trying to pass off immitations and stolen records contributed to more applicant denials of Swedish sanctuary than all other reasons.

People smuggling usually adhered to one of following scenarios. At a staging point either in Iraq, Iran, Jordan, Somalia, or Afghanistan, families liquidated all their material possessions for cash as a preliminary to traveling first either to Amman, Baghdad, or Teheran as an eventual departure point for either Istanbul, Trabzon, Yerevan, or Baku. From one of these assembly cities, migrants moved onward to Moscow for prearranged contacts with their mafia "travel agents." Dependent upon prior arrangements and greed, pricetags for stolen or forged documents and escorted journeys from the Russian capital to one of several Baltic Sea departure ports—St. Petersburg, Tallinn, Riga, and Kaliningrad were the favorite choices—for stealth movements to Sweden's east coast ranged from $1,000 to $2,500 for individuals and $2,000 to $5,000 for families. On rare occasions when no ships could be found, agents literally packed clients into truck trailers or containers for ferry travel. These persons were so desperate for a new life that they submitted themselves to a merciless class of smugglers who subjected their charges to vulnerabilty at each stage of their adventures. From initial departures under the supervision of the Russian mafia's Arab and Persian partners until entries into Sweden, there were risks from thugs ready to assault and murder defenseless migrants for their money. Moreover for female travelers, risk of rape always existed as a possibility.[61]

With an overabundance of individual stories to report and similarities in most of them, noting the horrible experiences of thirty Iraqi Kurds who arrived in 1993 suffices. Their awful tale is representative of what did occur for many thousands who paid for illegal passages into Sweden. After their arrival on an island off Sweden's east coast, they told of leaving Latvia on a cold November evening and traveling all night to a designated point. Thereupon the captain of the transit vessel ordered his passengers to board rubber dinghies. Watching as the escort boat steamed away into darkness, the discharged individuals rowed toward lights in the west. Six hours later they reached land at Gotska Sandön on Gotland's rather barren northern end. Walking to a farmyard, a delegation of the weary migrants spotted a tractor to use. Upon hearing someone trying to start its engine, a startled owner found five strangers obviously intent on taking his vehicle. Confronted by the Gotlander, a Kurd in understandable English explained how he and others had just come ashore on the island and noted the presence of several other people near the sea. Being cautious and aware of a need to notify authorities of his find, the surprised farmer telephoned police. Then he drove to the seashore to pick up the other Kurdish stowaways for a reunion with the intruders at his farmhouse. There the Swede became a kind host, charitably feeding his hungry, thirsty visitors tea, coffee, sandwiches, and rolls. Since none of them had eaten anything for more than twelve hours, there was appreciation for their good Samaritan's kindness and hospitality.

Within a short time police officers arrived to arrange transportation and temporary accommodations. Seeing the physical condition of some persons, the lawmen called for a helicopter to fly several Kurds, including a ten-month old baby, to hospital at Visby. Meanwhile a Swedish Coast Guard patrol boat began a search mission, but like many others before and after this effort, it did not track down smugglers. The Kurds' inability to produce any identity papers complicated the job of sorting through their case, but authorities did what they could. After a few days of rest and recuperation on Gotland, the illegal aliens left the island and police jurisdiction for the mainland and the responsibility of the Immigration Board. There is nothing more to report on these thirty Kurds' fates because news coverage about them stopped after their departures for a refugee camp. Odds were excellent that they did eventually obtain permits to stay because at the time of their arrival roughly seventy-five percent of cases ended favorably for asylum seekers. It would not be until early 1996 that the Asylum Review Board or ARB began imposing tougher requirements and ordering more deportations.[62]

It was also toward the century's end that eastern mafias first exploited a much more lucrative form of smuggling. By providing the Western European sex industry with girls and women, they found in white slaving a certain path to wealth. Risks were few, and penalties were light for convicted offenders. Best of all there was a constantly replenishing supply from which to draw in unsuspecting victims. With availability of literally millions of desperate, naïve teen-aged girls, the task of luring them to the West was not difficult. With job opportunities almost nonexistent in the villages and cities of Rumania, White

Russia, Ukraina, and the Baltic states, the effort of attracting young women's attention required only help-wanted notices in local newspapers and on bulletin boards for a supposed demand for waitresses, nannies, and maids in the West. Producing large pools of applicants in search of better lives in the West, these false announcements gave slavers a chance to screen respondents for attractive persons with market value for street solicitations, bordellos, and pornography. Once unknowingly snared by lofty promises of good paying jobs and help with immigration, unsuspecting victims agreed to "training." In reality it consisted of subjugation and dehumanization through debauchery, physical assault, rape, and addictive drugs.   Shamed, addicted, debilitated, and mentally conditioned, "broken-in" young girls and women had developed into dependable sex slaves for export. Thereupon agents sold the victims for a few thousand dollars each to sex overlords and pimps for smuggling into Western Europe and careers as whores.

Once sold the dispirited youthful victims entered involuntarily into new relationships with demanded sexual performance for pay. Among other things captors commonly informed their prey of indentureships and indebtedness for the costs of purchasing, transporting, and accommodating them into Western Europe. With alleged debts to repay and obligations went strict instructions; these rendered the frightened captives absolutely beholdened to their masters' commands and dictates. Victims soon discovered severe restrictions on their freedom in strange surroundings with nobody to trust and nowhere seemingly to turn for help. Trapped as unwilling prostitutes, they were forced to accept men sent them or to solicit their own customers. Harsh penalties awaited the nonperformers of sexual acts and unsuccessful escapees; beatings and denials of drugs followed disobedience, and death was often the penalty for persistent misbehavior.

With a modified script the misfortunes of a young woman in Malmö illustrate the fates of so many other gullible Eastern Europeans. On January 11, 2000, Lithuanian teenager Danguole Rasalaite's short life ended after her suicidal leap from an overpass onto an expressway. Tragedy had begun early in her life. After abondonment by her mother, a grandmother raised her in the village of Ziezmariai. Then at sixteen-years old, Danguole bought a friend's passport and flew to Sweden with a ticket provided by "Giedrius," a young acquaintance she had met earlier during an adventure to Riga. Soon after her arrival dreams of romance turned into nightmarish prostitution. Giedrius was demanding sexual acts as a repayment for an alleged 20,000 kronor "debt" that he was claiming she had accummulated for a passport, assistance with Swedish immigration, travel, and lodging. Locked in his apartment and deprived of all contacts except for the johns provided by her captor, Danguole after five weeks in Sweden managed an escape. Surviving during end-of-year holidays as best she could as a runaway on money earned again from selling herself, she likely concluded after two weeks that death might be better than continuing to live in constant fear of either being found by Giedrius or being arrested by police for prostitution and illegal entry.

Little had she known before a fatal jump that a return home to Lithuania would not have been so unusual or as disgraceful as she might have suspected. Help organization Missing Persons in her homeland was aiding young women like herself. Already it had assisted over 550 of them, first with comebacks to the Baltic nation from horrible experiences with Western European captivities and prostitution and then with readjustments to meaningful existences.[63]

Above all others Amir Heidare was Europe's master smuggler. Despite his lofty claims, judging him represented no special problems of interpretation for Swedish authorities. Comparing himself to Moses leading Israelites from Egypt, Iranian immigrant Heidare admitted in 1990 to aiding the escapes of some 20,000 countrymen from their homeland to Scandinavia. At $5,000 per exodus Swedish authorities saw more profiteering than a selfless Mosaic-like deliverance from bondage; found guilty in March 1990 by the highest court of Sweden of gaining personally from his activities, Heidare received a sentence of eight months' imprisonment. Incarceration was not a corrective experience for him, and the possibility of another sentence to jail did not act as a deterrent in his case because over the next ten years—whether during his seven different prison terms or his rare free moments—the smuggler remained busy, defending his organization *Solh* (freedom in Persian) and its activist program of arranging with counterfeited or stolen passports and identifications as many movements as possible from Iran to second countries. A recipient himself of sanctuary in Sweden after Ayatollah Ruhollah Khomeini's assumption of power in 1979, the Iranian Moses—as Heidare was describing himself in 2000—changed only three things between his first conviction in 1990 and new legal troubles in May 2000 after his capture with false documents at Göteborg's Landvetter Airport. In addition to claiming to have "led" another 10,000 persons into Sweden and to charging more for *Solh*'s services due to inflation, the indefatigable Iranian smuggler pointed to a Swedish hero from World War II as his role model. As he explained it, "Raoul Wallenberg worked in the same way as I. He provided people with travel documents." Although a reported 30,000 Iranians had come to Sweden as a result of Heidare's work, *Solh* did not limit itself to placing its people there. Altogether Heidare boasted of its assistance going to more than 230,000 Iranian refugees and of its success settling people throughout Western Europe and Canada.[64]

Whether detained after such clandestine passages into Sweden as thirty Iraqi Kurds had experienced or stopped after arrivals at regular Swedish border checkpoints, asylum seekers were at the mercy of the police or the Immigration Board for initial judgments about their appeals for sanctuary. At the first stage of processing, there were two alternatives, immediate deportation or movement to one of four refugee detention centers. Being returned usually resulted from personal origins, ethnic backgrounds, and paths to Sweden. Authorities were not hesitant about sending back residents from the ex-Soviet Union, gypsies, and persons whose obvious reason for coming was economic opportunities and whose circuitous routes to Sweden ended in departures from Baltic ports. For most hopeful entrants into the monarchy, final resolutions of their petitions to remain went on indefinite hold. Unlike many deportees who had not received more than a cursory decision that meant for one reason or another they could never qualify for asylum and therefore would be returned, other more fortunate newcomers received instructions to board buses for temporary residences; then a long ordeal would begin for an ultimate judgment. Seekers waited at times many months and even years for official resolutions of appeals.

Depending on available space, where these anxious people would spend their first nights in Sweden varied, too. For the many thousand escapees from Bosnia and Herzegovina's ethnic cleansing and mass destruction, who literally "flooded into" the Nordic kingdom during the first phase of Yugoslavia's civil war, tents awaited some of them. Although immigration officials encountered no major problems—other than the fright of Bosnians who left war only to be placed near a Swedish artillery range—from lodging people temporarily under canvas pavilions, results obtained from another temporary solution were not equally positive. Boarding admittees on out-of-service ferries moored at Malmö, Göteborg, and Stockholm's harbors had mixed but mostly negative consequences. First of all a typical compartment at twelve square meters was too confining to accommodate four boarders—whether only adults or children with their parents—for more than a night or two without causing cabin fever and nervous anxiety. By placing refugee households in such circumscriptive environments, immigration officials demonstrated a callousness and obvious disregard for basic human needs for mobility and space. Completely lacking in empathy, they had not imagined the difficulties of parents—likely without any available toys and games—trying to pacify and entertain young offspring for more than a few hours; nevertheless, there were cases of families being under these restrictive conditions for weeks. Aboard the *Winston Churchill* anchored off a Malmö pier, the four-member Eminoglu family from Bulgaria lived for more than five weeks in claustrophobic surroundings; they were not the only family with small children on board this ship. Although *Siv* personnel tried to entertain the 130 boys and girls living on the ship with a club especially for them, boredom and sickness existed, nevertheless. Living in close quarters without proper ventilation and often in windowless cabins, residents had no escapes from smells and germs permeating the *Churchill*.

Naim Mustafaglu, his wife, and two children occupied a typical nine-square meter, bottom-deck cabin for more than one month. They endured an engine's constant grinding sounds and a buzzing ventilation system. The adults suffered perpetual headaches, while the children developed irritating rashes. In the ship nurse's professional opinion, "these symptoms—such as headaches, indisposition and colds—are entirely to do with these people being under hard mental encumbrance and under stress."

Illness and fatigue were not the only effects of ship confinements. On May 24, 1990, a serious fight erupted between 200 Somalians and 75 Lebanese on the *Stefan*, a refugee ship anchored off Göteborg. Before police could intervene to separate ethnic combatants, considerable material damage to ship furnishings occurred. Although the outbreak of violence represented one of the most serious altercations between the two groups, there were others including attempted arson. Middle East natives, unable to live peacefully with Africans, lost their residential privileges aboard the *Stefan*. After a separation of adversaries, law officers escorted the Lebanese from the ship to other living arrangements. In a report on the incident for *Siv*, fighting was officially attributed to racism and insufferably long waiting in tightly packed quarters unsuitable for protracted periods.[65]

Conditions were better and more spaceous at most provisional onshore facilities and the four permanent staging residences, but the Immigration Board still lodged many of its charges more as prisoners than as sanctuary seekers. It was harshest on unaccompanied minors and all who arrived at Swedish border crossings without such proper identifications and documents as passports and visas. These individuals received the harshest treatments and caused the most suspicions. Pressed into service for detaining persons without papers were the wards of two hospitals. Göteborg's Lillhagen Psychriatic Hospital and Eastern Hospital of Malmö were among the facilities employed for this purpose. At the former institution sanctuary seekers lived together with mental patients who had histories of violence, sex crimes, and xenophobia, men to one floor, women and children to another. Inasmuch as staff members tried their best to prevent unpleasantries, they occurred anyway despite precautions. There were such complaints as the one by a refugee father after his children's contact with an exhibitionist. Although risks were minimal at the Malmö holding center, its alien residents lived as criminals, being restrained behind locked doors. Their incarcerations were so cruel that they attracted demonstrators who appeared outside hospital windows on September 9, 2000, protesting the lockups and demanding freedom for twenty-two innocent people kept inside the building.

Distrust also affected and prevailed against the many children who had traveled to Sweden without adult supervision. Following applicable rules and procedures for adults, officials requested data from young adventurers. When they had trouble responding to their questioners because of language barriers, only telecommunicational links to translators were often available instead of a human presence of someone with less hostility and more reassurance. In many cases it did not seem to matter that Swedish law required personal helpers. As traumatic as these interrogations were, even worse treatment could follow the hearings. It came especially whenever officials had doubted a child's testimony or had feared a boy or girl's disappearance. For such cases where any doubt or apprehension might exist, interrogators recommended a careful monitoring of the detainee at the Carlslund Refugee Center's special youth section. For half of 1991 the state secured down more than 300 youngsters there, with between five and ten percent of these held in lockups for more than ten days. Save the Children was among several organizations that demanded an end to the cruel practice of treating boys and girls as criminals.

The kind of experiences endured by thirteen-year old Samir from Iran would occur regularly. Fearing a son's required military service in the war with Iraq, the parents, over his protests and disappointment, sent him alone to Sweden in

1990. Taken into custody upon arrival, Samir suffered through an interrogation with only a little assistance from a telephone-connected translator; these were his experiences prior to Carlslund and an unrecorded fate thereafter. However, if his future in Scandinavian had been anything like that of fellow Iranian Ramtin Sabz Ali, it ended less than two years after his entry with seating on an airplane headed for Iran. Young Ali's departure was due to *Siv* officials' final judgment in 1991. The conclusion was that as a fourteen-year old he had lied at his preliminary hearing which had been conducted in English and which had involved several uncomprehended matters. With adversarial adults tormenting children with a battery of difficult questions and subjecting them to jail-like living quarters, the pithy conclusion of a young asylum seeker summarized appropriately and accurately a reflection of living for many children who had come unescorted to Sweden for many children; it had been, he noted, as if he "were in a prison."[66]

For dehumanization's survivors who had lived either under guards in a lockup at one of the four permanent refugee-staging centers or in a cramped quarter aboard a ferry, the next step was moving to a regular refugee center in one of Sweden's 276 communes that by 1990 had agreed to accepting asylum seekers. Eight townships did not cooperate with *Siv*. Of these Sjöbo gained the most attention and criticism. Its adamancy about not participating received so much publicity that Sjöbo became synonymous in the Swedish language for a community where xenophobia and racism existed to such extent that many if not most of the residents wanted nothing to do with foreigners.

Local farmer and politician Sven-Olle Olsson, as the leader of negative forces in Sjöbo, gained fame throughout Sweden for standing up determinedly for his neighbors against the national government's determination to override and encroach upon a local people's prerogatives of being hostile to accepting refugees. As a Center Party member, Olsson for his position brought outside pressures upon himself to capitulate, but—rather than conform to regional and national party leaders' dictates and policies—the feisty, jocular Sjöbo resident refused to bend to pressure. He formed his own political party with planks in its platform for an insular Sweden that would become off-limits to incoming immigrants and refugees. The Sjöbo Party slated candidates in several local elections during the 1990s. In the 1991 general elections it succeeded better than all the other so-called small parties, polling 27,637 votes. Naturally not every communal resident liked being associated with Sjöbo's reputation for hostility to non-Swedes. Embarrassed, they tried but failed several times at overruling Olsson's ruling faction in local government. Thus, for most of the period, 1990-2000, the added words to a sign noting entry into Sjöbo applied; someone had scrawled "WHITE only" under the commune's name. Finally in October 2000 the more cosmopolitan-minded citizenry overcame Olsson with enough favorable council votes for a Sjöbo reversal of a long-standing policy of resistance to accepting refugees.[67]

For Sjöbo and three other communes[68] in prosperous Skåne, choosing to rebuff *Siv* pressure and spurn financial incentives in exchange for refugees was not a difficult decision. Unlike many local communities in Norrland—as the northern third of Sweden is called—with high unemployment rates and many vacant apartments, the southern locales were not going to be enticed to accept refugees just because agreements with *Siv* might bring in extra revenue and jobs. Politicians in the north, on the other hand, welcomed and even solicited opportunities to host and lodge alien newcomers inside their borders. Across the region communes owned building complexes with many empty units, and they also had shrinking tax bases from which to maintain public services.

For evidence and comprehension of the effects that Immigration Board's monetary infusions had on local treasuries, citing a few facts about beneficial consequences should clarify matters and even raise questions about motives. Situations in Bjurholm and Vilhelmina illustrate what two financially strapped communes obtained from their contracts to accept asylum seekers. Vacancies in apartments owned by the former commune had averaged between seventeen and twenty units when it consented to taking in approximately fifty refugees. In the latter rural township's annual summary released in early January 1993, Vilhelmina *Bostäder AB* (Residences Incorporated) reported some substantial monthly income losses from its thirty vacant apartments. Four weeks later a solution to the problem followed the arrival of thirty Bosnians, nine Serbs, four Hindus from Sri Lanka, fifteen Croatians, and twenty-eight Kosovo-Albanians.

There is no better way to grasp the effects of foreigners occupying empty buildings than to examine the losses that resulted after their departures. Aliens evacuating fifty units in Åsele at the end of September 1993 caused an annual loss of 2,700,000 kronor to the commune. Closures also produced some other negatives consequences. First of all communes with asylum centers annually received fixed subsidies as compensation for borne costs of caring for charges. Respectively for each adult and child under township supervision, *Siv* paid out in 1993 138,300 and 84,000 kronor. Secondly refugee centers employed local people; Wilhelmina's operation, for example, yielded five jobs, and Älvboda Refugee Center at Älvkarleby had seventeen employees.[69]

Relationships between communes and the Immigration Board varied as a result of several factors. Both suffered considerably because of a lack of good leadership and consistent policies from the national government in Stockholm. The consequences of these inadequacies showed up in the fluctuating refugee statistics for the years 1990 through 1992. Just as communes had begun to be ready for an ongoing influx of people in need of shelters, the Lucia Law took effect, thereby ending many quests for a life in Sweden. Although first-quarter 1990 numbers had not shown any signs of a pending decline, what did become a trend appeared in second-quarter figures. As late as three weeks into March, *Siv*'s head had predicted 10,000 more arrivals in 1990 than during the previous year, and the increase, suggested Rogestam and then seconded by Immigration Minister Maj-Lis Lööw, would certainly necessitate an emergency budgetary supplement and additional communal cooperation. Neither their numbers nor their forecasted requirements were realized because to the women's surprise a combination of toughness toward illegal asylum seekers as evidenced by those

immediate returns of unwanted persons to Poland and by Swedish demands for
agreements for better cooperation and adherence to international law from this
nation and other intermediaries responsible for releasing migrants to Sweden.

Moreover the Lucia Law caused entries to drop sharply. Compared to how
many had gained places in the monarchy during the first quarter of 1990, the
6,000 acceptances during the next three months represented a decline of 4,000
incomers. Altogether applicant numbers remained low for twenty-one months.
Then on December 19, 1991, just as commentators and *Siv* analysts were
forecasting a continuation of this trend of slackened interest in Sweden, Prime
Minister Carl Bildt's four-party, nonsocialistic coalition government, in
response to liberal pressure, rescinded the Lucia Law. Before the reversal the
Immigration Board had begun to allow communal contracts to expire as well as
many refugee residences to close. For unlucky individuals whose cases for
residence permits had not reached the ARB, the shuttering up of facilities often
placed their lives in flux that resulted in authorities always seemingly ordering
moves from one location to another. During 1990-1991, the period of so many
closures, one Lebanese refugee, during a year in Sweden, was forced to endure
seven moves. *Svenska Dagbladet* reporter Lova Olsson called him and other
foreigners with so many address changes, "the moving carrousel" victims.[70]

At *Siv*, in what was quickly deteriorating into a planning tragicomedy of
great proportions, basing refugee quarters upon estimates of asylum seekers for
1992 proved disastrous; numbers were many thousands below eventual needs.
Escalations in the Balkan conflict—fought at first primarily between Serbs and
Croats over control of ethnically divided enclaves in Bosnia-Herzogovina—
caused more than 2,000,000 people to flee war-ravaged areas for shelters and
sanctuaries elsewhere. Ethnic cleansing by both sides contributed to additional
mass evacuations.

If numerically measured, Germany accepted more refugees from the war
than any other nation, but in proportion to national population, it was Sweden
that took in the most asylum seekers per inhabitant. By June 1992 as many as
2,500 people arrived weekly at Swedish borders in anticipation of safekeeping;
during the first five quarters of warfare, 40,000 Bosnians asked for asylum in
Sweden. In a desperate response to a surging need for accommodations, panic-
struck *Siv* officials accepted renters' contractual terms for residences, thereby
paying lessors an estimated 300,000,000 kronor more than a fair-market value
for temporary usages of their diverse properties; in many instances these were
hotels—like O'Henrys Hotel in Strängnäs—with low occupancy rates. For a
six-month right to utilize this 300-guest capacity facility, *Siv* paid 12,150,000
kronor, or according to *Aftonbladet* calculations, 6,210,000 kronor too much.
Stopping short of labeling these hotel deals scandalous, Sweden's most read
afternoon newspaper—known more for sensational human-interest stories than
for investigative reporting—criticized *Siv*'s negotiating skills. The question to
answer was why no attempts had been made in a "buyer's market" to "press"
down prices. As these panic contracts were expiring, negotiations started in
order to seal new deals with communes. The result was *Siv* and townships once

again involved with the desperate task of trying to find suitable living quarters for an influx of refugees.[71]

In different ways Sweden's generous acceptance policy evolved into a lesson-giving exercise for both Swedes and refugees. "Little Härnösand has become a part of the world," a newspaper-article conclusion by Bengt Falkkloo of *Dagens* Nyheter with a reoccurring theme. Like many Swedish reports written during the 1990s, this one also examines the many effects of aliens on the indigenous population of Sweden.[72]

Rather than repeat the changes that had come to Swedish society as a result of foreigners, the purpose here will be to look at Sweden's influence on asylum seekers. Children's health suffered during long waits for decisions. Altogether too frequently for young travelers coming by themselves, the experiences were traumatically unpleasant, or as a fifteen-year-old youngster described his ordeal, it was living as if "in a prison." After a sorting through a minor's papers by an official and a release from "protective" custody, communes assumed control of the young person. Under their maintenance arrangements varied. If relatives were willing to assume responsibility, placing a ward with extended family usually worked best. A majority of children were not so lucky that they had relatives with whom they could live. Communes placed most of the less fortunate boys and girls with foster families. Authorities dispatched all the others to refugee camps without much supervision or to boarding schools. Regardless of where officials dumped minors, there was psychological suffering. Living alone in a strange land for a child—often without knowledge of their parents' fate—was not easy. Psychic maltreatment at Carlslund Camp was so hard on the children that two staffers could not continue working there. In their opinion it was "no place where anyone working with Swedish children would accept the relationships that prevailed at Carlslund's group home."

It was rare for youngsters who arrived by themselves to benefit from direct adult assistance and counsel. Without such help they faced alone all the ordeals of uncertainty of refugees. Until a decision of their cases by the Asylum Review Board, these youngsters never knew from one day to the next if they could stay permanently in Sweden or would be returned to the dangers of their homelands. A case in point involved the struggle of a sister and brother from Uganda. For two years after their arrival alone from Africa, twelve-year old Faldha and one-year younger Brian Okumu lived with an aunt and older sister in Kinna. Then late in March 1998 they learned an ARB decision had gone against them. Frightened by the potential for dangerous consequences from a return to Uganda, the pair went into hiding with family friends' help. Meanwhile on the siblings' behalf, *Expressen* began a daily campaign to win sympathy for the children. The newspaper's efforts ended with good news for the Ugandan pair on March 30, 1998. The unkind publicity about bureaucratic cold-heartedness toward the children succeeded at winning a deportation-order reversal.

In another episode involving Ugandan children, Dorcas, at fifteen-years old, was the oldest child in her family. As such she assumed responsibility for the welfare of siblings Hassan, Sarah, and Elisabeth at Österbybruk, one of the four

Swedish orphanages charged with caring for orphaned youngsters. Given major responsibilities after her departure from Africa, Dorcas confessed a need "to be strong" for her sisters and brother's sake and a desire to be patient with taunters' racist slurs. For Jeff, a seventeen-year old Ugandan at Österbybruk, he simply wondered if anybody would want to "help me away from this f. . . king place?"[73]

For many single adults and families residing as refugees in Sweden, the same question also must have occurred to them. Whether boarding in hotels, barracks, or elsewhere,[74] these folk had boring existences, and their lives were filled with constant anxiety and conflicts. Excepting a special accord between a Jewish congregation and the Immigration Board, one that allowed members of a Stockholm synagogue to assume full responsibilities for Jews who asked for asylum, there seemed little regard for ethnic prejudices and animosities in refugee placements. As foolish and insensitive as it might seem, *Siv* officials did not take enough precautions to insure against "enemies meeting in exile." At the same refugee camps they placed Serbs with Croatians or with Kosovo-Albanians, thereby raising the risks for trouble and fights. Despite warnings about potential conflicts, Swedish idealism dominated assignments to camps. In placing someone from a war zone,"the principle prevails that if a person has fled a conflict in order to obtain calm and peace in Sweden, then the individual must live up to that."

Inasmuch as life in exile should be different and peaceful, as one official imagined it might be for the ethnic groups now safely in Sweden but who had countrymen now fighting each other elsewhere, statistics refuted the dreamer's hope. There were 159 reported cases of violence and threatened hostilities in 1992, while during the first half of 1993, police responded to 104 incidents. As a result of racial animosity conflicts like an Arab-African fight at Kolboda on March 18, 1991, occurred. In this instance a hundred or so Lebanese and Somalians pursued each other with knives, hammers, and fists. Other fights were rooted in ethnic prejudices of the kind that affected Serb Zoran and Croat Mira's relationship in Sweden. The pair encountered unpleasantries because of resentments toward their mixed marriage. The couple had expected sanctuary together in Sweden would bring them peace from ethnic hatred, but their hopes were quickly dashed. As Mira related in disillusion after continued chiding of her, husband Zoran, and son Vladica by fellow refugees, "We had believed that everyone who had fled the war had left antagonisms behind; now we know it is not so." This mixed family never felt safe and secure until it had isolated itself from fellow Bosnians.[75]

Existing in Sweden without a clarified status caused several problems. Restlessness and nervousness from not knowing if there would be a grant for permanent residence or a decision for deportation were the human symptoms that prompted reactions of every sort from drug addiction to acts of vandalism. Morover there were several reported rape and murder cases involving refugees. Resentments were obvious from refugee actions either directed randomly at Swedes and other asylum seekers or aimed deliberately at *Siv* personnel and facilities. A harbor incident at Oskarshamn aboard a ship was the likely effect of desperation and boredom. Here while holding a *Siv* advisor hostage in his office, thirty-some refugees were able to drive away police who had responded to the captive official's request for assistance. The combatants met the officers on embarkation with a barage of chairs, a table, and other missiles. Their acts of threatening and agitating government officials ended in two arrests after a detachment of security reenforcements had rescued the Swede and reinstated order on the mutined vessel.

All across Sweden there were instances of residents vandalizing their quarters. At Koppoms Manor, for example, "refugees went berserk," causing property damages estimated at 250,000 kronor. Moreover it was common for youth gangs to form at refugee camps and for them to wander away at nightfall from their compounds in search of trouble. This description seems to fit what occurred around midnight of April 13, 1991. A pack of nine to fifteen foreign teenagers—during a walk into Virserum, south of Hultsfred—exchanged some unpleasant words with town youths. A fight erupted, resulting in serious knife wounds to an eighteen-year-old participant.

With Swedes some nationalities had worse reputations for trouble and criminality than others. A Swedish law forbids journalists from identifying a suspect or a convict by name, but it does not prevent disclosures of criminally-involved persons' ethnic backgrounds. In August 1992, following the arrests of several Kosovo-Albanians for shoplifting, Minister for Immigration Birgit Friggebo—rather than showing discretion and wisdom—blurted out unwisely her candid opinion about this folk group being the one with more proclivities for pilfering and stealing than any other. For showing insensitive stereotyping, Friggebo, a public figure without an especially good reputation for tactfulness, immediately found herself at the center of a storm of controversy. In the midst of critics demanding her resignation and indictment for alleged racial agitation, she attempted to extricate herself by purporting "to have used an unfortunate formulation which gave an extraordinarily wrong picture of what would have come through Aktuellt [a Swedish television news program] if it had sent the whole interview."

Seeking solutions both to public perceptions about alleged incompetence and refugee outbreaks and crime, the harrassed cabinet officer called and then chaired a meeting that was attended by prosecutors and representatives from the ARB, police, and *Siv*. Two priorities emerged: the police should prioritize investigations of refugee suspects, and the Asylum Review Board should settle first all cases involved with the fates of asylum seekers with criminal records in Sweden.

As the seven-member Sali Kryeziu family would learn the hard way, the enforcing of a new "get-tough" policy toward all troublesome aliens did reduce tolerance and accelerate deportations. After spending almost four years in the Scandinavian nation, every member of the household was expelled following a conviction of one Kryeziu for an eighty-eight kronor theft of chocolate and shaving lather.[76]

Idleness was one of worst problems confronting asylum seekers. Confined somewhat by fear and logistics to the immediate surroundings of a refugee camp and quartered often in an overcrowded room, asylum seekers had little more to do than socialize and worry. Study opportunities—if they existed—were usually limited to Swedish instruction, a subject that motivated very few foreigners; not many saw the point of learning a language without a reason or any personal relevance. Not only were incentives often missing among many aliens, but there existed tremendous discrepancies in their abilities to absorb a second language. At many camps the range of educational backgrounds could spread from people with advanced university degrees to illiterates.

On the giving side many communes lacked both financial resources and trained personnel to educate everyone. Although offering meaningful Swedish instruction to everyone was a legal right, its availability varied from township to township. As a result only a minority of camp inhabitants received enough training to qualify as proficient users of the Scandinavian language.

Even when studying Swedish was an impossibility, suggestions as well as demands that the refugee population's passitivity could be met by allowing this group to work went nowhere except for the select few who had a medical degree. To meet national medical needs Sweden's health system literally was pulling physicians from refugee camps for placements in special programs to upgrade and adjust their credentials to Swedish standards.

At the start of the 1990s when Sweden's national economy prospered and unemployment was insignificant, there were demands from many societal sectors to allow refugees to work. Some experiments even yielded a few jobs. Despite an expressed interest then in changing both law and policy to allow the hiring of persons without residence permits, attempts at pushing through new rules in the *Riksdag* failed. When the economy was strong and jobs plentiful, adamant advocates of more liberal work requirements gained fair hearings for their proposals. After the plummet of 1992 with its rise in joblessness, almost nobody then dared to propose an opening of the job market to asylum seekers. Politicians—now obviously beholdened first and foremost to a Swedish-first policy—now had as their main concern the restoration of employment to the multitudes of laid-off Swedes. During the recession any attempt at offering jobs to foreigners would have met fierce opposition from the nation's strong labor movement. As much as xenophobic thoughts might have occurred, few union leaders or their political allies in the Social Democratic Party dared—lest they be called racists—to suggest as Gösta Brodin, a controversial, uninhibited colleague from Åstorp, had. Seeing conspiracy, he charged in an opposition speech that the admission of Yugoslavian refugees was an employers' association plot "to increase competition for jobs and press down incomes."[77]

Generally without opportunities for studies or work, asylum seekers endured more pain than pleasure during their stays at refugee centers. Reality at these macabre residences contrasted oppositely to the resort-like conditions described in *Ny i Sverige* and its successor *Migranter* (new in Sweden and migrants), *Siv* bimonthly magazines. An article appearing in 1992, for example, described the opportunities available to occupants of a facility in Värmland (a west-central region of Sweden). Residents at Älvsbacka had, because of access to a fully equipped theater, an opportunity to develop an interest in drama. Another in-house report told of a constructive educational effort experienced by six Eritreans. They had learned woodcraft skills at a woodworking shop near their Småland (an area immediately north of Skåne) camp. As a result of training associated with living at Aneby, noted the 1995 story, the Africans had designed and built 480 school desks for a shipment to and use in their homeland.

Positive activities were exceptions, however. Even such easy-to-fulfill requests as providing cable-television news from homeland stations met with obstacles. Bosnians discovered as much in Ängelholm after their request for access to broadcasts from Sarajevo. It, like so many other issues, had to pass through a bureaucratic maze. Although everybody living in Sweden—whether with citizenship or temporary residence—had entitlements to medical, dental, and mental care, there were many cases of ignored refugee needs. Even with an annual budget of 300-million kronor in 1991—with subsequent increases to cover thereafter inflation and a greater number of residents—and an average outlay of 200,000 kronor per refugee for that year, Siv often neglected its care group by not providing full medical coverage.

Inadequate attention was especially true for the thousandfold war victims who had arrived with such recently inflicted handicaps as blindness, amputated limbs, and trauma. If help were offered, it usually came after interminably long waiting periods. Worse staffs at refugee centers could tend to disbelieve residents' complaints. A failure to accept these at face value had unfortunate consequences on more than one occasion. A case in point was the death in 1995 of a Mongolian at Carlslund Refugee Center near Stockholm. Although the denizen had complained of severe abdominal pain, personnel on duty did not apparently want to believe his suffering was bad enough to require medical attention. As a result of the unwillingness to recognize a dire need for immediate intervention, the sufferer died the next morning from a ruptured appendix. Inasmuch as neglect had contributed directly to death, it resulted in no staff member dismissals or probations. Concluding there was not reason to punish or reprimand anyone for negligence or culpability, Swedish Prosecutor Sven-Erik Alhem did not pursue a case, thereby exonerating everyone.

If refugees did receive an expensive operation and corrective surgery, the procedures were so rare that they would become newsworthy events. A case in point involved a two-year old Kosovo-Albanian boy with club feet. Operating on each foot separately to correct talipes, a team of physicians at the University Academic Hospital in Uppsala surgically intervened on behalf of the toddler to alleviate his deformity. Costs of operating on him were not borne by *Siv* but were the result of a charitable drive organized by *Aftonbladet* on the child's behalf. Excepting instances of acute decay, routine dental care was generally 0unavailable to refugees because as one report noted, if work were to begin on refugees' teeth, Swedes would never see a dentist again.

As the following table illustrates, welfare payments were the only help that refugees could expect on a regular basis. These paltry allotments did not cover the price of a daily package of cigarrettes. In many respects *Siv* treated its charges as if they were irresponsible children incapable of making rational decisions. The agency decided and governed exactly how each refugee could spend an allotment. According to bureau rules distributed funds must only go toward buying food or clothing. Saving some or all of a grant for an eventual purchase of a capital good like a television or a stereo system violated agency regulations and constituted illegal usage of a stipend; the penalty for such spending meant denial of the following month's aid. *Siv*'s record of degrading and denying refugees convinced a Swedish critic of the system that "animals are treated better and with greater respect in Sweden than her refugees and immigrants."

Refugee-Welfare Allotments, 1991

Category	Refugee Buying Own Food:	Asylum Center Suppying Food:
Single Adult	76 SEK daily	25 SEK daily
Paired Partners	66 SEK ea. daily	25 SEK ea. daily
Child, infant to 3-years old	43 SEK daily	19 SEK daily
Child, 4- to 10-years old	50 SEK daily	18 SEK daily
Child, 11- to 17-years old	58 SEK daily	20 SEK daily

78

Three groups reacted against how refugee issues were being handled. Those cooperating communes that tried to provide comfortable living quarters and such services as language instruction complained to *Siv* about the long-term financial losses from contractual deals that governed accepting and provisioning aliens. A 1998 study of accumulated figures for asylum seekers who had come to Sweden in 1994 identified a contributor to problems. The compensation formula in place at the outset fixed aid as follows. First of all, for participating with no regard to the number of refugees involved, every commune received a flat grant of 500,000 kronor. During each of three years, *Siv* paid an additional 144,200 kronor for each adult in the program, and there was a one-time "stimulance subsidy" of 25,000 kronor per participant. Many townships complained of losing money as a result of their involvement. As an attempt to find the basis of grumbling, *Siv* ordered a three-year study of select communes to ascertain what had gone wrong. A survey of forty-one chosen townships revealed eighty-six percent of the refugee class of 1994 was living in 1997 in a household dependent in part upon welfare assistance. Even more startling to researchers, another thirty-six percent belonged to families whose entire existences were tied to receipts of dole payments. Herein was the rub.[79]

High rates of joblessness and welfare among ex-refugees resulted from many factors,[80] of which few could be blamed or pinned on alien recipients. Asylum outposts were training grounds for passivity and listlessness. Given a life of total dependence, no work, and few constructive activities, refugees lost confidence and pride. Self-doubts marginalized even the strongest individuals. Reactions to waiting months and years for rulings on their futures and feeling a native population's contempt were often enough to destroy all personal morale and optimism. For anyone who might have inquired, as these comments attest so aptly, refugees did express succinctly general feelings of frustration, agony, and pain: "The wait feels like a lonesome death," "The wait feels no boundaries," "Idleness becomes a compulsion," "Sweden is wait, wait, wait," "To wait is a way to live," "Sweden does not want to have refugees," "I die a little for every day," "People feel bad when they are inactive; it is almost like a prison with everyone pushed together in one cell."[81]

Although fears of consequences from a faceless immigrant bureaucracy left most refugees in pacific stupors, there were examples of protest. Many demonstrations followed deportation threats. Existing with uncertainties and inactivity might have been undesirable, but returning to homelands seemed a worse alternative. Refugees in most instances seemed to prefer slow deaths with mental torture in Sweden to what would await them in their native lands. Going back would mean either the dangers again of war, painful existences as a persecuted minority, physical punishment, or even executions.

To publicize discontent with ARB rejecting bids to remain in Sweden, refugees who had foreboded expulsion resorted to hunger strikes, sit-ins, and church occupations. At High Chaparall in Småland Lööw's arrival in January 1990 was met by sixty-some Turk-Bulgarians. With white sheets draping their heads and bodies, they greeted her appearance in a silent protest. One covered demonstrator then emerged from the group to deliver this message to her: "We want to show by this [action] that we actually constitute a substantial problem despite the government and the Immigration Board's refusals to perceive it" as such. What had prompted the protest most of all was—despite a suitability for many area job openings—an unwillingness to consider them as possible hirees. On other occasions refugees expressed discontents with *Siv* stooges who posed as creditable and trustworthy translators, program cutbacks, and Italian-fashion outlet Benetton. Using large billboard signs to dramatize the horrors of war by depicting a dead soldier in a blood-soaked uniform, the clothing retailer did not achieve its desirable objective with fleers from Bosnian death and destruction. Less a statement against war, the Benetton advertisement was more for victims and their children a horribly grim, personal reminder of all the bloodshed they had witnessed and had tried to forget.[82]

Prospects for and attempts at deportation caused most demonstrations and protests. Just the reality of knowing others controlled refugees' individual

destinies and lives also produced much anxiety.[83] Beginning upon entering the
Nordic nation at border patrols with two-to-eight hour ordeals and continuing
through months and even years of awaiting decisions on appeals for residence
permits, refugees demonstrated predictable nervousness about their futures in a
strange land. Uncertainty emanated itself in several ways. It could show up in
a protective display as a confrontation with police had at the Pontonen Refugee
Camp near Oskarshamn. Defenders foiled two officers who had arrived at the
site to interrogate a resident. Deterred by supporters intent on not permitting the
cross-examination of a fellow refugee, police were overwhelmed. Angered as
well as determined not to allow a pair of officers near a friend, a mob with an
estimated strength of thirty-odd people utilized chairs as weapons to force a
temporary police withdrawal. Made to abandon their efforts and flee, officers
had to wait for reenforcements before reentering the compound. Thereupon
police arrested the attack's two ringleaders as well as the shielded accomplice.
Each was charged with obstructing justice and threatening public officials.

In Malmö Swedish police faced a different kind of problem aboard the
Winston Churchill. Announcing upon embarkation a mission to fulfill orders to
deport all Turk-Bulgarians, the invaders caused panic. Instead of an orderly
procession to a waiting bus for transport to another vessel for departures from
Sweden later the same day, designees either hid throughout the ship, locked
themselves in their cabins, or simply sat, crying, screaming, and refusing to
move as directed. As a result of the tumult the act of removing designees from
the ship, a process that should have taken at most thirty minutes to accomplish,
dragged on for three hours and required a *Siv* official's promise of a temporary
reprieve. Rather than being removed as originally scheduled to Trelleborg for a
return to Bulgaria that afternoon, the bus transported them to another refugee
camp. Meanwhile blame for the snafu, according to Rune Gullberg from the
deportation department, must go to "communicational difficulties" between his
agency and *Siv*; these developed even though "we were almost sitting next to
each other."[84]

Hunger strikes, church occupations, and attempts at and threats of suicide
were the most common forms of resistance to and protestation of announced
expulsions. In Alvesta one man's receipt of upsetting information about
pending deportation resulted in attempted arson at his refugee camp's
administrative offices. Generally news spread quickly of ARB decisions to oust
an entire category of asylum seekers. Such occurred at different times with
Bulgarian Turks and Kosovo Albanians, and the results combined food refusals
with attempts at being havened in churches and cloisters.[85]

Believing churches could not refuse people in need and should possess more
compassion and sympathy toward refugees' plights than people at other
institutions in Swedish society, ministers and nuns freely opened their houses of
worship to desperate individuals of all faiths. Many parishioners objected as the
vestries of their churches became hostels for strangers, but as much as there
might have existed respect and empathy for such criticism from sisters, pastors,
vicars, and other ecclesiastics who had been behind receiving in refugees, there

was a consensus that compelled them as God's appointees to be more mindful of the church's evangelical call for openness to whomever should come than to what might prove to be popular and expedient with laypeople and government officials.

As direct repercussions of the Lucia Law, convictions' first tests came between December 31, 1989 and April 3, 1990. During three months or so more than thirty churches opened their doors to several hundred refugees and their supporters. Like early Christians during the time of persecutions by the Roman Empire, occupants gained shelter in the churches of Göteborg Bishop Bertil Gärtner's diocese. In his judgment there were ample justifications and a moral duty. Moreover, noted the churchman, any "nation that can spend 29 billion kronor on Christmas presents should also have money for a generous refugee policy." Gärtner also was willing to accept whichever punishments and personal consequences the authorities might want to impose as a result of his stand. It was the bishop's observation that "as soon as a person is positive to refugees, then the hate letters and even death threats follow." In notes and telephone messages, occupations' foes displayed boldness and belligerence, but their subsequent acts and responses—excepting the sporadic racist graffiti left by anonymous cowards who were unwilling to defend themselves in public forums—were timid and minimal.

Although there were many positive effects from opening churches to frightened people trying to avoid returns to their homelands, none was more important than its release of an ecumenical spirit. There was this coexistent benefit that tended to bind conscience-stricken Roman Catholics, Protestant free-church members, and state church devotees in agreement about the true importance of outreaches of comfort and aid to foreigners in crises; it united them behind common principles during a meeting with Lööw on January 12. Moreover churches uniting led to their joint effort of collecting signatures on petitions on behalf of refugees' pleas for a right to remain in Sweden.[86]

Periodically over the next decade churchmen sided with asylum seekers in their disputes with *Siv* by demonstrating solidarity with refugees in several ways. Most of these efforts generated only local interest and therefore went unnoticed by the general population,[87] but there were two major exceptions. A police raid of Alsike Cloister on November 24, 1993, caused a major reaction throughout Sweden. In the middle of morning mass law enforcement officers ringed the grounds of the religious order's compound near Uppsala as prelude to embarking at nine on a mission to capture runaway asylum seekers. This invasion of uniformed and civilian-clad police accompanied by an ambulance and a tourist bus came as a surprise and shock to sisters of the Sacred Order. It was no sooner that they had begun to grasp what was in progress, and thirty-six persons from the Middle East, Bangladesh, and ex-Yugoslavia were on a bus, heading for detentions in Uppsala. Like Sister Marianne who, as head of the cloister, was involved at Alsike Cloister with underground activities on behalf of aliens since 1978, the prisoners believed authorities would never disrespect the religious order's right to continue a mission of shielding refugees against deportations. After all some of the individuals taken during the incursion had lived under the sisters' protection for as long as two years. Asked by reporters for a reaction, the abbess seemed to be more dismayed with the police methods than with the result of the raid. "A provocation like that is unwise. The police could have sent a delegation from county headquarters to say it could no longer respect [the cloister] as a refuge. Then we could have explained which persons were here and how much time was needed to bring about new investigations of their cases."

Archbishop Gunnar Weman offered the first but unofficial archdiocesan response to the government's invasion of an institution under his jurisdiction. Careful to express some compassion for officers who had been ordered to carry out the awkward task of raiding a cloister, Weman noted his great concern was for how Swedish police would use 100-million SEK that had been budgeted for finding some 7,700 hidden aliens. It "should be used in a better way than conducting police raids at a protected church place."

Friggebo cautiously agreed, wondering if "it had not been possible to have found a better solution." In one of the rare defenses of the cloister raid by a public official, National Chief of Police Björn Eriksson judged matters very differently, "grasping that at Alsike it [the raid] did not stir a place of worship but a place to live." Aside from expressions from both religious and political leaders, the nation divided over whether the police had acted prudently or not. As for Sister Marianne's role, some individuals viewed her as an angel, while others considered her a lawbreaker. In spite of diverse opinions and reactions, the nun allowed neither a police incursion of Alsike nor negative reactions to stop her from reopening the cloister to refugees in need of assistance. As for a ruling on the legality of such raids as the one at Alsike, the ombudsman from the justice ministry decided in 1995 that the state does possess a legal right to seize anybody wanted by the police, even if the arrest occurs on church land.[88]

A second exception was the human drama that began October 19, 1993, with the occupation of an Åsele church by two Kurdish brothers' families. It attracted considerable attention because the news story involved determination by a little village in northern Sweden to fight *Siv* over a plan to deport people the Norrlanders liked and respected as friends, classmates, and neighbors. Agents from immigration viewed matters differently. Authorities accused the Kurds of lying in 1990 and 1991 to border police about their country of origin. They had claimed Turkish roots, but they had really come from Iraq. As for Åsele, unlike other places where thousands of refugees lived almost anonymously without any contacts with local people, its population was overwhelmingly supportive of Rashid and Ziya Sincari's families after an arrival in the small community two years before a move into the local church. Taking this step was a desperate effort to remain among friends in Sweden, but one which the fourteen Sincaris would find how solidified Åsele was behind them. Evidence of the degree of acceptance and support from Åsele residents for the occupants would be demonstrated often during the weeks and months of the encampment at the church. Classmates participated in efforts on the Sincaris' behalf, while townspeople held an ecumenical prayer service for the families.

Adhering to the rule that demanded asylum seekers' honesty during their questioning, the ARB was unwilling to overlook the Sincari brothers' lies. On November 26, 1993, it therefore reaffirmed an earlier decision for expulsions. Knowing the consequences of leaving a haven, family members did not dare to depart from their confinement's apparent safekeeping. The result for them was enduring whatever discomfort and limitations living in a church might bring them. The ordeal was especially unbearable for the youngest Sincari children, five-year old Nesibe and six-year old Sardar. They missed playing freely with friends.

During the holiday season Åsele residents did what they could to relieve the tedium of living in close quarters. On December 13, they bestowed upon seventeen-year old Rojda Sweden's greatest honor for a teenaged girl, the naming of her the community's Lucia. Then on Christmas Eve, the Norrlanders treated their Muslim neighbors to a holiday celebration that included a television for everyone to watch and presents from *tomten* (Santa Claus). Topping off the evening was a traditional *Julbord*, a table filled with festive foods eaten by Swedish households during the nation's most important holiday. At least during this occasion everybody could forget problems and enjoy fellowship with truly generous friends.

For more than a year there was a standoff with few noteworthy events. During this period a child psychologist in testimony foresaw dire consequences for the youngest Sincaris children if authorities should press ahead and remove them from a harmonious setting. Then in a joint protest, thirty-three authors of children's books, including Astrid Lindgren of Pippy Longstocking fame, tried to bring a happy ending to the Sincaris' quest. Hence there were moments for hope, and eventually circumstances seemed safe enough for the two families to abandon their places on the church floor for normal accommodations.

Then on January 11, 1996, at five o'clock in winter-afternoon darkness, worst fears became a reality. Coming with dogs, thirty police officers struck without forewarning, seizing as many family members as could be located. Word of a dreadful occurrence spread quickly through the little community, causing neighbors to assemble in protest against what was in progress. In an outward display of aroused emotions and panic, classmates and friends cried. There was also some slugging between people trying to stop the proceedings and law officials in self-defense. In the ensuing turmoil the two fathers and Siyar— at eighteen the oldest of the ten Sincari children—managed escapes. Despite valiantry citizens had lost their bid to protect the eleven other Kurdish wards. Police loaded them on a bus headed for detentions in nearby Lycksele.

Sweden reacted quickly and diversely to the raid. One day after police had acted, Carlsson, in an exclusive interview with *Aftonbladet* reporter Lena Mellin, placed blame on both sets of Sincari parents for "lying and exploiting their children"; he also insisted they had been behind "dragging out" the whole matter. Mellin concluded her questioning by asking the national leader for his response to Professor Tor Lindberg's assessment that the action in Åsele was reminescent of Germany in the 1930s. Obviously shaken by this insinuation, Carlsson claimed the chair of the Swedish Pediatric Association had offered "a tremendously iniquitous accusation" because in the case at hand "the parents actually have a responsibility."

Immigration Minister Leif Blomberg received more blame than anybody else for what had transpired at Åsele. "Blomman"—a prominent official with only six years of formal education—climbed upward from metal working on a factory floor to labor leadership. His payback for loyal service to the Social Democratic Party was Carlsson's reward of a cabinet post with responsibilities in a department that demanded sensitivity and knowledge. Åsele was a test of the minister's ability to resolve a difficult matter in a way that would ease the government through a crisis without offending Sincari backers or exaggerating the importance of rules against lying. Blomberg failed on both counts because of his adamant insistence that obedience was the paramount issue. Throughout the challenge the minister demonstrated stubbornness and boorishness and thus deserved criticism and censure. Olof Kleberg, editor in chief of *Västerbottens-Kuriren*, wrote that an overmatched cabinet member had left "Swedish refugee policies naked, unclad in all its meaningless word trimmings. Swedish rules, narrowly interpreted, are more important than [the United Nations] Children's Convention or humanitarian common sense. One minister's judgment is more important than pediatricians or humanitarian organizations' knowledge. Parents are depicted as rogues who have used their children as human shields."[89]

Deportation actions bifurcated into either individual cases or orders en masse. Whichever one, controversies arose frequently because of inconsistent applications of rules, nonconformity to the established international criteria for grants of asylum, ambiguous policies for judgments, or favoritism that aided some applicants but not others. Swedish citizens also had a hand in all of this. Dour and inexpressive generally as many have characterized them, they could be aroused—as events at Kimstad and Åsele have demonstrated—with passion about most matters associated with refugees. Public-opinion surveys captured with only marginal error the general trends of Swedish support and objection— usually wavering somewhere in the forty-to-sixty point range for reactions—to the different aspects of asylum, but they could not measure with any accuracy the degree of emotionalism that had entered into respondents' answers to the pollsters' questions.[90] In the case of Swedish government leaders—who were Europe's least educated and logically, therefore, the most likely to polarize issues—there were likely too many cases of judgment and enactment on alien matters on the bases of numbers and curves and rarely if ever on the possible temperamental ramifications of their actions and legislation.[91]

Usually when the Asylum Review Board ordered deportations en masse, strongest objections came from a targeted people's nearest affinity groups. As persons who either clung onto a nationality or identified with a specific ethnic group, they could often count upon support and demonstrations of one kind or another from individuals who had similar backgrounds but who now possessed

Swedish residence permits or citizenship. It would mean, for examples, Kurds acting as the champions of fellow Kurds who wanted to stay in Sweden or the Bulgarian Turks doing likewise for their compatriots. As with most everything concerned with refugees in the Nordic kingdom, there were exceptions. Native Swedes in small numbers did mobilize at times on behalf of certain categories of designees for expulsion. These efforts developed especially if the ARB was misjudging homelands as safe and respectful of human rights when all other indicators countered any hopeful outcomes for dissidents if they should be deported to these countries.

Iran was generally viewed as an unsafe country for deportees because most would be chanceless at obtaining normal lives there. Sending Christian converts, draft evaders, and female divorcees to this theocracy was an action tantamount to condemning such people to death sentences in the Islamic state. Humanitarian appeals also went out to officials not to force individuals to go back to African and Latin American dictatorships. Pressures from a minority of concern-minded Swedes, their organizations, and minorities seldom were successful because government and *Siv* leaders were more responsive to those segments of the Swedish population that wanted less ethnic diversity and more deportations. In terms of percentages the number of applicants for asylum who were obtaining favorable judgments from Asylum Review Board members was in decline. A study of eighty women under threats in their homelands revealed that, in clear violation of rules for granting automatic asylum established by the Geneva Convention on Refugees, only three candidates had gained permanent sanctuary in Sweden. The others either had gone into hiding or had returned involuntarily to their native countries and certain punishment.

Blindness to consequences of deportation even resulted after there had been alleged probes into the current situations existing in subjects' homelands. After an "on-site inspection" had amazingly found Bulgaria to be respectful of its largest minority, ARB ordered the ouster of Bulgarian Turks. Deportations, despite protests, then followed, often forcefully and brutally with the assistance of police. A similar conclusion by Swedish officials resulted during the mid-1990s when it was the determination of Swedish officials that Kosovo under the Serbians would pose no dangers to returning Muslims. In essence by this stand, the bureaucrats discounted the validity of Albanians' allegations about atrocities. By not believing victims of persecution and discrimination, judges at immigration concluded that the Kosovars were really nothing more than an anxious group after better futures in a more prosperous nation.

Interestingly enough Sweden did not receive Sarajevo's cooperation for deporting some Croatians from Bosnia and Herzegovina, especially ones who had migrated to the Nordic land from Croatia with Zagreb-issued documents. Regardless of the legitimacy of their papers and passports, there were several questions to answer about the wisdom and feasibility of returning persons to a war-ravaged, ethnic-cleansed place. Whether or not it could absorb thousands of returnees with diverse ethnic backgrounds from Sweden seemed to have had no effect on Minister of Immigration Pierre Schori's decisions. Finding truth and answers were obviously less important concerns to him than results. He sought a people's removal from Sweden, and a decision for this was final.[92]

Compared to groups, appeals on behalf of individuals carried more influence. During Sweden's greatest decade of reaction to refugees, there was abundant reporting about wretched souls whose cases for exile had ended in deportation orders. Such news as this not only tested the nation's conscience to review and reverse judgments, but stories also showed how embarrassing ARB with grim details could result in effective pressure. Decisions most susceptible to protest were either ones that threatened family unity or cases involving child welfare. After having hidden in approximately thirty different places around Sweden to avoid the same fate of capture and deportation as wife and mother Julia Dueñas had in November 1995, her Peruvian-refugee husband Rosario Boza Boza Dueñas, their son, and three physically handicapped daughters learned on June 8, 1998, of a humanitarian-based decision which would permit them to stay. Reacting to the news, oldest daughter Nancy told of "laughing and crying and almost not believing that it is true." By allowing the Dueñases to reside legally in Sweden and the mother to return, the Asylum Review Board reversed itself. The South Americans' deportation order had rested upon ARB's disbelief in an account of Peruvian violence and torture.

In a completely different story with an equally happy ending, a little boy who was reunited with his Kosovo Albanian mother after a week's separation won permanent residence in Sweden. The unusual mother-son episode began bizarrely on November 18, 1993, with the discovery of an abandoned boy in a baby carriage at a Norrköping department store. A note accompanied the baby to state: "Hi, I am Sebastian Svensson; I was born 92-01-01. They will pick me up as fast as possible—meanwhile can you help me; I am sad." After one week of searching, investigators found the mother responsible for abandoning her son and learned of circumstances behind her desperate action. The fact that she had given birth outside wedlock prompted her Muslim family to disown her. *Siv*'s first reaction was to deport the pair immediately, but it could not do so without a formal hearing. Finally three months later, on February 26, 1994, Ljuana accompanied by son Qundrim went before the Asylum Review Board for a verdict, but board members postponed a decision, thereby allowing the mother and toddler another six months in Sweden. Then on August 31, 1994, at the second visit to ARB, they received what she had requested, permanent residency in Sweden on humanitarian grounds.

There were many tales of woe and despair like the aforementioned two that came before the Asylum Review Board. Some ended with expressions of relief and joy, and others ended sadly in tears and deportations. In general two trends developed at ARB. Repetitious publicity in one of Stockholm's major daily newspapers could affect a happy conclusion, and stories about women—whether beaten or abandoned—had progressively better chances of garnering attention and sympathy than ones about men. Ultimately resultant decisions closing out women's well publicized appeals had better likelihoods of ending positively, too.

Moreover the presentations made to ARB by either Europeans or South Americans fared better than ones given by Asians and Africans. A Ghanaian common-law wife's bad experience with the Board—by all accounts a most unusual battery case to judge due to its many complications—deserves to be mentioned here because it illustrates just how distrustful Swedish authorities could be of non-Caucasians. After first filing a police complaint against her live-in boyfriend for a beating he had administered, the African woman arrived at her asylum hearing with bruises and blue marks. Requested to explain her appearance, she told of being assaulted. Deportation was the panel's verdict, nevertheless. An end to the victim-assailant relationship meant good riddance to her connections to Sweden as well. Then in an ARB postscript that would add insult to injury, there was speculation about her beating complaint being nothing more than a ruse to obtain residency based upon sympathy.[93]

As a logical consequence of a faceless bureaucracy dealing with several 100,000 refugees, asinine acts were bound to occur. Rama and Alfred Johnson were victims of the kind of mindlessness that can result when functionaries in a government body like *Siv* are expected to adhere strictly to rules. He was from Liberia, and her homeland was Tanzania. Both came to Sweden as strangers in search of asylum. Then like so many other love stories, they met, married, and started a family. There was a major problem in their case, however. With two citizenships to consider and deportation orders facing both mates, a regulation stipulated their separation, with the wife required to go to Tanzania and him to Liberia. As for the couple's two children, Swedish law stated in cases like this, paternal citizenship passes automatically to offspring, meaning here these two infants must follow their father even if the result would be a risk for the babies never reuniting with their mother.

In another absurd incident involving Africans, bureaucratic insensitivity to personal circumstances caused a serious problem for an entire family after the disappearance of a daughter. In 1997, with no clues of the whereabouts of missing eight-year old Mariam Adam, father Olar Adam turned into the prime suspect in the case because of the strange circumstances surrounding the status of his family with the Migration Board (*Siv*'s name after a reorganization in 1996). He had arrived first, coming at the end of 1990 and alleging flight from war-torn Sudan. After spending two years in Sweden, he received a grant for permanent residence from ARB. Later in 1992 Adam arranged for wife Adou Rokya and six children to join him, and his family subsequently would arrive in 1993. With their coming, personal testimonies about the Adames' African background began to unravel. Doubts surfaced about the family's true origins because of the mother's language and tatoos; these pointed to Ghana. Found guilty of lying, Adam lost his residency permit.

As plans were progressing to deport the family, the little girl vanished. Afraid to discount either obduction or disorientation, authorities placed a hold on everything. They were applying more caution to Mariam's disappearance than they had done three years earlier in a similar episode. In a well publicized case of missing siblings, six and nine years old, their disappearances had been the subject of considerable skepticism about their whereabouts. Both police and *Siv* officials doubted the parents' veracity. Rather than follow the mother and father's request and search thoroughly for the missing pair with a careful combing around the site of the refugee camp where the sister and brother had been living, authorities suspected parental involvement in an elaborate plot. According to suspicions the parents were keeping their offspring hidden as part of a ploy to secure asylum. Then six months later in a forest near the children's residence, their decomposed remains were found.   Subsequent autopsies attributed their deaths to exposure. As for Mariam and others in the Adam clan, reporters lost interest in them, noting nothing more about the family's plight or the eventual outcome of Mariam's disappearance.[94]

Offering asylum presented many controversies for *Siv* and ARB to solve, but none presented greater difficulty than the question of what to do with army deserters and draft evaders from conflicts in ex-Yugoslavia. More than twenty earlier in the midst of the Vietnam War, Sweden's offer of sanctuary to young Americans who were unwilling to fight in Asia almost destroyed the Nordic nation's relations with the United States, but unlike bloodshed in the Balkans, interference with another country's domestic law had not caused any special internal agonizing among Swedes. For them American fighting was foreign intervention in a civil war while the second represented a domestic dispute. There had been justification to intervene on behalf of men of good conscience in the first case but not in the second. Strange as it might seem, knowledge of how Serbian and Croatian forces were cleansing ethnic populations, torturing their prisoners, and committing other war crimes would not influence the outcomes of young male asylum petitioners who had refused to participate in brutal acts and would not affect others who had decided not to bear arms in a civil war.

Choosing to apply to the Nordic kingdom for sanctuary became a logical enough step even if the applicants had known little or nothing about Sweden's record of granting asylum to Americans years earlier or about the nation's laws concerning refuge to war resisters. Coming to Sweden made sense because of a reputation for peace, liberalism, and neutrality. According to arguments by Hans Göran Franck—a respected *Riksdag* member—for giving refusniks from the Balkans asylum, saving the lives of deserters who had chosen to escape to Sweden rather than carry out orders for heinous, inhuman acts or murders was paramount over the status of the war. Returning these men, Franck reasoned, would amount to signing their death sentences. Utilizing the Swedish press to build support for asylum and to force Carlsson's intervention on the deserters' behalf, the lawmaker wrote an article. Heretofore the nation had been neutral, disavowing the petitions of every deserter and evader. Franck's efforts along with those of others failed to produce any major policy shift. Lack of success can be attributed to a hardening of restrictions, thereby making asylum more difficult to obtain.[95]

Responses to rumors of and orders for deportation varied. With the aid of immigrants and idealistic Swedes who were foes of perceived restrictive, inhumane treatment of asylum seekers by wicked government policymakers, many candidates for removal found their way into a Swedish underground of safe havens. The network was akin in many respects to the Underground Railroad that had been responsible for liberating slaves in the United States before the Civil War. In both instances there were hideouts and dedicated individuals willing to risk breaking laws considered to be unjust and immoral. Moreover as a means of staying one step ahead of bounty hunters and officials, both "conductors" on the Underground Railroad and operatives in the Swedish system had to be clever, resourceful, and viligant. Due to helpers' dedication and determination, many runaways from deportation like the Sincari brothers managed to hide for several years without detection. According to estimates for 1993, roughly 7,000 people were in apparent hiding. Reservations about an exact number resulted from uncertainties about whether missing persons had remained in Sweden or had gone somewhere else.

Living underground was especially hard on preteenaged children. For Chilean siblings Christian and Ivonne Soto, it was a "feeling like cooped up animals." A child psychiatrist understood their reaction after several weeks of listening to a twelve-year old girl. From clandestine counseling sessions with his young patient, he concluded her ordeal of being concealed had turned this child into "a Anne Frank in Sweden," suffering from aggressive behavior, retarded social development, serious depression, and insecurity.

In dealings with young escapees, insensitive authorities could display ruthlessness. Just the act of seemingly placing a much greater premium on capturing runaway children than on the emotional consequences of actions was often enough to cause trauma. What transpired in the case of a Bangladeshi minor illustrates just how authorities could ignore completely young people's feelings. Hearing his mother was in hospital for severe depression and missing her, Shokel Rana left a hideout to travel across Sweden to visit her. Alerted he was at her bedside, police arrived to seize the teenaged boy, release his mother from care, and deport both to Asia.

A cruel aspect of being a child and living underground disappeared at the end of the decade. For securing care for sick children without risking exposure and automatic deportation, a change in rules began to facilitate the obtainment by parents in hiding of such medical attention as their offspring might require. Opportunities for school remained unavailable, however. Also repeated calls for grants of amnesty and residence to hidden people—especially children and families—continued to go nowhere. Maj-Inger Klingvall, a Moderate Party Youth Organization leader and a *Riksdag* member, was an outspoken critic of amnesty, arguing such capitulations to lawlessness would have an undermining effect on refugee processing and would legitimize an illegal activity.[96]

For scores of asylum seekers facing deportation, there were threats of and attempts at suicide. Since they were not backing their stated intentions with perilous acts, immigration authorities stopped taking these warnings of self-inflicted deaths seriously. Declarations had become so common without fulfillments that they appeared almost as tragicomic dramas with a somewhat surreal element. An excellent case in point occurred at Höganäs in 1990. An

Iraqi scheduled for departure fled police who had come for him. With officers in pursuit, the alien—brandishing an open-bladed razor—ascended steps to a church entrance, all to the amusement of a crowd that had observed the entire drama unfold before them. Standing there with a sharp blade pressed against his throat, the young man issued a death proclamation to pursuers. Onlookers who considered the ordeal entertaining yelled encouragement to the distraught man, shouting "good luck black head" and applauding whenever he had nicked his throat. Vicar Birgitta Cervin, in the accompaniment of the foreigner's legal representative, opened the door of the church and bid the stranger to enter. He accepted her invitation.

Thereafter townspeople telephoned Cervin, criticizing her cordiality and threatening to resign their memberships from the church. Aware xenophobia and racism existed in Höganäs, she was not shocked so much by confirmations of prejudice as by her parishioners' willingness to express openly their hatreds. This amazed and saddened her. "It feels bitter that a part of the congregation does not demonstrate greater love of humanity."[97]

Inasmuch as almost no seriousness had been attached to stated wishes for death, everything changed after November 6, 1996. It was then Iranian-native Mohammed Shakeri killed himself rather than face a return to a brutal Middle Eastern theocracy. All of a sudden there emerged multiple accusations along with wringing confessions of guilt. Although it was by no means the first case of a successful suicide, Shakeri's attracted more headlines and attention than all the previous ones. Lena Häll Eriksson, the Migration Board director at the time of Shakeri taking his life, admitted that she "should have lost her job" for not doing more to make asylum readily obtainable. In a debate article featured in *Dagens Nyheter*, Professor Bengt-Erik Andersson from Teachers' College in Stockholm argued Eriksson and Johan Fischerström, her counterpart at ARB, "took Shakeri's life."

Iranians living in Sweden tended to agree with this assessment of guilt. Acting through their organization, they and Merit Wager, the victim's legal deputy, asked the state prosecutor to file charges for a criminal investigation into the ARB members' actions to ascertain if they had played any role in the death of a countryman and client. According to the filing Shakeri had shown mental instability months earlier with a failed suicide attempt.[98] During the years that followed, there were critics who argued nothing had been learned from Shakeri's death.

Evidence suggests the opposite conclusion, however. Many officials were now taking precautions and attaching more seriousness to threats than most anyone had done prior to the Iranian's suicide. Proclamations of intent were still not enough to forestall deportations. Obtaining rights to remain in Sweden required more than some unsubstaniated utterance, but unlike all the distrust shown the Iranian after his initial failure, post-Shakeri attempters at suicide tended to be admitted to hospitals for psychiatric observation and care before escorts would eventually lead a distraught person out of Scandinavia.[99]

Just as authorities had failed at predicting a suicide in 1996, they did not succeed very well at undermining underground operations. Budgeted with millions of kronor for the job of capturing runaway aliens, the police seldom managed interceptions. In the rare cases when they had, tracking successes received publicity. Of the more than 7,000 refugees evading captures in 1993, police found only 220, this on a budget of 100-million kronor for this purpose. At this rate Swedish taxpayers paid more than 45,000 kronor per person taken into custody. Police proved so inept that occasionally even people under their guard escaped. The most celebrated case involved two men who had been in transit from Östersund to Luleå when they managed a dash for several days' freedom. Then it was an alert citizen's suspicions that would end one police-evader's flight. Observing from his automobile a truck driver giving a ride to a hitchhiker, the motorist used his mobile telephone to tip police about what had just transpired. The caller then followed the truck, keeping law officers posted of its location until the observed passenger's travels would end at a bus station. Within minutes police were there to capture the escapee.

To minimize underground activities, *Siv* officials became much less trusting of individuals destined for deportation. As a preventive measure persons without valid grounds for asylum went immediately into holding cells where they would remain until their movements from Sweden. Detainments could last for days or months, with periods varying in accordance to risks and circumstances. One Eritrean lived in an isolation cell at a Stockholm jail for more than eleven months. His case involved more than deportation, however. For petty thefts he had received a six-month prison sentence and deportation. Since authorities had confronted diplomatic obstacles in their efforts to return the African, his incarceration continued as insurance against him fleeing.[100]

At times with literally several thousand asylum cases awaiting ARB's adjudication, an expensive pricetag accompanied refugee seekers' choice of Sweden as recipient of their applications. Depending upon the caseloads, a one-day reduction in the waiting period could save the government several million kronor. Had the average period for a hearing been weeks or a few months instead of 300 days, as it was for arrivals coming in June 1990, there could have been significant savings. Each extra day spent in the monarchy cost Swedish taxpayers approximately 300 kronor per person who pursued a judgment.

Ridding Sweden of unwanted individuals was also a dear proposition. *Aftonbladet* published an exposé in 1998 based upon its research into charter-plane usage for deportations between July 1, 1995 and December 31, 1997. It found an outlay of more than 6.9-million kronor had been expended to arrange thirty-nine special flights to return ninety-seven men, women, and children. This averaged more than 71,000 kronor per deportee. Transporting the Sincari mothers and their seized children direct from Lycksele to Ankara, for example, resulted in the carrier invoicing *Siv* for 426,400; the bill for returning Nigerian John Adibe to his homeland on a Citation I was 270,185 kronor.

Not only were these flights costly, but passenger resistance could bring complications. To subdue and restrain deportees, police on escort duty often used straitjackets, handcuffs, tranquilizers, and sedatives to render their task easier but traveling more degrading for homeward-bound aliens. *Aftonbladet*'s report on Sweden's inhumane backside revealed how much cruelty and sadism authorities did at times employ in restraining stubborn, recalcitrant returnees. To emphasize maltreatment and demonstrate the grimness of methods in usage for the transport of undesirable aliens, the newspaper cited forty-three cases of restraint. These included everything from stripping a man naked for his travel to Poland to paying a Peruvian custom's officer a $200 bribe to let two people pass into the South American country.

From 1994 through 1997 Sweden deported 25,829 people of the 50,229 asylum seekers who had been processed. This means fewer than fifty percent of arrivals received residence. For the same four-year period Sweden paid out 514-million kronor to transport deportees home, or an average of about 19,900 kronor per person. To put the figure in perspective commercial travelers could fly six roundtrips from Stockholm to New York for the same amount. With a cost of deportation being so much, imagine then how frustrating it must have been when one deportee returned only six days after his escort from Sweden. It was the consequence of sending home a Hungarian in 1990, nevertheless.[101]

Excepting the costs and quantities involved in deportation, the previous paragraph should not be associated with typical returns. Its inclusion was only to show how Sweden treated uncooperative individuals; the process of sending home many thousands of people generally operated smoothly and without any dependence upon violence or coercion. Staff members who accompanied most returnees seldom resorted to force because leavers often were anticipating both reunions with friends and families as well as resumptions of lives in a familiar setting. To the end Scandinavia remained a cultural shock for many returnees. In their less progressive homelands, women were subordinate to men. Gender was a source of limitations. Swedes' nonchalance about sexuality perplexed and disturbed many foreigners. In addition as host to strangers, Sweden often made returning a more palpatable proposition by providing departees stipends with which to restart their lives and—when necessary—to rebuild their homes. Beginning in 1997 families who had agreed to return to Bosnia occasionally received as much as 40,000 kronor. According to the repatriation program in place, incentives followed a formula that rewarded eligible adults with 10,000 kronor each and provided 5,000 kronor per child. To qualify for this type of assistance, individuals usually had deadlines to meet, meaning persons would get subsidies only if they departed by the specific date set for their particular group. As with seemingly everything else connected with refugees, there were critics who questioned the ethics behind these schemes. It looked to them more like bribery than assistance.

Of all the minorities in Sweden, Somalians perhaps most suspected Swedish motives. Leader Abdi Egag found many of his countrymen interpreting the program as something negative and sinister. It was especially among educated Africans with no job prospects that "there has existed the rumor about the government wanting to be rid of us Somalians." Egag found strong desires among the group to leave for an anarchy-riddled African state, but almost nobody wanted to go before stability would be reestablished there.[102]

Swedish reactions to refugees ran the gamut from Sjöbo and Kimstad's negativism to Åsele's unwavering support and friendship. There were such reactionary foes as the arsonists who set ablaze refugee residences, and there were others like Stig Wallin and Sister Marianne, who befriended asylum seekers. After one had murdered Wallin's daughter, he demonstrated love and forgiveness, organizing the "Five to Twelve" movement on behalf of refugees. While it was helping with advocacy and transcultural friendship, the nun was busily defying laws by hiding escapees from certain deportations. In addition generous people were volunteering as refugee guides, helping strangers with life in a new country. Others either protested restrictive policies with letters to newspaper editors or demonstrated on behalf of refugees in one way or another. Even in supportive efforts, there was some negativism. Swedish snobbery and liberal paternalism could detract from goodness. Transcending often above Swedes' good deeds was a smugness that was rooted deeply in a superiority complex and in a notion other nationalities needed Swedish help. Both traits were inheritances from Protestant evangelicalism and from years of living in a benevolent welfare state with all its attendant propaganda about how much better life was in Sweden than elsewhere. The combination gave birth to obsessive self-righteousness and imbued Swedes with a spirit of intrusiveness that propelled indivdual citizens and the nation into the rest of the world with lessons to give about how human needs should be met.

A general conclusion of elitism developed among many Swedes that the outside world could benefit from Swedish intervention and assistance. Thus in effect it became Sweden's version of *noblesse oblige*. Obligatory this mission of leading desperate foreigners into a better society that had so many valuable lessons to teach became a zealotry equal to that of the many missionary efforts of Swedish Lutherans as they attempted to convert heathens or that of projects of *SIDA* (Swedish International Development Authority) workers who tried to improve the lives of Third World residents with inputs of Nordic knowhow. There was paradox in all of this, too. By twentieth-century tradition, Sweden's government possessed the dual roles of provider and liberal teacher, but with a clear majority of the population obviously opposed to more welfare extensions to aliens and refugees, three different prime ministers in the 1990s followed a gradual but steady retreat from historic generosity.

Herein was a rub for the most supportive people of refugee causes and programs. Since by tradition they had also been the strongest backers of the most generous government-sponsored liberal welfare policies, there existed a double-crossing of sorts at work. Veteran Social Democratic allies and friends were now the chief policymakers behind rejecting asylum pleas and increasing deportations. Liberals sensed betrayal from the likes of Carlsson, Blomberg, and Schori—one-time enthusiastic supporters who had favored and legislated liberal domestic programs—who had so easily become the willing servants of the new Swedish populists, the xenophobes and racists in the nation, who were opposed to Sweden continuing as the role model to the world and as the most generous provider of refuge and liberalism. Advocates of granting sanctuary on humanitarian grounds seemingly to everyone felt embarrassment after their nation had been the focus of criticisms from Amnesty International, the United Nations High Commission on Refugees, and the Court of International Justice. Each organization had chastised Sweden for inhumanity and for cruel policies. Persons who felt a sting of betrayal most painfully were often individuals who had been accustomed to pointing accusatory fingers at other nations because of their transgressions against human rights. Among the many factors accounting for a popularity surge by *Vänster Partiet* (the Left Party, the recast Communist Party) was its platform that contained planks which were promising to reassert a Swedish tradition of being a generous handler of asylum seekers. There is no intention here to assert that a shift in refugee policy deserves blame or credit for longtime supporters abandoning the Social Democratic Party, but there are indications that some of the organization's most adamant devotees—ones who had fought hardest first for maintenance of the status quo before and then for a restoration after the Lucia Law's adoption—were aggrieved to watch as two successive socialist governments responded favorably to what many old guard liberals considered to be reactionary, the demand that Sweden should not allow any more outsiders to enter.

Hence Kimstad's most important legacy would not be arson or protests against aliens moving there. Rather it was the attentiveness afforded thereafter to the town's most vociferous, simple-minded residents and to Swedes across the nation with similar agendas. The changeover came gradually. Carlsson at first demonstrated only a slight comprehension of the growing public opinion against refugees. Then he and his government—especially after his return in 1994 to the prime ministership—along with those of Bildt and Göran Persson surrendered to citizen demands for inwardness and halts to generous refugee acceptances. Unlike in France, for example, where LePen's success divided the right, Sweden's xenophobic and racist forces split the left, meaning that no ultraright political movement with a "Sweden for Swedes" policy ever would emerge with much chance for success in the Nordic kingdom. Even with the monarchy's slow drift toward the refugee stances of other European nations, the Immigration Board first and then the Migration Board could have done a better job of accommodating asylum seekers with meaningful experiences and of resolving their appeals expeditiously. After all with annual budgets varying from 7- to 12-billion kronor between 1990 and 2000, better results should have followed. Then again, as some critics argued, the newcomers to Sweden might have fared better over the long run if their fates had been left more to their own resources with fewer restrictive bureaucratic hindrances than under regulations and welfare. Then the majority of these people might not have been so passive and doubtful about their abilities to survive as strong, independent persons. Succinctly in a phrase, the problem that faced most refugees to Sweden was too much big brother and too little brotherhood.[103]

Chapter III

Inconsistent Policies, Incompetent Politicians

For explicable reasons social engineering and bureaucratizing have remained major parts of the Swedish state. Successively and increasingly throughout the twentieth century, these elements have had a dominating presence in public life because to a large degree both reflect and exist in the native citizenry's national character. After visits to the Nordic kingdom, most tourists—even ones who are not prone to sweeping overgeneralizations—come to a common consensus from their experiences. Visitors will invariably yield to temptation and ignore the inherent dangers and pitfalls which result from drawing oversimplified conclusions about ethnicity and nations. Stereotypes are often applied to Swedes and Sweden. As a rule coupled to what one often hears about beautiful young women, blue eyes, and blond hair are comments about the Scandinavian country's order and symmetry.

The latter two assessments are not without considerable significance and relevance. This is true even if they are based upon no more than at the marvel and appreciation for the coordination that exists between connecting trains and buses. Visitors who travel across the country often comment about the ease of transferring from vehicle to vehicle. Inasmuch as there are exceptions to most everything, even in a kingdom where conformity is taken so seriously that it is learned and practiced early in life, national pressure and chauvenism manifest in the joint production of a matter upon which there is little disagreement and much pride. Swedes are passionate about their reputation for precision. Few aspects of society and life, including even leisure activities and socialization, are allowed abandonment to chance or are left without control. Among the ethnic population, promptness has become more than a worthy goal. Swedes judge exactitude to be a serious matter not to be taken lightly. If, for example, a dinner invitation is for seven, it will be the only time when guests will dare to arrive. As a result there is a common Swedish scene of people sitting in their automobiles and taxis or remaining at apartment-building entrances. They will wait to knock or ring until that precise moment their minute hands are pointing to the time of an engagement.

The fanaticism and general enthusiasm for and acceptance of external factors' dominion and regulation over so much of Swedes' personal lives give as feasible an explanation as any for why the populace of this nation has also encouraged and embraced all-inclusive government. To paraphrase Joseph de Maistre's conclusion from St. Petersburg in 1811 that "every nation has the government it deserves," one could appropriately complement his wisdom by concluding that native Swedes do have a government that best reflects them.[104]

In this regard two odd factors emerge about a national citizenry and its democracy. After the Social Democratic Party had assumed dominance over the country in the 1930s, Swedes no longer began to demand or seek leaders with credentials which were conspicuously better than their own. Yet this electorate paradoxically has been willing to entrust so many aspects of life to ordinary people who do not possess much formal education and who have no special skills or experiences. Given voters' mandates and approvals, elected officials from one party have been able to dominate twentieth-century public affairs. This has translated into an expansion of governmental authority over most everything and a collection of taxes on incomes at ever expandable rates to pay for new services and more safeguards. None of this has passed without notice and study. According to a probe into backgrounds of Sweden's cabinet members under Prime Ministers Bildt in 1994 and Persson in 1997, leaders of these Swedish governments had educational levels which ranked lowest among the Western European democracies. Of 43 individuals who held cabinet-level appointments in these two governments, one third lacked a university degree. Two men of the group, Blomberg and Jörgen Andersson, never attended high school, and Friggebo had only a brief university experience. Ulrika Messing's formal learning ended with high school. Blomberg and Friggebo served as immigration ministers, and Messing supervised integration.

Not only were so many politicians lacking educationally, but most of these officials had little or no substantial exeriences outside politics. From an investigation Sören Edgar concluded from several conversations with leading Swedish businessmen that very few of these politicians possessed the merits, educations, and experiences to qualify them as private-sector managers. The deficiencies were also recognized outside of Sweden. Persson's appointment of high-school graduate Margot Wallström to the European Union Commission brought doubts about her ability to hold this position. Her interview with EU officials revealed just how little she knew. Statesmen who had quizzed her to determine if she comprehended the basic environmental issues—allegedly her specialty—were dumbfounded by her ignorance. It forced them to conclude with reserved embarrassment that in order to become an effective head of the EU committee charged with protecting natural resources, Persson's appointee would have much to learn. In another case that broke diplomatic decorum, an Austrian leader, after a frustrating first meeting with Persson, could not resist tagging the Swede with an unkind reference to a large mammal's stupidity.[105]

During the 1990s Sweden's political activities were a minefield with so many cases of incompetency that they exploded into the open for all to see on a frequent basis. Since foolishness respected no political boundaries, examples came without any partisan preference. At one moment or another during this decade, each major political party presented the Swedish press corps with the kind of buffoonry that made for sensational newspaper stories and mockeries of good leadership. Much of the ignorance involved immigrants and refugees. These subjects baffled public officials to the point of confusing and rendering them vulnerable to actions which would contradict their verbal commitments to uphold Sweden's reputation for generosity. Stating interest on the one hand in retaining an upbeat image in international circles of unbroken liberalism but finding determent on the other hand domestically among so many xenophobic reactionaries, politicians in befuddlement mixed kind platitudes for openness and justice with recalcitrant practices. Doubletalk was so easily detected that it caused reverberations and attacks from migration's friends and foes. Being not well schooled in diplomacy and people management, elected officials recoiled angrily to charges of inconsistency. With credibility virtually destroyed among the supporters of a pro-refugee policy, Swedish politicians experienced a great many difficulties as they tried to recover support from opposing sectors of the electorate. Like their political sponsors, the appointees to posts at Immigration and Integration did not fare much better because they were trying to administer nebulous programs. No matter how much effort they expended to defend their actions and organizations, there could be no escape from criticisms.

Carlsson's first government, the one that followed Olof Palme's murder in 1986 and that ended with a bitter electoral defeat in 1991, was somewhat doomed from the beginning by the inevitable comparisons of the successor to a predecessor. Leftists interpreted Carlsson's veers slightly to the right of Palme as deviations deserving of criticisms and consternation. Probably no individual would have found assuming the prime ministership an easy task to follow after one of Sweden's most controversial leaders. Palme was a complex person—hated or loved—with unabashed ambition and unabated ideological aspiration to revolutionize Swedish institutions into a fulfillment of his idealistic dreams. He wanted a *lagom* society with greater *jämlikhet* (translated roughly as a just-right society with relative income equality) and a Sweden with lessons for the world to follow. Unlike evangelical Palme, the commander of every matter of interest, his successor was a placid, reserved man who allowed matters to drift somewhat aimlessly without much intervention or personal leadership.

Inactivity on behalf of the so-called Lucia Law illustrated Carlsson's lack of control. Instead of preparing Swedes for the bill's adoption by giving explanations for its necessity, the laid-back Social Democrat simply ignored the legislation's potential critics. Consistent to his aloof style, he neither gave the nation rationale in support of the bill nor pacification to divert its attention.

Self-critical about his own shortcomings six months after losing out as prime minister, Carlsson admitted to erring: "The silence was well intentioned, but unfortunately it has done more harm than good." Thus considerable focus and energy went into attacking the law and memorializing Palme's compassionate refugee policies. As a result of disapprobation of Carlsson's policies, critics concluded the Social Democrat now in charge was a betrayer of his party's traditions because of his support of a harsh law.

Emerging after Palme's assassination, Carlsson faced in many ways the same challenges as Lyndon Johnson had in the wake of gunned-down John F. Kennedy in 1963. As a result of a common dilemma, both successors found themselves dealing with almost impossible tasks of finding endearment and gaining acceptance. Attempts by Johnson and then by Carlsson at stamping a personal identity on their respective administrations met disparagement and resistance, while adversely an adhering to predecessors' agendas generated charges of thievery and opportunism. In these no-win situations, it was either stealing a martyr's program or showing unimaginativeness for not developing original programs.[106]

Leading up to a general election set for September, 15, 1991, the Social Democratic Party and Carlsson were increasingly vulnerable to criticism. Of course incumbent officials and parties rarely escape targeting, but in the prime minister's case, there was just as much gnawing from within his own party as from outside it. Lacking leadership and discipline, its members were moving in all directions, causing embarrassment and confusion. For a political body with almost sixty years of advocacy and enactments of many progressive laws as well as consistent support for society's weakest members, having a person in a top local position like Göteborg's Terje Ahl making national headlines for a successful foiling of Muslims' attempts to build a mosque in his city did not coincide well with an image of fairness that so many other Social Democrats were trying to engrain in immigrant voters' minds. For saying, among other things, that "it would be horrible if the first thing a person saw in Bishop's Garden [a Göteborg neighborhood selected by Muslims for a sanctuary] is a mosque," Ahl became another "Swine Olle"—a reference to Sjöbo's alien-foe Sven-Olle—to his critics. Having such an obvious xenophobe in the party offended both its leftwing and alien portions, but his expulsion would have ramifications. Ahl's stand appealed to Bishop's Garden Swedes, who, for the most part, were assembly-line workers at a nearby Volvo factory and loyal Social Democrats.

Under pressures and in a dilemma, the party was caught, therefore, not wanting to lose hourly wage earners while needing at the same time to show goodwill toward Sweden's minorities. Timed to occur before election day, the Social Democratic-dominated *Riksdag* on September 9, increased subsidies to immigrant churches, and then two days later, after several years of postponing and delaying, Stockholm's municipal government followed the leadership of Social Democratic councilwoman Monica Andersson and assented to the city's 45,000 Muslims' wishes by approving a site for a mosque.[107]

While rightwinger Ahl's racist diatribes tainted the party's reputation, spokespersons from the left were contributing to disunity with harsh criticisms. Reflecting on the Palme Era's generosity, such veteran party leaders as Franck and Peter Nobel expressed adamant support for liberalizing rules for asylum and immigration and for expanding legal protection against different forms of discrimination. The former man, an opinionated member of parliament with definite views on many subjects, joined Left Party supporters and many fellow disgruntled Social Democrats to insist Carlsson and his supporters "tear up the refugee decision" adopted on Lucia Day and alter *Siv*'s entire *modus operandi*. Among other things Franck thought *Siv* was wasting too much time and energy on drafting agreements with communes, and he criticized refugee conditions in Sweden. In particular he saw no compelling reason for rules that kept asylum seekers from working, and he questioned their alleged "high quality" living standards. Franck contrasted these to what he could remember from World War II when "we in my home constantly had refugees living with us."

For different reasons but equally upset, Nobel disagreed as well with his party's actions. In his view the hardening of "policies has influenced opinion" negatively. During Sweden's worst-ever month of refugee-directed violence, Nobel as discrimination ombudsman linked his party's decisions to the attacks. Careful to separate ethnic intolerance from asylum opposition, noting the first had not worsened whereas the second had, Nobel concluded fellow authorities had erred twice. First of all "when the government goes out and says it now is going to shake the system to its foundation," what, he asked readers, should "the public then believe?" Thereafter from the regime officially designating all Bulgarian Turks for immediate deportation, "people have gotten in their heads that refugees can be graded." The general population, in other words, was left to conclude from governmental actions that it was fully acceptable to bifurcate asylum seekers into categories or putting everything in another context Swedes could look upon some as worthy of "our sympathy, . . . protection, and . . . aid" and others as so undeserving that "we can tighten the screws."

With less than seven weeks to go before the 1991 election, Nobel noted how weaknesses in Swedish antidiscrimination law limited his powers as the discrimination ombudsman. In a campaign that was marked by major parties' refrain from race-baiting tactics and blatant overtures to sway minority voters, party-maverick Nobel emerged, without party consultation and clearance, to advocate significant expansions of his agency's responsibilities and a complete overhaul of its enforcement mechanisms. As much as ethnic minorities needed protection from prejudicial treatment, Nobel suggested a broadening of whom to consider as victims of abuse. Notably he saw them as anyone who suffered because of their "age, sex, race, nationality, handicaps, sicknesses, memberships, language, opinions, or whatever it is that brings about unwarranted treatment." Arming the office of discrimination ombudsman with greater power and a wider scope of activities, it could become "ombudsman for human rights."

Carlsson's government unwillingly found itself contending with another powerful voice for change, and it came from Rinkeby, Stockholm's infamous immigrant ghetto. It was home to Juan Fonseca, an alien leader who had fled from Latin America to Europe and who had emerged as Sweden's most hated and conspicuous foreigner. Bold and fearless, the South American placed the welfare of immigrants first and his party loyalty second. Since the two often clashed, Fonseca's prioritizing irritated fellow Social Democrats. Among the matters on his agenda was his call for legal action against such hate groups as Nazi organizations. He also sought immigrant empowerment in Sweden's public and private sectors. Although the immigrant's words were a stinging rebuke of what was wrong with the kingdom and a prick at the conscience of the nation, other Social Democrats attempted to distance the party from them and from him. They obviously read public opinion polls and knew how these pointed to a strong nativistic leaning among ethnic Swedes. As much as Social Democrats wanted to bridle Fonseca, efforts proved unsuccessful. Since this man's principles proved stronger than their determination, there was no way to wring concessions or compromises from him. Not even slating him to hold a seat in the *Riksdag* three years later in 1994 would affect his will to battle.[108]

Insiders attacking their party's policies and priorities were not the only problems before the Carlsson wing. The incumbents found such longstanding Social Democratic supporters as liberal writers, academics, religious leaders, and organizations like the Red Cross critical of their party's alien and refugee positions and actions. These attacks came despite initiatives taken to fend off racism and xenophobic organizations. Building upon the 1985 foundings of *Riksförbundet Stoppa Rasismen* (the National Federation to Stop Racism) and *Bevara Sverige Blandat* (Keep Sweden Mixed), the first an umbrella body for twenty local groups opposed to racism and the second a national advocacy group for population diversity, the government also established *Kommissionen mot rasism och främlingsfientlighet* (the Commission against Racism and Xenophobia) in the autumn of 1987. Its mandate was threefold: ascertaining if current laws and their applications could become more effective; examining how knowledge and awareness of problems could be enhanced and extended through education and research; and determining how opinion-building efforts against racism and xenophobia could spread throughout society.

Although parliament had budgeted 12,000,000 kronor for these purposes, it gained little that had not already been known or recommended. Commission members in their report of 1989, for example, advised criminalizing extremist organizations whose missions were racial hatred and forbidding participations in such groups. Nothing new, these suggestions were simply a reiteration of the annually unheeded parliamentary appeals that had begun earnestly in 1984. In reality the inspiration for this type of legislation dated back to 1965 and the passage by the United Nations General Assembly of a manifestation directing member states to outlaw race-baiting bodies. For ignoring the mandate to act, Sweden received domestic as well as international criticism. A multifaceted bill with legal bans against racist groups and unfair employment practices did come before the *Riksdag* on June 2 and 3, 1990, but Carlsson forces postponed action, claiming both elements needed further study and promising resolutions of the two issues during the 1992 parliamentary session.[109]

Whether postponement had resulted from cowardice or civil libertarian concerns about the effects of legal bans upon free speech and associations, no definitive answer emerged. Few doubts existed about the presence of known tendencies among Carlsson appointees for racism, xenophobia, and prejudice, however. Many governmental entities were under their administrative control. For example responsibility for law and order ultimately depended upon police and the justice system. Management of these came directly from the offices of the national head of law enforcement and from the justice ministry, but Prime Minister Carlsson appeared to expect no accountability whatsoever from these. Media-reported cases of officer brutality against asylum seekers almost never advanced beyond denials of wrongdoing to the legal system. If there had been inquiries, investigations, prosecutions, and judgments, newspapers offered no coverage to internal probes and trials of misbehaving police.

In a news story that appeared on March 27, 1990 in *Dagens Nyheter*, Bo Westmar described denials by Swedish border police in Ystad of their alleged bad treatment of a boatload of illegal aliens who had arrived from Poland by ship at the port authority several days earlier. Speaking for his officers, Chief Inspector Lars Bergh claimed reports that police had hit children, women, and men with nightsticks and had confiscated these peoples' money and valuable possessions were "colossally exaggerated misrepresentations." Bergh simply attributed the aliens' complaints to their personal disappointments of having been turned around by the police for a trip back to Poland. If there had been any mishandling, "there surely would have been a reason for it."

At arriving back in Swinoujscie, the misfortunate travelers interpreted their experiences very differently. A young pregnant Lebanese woman in her second trimester complained from a Polish hospital bed of receiving a severe beating from Swedish police. Her injuries required hospitalization. Several refugees told of much seasickness on the ferry during its stormy voyage across the Baltic Sea because the police had locked returnees in buses parked on the bottom deck.

Aggressive law-enforcement behavior was not limited to incidents in Ystad. On a regular basis immigrants also had negative experiences with law officers. Take what occurred in Rinkeby one hour before midnight and 1991. Built-up resentments broke loose there during the remaining hour of 1990 after a teenager's arrest for allegedly shooting a skyrocket into a subway entrance. According to police, "absolute tumult arose when these people at the square began acting like wild animals, throwing stones and shooting rockets at us [police]." One hospitalized officer, two vandalized squad cars, and additional reenforcement of the residents' perspective of Swedish police as an invading force of storm troopers and provocateurs were the toll from this ordeal, the third consecutive New Year's Eve battle between police and local people at the most notorious ethnic enclave in Sweden.

Säpo (short for *Säkerhetspolis*) also figured in many controversies, first in following suspicions of Kurd nationalists for Palme's murder with illegal buggings and then for doing nothing substantial to track and identify racist attackers of refugees and immigrants. Almost without exception, the men and women involved with Swedish law enforcement were ethnic Swedes. As such, they likely had no more sympathy and empathy for aliens than the members of the at-large population with similar backgrounds. Moreover neither Palme, Carlsson, nor subordinates took steps to address the bias by and ethnic makeup of Sweden's police. As a result officers remained insiders dealing with outsiders, a situation certain to breed resentment, distrust, and hatred.

Matters were not better at the other side of law enforcement. Even with a sharp increase in violent criminal acts against aliens in 1989 and 1990, Hans Stark of the Justice Ministry claimed "the number of reported [racist crimes] which led to prosecutions were proportionately few." He attributed problems to "latent xenophobia." Although Stark failed to mention it, a general silence and inactivity from members of Carlsson's government contributed to the fact that racists were escaping detention and prosecution because arguments were not being made on behalf of aliens' rights. The unconvincing condemnations of xenophobia by politicians had an equally important role.[110]

Despite many outrageous actions and foolish comments from within a vast bureaucracy under Carlsson's control, no public chastisings of managers occurred. For example in 1990 when Soviet Jews were emigrating from their homeland in large numbers because of increased anti-Semitism, every reason existed to be understanding and generous. Case could have been made by the prime minister to grant them at least temporary asylum. It would have made sense since most of these migrants were choosing Israel while only approximately 150 had expressed a desire for Swedish refuge. In the end Nordic authorities' prejudices and ignorance doomed these Jewish appeals for permanent sanctuary. Veteran Foreign Minister Sten Andersson did not even want to grant them transit visums to the Middle East. He feared their eventual settlement in Israeli "occupied" lands on the West Bank might upset Sweden's sympathetic relationship with the Palestinians.

After the decision to deport a heavily burdened group to likely additional persecution, Immigration Board section head Marianne Brunfelt offered what amounted to a preposterously insensitive reason for the action. Namely it was her conclusion that "real Jews travel to Israel." Remarking about her tactless asininity and callousness for *Dagens Nyheter*, physician Henry Ascher could find only two explanations for such ridiculousness. Either Brunfelt believed herself as competent at detecting true Israelites from imposters as rabbis with this responsibility for the Jewish state or she thought all Jews belonged there. Whichever, Ascher demanded judicial intervention to determine if she had "overstepped the authority of her position." To this end the doctor urged the Justice Ministry "to try and see if prosecution for misconduct should be brought up." Moreover he wanted the Discrimination Ombudsman to charge her, and he sought to eliminate racists from the Immigration Board. Nothing happened.

Brunfelt remained at *Siv*, suffering neither penalties nor public reprimands for her outrageous claim that bordered on racial agitation.[111]

Carlsson insiders often sparred with politicians who were critical of the government's refugee program. Leading up to the 1991 election, Immigration Minister Lööw's policy defenses became a regular feature in several Swedish newspapers. Rebutting from the left for *Aftonbladet* readers on May 27, 1991, Lars Werner attacked Social Democrats' unwillingness to pass any legislation against employment discrimination and condemned the party's desire to enact a special law that singled out immigrant-perpetrated violence. The Left Party leader considered it appropriate in light of the fact all reports had been showing "the overwhelming number of terrorist deeds in Sweden have been committed by Swedish citizens." As a result "it was high time that this terrorism be given highest priority in police investigative work." In less than three weeks Werner appeared again in the same newspaper, this time claiming his rivals on refugee matters were both "nonchalant and uninterested." In particular he alleged the supervision of *Siv* by Lööw was so inadequate that it was leading to increased reliances upon child and adult lockups, illegal deportations, and infractions of laws meant to regulate the handling of aliens. In a political tit for tat without any substantive meaning to countering the criticisms, the beleaguered cabinet officer followed each article with ones of her own before finally categorizing Werner's charges as nothing but "tiresome mythicizing" and "trash talk."[112]

As Carlsson's appointee in charge of refugees and immigrants, Lööw did successfully fend off the wild accusations from Sjöbo's Olsson, but her efforts at rebuffing the more constructive criticisms from Folk Party spokespersons were not convincing. Claiming six-billion kronor did not represent a complete tabulation of everything involved with accepting asylum seekers, Skåne's now famous farmer-politician accused the cabinet officer of falsifying figures which Sweden was spending on refugees. By his reckoning, she had deliberately neglected to add into her total all the extra outlays that had resulted from the various residence grants. If the extra dental and medical costs, home-language studies, unemployment and welfare payments, and several other miscellaneous expenditures had not been omitted, the total would have reached approximately forty-billion kronor. Choosing to ignore Olsson's charge of a miscalculation, Lööw turned around the discussion to inform her critic how "every individual refugee is equally worthy as you are. Every person's life has the same worth, in my opinion, and that value cannot be measured in money." Inasmuch it was difficult to refute her line of argumentation, the minister's triumph was just another example of just how easy it was to obtain advantage over reactionaries in polemnical contests.

For *Siv*'s chief administrator, the liberal Folk Party's seamless attacks would have much more far-reaching importance. Unlike Olsson's Sjöbo Party and the more extreme and xenophobic *Sverigedemokrater* (Sweden Democrats, a group one Swedish historian described as "racists in new suits") who tried to arouse support by charging aliens had been advancing ahead of ethnic Swedes in queues for scarce housing and who wanted to stop refugee and immigrant acceptances, the critics who were charging Social Democrats with capitulating to such aforementioned enemies left Lööw and the Carlsson government with nowhere to escape. Abundant proof existed of tougher conditions for Swedish sanctuary. By eliminating through the notorious Lucia Law all supplementary grounds for asylum, by causing general mortification and embarrassment with anti-Semitic conclusions about Soviet Jews, by decreasing the percentage of successful sanctuary applications, by mollifying refugees into passivity, by permitting long waits for decisions, and by rounding up Bulgarians Turks for deportation, the incumbents had rendered themselves susceptible to attacks.

With this record, associating Social Democrats, as one Folk Party leader had, to policies "promoting xenophobia" required little imagination. Lööw tried her best to counter Peter Örn's conclusion, but maneouvering away from the Folk Party secretary's charges was not easy. Retrospectively from just an opportunistic perspective, a confession to all those terrible actions might have aided Social Democrats more in the election than trying to separate the party's from its activities and policies. Had Lööw conceded to Örn and agreed about the correctness of his claims, this response might have appealed to Sweden's growing recalcitrant majority. But to Carlsson and her credit, they were too rooted in party principles to attempt demogoguery. Especially for the prime minister, rousing ethnic Swedes against their country's aliens seemed never to be an acceptable option. Although he had already conceded much ground to restrictionists, he apparently saw no need in 1991 for any further concessions.

Hoping for the best outcome, the party ran on its migration record with no apologies or promises. Excepting *Nydemokraterna* (the New Democrats) with political novices Bert Karlsson and Ian Wachtmeister who attempted to turn public life into theater with buffoonery coupled to some populistic appeals for simple solutions to such complex societal problems as how to deal with a mass of refugees and oppositely the Folk and Left parties with promises to restore a generous attitude toward asylum seekers, the 1991 election would become less a referendum on Social Democratic refugee policy and more a mandate about which side could affect fiscal reform and reorganization. As the voting would show, the populace was disenchanted with exorbitant taxes, and there evolved in 1991 a majority consensus dictating needs for general reforms of and reductions to Sweden's overburdening bureaucracy; these were the key issues that brought down the incumbents and ushered in a new ruling coalition.[113]

After the Social Democratic Party's defeat of September 15, 1991, Moderate, Folk, Center, and Christian Democratic party members formed a government of divided powers and responsibilities. Installation of a new cabinet without Carlsson and the other remaining *Riksdag* socialists placed their party in a most unfamiliar role of governmental foes, a phenomenon that had occurred only one other time between the 1930s and 1991 and that more than a decade earlier when rightwingers and moderates had ousted a Palme-led government. Joining Social Democrats as outsiders in government without appointments or ruling authority were the Left Party and New Democrats. Unlike the other two affiliations, members of the latter newly formed political party theoretically did qualify as potential government partners as a result of their *borgerliga* (literally bourgeois but here nonsocialist) outlook and program, but their populistic and xenophobic extremism on so many issues rendered them too much of a liability for their inclusion.

From the party's formation through the election, cofounders and political novices Karlsson and Wachtmeister attracted crowds and much news coverage with iconoclasm and disrespect for Swedish political associations. Once in the *Riksdag*, New Democratic deputies—by altogether unlikely alliance with other shadow governments—had enough delegate strength to stall legislation and to dissolve parliament. Although there had been many threats and much bluster from Karlsson and Wachtmeister, attention from contesting and irritating other *Riksdag* parties seemed enough to satisfy these troublemaking instigators.

The Karlsson-Wachtmeister foray into refugee policies began during the 1991 campaign, and the attacking continued until they would tire of politics in late 1993. From the start of New Democrats' criticisms of the way Sweden was handling asylum seekers, Karlsson's dual roles as a renter to *Siv* and as one of its major faultfinders either represented a conflict of interest or a paradox. He was the owner-landlord of Stora Ekeberg, a large resort on wooded land near Karlsson's home in Skara and leased by him to *Siv*. Under this arrangement at the peak of alien occupancy, it employed a sixty-member staff. Yet after a 12-million kronor investment in renovations and modifications done to make the facility suitable for refugees, *Siv* was planning abandonment. Its justification resulted from the fact that fewer people had been seeking Swedish sanctuary. Karlsson was suspicious about this explanation because *Siv*'s decision to close Stora Ekeberg had too closely paralleled the December 1, 1990, announcement of plans to form the New Democratic Party for it to be coincidental. Leaders of the bureaucracy were so desperate to rid themselves of the embarrassment of an expose, the newcomer to Swedish politics charged, that an unnamed but highly ranked *Siv* official had been using bully tactics and extortion against him. Writing for *Göteborgs-Posten*, the novice in Swedish politics claimed to have been under threat from an anonymous bureaucrat whom he alleged had ordered him to choose between selling Stora Ekeberg or abandoning politics. To this unsupported supposition, the New Democrat added specific details of waste and implications of corruption that resulted in a doubling of the budget, or in other words a 3.5-billion kronor overexpenditure for Swedish taxpayers.

Ineptitude at spending public revenues providently was only one aspect of the New Democratic assault on alien policies. At other times allegations of refugees' alleged proneness to criminality characterized xenophobic diatribes from Karlsson and Wachtmeister. Resorting to raw demagoguery on July 26, 1992, to a crowd of Swedish vacationers gathered to hear the duo at the tourist town of Fjällbacka, Wachtmeister easily was able to secure audience approval and applause: "We are importing criminality which is formidable. We are allowing murderers to enter, and by doing this the society is applying the death penalty against you!" Whenever accusations of racism and xenophobia came as counters to such inflammatory utterances, the two rabble-rousing political neophytes managed reversals with clarifications, claiming their advocacy was for fairness and humaneness toward all legitimate sanctuary seekers. This, they maintained, was unlike their hypocritical adversaries who were guilty of disobeying laws, discriminating, and deporting en masse.

Karlsson devoted attention to b*orgerlig* Immigration Minister Friggebo's special handling of Kosovo Albanians in 1992. Through grants of temporary asylum, she did not offer them the same treatment that her Social Democratic predecessor had given Bulgarian Turks and Polish gypsies. It was Karlsson's understanding that without a change in law, the alternatives were either asylum or deportation and not something midway between these choices as Friggebo had been trying. According to his interpretation of the statute covering asylum applications and equal treatment, she had violated requirements for equality. She continued to be a favorite New Democratic target until strong electorate disfavor toward the 1991-elected coalition showed up in many opinion polls.

Thereafter Karlsson and Wachtmeister abandoned interest in her and began aiming wrathfulness at the Social Democrats because of their apparent rejuvenation of popularity. Responses in kind to Karlsson and Wachtmeister, as their critics were prone to do after the duo's provocative statements and claims, fulfilled the New Democrats' expectations. From distorting the truth about refugees and immigrants, they had obviously wanted negative feedback. Without foes' ill-advised recognition and attention—two necessary factors for demagogic success—the pair's race baiting could not have made headlines and pushed them to the center of numerous debate articles. In effect, by engaging them publicly, orthodox politicians legitimized two dangerous men.[114]

Resulting from the Moderate Party's success at obtaining more seats in the *Riksdag* than its coalition partners, leader Bildt emerged as Sweden's new prime minister. Since nobody in his party was especially interested in refugee and alien matters, the post of Immigration Minister passed to Friggebo. Her selection was logical. During the Carlsson administration, she and fellow Folk Party leader Bengt Westerberg criticized his refugee policy more than anybody else among *borgerliga* members of parliament. Although Westerberg as head of a political party generally synonymous with liberalism would take the post of Social Minister because of its greater status and clout than one in charge of immigration, considerable interaction occurred between him and Friggebo in the development and execution of asylum policy.

The actions and rules which resulted from their efforts contradicted in large part what their disapprobations of Lööw's handling of refugees and of her party's legislation might have implied if they should assume these duties. Excepting rescission of the Lucia Law on December 19, 1991 and a removal of the prohibitions of work by asylum-seekers on July 1, 1992, Friggebo's term in charge of immigration policy was not marked by any of the idealistic changes she and Westerberg had expressed as their goals for policy and practice prior to the 1991 election and their elevation to power. As inheritors of problems from the Yugoslavian civil war, they found themselves having to deal with several thousand migrants in search of Swedish sanctuary and a home populace weary from keeping outsiders in the midst of an ever deepening economic recession that was on its way to becoming Sweden's worst since the Great Depression. While the government was slashing domestic programs and employers were dismissing workers daily, the Folk Party relented, abandoning liberal idealism for a response to the pressures for less generosity and tougher terms for asylum than their Social Democratic predecessors had ever imposed. A more restrictive attitude began with enactments during 1992—the first year without the 1989 restrictions—when more than 84,000 people freely migrated into the Nordic kingdom.

Beginning on October 10, 1992, the Bildt government pushed through parliament a series of changes which aligned Sweden's policies closer to those of other European nations. The first of four acts imposed visa requirements on Serbians, Montenegrins, and Macedonians. Then coverage expanded on June 21, 1993, to include Bosnians. For ex-Jugoslavs migrating to Sweden became more difficult because the new rules demanded that they secure permission as a preliminary to coming. On the same day that the *Riksdag* restricted travel for the fourth group, there was somewhat a loosening of rules for the 40,000-some Bosnia-Herzegovina residents who were already in Sweden. As a result of the changes, they were allowed to stay. A few months later in an obvious response to silence critics, the legislature acted to correct what many refugee advocates had condemned as cruel, that is, the practice of deporting families who had had long waits for decisions on their sanctuary appeals. On April 14, 1994, Bildt's coalition stopped all further occurrences of this type by amending asylum law to reward refuge to such sufferers. According to particulars the change meant every asylum-seeking family with children and a residence application which had been registered before January 1, 1993, could now remain.

This effort at correcting one of the harshest aspects of seeking sanctuary in Sweden ended a series of *borgerlig* efforts at fulfilling Folk Party promises to reform inherited flaws. The first had come on July 1, 1992, with the lifting of bans against work by people who were waiting for asylum decisions. After the change of April 1994, parliament moved in the opposite direction with its direct concessions to xenophobic Swedes' complaints about a softness toward alien criminals. A *Riksdag* response on July 1, 1994, reflected the *borgerliga* lawmakers' swing to the right and signs of their capitulation to pressures from society's most reactionary forces. A parliamentary majority put into statutory law a demand for toughness against alien misconduct. Under the new statute an immigrant could now face a deportation hearing if found guilty in criminal court of a crime serious enough to be punishable by imprisonment.

Also in a final desperate move at winning Swedish majority support in the summer before a general election set for September 18, 1994, Bildt and his conservative-liberal government tried to demonstrate some empathy for the many Swedes who seemed to be concerned about press reports of completely out-of-control asylum seeking. The coalition did this by announcing a ban that would negatively impact most Africans who arrived in Sweden without visas. Overall the results from 1991 to 1994 were mixed. A *Riksdag* majority loyal to the coalition government had both adhered to and violated a component's liberal platform on refugees and immigrants. Given the lamblasting Lööw and Carlsson had received from Friggebo and Westerberg for allegedly abandoning the principles of Swedish generosity, the two Folk Party leaders could not—after a three-year period of setting and managing immigration and asylum policies—truthfully boast of having reversed a downward trend.

The pair could claim three things, however. Their appointment of Berit Rollén as *Siv*'s general director brought a person to the post with dedication to reducing agency expenditures. Under the Folk Party's watch, Germany awarded Sweden the 1992 Bertelmann Prize and 30,000 marks for constructive efforts toward people "living together in a multicultural society" and for conduct of a "long-range—and from a European perspective—very farsighted immigration policy." Friggebo also worked with the European Union to develop a mutual program aimed at encouraging Bosnians with asylum across Western Europe to begin returning to their homeland for its reconstruction.[115]

As critical outsiders before their takeover of migration matters, Friggebo and Westerberg had likely been sincere about doubting both the wisdom and direction of Social Democratic refugee policies. Once in positions to perform otherwise, they encountered forces which were aligned to upset their well laid plans to restore Sweden's reputation as a generous nation. For accomplishing this feat, they had expected praise from scuh world organizations as Amnesty International and the International Red Cross. As liberal as the twosome might have been on human rights, they were above all politicians who had worked in a coalition with unity based upon common resolve to unseat the socialist party. Public opinion and New Democratic stridency, as considerations and realities, also impacted decisions and policy. Although Karlsson and Wachtmeister did not endear themselves especially on a personal level with most ethnic Swedes, their inflammatory rhetoric about immigrants and refugees reflected nativists' feelings. Almost three months after the 1991 election, a quarter of them under 25-years old noted for pollsters an intention to vote for whichever party would pledge a stop to all migrations into Sweden. At fifty percent in June 1994—although down from 66 percent twelve months earlier—as the percentage of an ethnic populace that sought fewer refugees, it represented a significant force. If a political party were serious about winning at summer's end in September, some acknowledging of the Swedish electorate's anger and frustration would seem necessary. Although to a lesser degree for people intending to vote for the Folk Party than perhaps to the loyalists to the other seven political parties, negative feelings still prevailed as the following tables illustrate:

On how many refugees Sweden should accept; more, fewer, same?:

	more	fewer	same
Moderates:	05	50	42%
Center:	03	59	28%
Christian Democrats:	13	50	26%
Green:	26	49	18%
Social Democrats:	06	62	28%

Left:	10	34	45%
New Democrats:	03	90	06%
FOLK:	16	34	46%

Should authorities be encouraging refugees to return to homelands, actively or inactively?:

Moderates:	68	22%
Center:	70	15%
Christian Democrats:	58	24%
Green:	56	33%
Social Democrats:	66	20%
Left:	48	28%
New Democrats:	79	20%
FOLK:	51	41%

Do you think the latest immigration period to Sweden has been negative or advantageous?:

Moderates:	66	15%
Center:	68	07%
Christian Democrats:	72	19%
Green:	58	18%
Social Democrats:	63	14%
Left:	34	22%
New Democrats:	98	02%
FOLK:	51	32%

For asylum grantees without work, should they live off welfare or borrow?:

Moderates:	22	63%
Center:	24	59%
Christian Democrats:	32	53%
Green:	34	56%
Social Democrats:	30	55%
Left:	36	31%
New Democrats:	14	82%
FOLK:	39	49%

Have you personally had mostly positive, negative, or no experiences with immigrants?:

Moderates:	60	15	21%
Center:	32	13	47%
Christian Democrats:	61	11	19%
Green:	80	00	12%
Social Democrats:	50	15	29%
Left:	69	19	13%
New Democrats:	32	39	26%

Folk: 80   03   17%
*To every question, the remainder needed to bring line tallies to 100% had
no opinion.

As extreme as the New Democratic leaders and their followers were on
questions of asylum and immigration, their views, according to the results of this
public-opinion polling, did not differ so much from all the other partisans.
Consequences were piecemeal concessions to rabid foes of liberal policies and
less rhetoric from all parties on the general topic of immigration. Gone for the
most part between September 1991 and September 1994 was public debating on
a current Immigration Ministry's performance in relationship to what had been
promised and expected. Rather, attacks on Friggebo were personal and related
in effect more to her managerial competency than to whether or not she had
pursued worthy objectives and had followed Sweden's best interests. The
minister's parttime devotion to immigration was one matter that irritated such
old-line liberals as Ingrid Segerstedt Wiberg. She like others of her political
persuasion wanted in place an energetic champion of human rights and global
interests as well as a person who intended to return Sweden to the forefront of
righteous causes. Holding simultaneously two cabinet posts, Immigration and
Culture, Friggebo could never, complained critics of the arrangement, manage
both offices satisfactorily.

For obvious reasons Friggebo's classifying Kosovo Albanians as natural
thieves did much to damage her reputation among those who were advocating
both more refugee rights and acceptances. Her act of not pandering to liberals
like Wiberg had only a marginal impact on her standing because across party
lines they were outnumbered by the combination of restrictionists and status-quo
elements. Intemperate as her prejudicial stereotyping had been, it brought praise
to Friggebo from nativists and racists. Hence very few citizens—even if many
from diverse backgrounds had been expressing in letters to newspapers a worry
about Sweden drifting toward callousness—cared that the policies from a
borgerlig government did not reflect more humane and generous tendencies than
those of Social Democratic predecessors Carlsson and Lööw.[116]

Except for a few scattered volleys of criticism and inclusions of refugee-
immigrant positions in party white papers and platforms, politicians avoided
pro-and-con discussions of Friggebo's handling of asylum and migration so
much—even during the 1994 campaign—that suspicions arose of a general
conspiracy to silence critics and to remove these topics altogether from debate
and partisanship. Only confrontational Gudrun Schyman, Werner's successor as
head of the Left Party, tried to rally critics with the wild and unsubstantiated
charge that New Democrats had advised Bildt's coalition government. Liberal
Social Democratic backbenchers wanted generosity and commitments to aliens
and refugees written into their party's platform, but in the final document there
was no evidence of their appeal to change what a Blomberg-headed committee
had offered party-convention delegates.[117]

The Bildt years did leave one important legacy. In autumn 1991 to deal exclusively with appeals for sanctuary, the *riksdag* created the Asylum Review Board. Its establishment culminated many frustrating years of dissatisfaction with constant backlogs of cases awaiting decisions. Moreover placing judicial functions under an independent governmental unit gave politicians the escape hatch that they had been seeking from criticisms after unpopular deportations. With a title of general director and an original staff of 140, Fischerström began the job of clearing out some 12,000 appeals for asylum on January 10, 1992. It was his intention to cut the total downward by the end of the fiscal year to a more manageable 1,000-1,500 unresolved cases, but this achievement would not be reached because more than 84,000 people swarmed into Sweden that year.

During ARB's first years its failure at reaching a major objective was only one of several problems before Fischerström. In a June 8, 1993, article that appeared in *Dagens Nyheter*, 141 attorneys attacked the board's judgment with the claim that it had violated the rights of deported Kosovo Albanians. In response the general director defended ARB decisions with an "answer that the assertions about inadequate rules of law at the board are erroneous." To inform critics that only individuals with previous judicial experiences presided over sessions, Fischerström cited as proof his staff's credentials. "A homogeneous application of the law as the Board provides best guarantees rules of law. Thus subjectivity and common thinking are neutralized." As much as ARB's head tried to fend off criticisms with explanations and defenses, complaints persisted about the Board, and there were even several attempts at discrediting it altogether. Even after critics like left-leaning Sten De Geer and immigrant attorney Jesus Alcalá had called the ARB "a total disaster" and Fischerström "dishonorable," there was no escaping the veracity of the general director's rebuttal to such charges. "In conclusion, I want to underscore that neither I nor any of my staff reach decisions which obviously contravene the law."[118]

Whether decisions resulted politically from a department under a cabinet officer's control or more independently from the ARB, emotions and previous indifference could assert themselves into the process to complicate matters. Excepting the visa requirements imposed on aforementioned folk groups as a condition to enter Sweden, asylum law and policy exempted other classifications from special treatments. Thus when cases involving Jews from the ex-Soviet Union were before this special tribunal charged with evaluating their appeals, nothing in statutes or regulations could offer them extralegal protection or special consideration. Judging on merit and nothing else, ARB staffers had no choice but to conform to the highest judicial ideals at hearings and practice fairness and impartiality toward the subjects. Based upon presented evidence about the minority's status, alleged oppression, and appellant testimonies about personal experiences, initial decisions called for deportation. After verdicts for this, critics charged the ARB with anti-Semitism, claiming its decisions were reminders of Sweden's shameful dealings with Jews during the Nazi Era. Such transpired after a hearing on the appeal of parents Grigorij and Natalja Genin and their son Andrej. On their behalf several protests and emotional appeals followed which would move the national conscience and result in a judgmental reversal. In what would turn into a precedent-setting case, the Genins gained permission to stay in Sweden.[119]

Hate crimes and organizations perplexed the *borgerlig* regime. During its second month in control of parliament, newly appointed Justice Minister Gun Hellsvik expanded *Säpo*. In addition to its traditional responsibilities of counterespionage and counterterrorist duties, it began to chart and fight neo-Nazis and other rightwing extremists. General Director Mats Börjesson did not "see them as a political power and it is going altogether too far to say that they might form a threat against our democratic society," but "on the other hand they do create dread and terror in immigrant colonies and thus must be combated."

Meanwhile Sweden's regular law-enforcement agency was becoming increasingly confused about its role. In Göteborg there was the creation of a special corps with powers to uproot planned racist acts and seize weapons. Overall, though, police operated without much direction. Officers knew they were under a directive to hunt down deportation-judged aliens who were living in Sweden's underground, but when it came to dealing with demonstrators and protesters, they appeared lost. Whenever either leftwingers or neo-Nazis and skinheads secured permits to march and demonstrate, potential for trouble from one side or the other existed. Expecting as much, police were on hand to keep the hostile forces apart. If officers—in the course of trying to prevent violence and injuries—had used more force containing one element than they had with restraining the other, charges of favoritism followed. Leftist disruptors of the demonstrations by racists concluded police should always help and not hinder them because as Per-Åke Westerlund of the Coalition against Racism viewed these matters, "racists have no right to demonstrate."

In fairness to the police during confrontations, cabinet members had not issued a directive to officers for either neutrality or partiality, but leaders of the coalition indicated clearly enough that hate-generating organizations did enjoy a right to protection. *Borgerliga* officials like Social Democratic predecessors faced demands to legislate against racist organizations, but as with the left-of-center government the coalition refused to approve a prohibition, citing for its reason a law's potentially negative effects upon free expression and democratic institutions. Others claimed only minimum results would come from declaring hate groups illegal because rather than disappear, they would become more clandestine and therefore more difficult to monitor and control. Advocates, in contrast, viewed inaction as something tantamount to acceptance. If the *riksdag* had proclaimed hate-generating organizations illegal, belonging might have carried the stigmas of governmental disapproval and unlawfulness.[120]

To the general public Bildt was responsible for everything that went badly in Sweden during his three-year tenure as prime minister. It was his fault that the nation skidded into recession after the 1991 election, and it was his obligation and duty to respond to a race-motivated crimewave with words and actions. At least these were the opinions and expectations of dissatisfied Swedes accustomed to expect all major answers and solutions to flow from *Riksdag* leaders.   Resentment and bitterness, for example, greeted a Bildt visit to Rinkeby, an indication that aliens had begun to personalize matters as much as native Swedes.   Feeling he as the country's prime minister could be doing more about problems than he had been, local residents of the ethnic enclave booed Bildt unmercifully.

Across Sweden in Herrljunga, a fifth-grade class felt so strongly about Bildt's potential to promote harmony and comradeship that pupils wrote him a letter urging a condemnation of racism.   The children's appeal followed the ransacking of an Iranian classmate's home by prejudicial thugs.   Finally on February 9, 1992, or days after an unpleasant reception in Rinkeby and receipt of the students' request, the prime minister addressed the nation—a rarity for a Swedish leader—on racist crime and the need for national unity against it.   He also assessed why there was a problem, concluding "the xenophobia that exists here has its background in ignorance."   Looking at effects, the coalition head predicted suffering for the society if the cancer of nativism is allowed to take root in one segment of the population.   As he put it, "place some outside and sooner or later that influences one and all of us."

In the only exclusive interviews of Bildt's three-year tenure—one given to *Aftonbladet* and another to *Expressen*—two general themes emerged.   The prime minister believed immigrants just as ethnic Swedes suffered because of society's reluctance to set demands upon them.   Responsibilities and treatment, in his judgment, should be the same for every resident.   "Handle everybody alike, regardless of origins," was Bildt's advice.   Secondarily he saw language deficiencies as the basis of aliens' problems with adjustment.   The interviewee was emphatic about this point, stating that "immigrants must learn Swedish." Moreover their children should begin to sing *Du gamla, du fria* (the national anthem of Sweden with its beginning, "You old, you free") in school.[121]

In dealing with refugees, one segment in the *borgerlig* regime wanted to adopt a foreign policy that would integrate their nation's efforts to those of the European Union.   Success at doing this would have brought several changes, including the view of many Moderates in the government that help should be reorientated.   In their opinion greater emphasis should go to aiding people at sources of migration and less on granting asylum.

Riksdag member Gustaf Von Essen was one who envisioned advantages accruing from conformity and redirection.   Unlike the current situation with a literal flood of refugees continuing to appear at Sweden's borders because of a reputation for overgenerosity, responsibilities for receiving these people would be distributed equitably among European nations.   Moreover with the initiation of programs directed at assisting where problems existed, argued Von Essen, an efficiency would be achieved because the same expenditures going in 1993 toward asylum would provide more relief for many more recipients.   Insofar as terms for accepting refugees, the Moderate politician was of the opinion that Swedish offers of sanctuary should be temporary.   Although these goals might have been laudable, Von Essen's motives were not.   Stimuli behind his and the other conservatives' objectives explain why this party ran into so much trouble with both immigrants and Palme-style liberals.

Inducements behind their will to change so much about refugee and immigration policy also accounted for why Rinkeby had greeted Bildt abusively during his visit there and why there had been constant demands upon him to refute racism. In addressing reasons for a new refugee policy, Von Essen was frank and open, neither ignoring nor disguising the influential factors. The old way of dealing with people fleeing war and discrimination cost Swedish taxpayers too much money. In addition according to him, it brought into the country nationalities and ethnic groups which were unsuitable for Scandinavian society. As he put it, "integration of immigrants . . . in large part has failed, especially those who have come lately. Even several years after arrivals here, proficiencies in Swedish are insufficient. For many the job market is for the most part, putting it mildly, limited just as is active participation in society." Also worrisome for Von Essen were "the dangers [of these newcomers] becoming fourth-class citizens and permanent clients of the social security system." Once these motives leaked, even the sensational offer of exile to death-threatened Bangladeshi writer-critic Taslima Nasrin could not divert attention from the realism behind the Moderate Party's foreign-policy initiatives.[122]

Outside parliamentary and party inner-circles, two immigrant observers offered some freshness to an otherwise dull period of partisan nonbelligerence. Mauricio Rojas, a Chilean exile who became a Lund University professor of economic history, provided one insider's glimpse into the negative effects of Swedish policy on asylum recipients. In what many people would interpret as constructive conservatism, the Latin American's analysis points out the costs in human terms of refugees' total dependence upon state handouts. Passivity and a loss of self-esteem became two effects, and both have accounted for the development of a marginalized underclass. To return personal responsibility and initiative, Rojas advised a scrapping of welfare and a substituting of loans to foreigners. He suggested "such measures should make a 'new start' possible for Sweden's immigrants," but his remedy and conclusion would not set well with individuals who suffered from what might be called the Swedish bureaucratic syndrome. In their judgment the professor's plan seemed "dangerous" and "a simple solution to a complicated society problem."[123]

At the other end of the political sprectrum from Rojas but equally confrontational was Fonseca, another immigrant with South American roots. As an outcast Social Democrat whose support base was Rinkeby and not a campus environment, the politician from Colombia was also critical of foreigners' dehumanization. Unlike Rojas, Fonseca's culprit was not welfare, however. He preferred to spread blame throughout Swedish society, accusing political parties, employers, property owners, and ordinary Swedes of treating immigrants as "temporary guests in the Swedish society" instead of viewing them "as a resource." To alter a deplorable situation, Fonseca worked for the appointment of an immigrant minister who would be dedicated to a fourteen-point program for the elimination of discrimination and the improvement of opportunities. For a better social environment, "Sweden's immigrants need support and recognition for their contributions. Is it not time to put an end to disparaging immigrants and to give them a chance to integrate themselves into Swedish life?"

For believing and advocating such radical concepts, the ghetto leader not only emerged as the Nordic kingdom's champion of minority causes but also in all likelihood as its most hated person. Indicative of how much ill-feeling the Colombian was generating among Swedes was his need to implement some regular adjustments and changes to his living and traveling arrangements. As a person living under constant threats, this meant daily route alterations, frequent moves, and new telephone numbers. Unwilling to allow his Social Democratic allegiance to compromise a steadfast determination on behalf of fellow aliens, Fonseca never permitted his inclusion in the *Riksdag* after the 1994 election to affect his resolve. Rather than be ameliorated by his receipt of a parliamentary seat, he used a placement in this forum to gain more recognition for immigrant rights.[124]

Results from voting September 18, 1994, followed pollsters' predictions for the election. True all but two times since the first successful bid for control of the *Riksdag* during the Great Depression, the electorate again entrusted governing to socialists. Although they did not obtain a parliamentary majority, their mandate was strong enough to form a government with support from the Left and Center parties. Excepting the latter party which had made a deal with the Social Democrats for an advisory role, the other *borgerliga* parties were back in their familiar roles as government opponents. With labor returning to lead Sweden, it meant Carlsson's reemergence as prime minister. Several veteran politicians were included in the new cabinet, but there were some new people in Carlsson's entourage as well. Ministerial newcomers Laila Freivalds who moved from the radical ideology of her student days to political orthodoxy and Blomberg received cabinet appointments to oversee justice and immigration, respectively.

There were some other changes as well. As a result of lost interest in political troublemaking by menaces-to-democracy Karlsson and Wachtmeister, the New Democratic Party vanished altogether from the *Riksdag*, having failed to get a requisite four percent of the total vote needed for seating. Filling their places but with an altogether different agenda were delegates from *Miljöpartiet* (the environment or green party). Although they were left-leaning advocates on most issues, their Luddite proclivities and zeal for the environment and conservation could lead to temporary alliances with some *borgerliga* representatives.

Before and during the one month of official campaigning prior to the mid-September election, neither Carlsson nor any other prominent Social Democrat spoke about or promised any major changes to existing asylum policy. Rather than discuss it or criticize incumbent actions, their campaign focused on Sweden's worst economic downturn since the Great Depression. With no commitments to keep relative to migration and deportation, Blomberg, of course, could begin his duties without any encumbrances or confinements. Moreover his rule over immigration benefitted from another advantage. While the nation was fixed on adverse financial news and mounting joblessness, there was no particular interest in humanitarian efforts on behalf of displaced people and seekers of Swedish sanctuary. The resultant inward turn toward domestic problems meant a secondary role for international affairs. Through any degree of competence, Blomberg as the Immigration Minister could have easily had a conflict-free tenure.

This was not to be, however. Given Carlsson's passive tendencies and a union boss-turned government official with duties beyond his experiences and comprehension, a formula for disastrous results from his appointment to this post was obviously in place. Problems and criticisms began shortly after his installation as manager over a complex set of asylum and immigration issues and policies. The practice of rewarding and entrusting individuals without a basic intellectual capacity or academic preparation to do a job was engrained solidly as a feature of Swedish appointment procedure. Therefore selecting ill-advised choices for cabinet positions occurred without questions and protests.

Not many weeks passed before there would be consequences of having a person with Blomman's minimal competence in charge. On October 24, 1994, in an *Aftonbladet* debate article, Jurist Ann-Sofie Senkul directed a question with legal implications to the newly installed cabinet appointee. She asked, "Do you care about refugee children, Blomberg?" Her inquiry followed several deportations of individuals and whole families after household members had committed minor criminal offenses during their residences in Sweden. Senkul asked Blomberg to explain his policy with regard to linking expulsions to acts of criminality. She explained how the previous government had tried to tie common sense and the seriousness of crimes to its expulsion decisions. In contrast already after the Social Democratic victory of September, all signs seemed to be pointing to a prevalence of brutality in the handling of these kinds of cases.

Senkul wrote of being especially upset by two instances, hoping these in no way represented a trend or a future course of action. One involved a forced exit from Sweden of an entire six-member family because of a teenaged boy's physical retaliation against a classmate for repeated references about him being "a damn black head." The other departure occurred after a court had found an alien father-husband guilty of driving with an invalid license; he left behind a young daughter and Swedish wife. "With a view to perhaps never more meeting him as he is forced to travel to a land at war, which words of comfort do you have [Blomberg, she pondered] for a little girl who watches as her papa boards for such a flight?" Aware Carlsson had recently appointed the minister, Senkul wanted him to know how deportations related to petty criminality could cause direful consequences.[125]

Although Blomman never answered the immigration lawyer's questions directly, his actions supplied a response. During his first weeks as the primary administrator of immigration, while noting early his desire for an open forum on every aspect of asylum, he set a tone for confrontation by stating too "many [refugees] without reasons have gotten to stay." In an interview with *Svenska Dagbladet*'s Bitte Hammargren, Blomberg indicated why his ministry would be characterized by tension and strife. He complained of permanent residence having been awarded families because of the long delays adjudicating their cases. His answer prompted the reporter to ask the cabinet minister if he might consider such statements as inappropriate for someone in his position.

Given the seriousness of Hammargren's question, his reply indicated so obviously why he would be unsuitable for a job that required sensitivity and good judgment. Blomberg's response of "now we are there again with a man being unable to say what he thinks" summarized why Carlsson had not made a wise choice because the appointee was valuing outspokenness over diplomacy. It took barely three months at the head of immigration to provide an inkling of what would follow with this crude individual in charge of delicate issues. Already by year's end, he found himself at the center of accusations. Charges were leveled that his refugee program had been modeled after New Democratic suggestions. Left Party *riksdag* delegate Ulla Hoffman and General Secretary Anita Klum of the Swedish chapter of Amnesty International were among the many doubters and critics with worries and suspicions about Blomberg. Both women were upset with what sounded like a plan to challenge past asylum and residence grants. As much as Blomberg was proving a liability, Carlsson deserved criticism for not reprimanding an errant minister.[126]

Blomberg began the new year by challenging Klum's allegations that he had planned to deport holders of permanent residency. If, as he claimed, there was no truth to her charge, then he should have been wise enough to allow his actions to refute her. By first denying and thereafter trying to explain what he had meant, Blomberg, in essence, confirmed Klum's fears with an admission about there being aliens whom he judged as unworthy residents. Rather than trying to be the "world's conscience for all mankind in our world," Sweden, the minister advised, should distribute more aid to helping people near trouble spots. Then on November 24, 1994, on the pretenses of deciding petitions for asylum more equitably and quicker and of integrating aliens better into society, Blomberg told of the *Riksdag*'s split of *Siv*'s duties. The new Migration Board would have responsibility for immigrants and refugees, whereas the Integration Board would handle incorporating foreigners into Swedish society. Klum did not receive much satisfaction from Blomberg's explanations. If anything had come from his remarks, she surmised, there were more reasons for worry now about the minister's plans than there had been before his unreassuring reply.[127]

Blomberg quickly validated Klum's concerns. As a means of reducing the number of relatives coming to join alien family members already in Sweden, he hinted on January 25, 1995, of establishing a quota system. "You must do some sort of urgency determining to know which ones should get priority" or else, he warned, you would have to deal with everyone coming at once. During the same briefing he mentioned needs for persuasive measures and "positive stimulance" to encourage settlements by refugees in places other than Swedish suburbs. Obtaining no reactions to these suggested changes, the cabinet member in rapid succession followed with actions that would affirm a suspicion about his true intentions as Immigration Minister. First by defending Jewish deportations to Russia after a child psychiatrist had reasoned why one minor with her family should be allowed stay, Blomberg not only reversed the claim of Friggebo about the need for asylum going to Eastern European Jews as a result of a wave of anti-Semitism that was sweeping across the ex-Soviet Union, but his action also rekindled memories of Sweden's deplorable record of not helping many Jews during World War II. Thus for several reasons his action did not set well with a Jewish minority in Sweden. For refusing to take a medical specialist's opinion about what would be best for a child, Blomberg should, advised political satirist Salomon Schulman, "go to a gynecologist"; it was clear the minister did not believe in relevant diagnoses.

Second *Siv* under Blomberg's direction removed three Bosnian Croatian families to Croatia because they supposedly possessed its citizenship as well as guarantees of acceptance there. Help organization Caritas was critical of these deportations, claiming Sweden had "chosen to stick its head in the sand." Its basis for disapproving was the Croatian papers used for entering Sweden. The documents apparently had not been issued by the Zagreb-based government but had in fact been fakes purchased on the black market. Despite evidence of fraud and doubts about Croatia's willingness to allow in people with falsified papers, Blomberg proceeded with deporting 5,000 Bosnian Croatians, satisfied Croatia would keep its promise to give them sanctuary and not return them to Bosnia.

What Blomberg had not considered was the existence of some 400,000 Bosnian Croatians who were already living in Croatia without refugee status. At the arbitrary discretion of their hosts, these displaced persons could at any time be forced back to war zones and uncertainty in Bosnia and Herzegovina. As a result of the many questions related to the futures of Bosnian Croatians in Croatia, there were objections to Blomberg's insistence that no danger existed. Protesters sharply critical of Blomman's decision included Princess Christina Magnuson—King Carl Gustav's sister—and Leif H. Gustafson, the editor of *Brotherhood*, a Christian Social Democratic newspaper. Gustafson considered the minister "clumsy and without feelings" and was "shame to the government and the workers' movement." The editor demanded the recalcitrant minister's forced resignation from his cabinet post.

On the other side of the deportation question, Blomman had defenders who supported his order. Except for Professor Ingrid Björkman of Göteborg University, most were members of rightwing extremist organizations. As for the academician, one free-lance writer compared her to the French historian and holocaust revisionist, Robert Faurisson.[128]

Hints Blomberg gave during January of tightening rules for family members joining relatives came closer to reality several months later on June 30 as part of a package of new conditions for coming to and staying in Sweden. Among the proposals one regulation would not allow a husband to join a wife or vice versa without a means of self-support as identified by the Swedish domiciled mate's proof of self-sufficiency. The *Riksdag*'s Refugee Committee offered other changes to refugee management and maintenance, including an 800,000,000 kronor budget reduction, temporary asylum, and a lowered legal age for adulthood. Parliament did not act on the committee's recommendations because the release had come just as delegates and much of the government were recessing for July (a holiday month). After Blomberg's return from a month of fishing in Norrland, reporters were anxious to query him about the *Riksdag* advisory on refugees. Defensive about the suggestions, Blomberg did not want to concede that an acceptance of advised rules would constitute a departure from Sweden's traditional policy. Rather than concede and acknowledge "tougher" requirements for Swedish asylum, he preferred to speak of "giving places to the ones who really have needs for protection."

Blomberg's did not fully engage in a discussion on refugees until after a reporter had solicited his reactions to critics' charges that the plan's adoption would accomplish posthumously all of the New Democrats' objectives. "This debate is not serious. I do not care what Vivanne Franzén [leader of the few remaining New Democrats] bawls from the fringes. She is hostile to aliens, and we are not that." Although from early August through the first week of 1996, there were Blomman's usual involvements in refugee and immigrant matters and his typically candid replies to reporters' queries, nothing around him generated more than fleeting interest.[129]

Unfortunately for a person with Blomberg's background and record, he would find trouble or trouble would find him. Disaster struck with his stupid handling of the Sincari family's deportation. Although it had been the Asylum Review Board and not he who had ordered the expulsions, he allowed himself to be drawn into the controversy by making silly comments about how correct the decision had been and about his support for the order's discharge. Making matters worse for himself, Blomman attacked the Reverend Roland Haglund of Åsele for opening the parish church to the two Kurdish families. As he put it to the churchman, "You must see yourself as an accessory to that which has happened. It was of course you who hid them in the church."

Then adding an insult to injury less than 48 hours after the nation's exposure to television and newspaper coverage of police forcing two mothers and their children onto a bus, Blomberg visited Umeå, the closest large city to Åsele. There he gave a press conference to clarify why the raid had occurred. Claiming every law and international convention had been followed by the government and insisting no alternative to the families' deportation had existed, the cabinet official blamed everything on the Sincari brothers. "The husbands have split the families, not we." In answer to a question about what might await the wives and children upon their return to Turkey, Blomberg's response was vapid, claiming "we have no special responsibility for that; we are doing no special checkups on what occurs with them."

As soon as the ex-labor leader had finished, an escort was present to lead him past a crowd of chanting demonstrators who screamed loudly at Blomberg in unison "humanism withers when 'the Flower' bursts into bloom." In regard to what critics were calling the crime of Åsele, Carlsson—although as much in agreement about Sincaris' lies and as much in support of the police action as a subordinate—demonstrated better judgment and more tact than Blomberg, but what the prime minister was saying or doing about two families' deportations or any other issue did not really mean much at this point, however. It was long before any of this that he had announced plans to retire before the spring. His decision to leave office in several weeks passed almost all culpability to a man who knew no better than to raise his fists figuratively and dare critics to fight. Just as several times earlier after unpopular actions from Blomberg, demands once again were heard for his ouster.[130]

In a way opponents received fulfillment this time.   After Carlsson's departure and Persson's emergence as prime minister, there were changes, including a cabinet shakeup. What followed was a *riksdag*-shuffling of many administrative duties at the Immigration Board. Two divisions emerged from the reorganization. One section would deal with migration, while the other would handle integration. Their respective duties of working with logistics and adjustment of newcomers to Sweden (or would it be adjusting Sweden to newcomers).   Immigration and asylum duties were more or less cut and dry, whereas nobody knew what to expect from integration's implications. It began without any specific definitions or guidelines. Thus its rationale as well as its actions would unfold after studies. Only then would its general director and the Persson government decide how to proceed. The new prime minister appointed Schori to oversee the migration section, and he entrusted integration developments to Blomberg. By turning over responsibilities to these two men, Persson did not demonstrate any more competence at judging qualifications or credentials than his predecessor. This was one more instance of nothing being in candidates' backgrounds—either from work experiences or from academic studies—to promise satisfactory performances.[131]

Although Schori like Blomberg had tendencies for duplicity and needless confrontation over asylum questions, there were also conspicuous differences. The new minister's many years in politics made him more subtle and less blunt than the tough-talking ex-union boss. A good example was how Schori would explain why Sweden needed a new asylum policy. Appearing June 4, 1996, in *Dagens Nyheter*, his rationale began with a nostalgic recall of some Holocaust survivors coming to his parents' hotel in Malmö after Germany's surrender. These wretched individuals were, according to the minister, good examples of deserving applicants for asylum, and their treatment illustrated what a future policy must do. To be effective and acceptable, it must reflect the high ideals and purposes which had been in place as motivators behind the accepting of Hitler's victims. In practical terms it meant granting sanctuary again only to worthy candidates.

To rekindle a past success with refugees, Schori advised enacting into legislation four principles. They should include incorporating "comprehensive perspective on refugee policy, . . . humanitarianism and respect, . . . legality and effectivity, and . . . [a] process and judgment with ambiguity-free rules."

Sweden's deviation from the Geneva Convention complicated asylum matters and added uncertainty and arbitrariness. Nonadherence also tended to create false hopes because "people who do not have reasons for asylum should not be tempted here by the belief that Sweden would consider them as refugees." To these ends, Schori solicited Swedish ambassadors to accept a new mission at their posts. He suggested that they should be "actively informing about their nation's refugee policy." He called it "our responsibility, the politicians and authorities together." It was the minister's judgment that "more than at any time the global question" of refugee policy must closely follow international perspectives and not individual national aims. A casual analysis of Schori's blueprint for changes was certain to promt negative reactions because to the asylum liberals, it represented clear backtracking to the Lucia Law.[132]

During Schori's three-year association with refugee policies, critics—one after another—stated their cases for liberalization to no effect. Through press statements, petitions, protests, personal appeals, and articles written for publication in newspapers flowed sharply and kindly worded disagreements to Schori's obvious retrenchment from Sweden's earlier generosity. Hoping to stir him to an altered course, an archbishop, lawyers, journalists, immigrant leaders, leftist politicians, medical doctors, and Pippi Longstocking's Lindgren were among the many disillusioned individuals who reacted publicly at least one time. Such diverse groups as Human Rights Watch, Sweden's Red Cross, and Amnesty International were also expressing their disapproval and protests. Peoples at risk of deportation changed periodically, with the fates of Algerians a worry one moment and then the futures of Kosovo Albanians.

During these ordeals Schori was the villain whom critics charged with a range of disagreeable acts. These included everything from conspiring with Slobodan Milosevic to exhibiting "false humanity." For the most part he did not overreact to what his accusers were writing and saying about him, but there were instances when he did return in kind what foes had hurled at him. An oft-repeated favorite comeback was his reciting how much Sweden would benefit from policies like those of other nations. Pursuing a similar course, he liked to assert, would ultimately result in greater fairness and fewer complaints. In the main, if compared to Blomman, Schori's decorum and appeals to reason were a more difficult target to hit. Unlike a predecessor whose personal appearance did not generate much respect, Schori seemed managerial and professional. While Blomman appeared always to be wearing the same jeans, flannel shirt, and leather vest, his successor arrived at meetings well clad in suits or sports jackets, white shirts, and ties.

As foolish and superficial as initial judging of people by their clothes might be, such intangible factors as first impressions can be the most decisive. Blomman—always one of the workers—succeeded as an industrial union's shop-floor steward but failed at convincing skeptics about the correctness of his policies. In contrast winning over people was Schori's forte. By relying upon sanity and consistency, he approached a goal of restricting asylum with an emotional detachment that critics found difficult to combat. Labeling the elusive politician a "hypocrite," as one editorial had for his effrontery of claiming reactionary policies were really liberal, was appropriate. As many and diverse as Schori's foes were, their views did not alter a determination to harmonize Swedish policies to those of other EU members. Many cases of personal hardship were the consequence. People who had wagered all on the past reputation of Sweden continuing as the island of hope in a continent of xenophobia were forcefully returned to homelands disspirited and broken. Awaiting them upon their returns were encounters with uncertainty. As one editor sarcastically noted about so many expulsions, Schori's title should be "Deportation Minister." Seldom during a period of polarized opinions was the prime minister at the center of these controversies. Persson unlike Carlsson was generally able to escape blame for transpirings.[133]

Many factors explained why criticism was not having much effect upon Schori and a Social Democratic majority in the *riksdag*. Public opinion indicated majority support for tightened rules for refugee status in Sweden. Squabbling among the largest opposition party's membership over the wisdom of advocating an even harsher asylum policy than the government's accounted for escape, too. Deciding what course of action to follow on refugee matters deeply divided the Moderate Party, thereby nullifying its leadership's attempts at disrupting Persson's two parliamentary coalitions formed before and after the 1998 general election as his party's necessary ruling partners. As the most conservative major political organization, the Moderate Party claimed among its members individuals who were hostile to anything that suggested or implied liberalism and socialism. *Riksdag*-member Sten Andersson from Skåne was so blatantly xenophobic and racist that several internal calls came for his ouster, but he retained considerable popularity and support in southern Sweden. Not even an exposure of his associations and appearances with *Sverigedemokrater* hurt his standing.[134]

Opposite Andersson in the party's diverse makeup was Chair Thomas Idergard of *Moderata ungdomsförbundet* (*Muf* or the Moderate Youth Organization) Chair Thomas Idergard. He found himself "embarrassed for my party" in December 1996 after its move to the extreme right on immigrant and refugee matters. By supporting Schori-sponsored legislative initiatives, party parliamentary whips Bildt and Per Unckel upset Idergard. In his opinion, the organization should have supported a more humane effort. Idergard preferred giving sanctuary to more people but with less generous welfare benefits.[135]

Then during 1997 Moderates swung further right on the question of foreigners entering Sweden. In response a critic claimed they were seeking to "be the party for angry white men." An Unckel-led platform committee issued a manifestation entitled "Land for the Hopeful." It represented a combination of cultural conservatism and fiscal frugality, while stating two basic objectives. First it wanted asylum standards to follow the Geneva Convention guidelines. Second it sought a conditional return to free immigration into Sweden, but to enter, every newcomer must be able to prove self-dependence. In advance of immigrating, there would to be either prearranged employment or guaranteed sponsorhip. By themselves these goals were not so altogether different from what the Social Democrats had recommended in the spring of 1990. The rub came from the Moderates' preamble. Its tone was so extremely divisive and ethnocentric that foreigners were blamed by implication for the government's need to levy such extremely high income taxes on ethnic Swedes. Aliens were the cause of the burden because of their disproportionately high dependence on welfare handouts. As the Moderate document stated the matter, "You cannot simultaneously hammer taxes from the nation's inhabitants, sucking them—who have some kind of domiciliary rights in the country—out down to the bare bone, and with the other hand include innumerable multitudes and tender them a reasonable living standard. . . . It is inequitable."

As perturbed as Idergard had been with his party for aiding Schori five months earlier, he would emerge as an enthusiastic supporter of Land for the Hopeful. After an examination of the document's program, he approved it. He was so impressed with the plan's beneficial features of free immigration and its elimination of alien dependency upon assistance that the youth leader chose to overlook its venomous aspects. He like other backers thus became the focus of harsh treatment from antiracist forces. Biracial entertainer Camilla Henemark, immigrant boxer Paolo Roberto, and the chair of *Sveriges Socialdemokratiska Ungdomsförbund* (*SSU* or Sweden's Social Democratic Youth Organization), Niklas Nordström, responded negatively to the manifesto in a joint article for *Dagens Nyheter* on April 3, 1997. They wrote that "the Moderates are helping neo-*Nazis*." During the next four months, a heated dialogue followed; it pitted critics against Moderate defenders. A climax to opposition came June 8, when seventy-two public figures—some more famous than others—from publishing, entertainment, athletics, and politics joined to proclaim "we can now no longer remain silent" about the racism embodied in the Moderate Party's white paper. Enbattled and charged with being a "party for the prejudiced," it found itself in a position where retreating would be the only viable option; withdrawal of the most objectionable features occurred during late August in Umeå at the party's annual congress.[136]

Six-plus years of labor governing Sweden after the 1994 election netted several new laws and regulations related to migration, asylum, and minorities. Regarding refugees, desires for restrictions would characterize the ambition of *riksdag* legislation just as the Lucia Law of 1989 had proven to be a model for earlier Social Democratic curbs. Gone altogether was anything at all related to the pre-1989 era when Sweden had unintentionally beckoned many sufferers in the world to come with their palpable hardship stories and seek new futures.

As one might expect from the global masters of bureaucracy, their latest rules could be specific to the point of absurdity. Swedish rules and regulations that governed parental visitations illustrate how unnecessarily compulsive and exact matters had become. Parents who were younger than sixty and living in Bosnia could not obtain Swedish visas to visit a child with residence permits if the daughter or son was older than eighteen. Lajla Sandzaktarevic discovered this in 1995 after a frustrating experience with Swedish immigration. The rule

existed as a preventive measure presumably to keep mothers and fathers from
arriving and requesting Swedish asylum. One could ask—and likely twenty-
four year old Sandzaktarevic did—why just persons under sixty would be so
much more interested in asylum than older people, but *Siv*'s answer would no
doubt have been as asinine as the arbitrary age specifications.

Similar mulishness met *Flyktinggruppernas och asylkommittéernas riksråd*
(*Farr* or the Refugee Groups and Asylum Committees' State Advisory) in 1996
after it had advised a three-month grace period during which a refugee who had
lied for one reason or another to officials during a processing session could
resubmit honest data; *Siv* General Director Björn Weibo, with Blomberg
concurring, opposed this suggestion because "it would be rewarding lies" and
would be creating unjustifiable decisions. "Why," Weibo asked, "should they
who have received their permits on incorrect grounds be permitted to stay here,
when other honest persons are denied and forced to leave the country?" The
answer was clear enough for anyone with knowledge of other cultures; lying
often came as a defense mechanism for fleers coming to Sweden with reasons to
fear officialdom.[137]

Several times between the 1994 election and 2001, Social Democratic-
controlled parliaments embodied into legislation the labor party's considerably
hardened response to asylum. Its first law passed December 10, 1996. Taking
effect on New Year's Day, 1997, a set of new rules established a different way
for Sweden to determine eligibility for sanctuary. Now the nation would begin
to follow refugee-status bases which the Geneva Convention had established
more than 45 years earlier. The new law also clarified which relatives would be
welcomed to join family members already in Sweden; with one exception, only
nuclear members would possess the privilege. In cases from homelands where
there were verifiable experiences of other relatives living together in the same
households, these persons could come to Sweden and continue to reside under
such arrangements. There were additional provisions that entrusted the care of
refugee children's health and overall development to national medical
authorities and others that required a set of fingerprint impressions from every
entrant older than fourteen. Finally in order to discourage people smuggling,
convictions for illegal escorting could thereafter result in four years of prison, a
significant increase over the previous maximum one-year sentence. Pleased by
the new law, Schori praised it as "modern, brotherly, clear, and credible."
Critics found something else in the legislation; "accusing the government of
hiding behind EU walls," they charged its supporters had conveniently used
European Union standards as an excuse to satisfy xenophobes and stop needy
people from entering Sweden for asylum.[138]

Major changes occurred in 1997, but only two resulted from domestic
initiatives. Both related to aliens who had chosen underground existences over
contesting orders for their deportation. One corrective step removed all police
responsibility for these people, entrusting it now to *Siv*. Immigration Board's
Barbro Thorblad believed the move would reduce the fears which persons who
were hiding had of surrendering themselves to law-enforcement officers, and it

would increase opportunities to enlist the assistance of volunteer organizations such as the Red Cross. As facilitators and comforters, humanitarian groups would, according to the logic behind the change, minimize individual anxieties about eventual consequences from surrenders, and they could be employed to arrange details for escapees' returns to their homelands. In a separate action, Schori ended all amnesty hopes for the 5-6,000 individuals who were living secretly in Sweden. To do anything else, he reasoned, would "send a wrong signal."

In final analysis these were only a minor adjustment compared to much more significant decisions which came out of the European Union in Brussels. Justice ministers there were finalizing details for all member nations to follow in the granting of residence permits. According to the proposal drafted by EU delegates, offers of permanent residence to aliens could only result after a five-year trial; by Swedish law, a foreigner could obtain this after two years. For cases of long-distance love affairs and desired reunions in a EU nation, plans called for altering terms of these as well. By a procedure under discussion, couples would need to pass an eligibility test. First of all their bonds must have been binding for a minimal five years; a newcomer then could apply for permanent residence. Secondly as a prelude to entry, a "love" candidate who wishes to immigrate to an EU nation must prove that there is available housing and a personal capacity for self-support. In Sweden relationships had to hold for only six months, and there were no self-reliance tests imposed upon people who sought reunions with their lovers who resided in the Nordic kingdom. As recommendations for member nations to ratify, the EU changes would become effective only with their unanimous approval. Their very existence pointed to a trend for fewer national imprints and pan-European directions and influence over immigration and asylum questions.[139]

In 2000 parliament worked on two important issues. Of first importance Sweden divided over joining a growing list of European nations which had already begun granting double citizenship. During debates on a proposal Christian Democrat Johnny Gylling emerged as its primary champion and spokesperson. In his mind the time had come to eliminate an outdated identification concept. As he stated a case for change, "There is a mass of old holy rules whose time has come to penetrate. If persons are living in two countries, they certainly should be able to have citizenships in both." In June 2001, optional double citizenship went into effect. A second law set in motion minimum legal protection for women whose special vulnerability had long been an interest and a cause of Swedish feminist organizations. To protect the rights of foreign brides and girlfriends who were escorted to Sweden by male citizens, an amendment to the law that had required at least two years' domicile for permanent residence permits provided exceptions as long as applicants were meeting certain conditions. First evidence must point to serious intentions by couples at the outset of their relationships. Second police must check into a male partner's file to ascertain if there had been past complaints invovling physical abuse of women or abandonment of foreign women before the expiration of their two years in Sweden. To some extent, just by the *riksdag* finally acknowledging a possibility of these problems with mail-order brides, its members succeeded at satisfying most female rights' advocates, even if a militant minority of women   considered the parliamentary response as "toothless."[140]

Sweden—despite having so many societal woes covered by laws and regulations—continued to find no will to enact anti-hate legislation. Just as Social Democrats had failed during Carlsson's first run at governing and then after as a *borgerliga* regime of rightwing and liberal coalition partners had not done, the subsequent governments under Carlsson and Persson also found irrational, flimsy excuses for not extending legislative protection to ethnic minorities and fascism's most outspoken critics. Laws for dealing with neo-Nazis and other prejudice peddlers' violence were not passed.

The assembly would come closest on October 26, 1995, when there was serious debate on the pros and cons of outlawing groups whose reasons for developing had principally been to spread loathsomeness and disrespect for a democracy. Previous and present justice ministers Hellsvik and Freivalds—respectively, a Moderate and a Social Democrat—agreed "it is a symbolic measure" to forbid these types of associations. More importantly, a consent about the need from two individuals who usually were better known for their discord than accord showed how "we mean business with those laws that already exist." Currently on the books, reminded Freivalds, were laws that did criminalize every form of racist activity, and "perhaps the police should, more than heretofore, intervene against the aspects of, for example, a demonstration which are forbidden." A Left Party representative and two of parliament's three immigrants confirmed agreements with what Freivalds had indicated about doing more with existing laws, but they still wanted fellow lawmakers to join them in enacting a legal prohibition. Elisa Abascal Reyes, a *Miljö parti* delegate and Fonseca pointed to "racists of every variety," who used freedom to act openly without a fear of punishment. "They can have town-square meetings and demonstrations, sell t-shirts, and knock down folk on the streets although they are not allowed to do so," Reyes complained to the complementing of *Vänster partiets* Alice Åström who observed how "we see them time after time on TV." Also heard this day were three alternatives to the removal of racists' legal rights. Center's Ingbritt Irhammar asked for "everybody's help in starting local crime prevention work in the communes." Kia Andreasson like Reyes, a *Miljö parti* member, wanted a clear directive sent to schools to inform students about where "boundaries can be drawn for what is allowed and not." To Freivalds disconcertingly, the suggestion of Andreasson represented redundancy, for "they who work in the school must know what exists in school law and lesson plans about democracy training."

In an obvious attempt at drawing attention away from nativistic haters of foreigners, Moderate reactionary Andersson wondered how parliament should deal with the Latin Kings, controversial music-recording artists whose parents had come to Sweden. In one of their songs, the words called for "death to all blond Swedish vikings." Nongermane as Andersson's input was to the debate about outlawing organizations, it capped the frustration of trying but failing to deal this instant with a mounting problem in Sweden. With another day ended, it would mean one more session of the *riksdag* without legal action against fomenting racist thoughts. Later parliaments would also do nothing.[141]

Subsidies to festivities hailing Sweden's diversity and to authors became the nation's primary weapons for battling hate and prejudice. One of the first large arrangements against racism—and a model for subsequent ones—occurred in 1991 between June 1st and September 1st at twenty-one Swedish sites spread around the nation. The barnstorming festival featured a troop of Swedish entertainment headliners, including national favorites Kayo, Lill Lindfors, Eva Rydberg, Pappa Dee, Tito Beltran, and Titiyo.

Naiveté and innocence obviously laid behind investing public revenue in such a tour. It was the ambition of government sponsors that dispatching these popular entertainers to perform across Sweden beneath a sea of colorful, bright promotional banners ablaze in catchy slogans against racism and xenophobia would draw large audiences. The plan called for the well-known artists to mix their music with personal testimonials against hatred, thus affecting a rebuttal to racism and supposedly increasing openmindedness. Unfortunately from all indicators, these efforts did not change people's minds. As chapter five shows, racist crimes actually soared upward in the 1990s. If there were musicians or music with impact, its providers were bands and composers of lyrics with neo-Nazi and nationalistic sympathies.

By 2000 as a result of Swedish tolerance of hate groups and their outputs, the country emerged as the world production leader of so-called "White-power music" and the largest manufacturer-distributor of media products with fascist themes. Sick-minded people everywhere could choose among about fifty different internet homepages, many-thousand tapes and compact discs, scores of anti-Semitic and racist films, hundreds of magazines, brochures, and posters, original memorabilia and reproductions from the Third Reich, books, embroidered emblems, buttons, and t-shirts. In sum the Swedish mail-order and/or electronic businesses were international supermarkets supplying hate music, literature, and trinkets to whomever might want to wallow in disgusting stuff. As with outlawing hate groups, parliament and the Swedish legal system responded feebly and ineffectively. A law forbade a display of racist symbols such as swastikas on clothing, but it did not deter bearers. Its authors had put such an inept law in effect that a court of appeals in Göteborg overturned the only conviction which had resulted from it. Although Freivalds was "worried about the propaganda it [racist music] spreads and how it can set down tracks for the future" and the government proclaimed that Sweden should not host an international forum of racists, yet neither stopping a free movement of offensive lyrics nor halting known racists at the nation's borders occurred.[142]

Säpo was generally ineffective at preventing hateful acts and combatting the spread of racist materials. Raiding Nazi-organization Nordland's premises near Linköping in 1998—an act that included confiscating 200 racist compact discs and arresting two leaders—would represent the security force's most sensational effort against fascism. According to a statement from Chief Anders Eriksson of *Säpo*, "Nordland is one of the largest producers of racist music," and the revenues it netted from sales of racist music financed its hate activities. It, the Arian Brotherhood, and the National Socialist Front became *Säpo* priorities. Although they did not constitute a national threat in Eriksson's judgment, he was viewing them as dangerous to immigrant groups and their friends. As he assessed the situation, "Today there are not more persons who are engaged in rightwing extremist organizations than earlier, yet . . . some of these organizations . . . have escalated violence and threat of violence."

More familiar at directing investigations at the left and foreign spies than at dealing with the extreme right, *Säpo* also targeted immigrants and their most vehement supporters. Suspected of terrorism and PKK activities, Kurds living in Sweden became agency favorites for careful surveillance. Other aliens were targeted for scrutiny as well. Security police had listed Fonseca as a potential terrorist during the 1970s. Other centers of attention included Soviets as spies and leftist demonstrators as revolutionaries. Given the agency's inexperience with rightwing threats and plots before Kimstad and an upsurge in race-related crimes, there were ample reasons to question *Säpo*'s advice and actions.

With police records noting 940 crimes attributed to extremist parties and persons in 1998, or double as many as during the previous twelve months, the regional boss of the security force in Malmö in 1999 was advising politicians and public administrators not to publicize rightwingers' threats against them. "We know," confidently noted Jan Zelmerlööw, "that the Nazis try to obtain publicity. We don't want to contribute to them achieving their purpose. Thus, we are outwardly lying low." Following this advice, Municipal Commissioner Björn Fries of Karlskrona had been holding threats to himself until neo-Nazis murdered two policemen and a syndicalist. "I had believed for a long time in the police advice that the Nazis only wanted to derive advantage from all the attention. But after these events I came to a decision. I am convinced that the publicity does some good. People get damned furious and react." One media survey of reactions to the agency's suggested silence revealed much division of opinion among the secretaries of Sweden's major political parties. Except for *Vänster*, a firm supporter of *Säpo*'s advisement, other parties either vacillated or rejected outright the agency's recommendation.[143]

As much as failures marked the government's attempts to curtail racists' criminality, there was one area where Swedish authorities were enjoying some success. No nation was better at building public bureaucracies than Sweden, but her accomplishment did not always bring desirable results. Look at effects in the Nordic kingdom, and one might take more seriously the libertarian point that governments which try to solve every problem only become creators of the greatest obstacle to progress, themselves. *Siv*'s operation from 1990 to 2000 is a case study of an agency going awry. Begun in 1969 as a consolidation effort to remove permit issues from the Aliens Commission, citizenship matters from the Ministry of Justice, and assimilation work from a Ministry of the Interior's committee on immigrant affairs, the Swedish Immigration Board swelled into a Norrköping-based colossus with almost 1,700 employees at headquarters, five regional offices, and several local centers. A government-appointed eleven-member Executive Committee composed generally of *riksdag* delegates, the board's director general, a municipality representative, and two staff selectees was charged with oversight and review responsibilities. Resulting from an odd semantic twist that would cause *invandrare* to become a Swedish word vested in negative connotations, parliament—in a move toward political correctness—became a wordmonger, giving the board a less offensive, more nondescriptive name. Therefore on July 1, 2000, the Immigration Board officially became the Migration Board or *Migrationsverket*.[144]

During the 1990s, the decade with more asylum seekers to process and manage than any other ten years in Swedish history, *Siv* was often at the center of criticism. Dependent upon current situations, complaints varied from year to year. Although it had been the governments headed by Carlsson, Bildt, and Persson that deserved blame for their inadequate oversight and inept policies, it was the Immigration Board and its leaders who absorbed altogether too many of faultfinders' objections to asylum's management. For example when there were long delays in deciding the fates of thousands of individuals, frustrations were directed at *Siv* for not settling cases expeditiously. It really was *Riksdag* rules and budgets which had the ultimate responsibility for bottlenecks because had its regulations not demanded such thorough checks of sanctuary candidates and had it allocated more money for additional hires, the severity of problems could have been lessened.

Five different parliaments during the 1990s set up various standards and requirements for hiring personnel and appointing general directors. Like so many governmental entities in other countries, *Siv* certainly was not drawing from society's most talented job bank; simply put, it was not an especially desirable place for showing off creativity or being resourceful. Silly rules that forbade fraternization between employees and refugees, for example, hurt staff morale. Advancing cronies to general directorships and subjecting them to politicians' absolute control also did not facilitate success. *Siv* personnel absorbed blame for whatever skewed in the wrong direction, nevertheless. Rogestam's abandonment of train travel in 1991 illustrated this absurdity. As the recipient of citizens' hate and threats because of their disagreement with Sweden's record of alleged overgenerosity toward distraught peoples, the general director took precautions, substituting a motorpool car for her travel instead of public transportation. Several times in the 1990s, following media reports of asylum-related problems, demands for a disbandment of *Siv* increased. Critics occasionally added a degree of levity to their otherwise sober appeals, advising the government to "deport the Board's personnel."[145]

Disillusioned Swedes who demanded *Siv*'s dissolution were not offering a serious, realistic suggestion; most of all accountability and reforms were the major needs of the Immigration Board. Carelessness abounded, and the leadership shunned outside advice. With an annual refugee budget greater than that of the United Nations, *Siv* gave its harshest observers justification for wanting better results. Even when there had been reforms and cutbacks, the beneficial results were rarely noticeable. Paying excessive amounts for refugee residences and flying deportees to homelands in chartered airplanes represented waste, but no activity would irritate as much as outfitting Swedish newcomers with all new furnishings. As a reflection more of a Social Democratic philosophical ideal of making a commitment to social *jämlikhet* (meaning much more than a lexicon-defined equality, it is an attempted leveling of society by bringing down people at the top to elevate people at the bottom) than either a prime example of gross financial incompetence, fiscal mismanagement, or extravagance, the purchases ruffled most working-class Swedes. Excepting a minuscule gentry in Sweden, ethnic Swedes did not object so much if the state excessively taxed society's richest people to raise living standards for people with their backgrounds, but there developed considerable resentment whenever public revenues had gone to newly arrived outsiders.

With many examples to cite, a new-start package given the five-member Benjamin Garate family in 1990 highlighted adequately what served to irritate many Swedes. On January 30, 1990, the Garates arrived in Simrishamn, a port city located at the southeast corner of Sweden. Awaiting this mother, father, and three children with roots in Chile were an empty apartment and 28,400 kronor; the disbursement was for the purchase of furniture and household necessities. This family of a politically active construction worker who had worried about being the victim of an "accidental" fall in Chile and who had become aware of Sweden's reputation for kindness from relatives already residing in Stockholm would eventually receive much more than housing and furnishings. The state also offered daily adjustment assistance from personnel at the local refugee office, and for studying Swedish, the Garates were "entitled" to a monthly stipend of 7,104 kronor and subsidies to defray outlays for rent and medicine. Spoiled by an indulging system, refugees could complain as Poles had in 1990 after their placements in a Finspång housing complex. Finding every unit identically furnished, they protested because of governmental disrespect of personal-taste differences.[146]

Siv participated in 1997 with the Education Board, National Board of Health and Welfare, Federation of Communes, and Labor Market Board in a joint internal investigation. The effort produced a report that criticized the handling of refugees. One main charge was brought against the Immigration Board. According to the study, it was guilty of procrastination in application processing and refugee settling. On average, refuge seekers waited eighteen months for decisions, a period that created voids in their lives. Coordination between different governmental entities did not exist. Among other things it meant different agencies were not recognizing completions of Swedish-language studies at refugee camps. Hence individuals who had gone to communes with degrees of competence began their training allover again. As for Labor Market Board errors, its employment officers "are standing in the way for refugees when it comes to finding jobs." Problems, the report cited, were the result of inflexibility. By adhering to agency rules, employment counselors were unable to register aliens in the job market until the board had graded their *svenska för invandrare* (*SFI* or Swedish for immigrants). After release of this report, neither Häll Eriksson nor Blomberg commented immediately.[147]

Siv officials seldom reacted with silence to criticisms. Judging by their many rebuttals and justifications in Swedish newspapers, cynics could easily have contended that the general directors were overly sensitive and reactive and spent altogether too much time and energy on either defending or justifying personal and agency decisions and actions. The foursome who held the post during the 1990s shared a common resolve to respond to critics. Rogestam—after attacks against the Board, refugee policies, and her administration—set a precedent of utilizing the media for countercharges. Before leaving the general directorship in 1993, she explained why people had been waiting so long for settlements as well as how the process could be shortened, advised the government—after the eruption of disruptive violence at refugee camps—to stay the course and stick to its current refugee policies, reiterated immigration's positive effects on the development of Sweden, answered critics, suggested a clarifying of Swedish asylum policy, and justified *Siv*'s budget requirements and expenditures.[148]

On February 1, 1993, at the start of Rollén's tenure as *Siv*'s new head, one newspaper headline described her as a "positive boss who likes power." She left a managerial position at *arbetsmarknadsutbildningen* (*AMU* or the Labor Market Board's vocational training sector), expecting to find "an interesting and stimulating job" ahead of her at the Immigration Board. Before finishing 21 months as general director, she resigned, citing her inability to cope with "too hard pressure from [Sweden's] mass media." At explaining her short term of leadership, Rollén could have added her difficulties with Hedi Bel Habib, one of the Board's nine internal experts. Whether it had been genuine disappointment with her job performance or the anger he had felt after having been overlooked for the general directorship, Bel Habib, through many critical articles for newspapers, led to questioning Rollén's competence to run *Siv*. It did not help matters that 141 lawyers had criticized the Board handling of Kosovo Albanians midway through her fourth month. Their harsh remarks had provoked the general director so much that she wrote an article for *Dagens Nyheter*, defending their treatment and that of others as ideal examples of how the Board had correctly followed exemplary procedures.[149]

Weibo, Rollén's successor, resigned after only eighteen months as *Siv*'s general director, he noted, to assume the challenge of managing the attempts by Sweden to stop people smuggling in the Baltic Sea. There was speculation about Weibo-Schori differences ending in the former man's dismissal by the cabinet official, but neither the general director nor Schori would acknowledge friction or admit to differences behind a change of leadership. Weibo's actions soon after Persson's elevation as prime minister implied conflicts. For *Svenska Dagbladet*, he noted strong disapproval of the new government's plan to separate integration from the Immigration Board's control, arguing it "was threatening to obstruct immigrants' integration."[150]

Seemingly chosen by Schori even before Weibo had resigned, appointee Häll Eriksson was already known as a hardliner on refugee questions from her working closely with Blomberg as his undersecretary of state. Her selection did not please Chair Anita Dorazio of the Asylum Committee in Stockholm: "With thoughts to her participating in the Åsele Kurds' deportations and her leaking out smears against them from the department, then it is most worrying to know she is becoming the Immigration Board head." Others were equally dissatisfied with the appointment, and as general director, Häll Eriksson did nothing to disspel their fears. Deserving of recognition as *Siv*'s Iron Woman because of her stamina to withstand more criticism than any predecessors at Immigration, she seemed willing to do Schori's bidding and fulfill a demand for consistent toughness.[151]

As often as the Immigration Board was a favorite target for criticism, there were times when the Asylum Review Board received as much. Faced with the difficult tasks of hearing and judging appeals for sanctuary, the body had no freedom to operate independently of laws and policies from the *riksdag* or governments, but like court decisions throughout Sweden's judicial system, cases did come before ARB where precedent and reliance upon interpretation would determine jurists' verdicts. To be fair, justice must be blind and result without emotion; not always appreciating these qualities, critics could look at results differently. For example, as much as asylum seekers might face many hardships from deportations, Swedish law mandated a ruling for expulsion if a registrant had based an application on lies to Swedish immigration officials; it was clear enough that it required no interpretation. Nevertheless, in a number of special cases with mitigating circumstances that seemed to present reasonable arguments for an exception, ARB jurists disappointed applicants and Swedish sponsors by refusing to budge. Legally correct rulings based upon law and not on emotional often produced unfair outcries against prosecutors and judges, or here, the Asylum Review Board, rather than parliament and a cabinet.

Simply put, many criticisms surfaced in newspaper articles because their authors refused to fathom the degree to which policy restraints and legislation had hamstrung Fischerström and the Asylum Review Board in issuing asylum. It was easier to pin all blame on him and ARB than to convince legislators and prime ministers to ignore the popular will and reopen Sweden to all who would call. ARB's first general director fully comprehended and acknowledged those constraints under which he must operate, and he acknowledged as much in his clarifying statement of 1996. As he explained it, "We [Fischerström along with the Board] must ask all along when we take a position if it conflicts with some point of view the government had taken earlier." Therefore ARB critics and callers for its disbandment were unfair to Board members, Fischerström, and Göran Håkansson—the second general director—for requesting parliament "to get rid of the Asylum Review Board bums!" As much as the petitioners—five liberal- or left-leaning *riksdag* members—behind a call (or the several others with a similar objective) to dissolve a body charged with adjudicating asylum appeals were sincere, their actions failed at targeting the real culprits. Their directive should really have taken aim at *riksdag* colleagues, the ones who were leading and belonging to incompetent governments and who were drafting all the insidious laws. ARB lawyers who acted, according to Fischerström's honest description, as mere functionaries in the deportation process should not have been recipients of asylum defenders' anger and frustration.[152]

Integration policy was another Social Democratic folly. As with many other of the party's intrusions and mistakes, it represented another example of government becoming half committed to a concept that few people seemed to understand or accept. As percentages of immigrants in Sweden's population kept growing, debates began about what role aliens should have in the general society. While social engineers used demographic models to advocate either assimiliation or integration, a majority of ethnic Swedes showed ambivalence and inconsistency about what they considered to be the proper role of aliens in Sweden. On the one hand advice was for foreigners to adjust to Swedish ways, acting as Swedes but not interfering with or challenging the indigenous population in any significant way. Among assimiliationists, a most common conclusion was for a policy of absorbing newcomers in a process somewhat akin to what Francophiles had been doing with extraneous peoples who had entered France. In Sweden's case it would mean literally turning everybody into Swedes. Others argued against such a plan, citing its disrespectfulness of other cultures. Rather than advocating a homogeneous outcome with Swedish elements retained and everything foreign absorbed through centrifugation, the second group argued for integrating different attributes. This group spoke and wrote about bestowing honor and respect to diverse cultural accomplishments. According to the scheme, Sweden would emerge as a land where multicultural expressions could live side by side with majority values and ways.

Eventually an altogether "new Swede" would emerge as a diverse amalgam from allowing only the strongest cultural characteristics to triumph. In effect then what these optimistic prophets were imagining would be every different element in Sweden being tossed together into a cultural salad. Survivals of only superior institutions, whether Swedish or alien, would mean an example of Social Darwinian. As its result in the culinary world of a New Sweden, the traditional meatball might emerge with flavors of various Persian spices and under a thick Slavic sauce, and in deference to an emergent Islamic majority, made from a recipe without a blending of ground together pork and beef. Unlikely as the latter plot might have been as a possible outcome, many Swedes feared it. Despite Persson-controlled governments' earmarking billions in tax revenues for multicultural integration projects after April 1996, Sweden did not move toward cultural submersion or cultural submission. If anything did apply at the end of 2000, it was a triumph of segregation over integration. Efforts at reversing negative trends failed almost completely. For declaring "integration is a political cuckoo," Moderate Party reactionary Andersson was not altogether wrong because as Jan Molin, the ex-head of the immigrant affairs office in

Göteborg, noted, desires to stop progress "lies in the majority of inhabitants' attitudes."[153]

Factors behind their views were striking. First of all, as with other alien issues, leadership was either missing or lacking. Prime ministers did not go to the nation with reasons for or benefits from integration. Moreover none of the governmental agencies, boards, and ministries were showing by example what might result from equal opportunities. Even during the European Year against Racism, there was not enough preaching or practicing to generate awareness of the event and its meaning. The thought seemed to be in 1997 that an allocation of public revenues to underwrite a series of activities and events would cause a change. To build respect for Sweden's different cultures and nationalities, the nation's museums sponsored various programs, worked with schools, and used displays to capture images of global variety and contributions. Impressively the People's Ethnographical Museum of Stockholm devoted the entire year to the promotion of multicultural appreciation. Funding from immigrant groups, the Immigration Commission, and SIDA enabled the museum to utilize music, dance, drama, lectures, films, and exhibits to promote human diversity. There was also a school-outreach program. Its goal was to implant a simple message in students, "We are alike and different."

In preparation for and during 1997 government-subsidized "Youth against Racism" continued its sponsorships of retreats and programs aimed at emphasizing and fostering unity and solidarity among all youths in Sweden. In an effort to foster solidarity among people from all backgrounds, the National Committee for the European Year against Racism conducted an essay contest. For the best composition on the evils of prejudice, the Swedish body awarded a first prize of 30,000 SEK. The contest winner was a 28-year old man who had been born in Sweden to parents from Senegal. His entry was titled "Racism: A Different (Appearance) Vision." It was the author's recollections of a painful experience of being raised in Sweden as well as some perspectives about what could be done to make life easier for aliens. In the victor's opinion, the nation had been doing too little "to avoid, diminish, or alleviate" what had given "rise to racially patterned exclusionary or discriminatory outcomes."[154]

A check of bureaucratic efforts at overcoming or minimizing problems as exposed by a victorious essayist reveals why there was little or no progress. Appointments to lead the Integration Office resulted more as rewards to good Social Democrats than as culminations of searches after the most competent candidates. With the establishment of the Integration Board in 1997, *riksdag-*provisions vested governmental control in another ministerial-level officer and entrusted a general director with operational matters. Just like the Immigration Board, the Integration Board through its general director answered to a cabinet minister. Including Blomman after his transfer to Integration from *Siv*, the first six holders of these two new positions did not possess the personal experiences or educational qualifications which were needed to deal with segregation and discrimination. All but Andreas Carlgren were professional Social Democratic hacks who had moved upward in a party's hierarchy; the exception had been a

Center Party vice chair. Like careers of so many other Swedish politicians, the dominant feature of each selectee's adulthood was partisanship. Their resumes attested in large part to one-dimensional existences. Lars Engqvist had served briefly as the president of Sweden's semi-public Film Institute, but he, like the others who vaulted into high positions in immigration and integration, spent an adulthood close to partisan politics. For Blomberg, Engqvist, Ulrika Messing, and Maj-Inger Klingvall receiving ministerial appointments and for Carlgren and Lars Stjernkvist gaining general directorships, appointments should have recognition for what they were: rewards that enabled political careers to begin, continue, or restart.

Whether deliberated or planned, the placements at Integration illustrated just how little interest Persson's government was giving immigrant problems. Had they been a priority, the prime minister would have appointed persons of Bel Habib and Fonseca's caliber as general director and minister. Both were Swedish citizens, although to ethnic Swedes they seemed like foreigners due to names, appearances, and accents. Compared to an unprepared, undereducated sextet, the pair could have provided personal experiences as immigrants along with university educations. Barring a key fault, the twosome seemed to have possessed ideal credentials for these posts in immigration affairs. Neither the veteran researcher at the Immigrant Board nor the leader from Rinkeby would accept muzzling. Candor and criticism were their responses to whatever and to whomever irritated them. Persson resisted challenges from underlings, and he did not want provocateurs around him who might disrupt with unsettling ideas such as quotas. He preferred to distance his regime from persons with radical proposals. Instead Persson used a well funded integration agency as a sop for appeasing Social Democratic backbench liberals and his coalition partner from the *Vänster parti* and for countering complaints about his government having a low commitment to correcting Sweden's dismal integration record. Of course, the prime minister could not fool alien outsiders like Bel Habib and sociologist Masoud Kamali. As the latter man indicated with indignity, "You [Persson as well as your government] must stop throwing tax revenue into a wealth of grants to . . . projects for reducing crime statistics or helping problem-burdened immigrants . . . . Change must begin with a drastic, responsible organizational distribution based upon well cultivated and grounded integration theory."[155]

To achieve what Ministers Blomberg, Engqvist, and Messing considered as integration, the trio followed essentially a similar painless approach that was centered between two extremes. Moderates were at one end, and their program advocated a removal of governmental obstacles from immigrants' lives. Since the source of problems to conservatives had been excessive meddling from an interventionist immigration bureaucracy, they concluded the consequences to be a fostering of passivity among newcomers to Sweden. The result for them was dependency upon public handouts. With these conclusions it would have been irrational and illogical to expect solutions to flow from Moderate Party leaders for the development of additional public programs to assist aliens. To the satisfaction of members of Sweden's rightwing party, offering residents a new national environment free of restraints would allow everyone—including immigrants—to have the wherewithal to improve and develop themselves. In sum their vision for Sweden was centered on more opportunities for individual initiatives.

In sharp disagreement at an opposite pole were Left Party members who believed the fault laid not with too many but with too few public commitments to eradicating obstacles to immigrant progress and development. As a result to insure equal protection and more opportunities, they urged the parliament to pass a sereis of tougher laws against discrimination and for more intervention on behalf of immigrants. Through a program of revisions to reorder priorities and revamp tax law, *Vänster parti* leaders, in hope of appropriating more aid for less fortunate people, favored a generous program based upon increasing taxes. In their judgment immigrants—as the most underprivileged residents of Sweden—could benefit from a restructuring of society that would impose upon the highest-income earners even more confiscatory taxation than what was in place. According to leftists, extra revenue would go toward reforming and improving life for people with lower than average incomes. Then as a plan for bringing foreigners into the Swedish job market, leftwingers advised an imposition of quotas.[156]

Although discrimination was the main factor why aliens seldom found employment that reflected their levels of education and experience and was a major reason why they had a much higher jobless rate than ethnic Swedes, the *riksdag* never gave any serious consideration to implementing a program that would resemble an affirmative-action approach to solving job discrimination. Reza Banakar, whom fellow aliens might easily have characterized Sweden's equivalent of an "Uncle Tom," cited three reasons in *Siv*'s official magazine why his adopted nation should avoid anything similar to America's program: it would stigmatize its intended recipients, prioritize aliens who require no such help, and harden attitudes of racism and prejudice against its beneficiaries by reenforcing xenophobic beliefs about foreigners as people who must require special treatment to succeed. In addition to repeating some of these arguments, reactionary Thomas Gür supplemented with what he viewed as a more cogent argument against instituting special treatment to immigrant job seekers. To his reasoning it would neither make sense nor be fair to favor one group at the expense of another group.

Four integration ministers were obviously afraid to disagree. As soon as a statement could be construed as hinting favorably at some form of special treatment, reactionaries' protests would force immediate retractions. What politicians and all other foes of quotas and affirmative-action programs failed to acknowledge was the degree to which special handling already existed; in reality real competition for jobs did not exist because of the favoritism ethnic Swedes had been receiving at the expense of often better qualified immigrants. The indigenous population in effect was the true beneficiary of special treatment, gaining more advantages than what would have resulted from a legislated or mandated quota system for outsiders.[157]

Generally when aliens did offer views on integration, their articulations on the subject varied. Harry Schein, an Austrian emigrant, was an avowed foe of multiculturalism; he did not consider it a worthy goal. He had worked hard at assimilating himself into his adopted nation's life soon after coming in 1939, and he advised others to do likewise. Not only did Schein believe in personal assimilation, it was his opinion that culturally diverse societies had tendencies for dysfunction. Emmanuel Morfiadakis, in contrast, did not believe outsiders could ever glide completely into Swedish society. After many years and even a seat on the Malmö council, the Greek immigrant asked what "in hell he was busying himself with" because "immigrants' knowledge is not valued. It is enough to have an accent when speaking Swedish to be stamped" as unworthy of contributing anything substantial. Stojka Lakic was not as pessimistic as Morfiadakis. Although understanding the Swedish mentality had taken twenty years, he found it both possible and advantageous to comprehend how Swedes functioned.

Kurdo Baksi and Rojas—like many other aliens—were distrustful of the Swedish government. They had suspicions the Interior Ministry might in fact be guilty of defaming and blacklisting an "immigrant elite." They also singled out for dislike the campaign that was being conducted by close subordinants of Blomberg. In particular Baksi and Rojas resented how Blomman's assistants had been pointing out the two immigrant intellectuals as members of an elitist group of aliens who supported themselves by creating "ethnopanic." The two accusers, suspecting the existence of a "discrediting campaign" against critical alien debaters, demanded that Blomberg distance himself from such activity.[158]

It was against a backdrop of mixed immigrant opinions and grave fears of anything with a remote resemblance to quotas that integration ministers and the Integration Board feigned work at achieving three evasive goals set in 1997 by the *riksdag*. Without regard to ethnic or cultural background, Sweden went on record as wanting to provide the same rights and possibilities to everyone; as seeking to promote social solidarity, with societal diversity as a foundation; as desiring to develop a society in which mutual respect and tolerance exist for all and one where, irrespective of background, every resident shall participate and have equal responsibility. As an agency charged with fulfilling some lofty idealistic goals, the Integration Board was budgeted to work with and dispense grants to communes, counties, and organizations in order to develop projects whose purpose was to combat racism and xenophobia.[159]

To some degreee each of four ministers responsible for administering integration policy personalized their interpretations of these three objectives. As the first one charged with dealing exclusively with integration, Blomberg seemed content to explaining in assorted newspaper articles the importance for Sweden's "destiny" of melting in diverse elements in society and maintaining cultural diversity. He advised readers not to expect fights against segregation or unemployment from his office because they were not the ministry's charge. As he interpreted instructions from parliament, the mandate before him was to struggle actively "against discrimination, create a consciousness of diversity's competence," and develop a better atmosphere for unhampered participation in society. Blomman in other words saw the ministry more as a promotional agency than as a provocateur directly engaged on behalf of victims' interests or as a judge empowered to punish wrongdoers. As part of keeping the role limited the minister visited communities to present a message of respect for diversity. After a young African's racist murder in Klippan, for example, Blomman came and lectured adults and young people on toleration. Assuming favorite roles of sage and father figure during one of his three appearances on August 27, 1996, he suggested that "we adults must wake up, begin to pay attention, dare to take positions, and show civil courage and put our feet down. It is more important than ever. The question is: Are we with people or against people."[160]

As a replacement after Blomberg's sudden death in March 1998, Persson recruited an old friend. It was clear from the start Engqvist's ambitions would never be satisfied by holding this obscure post. Except for a scattering of some rebuttals and comments, he did not do anything at the ministry.[161] Finally after approximately an eight-month wait, he gained a more prestigious post. During November after having left the Integration Ministry at the end of summer, the prime minister's friend—from their time together working as young men on behalf of *SSU*—became the new Social Minister. Meanwhile his departure opened up the post at Integration for Messing, a twenty-five-year-old without any prior experiences dealing with immigrants or administering a ministry. Her shortcomings had not seemed to matter because she received Engqvist's position as head of Integration during the summer. Choosing her demonstrated just how little importance Persson's government was attaching to integration.

Although this unprepared young woman struggled to do a commendable job, her unsuitability was apparent almost from the beginning. In one of her first acts, she tried to explain for local governments and public officials at all levels what she envisioned as their role. Messing hinted immigrants belonged in schools as teachers, in law enforcement as police officers, and in councils as representatives, and she expected townships and counties to work toward the systematic development of more diversity among their work forces. Her goals were worthy as one newspaper editor noted in wishing her well, but there was little likelihood she could achieve them with what was at her disposal. A *Gefle Dagblad* editor seemed skeptical about her chances of succeeding, but "would [be] very willingly to pay tribute to Ulrika Messing's efforts when, or if, she is successful." Among other things she expected ministerial colleagues to work toward integration's three goals in their offices, and she expressed an intention to banish "immigrant" from the Swedish language. To her, it was so loaded a word with negative and wrong connotations that it diverted from and distorted Sweden's new diversity. Naive and thin-skinned, the young minister could not deal with criticism. After suggestions from Baksi and Chair Anyasi Sabuni of the Afro-Swedes' Youth Association that Social Democrat Mona Sahlin would be better suited as the Integration Minister because of her broader experiences of dealing with the problems of immigrants, Messing became defensive, citing in a rebuttal article all the accomplishments which had occurred on behalf of aliens after her installation.

If the consequences of immaturity and insufficient knowledge had not been so disastrous for aliens, reason might exist for empathizing with an overmatched minister. In point of fact, however, Messing's failures had dreadful effects. In an attempt to attack immigrant unemployment and segregation in seven large cities, she supervised a 1.9-billion kronor boongoggle. *Sydsvenska Dagblad Snällposten* reporter Marianne Hedenbro investigated and found that program recipients had neither been consulted nor involved in Malmö plans. Moreover, it was her discovery that a huge investment had netted generally disappointing benefits.

Outsiders also found Sweden's record on civil rights for immigrants wanting in results. The most damaging incrimination came on August 5, 2000, from the United Nations Convention on Race Discrimination; the international body singled out the Nordic kingdom for failures to combat racist groups and to discourage prejudicial hiring practices. Perhaps of equal embarrassment for the egocentric nation, the UN report criticized a lack of progress in eradicating de facto segregated housing. In sum neither the efforts of four ministers nor of two general directors passed UN muster, and none of the *riksdag*-enacted legislation under Persson's two hesitant-to-act, afraid-to-offend coalitions was adequate for the large tasks of facing down Sweden's prejudicial practices and endowing her alien families with equal opportunities. Moreover a question must be raised why only political hacks, without clues or knowledge about how to proceed effectively against racism, emerged consistently as Persson's appointees. With an educated, experienced talent pool available to the prime minister from which to select competetent appointees, the only conclusion to reach about Persson is that he seemingly preferred making political paybacks to hacks to endowing immigration posts with qualified personnel.[162]

Immigration by the end of 2000 had become a bureaucratic hydra centered in Norrköping at the Migration Board and at the Integration Board. From these headquarters its tentacles spread in many directions across Sweden. Borås became home to the Immigrant Institute, a center whose primary functions have been to collect information and documents on immigrant and refugee questions. Begun in Stockholm in 1973, the Institute moved after two years to its permanent location. For the most part the Borås-based facility has operated as a specialized library; its holdings include written works by immigrant writers, reports on alien questions, immigrant newspapers, and an archive with letters, protocols, photographs, posters, and paintings by non-ethnic Swedish artists.

On the outskirts of and in the capital city of Stockholm are two immigrant-related centers. The Immigrant Institute and Museum is a facility located in Botkyrka, a ghetto suburb populated primarily by migrants to Sweden and their descendents. Working there is a cadre of ethnographers, anthropologists, sociologists, and other behavioral scientists. Their job is researching Swedish immigration. Begun in 1987, the institution also contains a reference library and sponsors publications about Sweden's newcomers. At the other end of the capital, Stockholm University hosts *CEIFO* (*Centrum for invandringsforsking* or the Center for Migration Research). Here in the midst of an academic setting, scholars and their students focus attention on Sweden's alien population. Each of these facilities fully depends on government funding. It might be fair to inquire why with so much attention given to aliens that the results for them have not been better programs for and more comprehension of their basic needs for fairness and equality.[163]

Thousands of immigrant organizations are nodes on a large bureaucratic hydra's tentacles. For many years these bodies have thrived on government subsidies, a dependence which has forced them to adopt and follow strict nonpolitical agendas. Therefore because of centralized governmental control, a logical placement of these ethnic clubs is within immigration's bureaucratic structure. Whether by design or accident, the government found in funding a method to choke off and moot alien protest. Aiding simply made immigrant organizations' survivals dependent, and it regulated effectively against their active participation in political activities. In effect by forcing them to register their charters with local governments and to agree to terms and conditions for such bodies, members exchanged integrity and independence for financial support. In practice they surrendered all possibilities to protest and lobby for or against legislation or represent their interests in governmental agencies. Also by agreeing to become tax-funded entities, organizations committed to not emerging as forums for the purpose of galvanizing their members' participations in protests and demonstrations on behalf of such causes as rights and jobs.

In Lund, according to Madubuko Arthur Diakité, developer and head of English International (one of more than forty ethnic organizations which exist in this southern Swedish community of 100,000 residents), the commune has set rules and regulations which govern all local organizations for minorities. To qualify for financial assistance, a group must have a minimum of twenty dues-paying members, bonds to an ethnic group, and no political agenda. In return for a written pledge, Lund awards fifty kronor for each certified member and provides a flat grant of 5,000 kronor to each organization. Many opportunities also exist for project subsidies. As examples an organization can receive extra support if it publishes a newsletter or posts an internet homepage.

English International, the umbrella body for English-speaking residents of Lund and Diakité's home organization, enrolled 140 members in 2000. For the next year its roll entitled the organization to a grant of 12,000 kronor; for publishing a monthly newsletter called *The Lundian*, the body received a supplementary 30,000 kronor. Moreover the commune provided members with a completely equipped office and meeting place. In addition to forty-one diverse organizations in Lund, there was *LISO* (*Lunds Invandrarföreningars Samarbetsorganisation* or the Cooperative Federation of Lund's Immigrant Organizations). In many instances leaders of diverse immigrant groups literally became professional immigrants. Diakité for instance has been a full-time worker at English International for more than thirty years, and during this time he has spent several hours weekly as his organization's representative at communal board meetings and *LISO* sessions. For attending and participating at these, the commune has compensated him.

The Chilean Organization during its peak operated on a much larger scale; in 1996 Freddy Weitzel headed a group with an annual turnover of 1.3 million kronor, of which all but 40,000 came from public coffers. During the period of Chile's rule by a military junta, many Chileans were critical of the organization and of Weitzel because both had refused to lead campaigns against a homeland dictatorship. "But," as the chairperson rationalized, "our response to critics was simple. Many of us will be spending the rest of our lives here. Somebody must see to it that our lives [in Sweden] will be as good as possible."

Athletic teams and participation at fairs represent what many immigrant groups have sponsored from their beginnings. Although only a minority of Swedes have ever been concerned with immigrant organizations, there were some exceptions. Social Anthropologist Aje Carlbom from studying Malmö-ghetto community Rosengård found much to criticize. To him it was more an Islamic society than a Swedish one, and indirectly the work of its immigrant groups preserved various ethnic cultures and promoted segregation. In effect then government grants to these bodies subsidized separatism. In the judgment of Carlbom, "They should be distributing money to other activities which stimulate integration instead; they should be pumping in money to trade and industry in order to produce jobs and practical training places."[164]

As for these expenditures by government to ethnic-club programs, the social scientist and other critics should have recognized immigrant control and curtailment as the true reasons behind governmental assistance. Swedish governments from Carlsson through Persson engaged in an effective shellgame of charading true objectives. They knew their political survival would depend more on following the pulse of the populace than on offering radical solutions such as quotas. At avoiding confrontations, the key politicians who dictated and formulated policy demonstrated a degree of genius by scheming to nullify immigrants and divert them from political acts by funding their organizations. To give the appearance of interest in minorities, governments passed a bevy of worthless laws against discrimination and established useless agencies like the Integration Board. With immigrants pacified by money and without any truly painful legislation imposed upon native Swedes, two Carlsson regimes, Bildt's coalition, and a pair of Persson-led governments foiled Swedish xenophobic equivalents of LePen, Haider, and Glistrup from grabbing political footholds. Following a Swedish formula where everything should be *lagom*, politicians have stimulated bestowals of just enough concessions to minorities to indicate interest and not so much as to attract notice or affect anybody. From the right, there were objections from extremist elements, but nothing short of returning all minorities would appease a miniscule element in society. From the left and among immigrants, there was dissent. Excepting the intellectual aliens—those so-called purveyors of "ethnic panic"—with no base with which to organize a movement, the government silenced and nullified disgruntled minorities with money for their groups. Although *Vänster partiet* was growing stronger, its increase in popularity had not resulted from its promises to non-Swedes. The party's bread-and-butter proposals attracted followers, and not the leftwingers' generous immigration-and-refugee planks. Only Marxist egalitarians among the party's faithful showed any enthusiasm for aliens. As matters stood at the end of 2000, the only true hope for immigrants in Sweden came from the European Union. On June 29, 2000, the council passed directive 2000/43/EC; it mandated member nations to implement a program to provide equal treatment by 19 July 2003, to all Union residents irrespective of racial or ethnic origin. Unless the Swedish politicians decide either to ignore EU membership responsibilities as they have done several times with mandates from the United Nations or to use subterfuges for honest efforts and escapes, change will come as a result of a forced imposition by an outside body. If the latter alternative occurs, politicians will be able to absolve themselves of blame much as British MPs did with an unwanted declaration on worker rights; they assumed the role of victims, claiming there was no escaping compliance to the overriding demands of an ever more intrusive European legislature.[165]

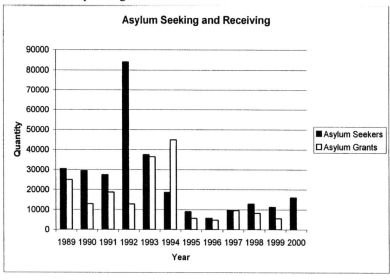

Chapter IV

Immigrants Lost on the Middle Way

In the global contest between capitalism and communism, neutral Sweden liked to describe her position as "the middle way." The purpose here is certainly not to conclude one way or another if the nation credited too much objectivity to her foreign policy. Whether the kingdom was an ostrich burying its head in the sand or an in-flight eagle pointing its beak condescendingly at two wrong forces is not a relevant question here, but there is legitimacy to see if Sweden actually intended a "middle way" for everyone inside her borders. As is true about any country under examinination for evidence of racism and xenophobia, checking out the kingdom's record involves a multifasceted probe and generalization. For the years 1990 through 2000, a range of her ratios of natives to immigrants in the population[166] went from six to one down to four to one. Thus a sizeable "minority" has existed long enough for there to be an abundance of materials on the subject. Available to study are records of past actions, contemporary and retrospective opinions, and numerous statistics. In sum these materials provide a sound basis with which to confirm or negate the appropriateness of applying the phrase middle way to the general experiences of newcomers to Sweden.

In pursuit of answers and conclusions about the matter, a researcher must inevitably compare "immigrants" and "natives." Without looking at one group in relationship to the other, no discovery of the impact or degree—if any—of such factors as national origins, ethnicity, religion, and race on treatment and development is possible to ascertain. If differences and barriers have been found to exist, then did they result from foreigners' inadequate educations, difficulties with a new language, and an unwillingness to adapt and adjust or were they the deliberate or inadvertent consequences of Swedish society and an intention and plan to set down legal or de facto restraints and obstacles in order to guarantee advantage for natives and insure a separation from aliens? Put alternatively, did the non-Swedish elements in the nation bring problems upon themselves or were these imposed by the native population?

In order to discover what happened and why, every aspect of immigrant life underwent a thorough examination and analysis. There were no shortcuts. To appreciate, comprehend, and understand minority-majority relationships, each of following was placed in a migrant-Swede context: employment and joblessness, entrepreneurship and exploitation, success and failure, crime and punishment, law and justice, religious conformity and diversity, integration and segregation, military advancement and stagnation, educational opportunity and prejudice, political involvement and exclusion, and healthcare provisions and neglect. To find patterns and ascertain which segments of the immigrant population fared best and worst and to see if success in Sweden was dependent upon race, origins, religion, education, or training, the different components of the immigrant population were investigated.

One thing is clear; prejudging people was easy. Utilizing many available clues, Swedes rarely had trouble with identifying outsiders. Accented speech represents an obvious indicator; it will readily designate an individual's foreign birth and background. With only about 8-million native speakers, Swedish is a language which is almost never studied or spoken outside the Nordic region. Thus it was rare for a non-Scandinavian to come to Sweden with any working knowledge of or firsthand experience with the language. With this being true, it has taken only one word or a syllable—a vowel will usually suffice for most American speakers because of their lazy vowels—to tip off a Swedish listener that a talker was a foreigner. Appearance is another giveaway about a person's non-Nordic roots. Almost any person with either Far Eastern, Middle Eastern, sub-Himalayan, Native American, or African physical traits and the individual with prominent non-Nordic features such as curved noses, tightly curled and/or dark hair, and brownish skin could not possibly be an ethnic Swede.

Factors heard and seen are then often complemented by a non-Swedish first or family name, a peculiar-to-Sweden religious practice, a set of different traditions and customs, and a diet of unfamiliar foods. Moreover just as United Kingdom residents know by the smell of curry waffling in the air that an Indian neighborhood cannot be far away, Swedes sense awareness of their entry into an ethnic enclave. Signs are clustering menfolk, booming voices, and gesturing hands. Natives of Sweden seldom gather in groups, and their speech is muted and unanimated. Moreover as much as Greta Garbo's isolation had characterized the Swedish-celluloid queen's retirement from motion pictures, a tendency for wanting something similar has figured into the lives of many other people from her homeland. For a nation whose indigenous population is only a few generations removed from forested isolation, a widely held stereotype holds that a Swede cannot express any emotion without first an intake of alcohol; with no intoxicant to release inhibitions, at least according to reputation, courage does not exist to express any personal or intimate thoughts. As lovers of privacy and separation, these Nordics find daily escape from other people through a personal sequestrating behind closed doors, and they use prolonged leisure periods to cocoon themselves in cabins on remote islands or on wooded land. Swedes refer to their vacations as a nature retreat, but many immigrants doubt the validity of this assessment. Rather than praise a desire to connect to nature's simplicity, aliens see in these disappearances acts of desperation and symbols of introversion by an essentially antisocial people. Whatever the typical Swedish holiday might be, sharp differences of opinion about seclusion illustrate why a polarity exists between two societal elements and why neither side could trust and comprehend the other's position.[167]

One negative manifestation of division was how the majority chose work companions and employees. In hiring decisons background often could mean everything. During Swedish prosperity and low employment, immigrants had found little difficulty in gaining and retaining lower-status jobs, but the outset of an economic downturn in the 1990s changed everything. A high percentage of aliens either found their entry into the Swedish work force blocked or were the first workers to suffer redundancies. In some areas of immigrant-populated Rosengård and among some minorities such as Somalians, percentage rates of joblessness were soaring into the nineties. There were even blatant admissions by some employers that they would not offer a job to a non-Swede. Anybody working with immigrants knew about this attitude. Counselors Jack Nilsson and Anna-Greta Bergman of the state-employment service freely admitted to jobless alien academicians on February 27, 2001, that "there had not existed hope for their placements earlier, but with Sweden returning to prosperity, job opportunities should finally develop for everyone present." Obviously there is only one conclusion to draw from the rejuvenated optimism; outsiders should expect to be hires of last resort.[168] Even if most officials have shown neither the penchant for candor of Bergman and Nilsson about alien job phenomena nor their implications about prejudice, there is no need for admissions.

Sweden's hiring record has voluminously documented an unwillingness to deal fairly with immigrant job seekers. Anyone with doubts about the mishandling of aliens in search of work should consult unemployment statistics; the numbers substantiate the realities and frustrations that were associated with desires for work during the 1990s. Recession-decade data about joblessness is only one source that counters irrational denials of and excuses for a regretable situation. There are also recorded personal testimonies from thousands of well qualified immigrants who had been so naive as to think that they might be in a fair competition for jobs if only they responded to help-wanted notices with application letters.

To all of the disappointment felt by aliens unable to land jobs, Swedes had a stock reply. They claimed Swedish-language competency would provide entry in the job market, but the argument was specious and illogical because nobody had worried about proficiency as a requirement for employment during periods of prosperity and active recruitment of alien workers. Seemingly then it had not been important as an employment issue because a desperation for workers had been forcing employers to hire whomever had been available. A shortage of labor had negated the need for entrepreneurs, politicians, and other rationalizers to find flimsy excuses for avoiding aliens because the options had been compromises with foreign hires or corporate retraction. A contrast to this state of affairs came during the 1990s when Sweden's economy was in process of receding to its lowest point since the Great Depression. As a result Swedes showed no desire to employ or advance foreigners at the expense of their own nationality.

Immigrants attained undesirability in a dwindling job market, and their lack of opportunities and importance became all too evident after Sweden had failed to use European Union funds that had been earmarked specifically for a campaign to move newcomers into gainful, productive work. If Swedes had an interest in finding work for jobless immigrants, the nation would have certainly spent the entire allocation and would have perhaps lobbied for even additional money the following year.

Looking elsewhere for evidence of no sincerity about or real intentions for fairness and complete access to the middle way, one should not ignore the role of government. Inasmuch as the public sector in Sweden was intervening so much in people's lives, there might be expectation to find it enforcing equal opportunities and pushing immigrants into workplaces and professions. By not pursuing these goals on behalf of non-Swedes, political leaders and bureaucrats showed both a lack of personal motivation to act and a fear of outrage from the indigenous Swedish majority's negative reactions. This was certainly the case insofar as offering immigrants any special initiatives or jump-starts into the job market. Intimidated by potentially negative responses from ethnic Swedes for anything that even remotely resembled a quota or an affirmative-action effort for qualified minority workers, Swedish politicians consistently refused to take seriously any program intended to upgrade immigrants at natives' expense. No matter how much wasted human resources might have been costing individuals and society, the governments of Carlsson, Bildt, and Persson preferred to drain treasuries on welfare over direct intervention on behalf of alien unemployment sufferers and immigrant victims of talent underutilization. As prime ministers, this trio of elected leaders did not dare to do more than promise outsiders better future opportunities for jobs, promote worthless bureaucratic agencies, and be sponsors of meaningless, toothless antidiscriminatory legislation.

Degrees of wastefulness involved with denying immigrants employment commensurate with their abilities and pacifying them with only half-baked acts and programs never seemed a concern. To deal allegedly with the problem of unemployment among aliens living in Malmö, one example of an inept action cost several million kronor and yielded fifteen positions. One cynic who had participated several times in asinine job-training programs without any tangible benefits called these vocational efforts "nurseries for adults." Outspoken and frustrated as always with excuses from government and with a lack of serious commitment to aliens, Fonseca concluded "the authority's time has passed." Elaborating on this point, he indicated why immigrants should stop adjusting to Sweden; they had waited long enough on their adopted nation to divide power and jobs.[169]

Just as the best and the brightest African Americans rarely found their way into leading law firms, outstanding universities, and corporate boardrooms—

except as cleaners—before Affirmative Action, Sweden's educated immigrants experienced prejudicial denial. In 1992 *Göteborgs-Posten* reported that after five years in the northern kingdom, only ten percent of university-educated aliens were working. Women and men suffered equally, and if gifted people originated outside the Nordic region, Swedish employers dismissed them entirely as worthy candidates for professional employment. It almost seemed as if natives derived pleasure from subjecting individuals with better educations than the average Swede to a second-class existence. In terms of educational levels, the following table compares the different folk elements present in Sweden:

Percent of People with 3 or More Years of Post-Secondary Education

GROUP	MEN	WOMEN
Born in Sweden	12.3	11.7
Foreign Born	13.6	11.3
Foreign Citizens	15.3	12.9
Born in Iraq	27.3	16.7
Born in Iran	19.9	9.3
Born in ex-Yugoslavia	8.2	6.5
Born in Lebanon	6.9	3.7
Born in Somalia	20.5	8.7
Born in Turkey	6.3	2.5
Born in Germany	18.1	15.2
Born in USA	43.3	42.6

The fact that an education had little or no impact upon the possibilities of an alien finding employment related to a general refusal by natives to honor foreign degrees and to a preference for Swedes who held Swedish diplomas. Discrimination would also affect aliens who possessed credentials from Swedish universities. The author met several immigrants who held two degrees—one from an institution in their homeland and another from a Swedish university—and who worked in restaurants and drove taxis. In an attempt to understand aliens better, he made a point of asking them to talk about their experiences. As a result of many informal inquiries, there were discoveries of a native of Greece with a Swedish doctorate in chemistry, who was working as a cook in a restaurant, an Ethiopian taxi driver with both English and Swedish electrical-engineering degrees, and an ex-professor of economics from Santiago, Chile, who was slicing meat for giros, this after, he said, a second earned Ph.D. in his specialty from a Swedish university had not yielded one job offer.

These three examples and many more like them were representative of a waste of immigrant talent found over a ten-year period from talking to persons denied the middle way. According to a report on outsiders and jobs done for a Swedish television news magazine, the Nordic kingdom has Europe's highest percentage of academically educated immigrants. It is no wonder then that at the main postal distribution center in Stockholm, mail sorters have included dentists, physicians, and engineers. On the same program there was a frustrating story about a Pole who had earned a master's degree in business administration from Sweden's most prestigious college of commerce. After ten years and by rough estimate 350 applications for jobs which matched his education, he did not find anything until a tip from a fellow choir member yielded a temporary position as a purchasing agent at AstraZeneca. In the Pole's case everything seemed favorable—including flawless Swedish—except a kiss-of-death matter of a surname that made his foreign heritage too transparent.

Unlike the Polish man who had suffered years of self-doubt, hardship, and joblessness essentially because of ultimate ethnic pride, other immigrants compromised to alter their personal identities in order to enhance their chances for employment and acceptance in Sweden. Each year for example an average of 2,000 foreigners spend 1,100 kronor each to change their original names to ones that are Swedish. Other immigrants, to insure the majority's approval and perhaps to deceive, have resorted to the more drastic step of undergoing plastic surgery. For several years one Malmö surgeon was "Nordicizing" as many as 100 alien faces annually at 25,000 kronor each, and in Stockholm during 1994 no fewer than 452 immigrants paid doctors for "new" noses. Of the number of foreign-appearing patients who had endured operations to have their facial appearance altered, 126 of the plastic surgeries were administered to women from the Middle East. Rima Jacob was one of the women who underwent comestic surgery. Content afterward with her new appearance, she was predicting "now the treatment [expected from Swedes] becomes quite different."

The adoption of new names and dear payments for facial operations by Sweden's newcomers confirm two things about life in the Nordic kingdom. In the first place immigrant willingness to forsake easy identification with roots and families in exchange for inappropriate Swedish names must have followed desperation and frustration from the futility of having to deal with prejudice; there otherwise would not have been comtemplation or fulfillment of personal denials of identity. Secondly an alien's willingness to sacrifice large sums for an operation to ape Nordic images of beauty resulted from progressively lower self-esteem that had accumulated from a continuing life as an outsider in Sweden. Plain and simple prejudice had induced these facial distortions.

Studies of the mental health of Sweden's immigrant population have confirmed risks and have shown early beginnings of the first signs of feeling inadequate. Physician Anders Hjern studied a blended group of children from Stockholm, and he found a significantly higher suicide rate among the offspring of foreign parents. Children with alien backgrounds were also more likely to engage in criminal activity. As 1996 crime statistics for Norrköping convey, 60 percent of youths whom police had taken into custody in this city had roots outside Sweden. In another study about children born in Sweden to non-Swedish parents, startling results emerge in a 1995-published book with the suggestive (translated-to-English) title of *Sweden's unloved children*. Rojas related what had been implied by suggestion. The Lund University professor concluded boys and girls born in Sweden to immigrant parents often have an "identity problem" that leads to "identity conflicts" and to "personality disturbances."

Like Rojas Lund psychologist Binnie Kristal-Andersson found children from two-world existences at risk, but she did not agree completely with what she was considering his oversimplifications and gloom about immigrants' abilities to raise sons and daughters successfully in Sweden. In contrast to the economic historian from South America, Kristal-Andersson discovered from questioning and comparing outsiders' offspring to ones with Swedish parents that residing in an immigrant household could have either positive or negative effects for youngsters. A correct channeling of a child's life could lead to wholesome integrations of two worlds, while an unsuccessful combining of diversity might result in "an identity ridden by conflict and incongruity."[170]

With adult immigrants willing to change their names and appearances in desperate attempts at finding jobs and gaining acceptance in Sweden and alien children suffering mentally and physically, foreigners' expressions of anguish found many other outlets. Although Swedes could show compassion through newspaper articles which attempted to convince countrymen why they needed to reassure aliens of their worth to society, harsh everyday realities for an alien population tended to be more effective at countering the kind efforts at making outsiders feel wanted and appreciated. Thus it was no wonder that minorities were more likely to become ill than natives. According to details of a 1995 study of registered sick days and of all injury- and sickness-induced early retirements, the rate of job absenteeism due to illness among immigrants was 70 percent greater than among ethnic Swedes. Moreover foreign workers were 10 percent more likely to retire prematurely due to disabilities than native employees. For the Southern European worker in Sweden, illness and injury figured in receipt of premature pensions as much as 30 and 40 percent more often than among members of the nonethnic workforce. A study completed some five years later yielded more or less similar results, while a survey of Chilean, Turkish, and Iranian women who had arrived in Sweden during the 1980s when sample participants were between twenty to forty-four years old found over 50 percent reporting generally poor health in 2000. For Turkish and Iranian males 40 percent did not feel good, whereas a quarter of Chilean men registered complaints about their physical conditions.[171]

Logical reasons explain the sapping of immigrants' vigor and vitality. Readily available information and statistics make comparing the lives of Swedes and aliens relatively easy. Doing the exercise yields two obvious conclusions: the jobs delegated to foreigners by natives have often involved more danger and monotony, and Swedes have enjoyed better living conditions. A team of Umeå University researchers found, for example, that non-Swedish workers at Volvo's large Torslanda assembly plant not only performed the most physically demanding tasks but they seldom advanced to better positions. According to one of the observers of conditions at the factory, "the result becomes a workplace with young Swedish men as well as older, bitter, and worn-out

Yugoslavs who had either tired out or no longer desired to work especially hard."

Another study reached similar conclusions about foreigners at work in Sweden. Generalizations by Ylva Brune, in a *Siv*-published book on the alien work force, collaborated the university investigators' findings at the automobile factory. Swedish job counselors' biased judgments about men and women from southern Europe and the Third World—without any attention to previous cultural, educational, or social attainments—led to categorizing these people and placing them in low-status employment. Overall compared to Swedes, immigrants, concluded Brune, were more likely to work in worse environments, to be on shifts or have odd schedules, to sit or stand at conveyor belts, and to perform the simplest service jobs. In addition an underutilization of educations was occurring, and for the same categories of employments non-Swedes earned less. Worst of all for an individual's self-worth and ego, she felt, employers and Swedish coworkers invariably judged and treated foreign jobholders—and prospective alien employees—more as problems than as assets. Elsewhere in reports on outsiders at work, many incidental factors have received mention; each contributed to job-related misery and anxiety. For immigrants with jobs they often suspected their employment was on the bubble. Recognized as well after only a few months on a job in Sweden was the reality that there was no need to expect any assistance with or protection from job-related problems.[172]

With prospects of layoffs so much more likely to come to aliens from unions exercising their last-in, first-out rule than to veteran Swedish workers, job-security issues caused them much work-related tension and stress. Labor organizations did not generally help immigrants. Concerned foremost with working conditions and salaries, unions were not going to battle to allow a leapfrogging by newcomers over senior dues-paying members. With entirely Swedish leaderships and with seniority overwhelmingly in possession of native Swedes, union investigations into immigrants' complaints were partial. As a case in point instances occurred when labor organizations defended the right of neo-Nazis to belong and hold jobs and refused to expel these racists as members or to support their dismissals from jobs. Thus the conspicuous immigrant could not count on organizational backing against hateful activities. For Muslim women who wore chador (their hair-covering scarf), disrespect and ridicule from employers and coworkers often deteriorated into harrassment and even to unlawful demands that their continued employment would depend upon them removing their head garment. If the female worker complained to a union shop steward, the matter would die without any repercussions from the offense. There were also no protests from union bosses whenever well educated foreign men and women faced the choice of forfeiting their welfare benefits or accepting job training to perform demeaning hospital tasks as orderlies and nurses' aids. *Riksdag* immigration chair Björn Rosengren, a powerful Social Democratic politician and the ex-head of *Tjänstemännens Centralorganisation* (*TCO* or The Central Organization of Salaried Employees), even went so far as to suggest unemployed female aliens should either work as maids or give up their rights to social-welfare benefits.[173]

This is not to imply that there were not exceptional cases when gifted immigrants had positive work experiences. Axis Communications, a computer-related manufacturer in Lund, was one company with an excellent record of hiring and rewarding aliens with expertise in electronics, and as an open-minded employer, L M Ericsson also compiled a commendable record of utilizing the skills and talents of anyone capable of contributing positively. In addition for many aliens who had arrived without training or experiences, possibilities did exist to learn new skills such as baking and bus driving. *Mormors* (Grandmother's) bakery in Lund opened in the 1990s as proof of what such training could achieve. At this immigrant-owned establishment, Middle Eastern bakers began offering an assortment of typical Swedish and Mediterranean pasteries and breads at lower prices than their Swedish competitors. There were also rare instances of aliens being able to practiced again their homeland trades in Sweden. Upon coming to Malmö from Lebanon, Ahmed Elali, for example, resumed a career as a sheet-metal worker. At the other extreme of moving into something else, Iraqi architect Husam Alkhamisi became a wholesale grocer after having failed at landing a job in his profession.[174]

Entrepreneurship as an alternative either to unemployment, marginalization, or job discrimination provided an increasing number of immigrants with degrees of independence and financial reward. Earlier before the government began a drive among aliens to encourage and promote their development of businesses with advice and low-interest loans, thousands, on their own, had experienced the benefits and advantages of ownership. Statistics illustrate the degree to which foreigners had turned to capitalistic pursuits by the end of 2000. They owned cumulatively 65,000 companies with 250,000 employees; these enterprises represented 12 percent of Sweden's total number of small businesses. Among alien owners, 16 percent did not have European roots. At seventy-eight startups per thousand inhabitants, East Asians were most likely immigrant segment to start a business. Turks were also enterprising, with seventy-two for every thousand residents. Northern Europeans were the least interested in running a business. Moreover as a group, non-Swedish entrepreneurs had more schooling than their native counterparts, with 47 percent of aliens having attended an educational institution after high school in contrast to only 23 percent of ethnic Swedes.

By the end of 2000, immigrant-owned businesses were prominent—and occasionally dominant—in certain commercial fields. In terms of customers their cleaning services, restaurants, kiosks, tobacco stores, small grocery shops with either specialty foods, long hours, or both, and fruit and vegetable stalls at open-air markets were the enterprises with the most mixed clientele, whereas outsider-run services such as barber shops, beauty salons, and travel agencies usually provided service only to fellow immigrants. In addition many alien-owned taxis were affiliated to networks that controlled dispatching and accounting. In some instances cases existed of immigrants banding themselves into cooperatives such as the eighty women who jointly owned Livstycket, a producer of colorful textiles in Tensta. Among all of the alien-owned businesses operating in Sweden, Sandra and Rune Danielsson probably ran one of the most unique. The pair—she was from Poland and he from Sweden—operated a mating service to introduce Polish women to Swedish men. As the couple interpreted a "mission," their matches allowed Poles to benefit from opportunities in more affluent Scandinavia and provided Swedish men with prospective brides allegedly "less spoiled, more appreciative" than what Swedish men would have found domestically.

In general for aliens starting all types of businesses, success would, as is almost always true in the beginning of entrepreneurship, depend upon a sound operating plan, willingness to work long hours, and novelty. All three factors have had especial applicabilty to ethnic restaurants because their viability often has related to young customers. Always on the lookout for something new and cheap, this segment of Sweden's population traditionally has been in the vanguard of trying new food. Pizza and Chinese food, for example, were popular in the 1960s and 1970s, but among trendsetters in larger cities, subsequent favorites would become Thai, Mexican, and Persian eateries.

As Haydar Akan from Kulu, Turkey, proved, ownership of thriving alien businesses in the Nordic kingdom could provide both personal satisfaction and prosperity. From profits earned from his ownership and operation of a popular patisserie and restaurant in a large suburban Stockholm shopping center, Akan purchased and furnished luxury apartments in both his hometown and adopted city, and he also owned a villa with a spectacular view of the Mediterranean Sea. As everywhere else with self-made men and women, immigrant success in Sweden came with braggadocio and condescension. Successful Palestinian shopkeeper Fawzi Khattab of Malmö expressed the universal feeling of many proud nouveau riche when he spoke of climbing upward from nothing. "I have sweated in order to take care of myself during all of my years here in Sweden. They [less fortunate aliens] must also have to sweat. If they do not want to do that, yes, then they should not be staying here in this land."[175]

Khattab's "sweat" netted a flourishing business, but that of several other alien gamblers on enterprises yielded only frustration and disappointment. Matters beyond their control could often cause entrepreneurial failures as well as fear. Shop and restaurant proprietors were often vulnerables target for racists' attacks. Hamid Jalivand's experiences were typical. A horrific experience for him, ownership of a small convenience market in Hofors lasted only for one miserable year before violence and vandalism would dictate a decision to forego continued operation. During the short period of working sixteen-hour days and trying to run a business, he agonized as racist hooligans smashed display windows six times, totally destroyed two cars, broke into and vandalized his transport vehicle, disturbed the refrigeration system, and stole early delivered morning newspapers left at the store's front door. Jalivand suffered as well from robberies, personal injuries, and insults. Among the several provocations and unplesantries which he endured, one incident was especially memorable. It involved two young men who entered the store with an apparent resolve to steal and irritate. After one had asked if he could pay half price for ice cream, Jalivand naturally said no. Thereupon, in response, the man returned to the freezer and began emptying its contents onto the floor. As he was doing this, his accomplice simultaneously stuffed small items into his coat. Jalivand's attempt at intervention ended with a hard kick to his side and two broken ribs. Reflecting on his one-year ownership of a little shop of horrors, the immigrant shopkeeper did not know what to conclude: "I do not understand what the Swedes want in reality. We [immigrants] take a job, then we hear the comment that we are taking the job from the Swedes. We sit home, then we are taking tax money from the Swedes. We stake money on something, and the first question is where we got the money from." Responding to Jalivand's nightmare, local police chief Bertil Larsson was somewhat sympathetic, but he did imply that the shop owner had only himself to blame for much of an awful ordeal because he had been "perhaps [a] little too nice."[176]

As much as one could explain away racist thugs randomly using murder, bombs, arson, vandalism, threats, assaults, insults, and disrespect to intimidate and discourage alien shopkeepers as an aberration not at all representative of a general Swedish attitude toward foreign entrepreneurs, there were other, more subtle occurrences available to confirm permeated, deep-seated prejudice in the kingdom. Easily decoded newspaper headlines illustrate just what an alien proprietor could confront. Often when "pizzeria" appeared in bold-faced type, what followed was a connection to a negative phenomena such as tax evasion and uncleanliness. Given the stories in print about these restaurants, the word could just as well have been *invandrare* because of an automatic association by Swedish readers of pizza and immigrant.

Hidden agendas, consciously or unconsciously, must have existed behind an editorial willingness to publish and an interest of reporters to write stories whose only immediate consequence would be turning Swedes against all alien-owned restaurants. What else could have motivated newspapers to print such alarming lead captions as "Warning for filthy pizzerias," "Pizza bakers don't have clean flour in the bag—The branch cheats on taxes for hundreds of millions," "Pizza filth in Jönköping," "Pizzeria withholds income," "Successful tax hunt in Östergötland—Some 50 pizzerias in the county are demanded to pay 50 million in unpaid taxes and fees," and "Black-market pizzas are sold in Borås"?

At the other end, one must also question why health inspectors and tax authorities focused on pizzerias. As anyone slightly familiar with bakeries and restaurants will attest, flour and mice find each other, and temptation exists for many restaurateurs to "cook the books" as much as food. Nevertheless, from a survey of thousands of newspapers for 1990 through 2000, the author found no reports on tax fraud by or filth at a Swedish-owned konditorei or bistro.[177]

There were other forms of harrassment and prejudicial treatment, too. Alien grocers who specialized in imported delicacies and spices became the primary targets of "consumer" inspectors. Among other things, according to Sweden's truth-in-labeling law, all food packaging must disclose in Swedish information about content ingredients, weight, and additives. Since the sales volumes for many items were so low that the extra cost of affixing new labels would have priced many imported foods beyond affordability, most of the distributors—aware few Swedes used these products—simply ignored the law, leaving in place original foreign-language inscriptions. The results were periodic raids of immigrant-owned specialty food stores and subsequent fines and warnings. Ewa Björnberg, a food-label surveyor, was satisfied "we have gone out with information earlier so all storekeepers know about what is illegal. We not only remove foreign-texted goods from storage or stamp them with sale prohibitions, but we are also responsible for reporting the matter [of incorrectly marked products]." Criticism of her work is not intended to be an indictment against consumer protection for there is obvious value in cautioning against unhealthy foods and in revealing contents for the prevention of serious allergic reactions. What should be pondered was the agency's true motivation. If the government's main goal was enforcement of the data-disclosure law, then there could have been allowance for greater rule flexibility. Accordingly the modification could have required distributors and resellers to provide on a customer's request a full information printout in Swedish for any shelved item in a manner not unlike what Swedish apothecaries have for prescribed drugs. Such data sheets would have been sufficient for consumers, and as for grocers these would have proven less offensive and equally effective at protecting consumers as costly product seizures.[178]

From systematically examining forty-five Swedish daily newspapers, the author gained a general impression about Swedish rule and law enforcements. Authorities applied much tighter standards and less flexibility to alien-owned enterprises than to companies operated by native Swedes. In addition banks and insurance companies engaged in discriminatory practices against foreign-owned businesses. In many instances financial institutions withheld loans to immigrant entrepreneurs, and due to no fault of foreigners, it was common for their business to be declared uninsurable. For example, regardless of pizzerias' locations in Sweden, insurance coverage was not available. Being profit-driven companies, insurers did not want risks associated with underwriting potential vandalism and arson at racist-targeted eateries.[179]

Third-world adoptees were another test of Swedish tolerance. By the end of 2000 the Scandinavian nation—the European country consistently with the highest per-capita rate of providing new homes to babies from orphanages in the developing world—was the setting of more than 40,000 placements of this kind. Adoptions were a logical outgrowth of a domestic-infant shortage that had resulted in part from a loss of stigma attached to unwed mothers keeping and raising their infants. Although many thousand older children lived in Swedish institutions, childless couples generally ignored them, preferring unwanted babies from Latin America, Asia, and Africa. Lives of these foreign adoptees, therefore, have provided scholars with some interesting case studies. As these boys and girls reached adulthood, their physical characteristics matched those of immigrants and their children from the same geographical regions, but everything else about the group mirrored the characteristics of children raised in an ethnically Swedish home environment. Adoptees spoke with the same regional accents as their adopters, had Swedish names, and developed Swedish outlooks, manners, and other intangible traits. There was one major problem, however. Among the indigenous population with only visual observations to guide and base first impressions, these strangers most often viewed the confronted foreign-looking person as Asian, African, or something other than Swedish. Then with spoken words the inevitably routine question routinely would be, "where did you learn to speak such excellent Swedish?" As an adoptee born in the Republic of Korea would note, he had considered himself a Swede until the day he looked in a mirror.

Others who had come to Sweden as babies from Ethiopia suffered the same forms of racial discrimination as adult African immigrants and their children. "Anders," one of these adoptees, told of being denied entrance into a Malmö tavern in 1994. As the owner confessed, "we do not want to have any niggers!" In the case of "Alfred" from Skellefteå, an unprovoked kick to his jaw and knowledge of a Somalian's death in the same Norrland city from a slit carotid in 1993 after a conversation with a white woman, would suffice to remind the adopted black son of Swedes of the dangerous consequences that might occur from attempts at interaction with female strangers in bars. "Tedros" learned firsthand about racism and stereotypes in Stockholm. Upon entering stores, he sensed suspicious eyes always fixing on him. In order to remove suspicions he learned to stretch his arms upward as if to communicate no intentions of shoplifting merchandise.

In addition to personal experiences with racist manifestations, Swedish vocabulary includes many words with negatively suggestive meaning. While reaching maturity in Sweden, Anders, Alfred, and Tedros had exposure from playmates and family members to *negerkyssar*, *negerbollar*, and *negeridiot* (the first two—literally "nigger kisses" and "nigger balls"—refer to popular Swedish confectioneries and the last—"nigger idiot"—is a derisive term used to demean a dumb action by an individual or general stupidity). An awkward connection must have occurred so soon as an African-descended adoptee had developed an awarenesses of the racial differences that were distinguishing a dark-skinned person from an ethnic-Swede. Parents of adopted children also confronted stares and stupidity. One grandmother even was so naive that she wondered about the future after a first visit with her granddaughter's adopted four-month Indian girl. Considering the infant "sweet and cute," the older woman asked "how will it be when she begins to talk?; you do not understand Indian."[180]

If the most perfect immigrants—foreign babies immersed in everything Swedish—suffered from prejudice, insensitivity, and racism, use imagination to visualize how much worse an ordinary outsider fared in a racially charged nation. For skinheads and neo-Nazis, any person without an ethnic Swedish background did not belong in "their" country. Although blatant racists' responses to the presence of aliens exceeded the parameters set by most Swedes for residence, it captured a majority's perceptions of what background should be required to hold truly Swedish credentials. As elsewhere in Europe about a connection of ethnicity and nationality, most indigenous Swedes tied two no differently. As a result, it would not help in the final analysis for either Jews or Roma to trace their roots in Sweden back several generations because members of the larger society would consistently identify both groups as special entities and not as "true" Swedes.

For an active racist, identification assumed an extra meaning. Just as Hitler's forces easily rounded up Jews in invaded countries, Sweden's neo-Nazis did not encounter many problems finding a Jewish minority for hate crimes and harrassment. Although to Per Ahlmark's credit as the Folk Party's leader in the 1970s, he had never made background an issue, there existed a conscious awareness from the start of his public career to see him as a Jew. Almost two decades after the end of Ahlmark's political career, people still remembered him as the only Jewish leader of a major political party. As a result television news producers earmarked him regularly to interpret most any domestic event that affected the Jews of Sweden. For example during late autumn 1992 when leader Ahmed Rami of Radio Islam in Sweden was planning an international anti-Semitic congress in Stockholm, Channel 4 solicited Ahlmark's opinions and reactions. He could report with satisfaction "the threat to turn Stockholm into the center for neo-Nazism has been warded off. Only some weeks ago there was a green light for Europe's neo-Nazis to come to Sweden." The guest commentator advised diligence in fighting anti-Semitism because "hatred of Jews is a snowplow for racism. It begins with Jews and continues later with other minorities."[181]

Ahlmark's reference to a beginning point was correct. Unofficially at least the starting point for racist acts in Sweden had been negative reactions to Jews. Remnants from pre-1945 remained latent until an arrival of large numbers of immigrants and refugees after the war. With them active anti-Semitism revived. Noticeably after forty-five relatively dormant years, active Jew baiting resumed on many fronts during the 1990s. With only sporadic reaction and mild governmental interference, blatantly anti-Semitic, anti-Zionist Radio Islam broadcast vile nonsense about Jews. Rami gained more recognition than punishment from several police citations for hatred-filled commentary and his denial of the Holocaust. The penalties were never so severe that they kept him from reemerging with more ignominy. The fact that Sweden returned Jews to the former republics of the Soviet Union to face maltreatment and torture might explain why Rami and Radio Islam were pampered by some of the same judicial officials who had given harsh sentences—including deportations—to other aliens for such misdemeanors as petty theft.[182]

Inasmuch as skinheads and neo-Nazis generally disliked Muslims, it was not so odd Rami would become an admired exception to the rule; simply put, it was his anti-Semitism. As followers of Hitler on race doctrines, the rightwing extremists naturally hated Jews and expressed their negativism toward this group by committing various noxious deeds. In several cemeteries hatred-inspired vandals vaulted star-of-David marked tombstones. There were also instances of haters firebombing Jewish-owned buildings and a school building where a Holocaust survivor was scheduled to talk, placing Jews on published hate lists, and communicating threats both to synagogues and individual Jews.

Being a Jew in Sweden during the 1990s could be dangerous. As music conductor Ilya Stupel and his daughter were walking their dog in the normally pleasant and safe Malmö suburb of Vellinge in 1999, two neo-Nazi teenagers attacked and threatened the pair. In explaining why an unprovoked assault had resulted, Stupel minced no words; "they hate me because I am a Jew." This was not an isolated incident. For a Jewish army recruit, his unpleasant experience occurred at military bootcamp. While in training for the Swedish army, he could not escape the downside of a Semitic identity. Two fellow recruits confessed to writing—"It was good that Hitler had taken the lives of Jews"—on the Jewish trainee's locker and also to waking him in the middle of the night with shouts of "gas, gas, gas!" Admissions from the two young culprits resulted in fines but not court martials, light penalties that were consistent with the sentences administered by civil courts to individuals found guilty of anti-Semitic hate crimes. It was also an especially difficult ordeal to be an Orthodox Jew in Sweden. The determination required to find Kosher meat symbolized in some ways what one minority was confronting in Sweden. Slaughter houses refused to follow Hebraic law, and stores avoided rabbi-sanctioned poultry, lamb, and beef because stocking special meat for so few patrons represented too many "logistic problems."[183]

If Jews were at the center of Ahlmark's snowplow, persons of African heritage were not far away. As the most conspicuous minority, they became a source of mystery and fascination in Sweden. Dark women, especially ones from an African-Nordic sexual relationship, often became exotic goddesses for Swedish men with erotic fantasies which were based upon their stereotypical images of black sensuality and unrestrained passion. When coupled to talent, the allure and temptuousness of Euro-Afro women in the Swedish mind perhaps explains why national entertainment moguls elevated so many of these women to stardom in show business and why they almost totally ignored possibilities of equal talent existing among other gifted female outsiders.[184]

Similar factors affected success in athletics; basketball, soccer, sprinting, and boxing were sports with a disproportionate representation of black participants, whereas Swedish society did not offer much encouragement to young blacks to excel at golf, hockey, tennis, skiing—whether slalom, cross country, biathlon, snow boarding, or jumping— in all forms, bandy, handball, gymnastics, sailing, orientation, shooting, diving, and swimming. Obvious prejudice dictated that these latter athletic events suited Swedes better than a descendant from Africa. Hence, Martin Dahlin, Pascal Simpson, Henrik Larsson, and Martin Pringle achieved fame in soccer, George Scott in boxing, African American imports in basketball, and Maria Akraka in sprint events, whereas Björn Borg, Stefan Edberg, and Mats Wilander became Swedish tennis legends, Swedish men won international titles in handball, golf produced such outstanding Swedish professionals as Jesper Parnevik, Annika Sörenstam, and Robert Karlsson,

Swedish skiing introduced Ingemar Stenmark and Pernilla Wiberg to the world as consistent winners of Alpine events, and in ice hockey several North American teams began depending upon imported Swedish talent.

None of this resulted from coincidence. Just as white Americans had long suspected that African Americans could not excel at certain key positions in American football, long-distance running, or sports that required intelligence and strong nervous systems, Swedes steered black youths from certain athletic activities and into ones with emphases on speed, jumping ability, agility, and brute strength. In ghetto communities Rinkeby and Rosengård, for example, their facilities encouraged alien young people's participation in boxing, soccer, and basketball. Athletic budgets deliberately did not fund many programs aimed at developing darker outsiders into world-class skiers, tennis players, swimmers, golfers, or participants in any "white" sports. Yet when Afro-Swedes competed in a "black" sport, their presence produced resentment. The implications were that they provided unfair competition or gave special advantage to their teams. Nowhere was this hostility to their participation more in evidence than during league soccer matches. Black players suffered through derogatory insults from opposing players and fans, and after failures—while competing for Sweden on the national team—to score goals that nationalistic-minded armchair "experts" had judged as automatic, black competitors suddenly went from status as Swedish sports heroes to "damned niggers."[185]

Elevations in show business, unfair expectations in sports from Swedish spectators, and racist expressions coming from angry fans represent examples of behavior and attitudes which were engrained early in Swedes from a variety of sources. First of all the most used Swedish-English lexicon cites fifty-three negative connections to and derivatives of *svart* (black), including references to everything from illegal transactions to jealousy whereas *neger* (an inclusive word in Swedish for Negro, darkey, and nigger) can be a stand-alone word or a prefix such as in *negerblod* (Negro blood, whatever it might be), *negera* (as in to negate), and *negerande* (negative). Subconsciously then as a Swedish child learns to speak and to play *svartepetter* (Old Maid), a youngster inadvertently will begin a process of picking up associations and concepts about the awful dreadfulness of *svart* and *neger*. As a boy or girl matures and attends school, Swedish textbooks include pictures that cultivate a prejudical image of Africa and Africans. Several generations of students have been left with impressions of a monolithic continent inhabited by lazy, wild, and heathen people with no history until the arrival of European colonizers. According to Maj Palmberg, a surveyor of many schoolbooks used in Swedish schools, the biggest problems were tendencies to treat Africans as objects and not subjects and as takers and not initiators.[186]

Swedes by adulthood had obtained—both abstractly and concretely—a negative composite of Africa and persons of African heritage and a personal feeling of superiority. Also present were factors of submission and control. Feeling more disciplined than outsiders, natives refused to allow emotions to become their masters as they surmised was true of "more primitive peoples."

Herewith was a double standard, however. It was acceptable for Swedish men and women to turn their lust into sexual activity with perceived overpassionate Africans because these acts would only fulfill a temporary curiosity. Often with Swedish men, a fear of inadequacy existed. In their competition with alleged out-of-control black men, "penis envy" caused worries about a possibility that could develop as permanent, negative consequences from Swedish women becoming sexually involved with black men. Reminiscent of the prevailing fears in the American South, white-male efforts in Sweden to exert dominance and insert mechanisms to control African men evolved similarly in Sweden. Native men, without any deliberate plan to gain this objective, spontaneously nevertheless belittled, humiliated, and tormented darker-skinned males, fomenting in the process fear, respect, and subordination.[187]

The humbling process took many forms. It meant either not employing African men or giving them only the most undesirable jobs. An offer of office work to a black male, for example, was so rare that its occurrence in the capital resulted in a magazine article.[188] Problems with finding jobs or receiving only ones unacceptable to Swedes represented one aspect of intimidation. A third of Sweden's African population reported having received natives' threats, and a staggering 65 percent noted problems from entering public establishments at night. Case after incriminating case occurred without consequences for either nightclub owners or their guards. Even a sting operation caught on film by a newspaper team failed to bring convictions, leaving two obvious conclusions: legislation against such discrimination was meaningless, and both police and judges lacked empathy for victims.

What Kenyan Kuria Ndung'u experienced in 1999 at a popular Lund sports bar and restaurant typified multifold cases in the 1990s when bouncers addressed blacks at the entrances to popular Swedish night spots. In line behind student colleagues from the Analytical Chemistry Department of Lund University, the African—and fellow classmates had gone there to celebrate a final Friday night together—advanced to the front of line's front. Thereupon the guard gestured with his hand for a halt. Curious about why he could not follow his friends into the establishment, Ndung'u asked for an explanation. After all he and the others had been at the popular restaurant hours earlier for dinner and had experienced no complications. "You cannot go in because you are drunk," replied the doorman. Steadfastly determined to disprove the allegation with a demonstration of capably walking in a straight line, the spurned man asked if race might have provoked the stoppage at the doorway. The guard, obviously sensing more stubbornness than he had expected, motioned and ordered the chemistry student to enter, but Ndung'u chose instead to file a formal complaint with police. His effort did not yield any better results than a hundred others like it. The law against discrimination was so open-ended that a defendant could be freed from racial discrimination charges by simply asserting that bias had not entered into a decision to close a facility to a minority member but it had followed judgment of a plaintiff's insobriety. As a precaution against potential rowdiness by unwanted patrons who had shown clear signs of apparent intoxication, guards had as an essentail part of their jobs the task of determining drunkenness.

Even if blacks became patrons at night spots, there were no guarantees of positive experiences. A Ghanaian discovered this at a bar after stretching his hand in front of another customer to lift over an ordered beer. Excusing a need to reach had no placating effect upon the other patron. Not satisfied by an apology, the Swede broke a glass over the African's hand. Sensing a possible disturbance from the incident, the bartender telephoned police. Entering and moving directly toward the black man, a female officer approached him with an exclamatory question, "what have you done, you damn nigger!"[189]

The law-enforcement representative's inappropriately offensive reaction exemplified why distrust and even hatred grew among blacks toward Swedish police. Hiphop artist Martin Carboo—born to Ghanaian-Finnish parents in England and raised in Sweden—captured the mood with "Policeman," a song about a threat to a young man after his failure to follow police instructions to lower the volume of his "boombox"; according to lyrics, the Swedish officer advised the disobedient listener that "tonight you are going to sleep in jail, Nigger."

It was not just police whom Africans distrusted. In general all Swedish authority figures were viewed with equal suspicion. In the struggle against the spread of the human immunodeficiency virus, lack of cooperation had existed as a problem in the Malmö region until health officials hired Togo native Povi Foly-Lawson. Against the deadly disease, she could do what Swedes had not been able to accomplish. She succeeded at convincing fellow Africans to be tested and to be protected. As a result of confidence she had sealed with men and women, a routine was established to collect blood samples which would lead to an uncovering of sixty African virus carriers. For officials in Sweden, the aforementioned examples represent a small sample of the consequences of black resentment. Indicators of dissatisfaction and unsuccessful prosecutions of persons accused of discrimination and prejudice at public facilities provided enough reasons for black freelance journalist Cecil Sondlo to proclaim that the "time [has come] for a black DO [Discrimination Ombudsman]."[190]

Being barred from nightclubs and being subjected to police insults were unpleasant experiences for African men, but the root of these occurrences was even more disturbing because the source was a need by many Swedish males to humiliate blacks. Abilities to terrify and terrorize boosted inferior egos. Swedish perpetrators and black victims of bullying consequently deserved pity for different reasons. For factors beyond the scope here to explain, something had occurred to Swedish men during the twentieth century. Whether the cause had been neutrality through two horrible European wars, fatherless childhoods and divorce, changing gender roles in Swedish society, or something else, the result submerged violence unlike anything the nation had ever experienced in modern history. Altogether too often, the presence of black males triggered its eruptions in both minor and major manifestations that were intended to convey manhood; yet these were largely acts of cowardice.

Ben Holm's introduction to racism occurred in Malmö on October 26, 2000, when he discovered damage to his pampered Alfa Romeo. This son of Swedish-Nigerian parents found etchings allover his automobile, a swastika embedded into motor hood and "die nigger" spray painted on the vehicle. At first Holm reacted to the vandalism by claiming to "have never been affected by racism before," but after giving more thought to the subject, he concluded subtle forms of prejudice had been a regular feature of his life. "Almost every time I drive home on the Bridge [binding Denmark to Sweden] from my job in Copenhagen, I am stopped for passport control only because I am colored. One time customs officials searched my car for narcotics."[191]

Holm was by no means the only victim of targeted property. Among the many cases, one of interest involved racists in Göteborg, who damaged a store specializing in imported African goods. This time, police questioned but released a twenty-four-old male suspect; without witnesses, evidence, or a confession, he could not be charged with painting a swastika on the building and writing "Nigger Go Home" on a display window. During tours throughout Sweden, rap performer and Nigerian immigrant Alban U. Nwapa—a dentist better known to his fans as Dr. Alban—had several Swedish concerts disrupted by racists. As a precaution during offstage walking ventures around the Nordic kingdom, he employed personal bodyguards to accompany him. Yet during an interview, Dr. Alban downplayed racism, claiming "it has occurred now and then with people calling me nigger or whatever, but it is nothing to be concerned about."[192]

Had retainers been available to shield less famous Africans, nonchalance might well have depicted their reaction to racists, too. Such was not to be their good fortune, however. In 1993, as soon as a skinhead gang observed African American James Gray alone one night in Sundsvall, one of the racists jabbed a knife into the black passerby, causing serious blood loss but no serious internal injuries. As usual in cases that involved natives on trial for assaulting aliens, a Norrland court showed customary leniency, sentencing the attacker to a fine as well as a brief stay in reform school. The result would be no different in 1995 after a twelve-year old Eritrean boy in Örebro had become the attack victim of two racist brothers. In a stairwell leading to the youngster's apartment, young men aged sixteen and twenty-three met a candidate for violence. For no reason other than "we are racists, [and] we do not like nigger kids," siblings kicked a defenseless African child and cut him so severely several times with a knife that the jabs severed his thumb and required stitches to both his forehead and forearm. One month after the unprovoked attack, a county court announced punishments; it placed the younger assailant in a juvenile-detention center and gave his older brother a two-year prison sentence. Additionally the defendants were under judicial order to pay their victim 40,000 kronor. At a spring dance in 1996, a fatal knife wound became the price that an Ethiopian would pay for having shown too much interest in a thirty-year old Swede's girlfriend. Many times, such as an incident that occurred in Borås in August 1992, racist gangs attacked Somalian refugees. In the specifically mentioned case, head injuries and a broken arm were the physical inflictions sustained by four African men after a confrontation with a roaming pack of crazed Swedes on the prowl to find and manhandle foreigners. After arresting four of the tormentors, police released one of their typical conclusions about such unprovoked assaults; according to the official report, Borås police denied that racism had motivated the natives' attack of Africans.[193]

None of these attacks resulted in deaths or life-threatening injuries to a black resident of Sweden, but there was one that did. The wanton murder of Gerard Gbeyos on September 9, 1995, affected and sobered the nation more deeply than any of the earlier beatings. Just before midnight on a Saturday in the sleepy Skåne village of Klippan, a gang of local fascist youths spotted a young black stranger at a busstop; he was waiting for a bus home to Alvesta. Drunk from *hembränt*—Sweden's illegally distilled and sold white lightning—and fueled with hatred from having listened an entire afternoon to "white-power music," the young neo-Nazis found a common thought racing through their warped minds: "Let's get that Nigger!" Upon approaching Gbeyos, one of the youths, a sixteen-year old with a long history of juvenile offenses, pulled out a knife just as the African was about to greet the fellows who were coming toward him. Within a flash, the assailant's sharp-bladed weapon embedded deeply into the chest of the twenty-two year old native of the Ivory Coast. As the wielder removed his knife from the victim, he yelled "Wow!" with both his arms raised up as high as he could stretch them as if to indicate an awful action had been a great triumph to celebrate. Losing blood rapidly and struggling to find help, Gbeyos managed to move himself to bushes on Klippan's main business street before collapsing and eventually dieing. About eighteen hours later, a pedestrian discovered a lifeless figure and notified police. Within an hour of a senseless deadly deed, the killer concluded his day by eating a large bowl of chocolate pudding covered with whipping cream. On page six with a medium-size caption, Malmö's *Sydsvenska Dagbladet Snällposten*—Southern Sweden's leading newspaper—simply informed readers "Man found dead in bushes in Klippan." Insignificantly reported the first day, news of the murder became one of Sweden's most followed human-interest stories of the 1990s.

For African—and other—immigrants, Klippan, and Swedish liberals, the murder was an epiphany. Before it could reach this point, certain clarifications had to occur first. A first one involved police investigators. The blood-stained body arrived without any identification, and with no reports of a missing young black male, officers did not know whose murder they would be solving. Not even certain the death had been race-motivated, police speculated about the victim's possible involvement in a spat among rival refugee groups. By the third day, pieces of the puzzle were fitting together. There were an absolute identity, some details about his movements on the fatal Saturday, and a better comprehension of racial attitudes in Klippan. Meanwhile as some local residents were engaged in soul-searching to ascertain why their community had been the one for a young African to bleed to death from a knife wound, others were pondering and placing flowers and condolence notes at the site of Gbeyos' death.   Reflecting on past events that had involved residents and outsiders, Police Chief Ulf Svensson remembered from two years earlier that tensions had culminated in a cross burning, but relationships thereafter, according to his perspective, were by all indications relatively calm and peaceful.   The head of local law enforcement—like so many other Swedes in responsible posts— missed the significance of neo-Nazis.   As with a naive *riksdag* majority, Svensson apparently had viewed the often boasted intentions of hate-filled ideologs as nothing more than youthful fantasies that would never have any serious consequences.   A false illusion about their potential danger to society abruptly ended with the arrest of two of these young men.   In the minds of many followers of the case, Klippan was just as much on trial as two arrested neo-Nazis.   One newspaper article even went so far as to refer to the community as "Sweden's Birmingham," a reference to hateful polarity found in the Alabama city during the protests of 1963 when the world via television had witnessed city policemen's use of mean-spirited dogs and high-powered water cannons to disperse peaceful, nonviolent young African Americans demonstrating for rights.   An exaggeration without basis or substance, the comparison was sensational and inappropriate.   Assigning a surreal distinction to Klippan as the hate capital of Sweden, news coverage wrongfully generalized and simplified community attitudes.   Television crews, newspaper reporters, and delegations who claimed to represent the nation's black inhabitants descended on the community to see for themselves and produce articles and documentaries.   What they found for the most part was a small town more or less like scores throughout the kingdom.   Although few Swedes wanted to accept truth about themselves in regard to their racism and convictions about aliens and natives, there were no basic differences separating Klippaners from other Swedes.

The trial was not so much about guilt or innocence as it was about other matters.   A local court had to decide whether Gbeyos' death should be judged a premeditated first-degree murder or a manslaughter.   Regarding the seventeen-year old defendant, should he be judged and sentenced as an adult or as a juvenile.   Given the murderer's youthfulness, the question became should he recieve a harsh sentence or a light penalty.   As for the victim's family in Africa, the legal question evolved into determining whether their compensation should be as much as the court would award Swedish surviving relatives under similar circumstances or should the amount be lessened because of the Ivory Coast's lower cost of living.   At the lower and appeal levels, verdicts on these pivotal points dissatisfied either the prosecutor or the defense lawyer.   Hence everything rested on decisions by *Högsta domstolen* (*HD* or the highest court).   First of all *HD* judges ruled the murder had been deliberate.   Although they found racist motivation for the knifing death of Gbeyos, it was deemphasized.   As for punishment *HD* sentenced the seventeen-year old killer to a four-year prison term.   Finally it awarded 20,000 kronor to Gbeyos' family.   Thus the case ended, leaving almost as many questions unresolved as settled, with the biggest one being why had the African relatives received so much less than Swedish survivors would have garnered and how could a four-year penalty be justified in light of a Klippan court subsequently punishing more severely a bootlegger for selling untaxed alcohol than what the high court had administered to a cold-blooded killer; the court sentence for selling illegal spirits was four years and six months. Even his jail term was mild if it is compared to the nine years given two Kosovo heroin smugglers. For Klippaners there was no escaping the terminal effects of "the murder"; scarred by a few young racist thugs' sadism, the community remained in the national conscience as the setting of the most memorable racist murder in recent Swedish history.[194]

To varying degrees Ahlmark's "snowplow" was wide enough to catch other minorities. As an alien in Klippan responded to a reporter's question about the relevance of Gbeyos' murder, "all foreigners have a bullseye on their foreheads; every Swede sees the bullseye, but we do not." An exaggeration to be sure, but it captured how many outsiders viewed a country in which their position always appeared tenuous and prejudice seemingly permeated every institution. Concerns about personal safety had become an inescapable factor in how aliens reacted to daily routines, but worries about becoming an assault victim would not be the only problems that faced immigrants. After all, as a population segment that accounted for almost 2-million people of a national total of nearly 9-million inhabitants, the risk of being harmed was slim if the official statistics were accurate. In 1998, police recorded 2,622 cases of racist crime or slightly more than 1.4 reports for every 1,000 immigrants. During the first two months of 2000, approximately 200 acts had reached police attention.

To put Swedish figures in a statistical context of tabulations elsewhere in the world, they purport to show just how relatively infrequent reported violent racial crime was against foreigners in Sweden. In Australia and Great Britain for 1999, more than 4 and 3 percent of their respective citizenries had become victims. Even in relatively crime-free Japan, violence affected 0.4 percent of her population. At first glance for the Scandinavian nation without examining deeper and elaborating further, one could easily reach a false sense of security and could conclude that it was not so much crime's reality that likely mattered most to immigrants but its specter in relationship to their expectations. They came with hopes for a peaceful life in Sweden. After all many of these people had escaped horrible experiences in their homelands and had chosen Sweden in many instances because of visions of tranquility to be found there.[195]

The Nordic nation's crime statistics were meaningless for many relevant reasons. First of all police were not motivated to collect them because of their failure to see any reason for suddenly subdividing criminal acts into ones with and ones without racist motivation. As late as December 1995 Sweden's chief prosecutor was requesting this type of breakdown of crime information. In the second place the corps was with few exceptions a homogeneous ethnic-Swede force. Thus members were likely as prejudiced—if not more so—toward the outside element of population as any other segment of Swedish native society. Just as the black victim in a Stockholm bar experienced, police officers tended to use derogatory racist terms when addressing and discussing aliens. Police as a result maintained two distinct standards—one for fellow Swedes or "we" and another for outsiders or "they"—when sorting out multiethnic conflicts. Then a tendency was to ally with natives. Most often patronizing and condescending toward aliens, police could also become brutal such as they were with Osmo Vallo. During his custody in Karlstad, police beat this person of Swedish-Finnish heritage to death and thereafter denied any responsibility for his fatal wounds. Also the curricula of Swedish police-training schools ignored racism and minority issues. It meant police cadets being unprepared to deal with problems in a multicultural nation.

On the other side aliens neither trusted nor respected Sweden's police. According to one scientific opinion poll, many more immigrants experienced racial crime each year than would be recorded in official statistics. The answers collected from questionnaires distributed to randomly selected Arab, African, Asian, and Yugoslav aliens in 1996 revealed that one-third of respondents had suffered some form of racist victimization during the past twelve months. In another survey only 11 percent of the participants sensed equal treatment from police. In fairness to Swedish officers a part of distrust had accompanied many immigrants to Sweden, and the remainder was acquired from unfortunate experiences after their arrival in Scandinavia.

Aliens learned both firsthand and through colleagues how police handled complaints about racists. It seemed altogether too often when their testimonies were countered by Swedish offenders, police either did not believe a victim or jointly charged a victim and an aggressor with crimes. Hassan Labadi suffered the latter nightmare Easter Sunday 1995. After a gang of neighborhood punks had gathered in front of the Labadi home in Vålberg outside Karlstad to pelt it with apples and eggs, fire airgun pellets at windows, and shoot up skyrockets at the roof, Labadi bravely charged from his house to disperse the tormentors. Once outside he challenged the mob to disband. Thereupon an assailant hit Labadi on the head with an iron pipe. Seeing her husband struck and on the ground, Kamela Labadi tried to come to her spouse's rescue, but before she could do anything, someone hit her with a rake, felling her to the ground. In the process of attempting to raise herself from a defenseless position, crazed assaulters kicked and called her a "black headed whore." In response to the disturbance at the Labadi home, police arrived and immediately arrested three Swedish youths and Hassan. In association with defending property, the alien homeowner faced felony charges for aggravated battery, but the police did no more than question the boys before releasing them to their parents with advice to behave.

Among foreigners a general consensus existed about prevailing bias in the police corps. Many outsiders were cynical, surmising a total pointlessness in reporting offenses because sharing information and filing complaints with a law-enforcement officer would prove meaningless. From a typical immigrant perspective law-enforcement agents had tendencies to reduce threats by racists to immigrants as no more than child's play. As a consequence of their assessment cops either responded slowly to or ignored hate crimes in progress.

Just being perceived as the potential target of young men who paraded around Sweden with illusions of being Hitler's nouveau guardians of Nordic purity was enough to terrify escapees from fascism in Chile, Iraq, and former Yugoslavia. No spectacle illustrates the fear more conclusively than the fright television personality Alexandra Pascalidou experienced after she had opened her apartment door to armed neo-Nazists who were standing there before her. Unknown at that instant to the popular host of a program for immigrants, she had been targeted by a young *Aftonbladet* reporter who had staged everything to obtain exclusive photographs of and information for a news article about the famous Greek-born TV-program leader. For Pascalidous, like reactions from so many other aliens before and after her ordeal, relating a nightmare to police was not a positive experience. As a result of having been taken to Sweden as a child by her parents, her Swedish was flawless. Imagine then how it must have been for other immigrants who could not convey accurately to authorities what had happened to them in understandable Swedish.[196]

The Pascalidou incident was significant because her trauma duplicated in many respects what other immigrants experienced with a sudden appearance of skinheads. Under these circumstances, an alien could expect the eruption of trouble without provocation. Perhaps the most terrifying ordeal of all for aliens occurred in Stockholm. Spanning almost two years across the capital from 1991 to 1992, a crazed-with-hatred madman known simply as the "laserman" stalked immigrants in a shooting spree until his capture by police.[197]

Sweden also suffered her own version of "ethnic cleansing" on several occasions. It occurred whenever racists used violence and threats to force out immigrants from their residences. In one case police found enough explosives that was set to destroy an entire multi-unit structure that was housing about 200 aliens.[198] Moreover there was an annual day designated by racists for attacking anything and anybody foreign in Sweden. Each year on November 30, the date of idol King Charles XII's battle death, xenophobes have paid homage to their fallen hero with marches and assaults on aliens.[199] Taken collectively to coerce and to intimidate, racists carried out attacks with bombs,[200] guns,[201] knives,[202] arson,[203] communicated threats,[204] such symbolic hate gestures as Nazi salutes, burning crosses, and spray-painted swastikas,[205] and brute force.[206] They beat, stabbed, and shot victims as well as bombed and gutted alien properties. In one case of hatred a motorist deliberately drove his automobile into immigrant children.[207] Acts could also be sadistic. For example four neo-Nazis pinned down an alien teenager in Gävle's "foreign quarter" as their accomplice carved a swastika on a young victim's arm.

In 1996 during a two-week period in the mid-sized city located 175 kilometers north of Stockholm, sixteen-year old Ammar Feyli was one of three immigrants whom skinheads attacked. What happened to him in a parking lot on the night of April 14 was a good indication of just how savagely brutal racist attackers could be. For no other apparent reason than a teen's ethnicity, "they slugged me down, kicked and marked me with a Nazi cross; I observed their shaven heads."[208] Violent acts also came as reprisals. A sixty-year old Polish immigrant who lived alone outside Göteborg in Lerum paid dearly for befriending refugees. For not heeding telephone warnings to stop "chatting with blackheads," she had a visit from three hooded men who proceeded then to scratch her with a knife, smash furniture, and wreck paintings and clothes.[209]

Although Swede-directed violence at aliens would be the stimulator that aroused normally unopinionated King Carl Gustaf to express worries about its consequences in his realm, more subtle forms of prejudice had perhaps equally detrimental effects because of their impact on so many more individuals. On account of "nonpunishability," felt Discrimination Ombudswoman Margareta Wadsten, "daily racism is worst." She could have added strangeness as well as variety because Swedes had found so many novel ways to assert their authority and power over outsiders.[210]

In many respects bias in media news reports and the depictions of aliens either solidified existing negative images or created new ones about outsiders. Among wrong concepts reporters implanted in readers' minds was associating spousal abuse with immigrant husbands; this linking completely ignored the problem of domestic violence in Swedish marriages. Seldom emphasized was a fact that native men were responsible for approximately 80 percent of all recorded wife-battering incidents. The press was also guilty of dehumanizing immigrants by dealing with them collectively instead of individually. Moreover, by using sensational headlines such as "Young immigrants in narcotics ring," "Polacks dump the prices," "Foreigner jailed for drug crimes," and "New immigrants behind Malmö's Social Welfare," publishers were guilty of aiding and abetting prejudice against aliens. Inflaming an indigenous population with article titles in bold print might have sold newspapers, but it also represented irresponsible journalism because native-immigrant relations suffered from sensationalism. Even in the choice of photographs, editors inscribed—as the phrase goes—a thousand words with a picture. Except to amuse readers at another culture's expense, *Dagens Nyheter* would be hard pressed to explain why it published a picture of a head-covered Muslim woman in an undergarment store, and only editors at *Sydsvenska Dagbladet Snällposten* could note why on two occasions photographs appeared in their newspaper of scarf-wearing Muslim girls at play kicking soccer balls. At least an editor from Göteborg was honest enough to confess "we write about them (refugees) when something dramatic happens or when there is a particular sin involving them."[211]

In Sweden's cradle-to-grave welfare system, sick and senior immigrants occasionally did not receive the same care and considerations as their Swedish counterparts. Had it not been for *Expressen*'s campaign and then the Handicap Ombudsman's resultant involvement, twelve-year old Arash Ghelichkan with Duchenne's disease might well have remained "a prisoner in my apartment," notwithstanding laws written to protect him as a mobility-challenged person. For three years the boy's mother had struggled with commune officials at the Solna housing authority for living quarters suitable to her son's special needs, but her efforts had gone nowhere. Then a combination of her hunger strike and an unrelenting publicity campaign by the newspaper finally yielded more suitable living accommodations. The case illustrates just how legislation could fail immigrants because of their inexperience with Sweden and bureaucratic indifference. Herewith medical personnel was most supportive of the family's special needs,[212] but such was not always true. Through work as an interpreter and personal experience, Noushin Nadjafi knew all about the ongoing effects of prejudice on the treatment of immigrant patients. "Many Swedes," she found, "have perceptions about foreigners beating their children and men mishandling their wives. . . . Women often get questions about men, and if the husbands are abusive." She also noted an episode of accompanying her five-year old son to Helsingborg hospital. As a trained nurse, the immigrant mother knew enough medicine to realize the boy's high fever and abdominal pain had resulted from infection, but rather than examine him thoroughly, the attending physician simply advised Nadjafi to "give him hugs and proper love" for what would later be diagnosed as a urinary-track infection and clearly not "parental lovelessness." Not only did doctors make false judgmental assumptions, they also tended to disbelieve immigrant patients. In Ridha Bouhlal's case, dentist Ola Saav was so afraid that he would not collect a final installment of 20,000 kronor from the alien that he locked the patient's lower dental prothesis in a cabinet as security against a final payment, thereby depriving Bouhlal of his bottom denture plate.[213]

For a majority of immigrant pensioners, another serious problem existed. Few 65-year old immigrants had reasons to expect Swedish retirements to begin their golden years. Coupled to nostalgic longings for their homelands, relatives, and friends left behind years earlier for new lives in a new country in northern Europe were the realities of spending time as outsiders in a strange land whose extraordinary programs for elderly people and excellent pension programs had not been established to accommodate the special situations and needs of diverse aliens. If they had never gained proficiency in the Swedish language, serious communications difficulties occurred at nursing homes and retirement centers. Since staff members, other patients, and fellow residents at these facilities were primarily Swedish, barriers to obtaining needed assistance and socializing existed to such extents that aliens found themselves depressed in lonely isolation and their caregivers with a major handicap to overcome in discharging proper aid to people who could not comprehend their instructions and questions.

For a majority of immigrant pensioners, another serious problem existed. Their years working in Sweden did not qualify them for fully vested pensions. Without enough registered quarters of Swedish employment, options became fourfold. To survive immigrant senior residents could depend upon children as many would have done had they remained in their homelands. Secondly they could apply for and live on welfare. For especially proud aliens, the ones who did not want to turn either to their children or to the state for help, choices then were working after age 65 or living in poverty. Finally and a preference of many retirees, the temptation of leaving Sweden and returning home lured many immigrants to the lands of their dreams.[214]

Sickness and old age obviously were not prerequisites for making aliens to feel special in Sweden. In one of many surveys conducted about attitudes, the following table demonstrates how ethnic Swedes judged the treatment of immigrants in relationship to their own. Participants were asked how often they believed immigrants in Sweden had been handled poorer than they had been by the same categories of interfaces. Stated in percentages, the opinion-poll results were:

Aliens Experiencing Specific Forms of Discrimination, given in percentages

Where/Who	NEVER	SELDOM	SOME	OFTEN	ALWAYS	UNSURE
Stores	8%	23%	44%	20%	1%	3%
Restaurants	8%	22%	39%	19%	1%	11%
Police	11%	19%	34%	24%	2%	10%
Caretakers	24%	34%	24%	6%	1%	11%
Employers	12%	23%	39%	21%	1%	6%
Neighbors	6%	16%	44%	26%	1%	7%

215

As much as the survey noted awareness of Swedes being prejudiced, its extent probably did not occur to them. In reality few institutions and actions were without some effects of unfairness and discrimination. These included a tour-bus company that restricted the number of immigrants on its shopping excursions to Germany, this measure to avoid travel delays on return trips to Sweden as a result of greater diligence paid to inspecting aliens' documents and purchases than to that of natives. Prejudged suspicions about foreigners being more likely to shoplift caused a Höör department store to prohibit foreigners from shopping there; uniformed security guards stood at entrance doors to enforce the policy. Restrictions in Malmö included selective realtors who refused to show, sell, or rent available houses and apartments to aliens.

Nonethnic-Swedes often experienced problems during military training. A Muslim in training to be a Swedish soldier abandoned without leave a post in Hässleholm because of fatigue; he had tried to live on rolls and milk because so much of a Swedish ration either consisted of pork or came in contact with Islam's forbidden meat. Hearing of the problem, the major in charge of the runaway soldier's training unit became defensive about the diet. As the officer responsible for armored-vehicle exercises, he justified the action with the claim that catering to special diets would be unrealistic during war. As he put it, "We should be in a drill for wartime, and then we could not continue to serve up special food to certain people." Many neo-Nazis and racists were in the Swedish army, and just their presence could make military life unbearable for ethnic recruits and explained in part a reluctance to serve. Thinking about Swedes and their relationships to outsiders, Uppsala bus driver Pradip Datta from India concluded Nordic natives were somewhat peculiar; he noted how "Swedes kiss dogs but will not sit next to an immigrant on the bus."[216]

A tendency to avoid people of different racial and ethnic backgrounds was strong, but nothing alarmed the native population more than immigrants who followed non-Christian religions. To grasp the roots of the intolerance, it is necessary to look back at a religious revolution that swept through Sweden between 1850 and 1950. At first in the aftermath of pietistic influence in the mid-1800s and a subsequent spreading of "free" churches, oppression by the government followed, causing an emigration to the United States. Toleration eventually replaced suppression, and the state guaranteed freedom of worship. Attitudinal change brought more fairness to churches which were independent from the established, state-subsidized Lutheran Church. Parliament approved tax-exempt status and subsidies for free churches. With better incomes, evangelical, penecostal, and baptist denominations built splendid houses of worship, expanded programs, sponsored missions, and hired full-time pastors. Everything was moving along acceptably; even a revival in Sweden of Roman Catholicism with the arrival of immigrants and refugees from Italy, Hungary, Croatia, Poland, and Chile did not upset *Pace di Gesù Cristo*. Martin Luther's relevance faded as Swedish adults no longer worshipped and children avoided confirmation. Growing ecumenical spirit and toleration seemingly correlated with dimishing faith and dropping church attendance. Achieving peace and harmony among Christian confessions represented modest achievement for a nation once as dogmatic about religion as any European country, but once it had become a reality among Christians, a much greater challenge to religious tolerance arose. It involved Muslims and the question of whether or not the same concepts of respect and religious freedom that all Christians were enjoying in Sweden should also be extended to followers of Islam.

Even when there were few Muslims in Sweden, their appeals for equal treatment caused difficulties. Quite simply Islam's organizational structure did not correspond to rules established for aiding "free" churches. Eligibility for a subsidy—according to a century-old church assistance model—was one that required a volunteer membership, a common ideological expression and interest, an operation dependent upon responsible members, and a democratic decision-making procedure. With Islam meeting none of the parameters, no legal grounds—without major special concessions and compromises—existed for state-sanctioned financial assistance. Moreover there were other obstacles to circumvent such as Islam's undefined structure. Whereas free churches had synods and councils, Muslims lacked a comparable representative body to tend to their interests. In addition their membership did not appear on rolls, and no believer could leave Islam. The notion of an individual having free will to quit the faith was an alien concept. Since Islam's faithful were more interested in obtaining help than Swedes were in granting it, the final outcome would not be doubtful. Muslims blinked first. In order to learn how to organize boards that would conform to Swedish standards, they attended democracy workshops in Flemmingsberg outside Stockholm.[217]

For Muslims adapting proved to be the easiest hurdle. Tougher tasks were gaining authority to construct mosques and winning acceptance in Swedish society. Even inactive state-church members reached a consensus about Islam's devotees. In general Swedes viewed Muslims as heathens who would benefit more in their new nation from converting to Chrisitianity than from being encouraged in their own faith. Researchers Åsa Brattlund and Jan Samuelsson discovered that "a negative position against Muslims exists among all categories of Swedes, even the well educated and those whose employment brought them into contact with refugees." They blamed this prejudice on mass media's depiction of Islam as the religion of ayatollahs, wars, fanaticism, and maltreatment of women.

No matter the roots of bias against Muslims, problems unfolded for them wherever and whenever permits were sought to build mosques. Clearly by the actions and deeds of foes, Swedish religious freedom applied to Christians and not to Mohammed's followers. A clear message went to faithful Muslims: if they wanted to face east and pray to Allah, Sweden was the wrong country. Hence as preludes to the relenting by local politicians with authorizations to build mosques, petitioners were forced to appeal often and fight protracked battles with communal councils over what supposedly was a guaranteed right in Sweden. Stubborn insistence in Göteborg ended in Strasburg at the European Court, and in Lund, after many frustrating years of rebuffs by local officials, Muslims finally gave up all hope of ever being able to erect a mosque there.[218]

Despite fears of Islam and Muslims, Swedes had insatiable curiosities about the religion and its followers. In response to the interest press editors responded to inform their readers about the different aspects of the religion and its influence over practitioners' lives. Thus articles covered such topics as *halal*-slaughtering rituals, burial procedures, observances during Ramadan, Koran teachings, gender roles, *Hajj* pilgrimages, honor murders, and feminism. In addition there were clarifications about how a "modern" Muslim woman could rationalize beliefs in Islam with liberation and women's rights.[219]

Information affected ethnic Swedes both negatively and positively. For intolerant reactionaries it reaffirmed opposition to having a group in their land with such different beliefs. Annoyed and displeased with an Islamic presence in "their country," foes expressed themselves in several ways. In Trollhättan the local mosque became a favorite target. In front of this house of prayer on March 14, 1992, xenophobes planted and set ablaze a gasoline-soaked, seven-foot cross. Then eighteen months later, direct protest escalated to arson. As a result fire totally engulfed the building before gutting it. Elsewhere phoned threats were common. Callers noted their intention to blow up mosques with bombs. There were also milder offenses against Muslims such as intimidating women and girls to remove their head coverings.

In Landskrona Muslims were at the center of a unique conflict. To save money in the operation of school cafeterias in the city, local authorities decided on a solution without considering its neglative effect upon children whose faith forbade pork consumption. School officials announced a plan to stop offering alternative hot lunches on those days when the forbidden meat would be on the menu. Responding with a city-wide portest, Muslim parents kept their children at home. Finally after a week-long boycott school officials relented, dropping their disrespectful savings plan.[220]

In fairness to good Swedes, genuine efforts at comprehending different religious traditions and offering compassion to victims of hate and ignorance were made as counters to violence and disrespect. In Trollhättan, for example, during rededication ceremonies to celebrate the completion of a replacement mosque for what terrorists had deliberately destroyed, the new prayer facility filled to capacity with Muslim, Christian, and Jewish celebrants for a joyous occasion. As the city's representatives from the Swedish established church, the Reverends Gunnar Prytz and Bengt Wilgot Johansson came with presents and support from their parishes. Citing the Koran, Johansson gave a message of hope about how "Good deeds come through belief, and gardens come into existence from forward-moving brooks." Demonstrating respect differently at a graveside service, Vicar Anders Nisbel of Linköping's Berga Church reached out to Muslims while presiding over a burial service that mixed Islamic and Christian elements. To the usual God in three persons, the church official added a fourth for this solemn occasion, causing the Trinity to become "in the name of the Father, Allah, the Son, and Holy Ghost," an inclusion that would raise questions about whether or not Nisbel had violated his ordination vows. After noting personal doubts about the wisdom of the pastor's inclusion of Allah, his bishop, Martin Lind, wishing no ramifications or ill will, let the deviation pass.[221]

Insofar as education's relationship to church and state, the two estates had been integral parts of Swedish schools until secularizers increasingly tried after 1950 to separate the two elements. Under supervision and control of the parish priest from the establishment of the Lutheran Church, connection found expression once in such school activities and traditions as reading the Bible, praying, studying Christianity in religion classes, singing hymns, observing church holy days, and worshipping in parish churches. By 1990 with the official legal status of Swedish public education supposedly neutral, environments at state-run facilities still retained much of the old system. A visit to almost any public school in Sweden during the weeks leading up to a December recess would result in observing and hearing much that was partial to Christianity. Manifestations include advent lights in school windows, Lucia and Christmas pageants, carols about Jesus Christ's birth, and wishes of God Jul (Merry Christmas) to everyone as schools closed for a fortnight to mark a celebrated religious event. In contrast during Ramadan, or the ninth month of the Islamic calendar when Muslims fasted, nothing special was evident except perhaps pupils skipping lunches and arriving at school somewhat more exhausted and unprepared than at other times during the schoolyear. In terms of inappropriateness for alleged neutral education, skolavslutningarna (the formal ceremonies that ended schoolyears) offended many non-Christians most of all. To honor the conclusion of another academic year and the start of summer holidays, students—dressed often in their best clothing—followed an old tradition of parading from school to the parish church for a semi-religious ceremony in music and verse.

As much as firmly implanted Swedish school traditions embarrassed and offended non-Christian pupils, other equally negative attributes of the state-run school system affected and impacted immigrant students. Cities of 50,000 or more inhabitants were home to the overwhelming majority of Sweden's aliens, and their residences were generally found in foreigner enclaves on municipal outskirts. With children from these areas attending neighborhood schools, it meant that a large proportion were effectively enrolled in "segregated" institutions with few ethnic Swedish students. Beginning with preschool and moving through grade nine, Sweden operated what amounted to two separate school systems, one for the offspring of foreigners and another for native children. During schoolyear 1995-1996, for example, the enrollment of the junior high school in Rinkeby exceeded 400 students, but only sixteen of the youngsters had Swedish ethnic backgrounds. Johanna Gustavsson was one of them, and although she had an awareness from an early age of her special status, adjustment came easily for her in this environment: "I am born and raised here in Rinkeby. I do not think that I am different, and I feel much more like one of them [nodding toward schoolmates] than I ever feel Swedish, you know."

Attending a school where classmates had begun their studies in Sweden with 35 different first languages was not particularly beneficial to developing language skills among native speakers. Exposure to incorrect Swedish often affected their speech, and needs for help and remedial work among immigrant children generally held back classroom progress and slowed advancement to new concepts. Here in Rinkeby like at other schools that served primarily an alien student body, a high percentage of pupils had refugee backgrounds. In many cases it could mean lag periods in their studies both before and after their arrivals in Scandinavia. Although Swedish law entitled children to instruction during their residence at camps, many negative forces operated to impede satisfactory educational development.

In similar way legislation in principle guaranteed extra assistance to all youngsters from homes where Swedish was a secondary language. There was to be additional instruction both for mastering a new language and improving an original language, but funding for these twin goals was almost always subject to reductions whenever budgetary cuts occurred. Worse the revenue lost for immigrant language training was often disproportionately more severe than the suffering by other educational programs.

Results from disparities, of course, were evident. Swedish youngsters were much more likely to begin and finish *gymnasieskola* (secondary school) than alien counterparts. Grades proved another indicator of student progress. At the end of the 1999-2000 schoolyear for Malmö ninth graders, 2 percent of students at Berga School in affluent Limhamn received a failing mark in least one key subject. At predominantly alien Rosengård School, 52 percent flunked a course. Interim rector Johannes Schad understood why the failure rate had been so high at the latter institution; "when parents are jobless . . . many pupils do not think making an effort is worthwhile." Among the 427 teachers in Rosengård, burnout was high. The cause was having to deal with troubled youngsters who "steal 95 percent of all time." As remedies these instructors wanted smaller classes and a school psychologist assigned to the worst problem children.[222]

The ministry of education's primary task was providing every boy and girl with equal school experiences, but Swedish parents like American fathers and mothers knew better educational opportunities existed at some schools and not at others. Hence when family finances permitted moves to better districts, Swedes, like counterparts in the United States, fled areas with bad schools for different neighborhoods with better ones; young Gustavsson's family was on a waiting list to move, too. Efforts at times to find a more suitable school than a facility where outsiders predominated could be based more on perception than on reality. Natives, and to some degree non-Swedes, simply assumed a school without many foreign pupils would be superior. In some instances, according to a nationally administered standard test, students at ghetto schools did as well as or better than boys and girls at institutions with mostly Swedish youngsters. Yet whenever ghetto children performed better than Swedish pupils, it would become newsworthy as an astonishing accomplishment.[223]

As much as possible the Ministry of Education seemed to try to achive its stated goal of equalizing of schools, but some immigrant parents wanted nothing to do with public education. Muslim parents did not appreciate their children's exposures to family-living, sex-education, and coeducational physical-education classes. Dancing and course work that subjected pupils to such controversial western ideals as male-female equality and respect along with nondiscrimination for homosexuals caused parental concern. On the outskirts of Göteborg in Bergsjön, a group of Somalians had become so upset with Gärdsmosse School because of their children's contact with alleged "bad" influences that they met with administrators and teachers to express their concerns. In this case, except for both sides having heard arguments for different perspectives, discussions yielded neither major changes nor breakthroughs in school policy.

In efforts to escape either Swedish propaganda and liberal perspectives about contemporary issues or immigrant children, two groups with opposite agendas found a common solution in private schools. Despite the objections to independent and parochial institutions from old guard socialists like Blomberg, who were adamantly opposed on the grounds these schools promoted elitism and isolation, the popularity of private schools proved greater than their foes' determination to stop them. Every year between 1990 and 2001, several new free schools opened in Sweden. They offered alternative educations either for pupils whose parents disliked the academic standards and discipline—the code for too many immigrant students—at public schools or for the children whose families sought Islamic-inspired training.[224]

There was another reason why alien parents preferred either private or ghetto schools to ones with largely Swedish enrollments. Their children were less likely to be bullied. As the products of homes with adults who expressed prejudicial opinions about foreigners, native children naturally came to school with what they had heard their elders say about certain nationalities, religions, races, and ethnic groups. All too often such talk resulted in intimidating and teasing outsiders. For evidence look at the experiences of Elham Sateei and Zoya Yusefi. The first child arrived in Sweden, expecting a pleasant life filled with new friends, but her schoolmates quickly dashed her dreams. Teased and humiliated, she lost all sense of belonging. Due to incessant badgering, Yusefi wanted to leave school. Afraid incorrectly spoken Swedish would only worsen matters, she did not dare to participate in class discussions.

Given a numerical advantage, alien children did not behave any better. Learning a substitute teacher was Jewish, three fourteen-year old boys from the Apelgård School in Rosengård verbally assaulted and taunted him with racial slurs. The students' repeated use of "sieg heil" and "Jew swine" resulted in the victim going to police to file charges against the boys.

To many alien students with Swedish friends, enduring dark moments were an important right of passage to acceptance. In attempts at removing the obstacles to understanding, schools of education devoted pedagogic training to intercultural activities and to textbook-content alterations. According to logic behind these moves, future teachers needed to have their consciousness raised in order to give issues an international perspective. Therefore a cleansing out of objectionable materials from course-lesson plans was necessary.[225]

Desperate at times because of pressures to act, school officials suggested both reasonable and ridiculous solutions to the cleft between foreign and native students. Concluding Malmö already had enough non-Swedes in its schools, Superintendent of Schools Hans Persson proposed a stop to additions. To keep more immigrants from settling in the city, he advised that new settlers should not be eligible for welfare payments. As expected the city's alien community reacted angrily to Persson. Enraged by the implications of this undemocratic, racist plan, Social Democratic youth-section member Luciano Astudillo led a protest by foes to Persson's idiotic scheme. "As immigrants we feel ourselves being pointed out as a virus, a sickness in an otherwise healthy body." Fearing evil consequences from Persson's statement, Astudillo imagined it—and others like it—would stir xenophobia to a level when "within ten years we risk having the same development here in Sweden as they have had in Austria where most recently rightwing politician Jörg Haider almost won election with practically Nazified opinions."[226]

Since classroom overcrowding in Malmö—as in many Swedish cities with concentrated immigrant populations—existed primarily in Rosengård, there were proposals to transport children to the neighborhoods where schools were not experiencing density problems. With extra space and too few pupils, Limhamn's Berga Junior High School agreed to participate in a pilot program. By the experiment twenty-seven carefully chosen students from Värner Rydén School in Rosengård attended classes at Berga on March 21, 2000. Reflecting on a day of amazement, visitors expressed astonishment that two schools could be so different. As Enisa Salja summarized differences, "Here [at Berga] is so calm and nice. We are used to disturbances and fights. . . . I hope that I have permission to go here." It was her wish after a positive school day.[227]

Given Sweden's inability to react positively to the educational needs of immigrant children, aliens who expected better from national universities and specialized training institutions only found disappointment. Asked to provide statistics about outsiders in attendance or on the faculty at Lund University, an official claimed such information as this had never been collected, a somewhat odd confession in light of Sweden's passion to gather data on every other conceivable subject. Therefore only circumstantial evidence exists from which to form bases for a judgment about whether Lund and sister institutions were guilty of practicing discrimination. Through stories that have highlighted non-Swedes' attendance at various institutions of higher learning, newspapers have inadvertly offered some indirect evidence. If one follows the old adage about dog bites man is not news but man bites dog is news, then the coverage occurred because of its newsworthiness as a Swedish rarity. Clearly reflecting a "Sweden-for-Swedes" mentality, universities have long suffered from inbred faculties. Lund University always formally introduces new appointees at gala installation ceremonies, and if the 2000 event was any indication of whom the university has been hiring as professors, then its professional staff suffers from insularity and provincialism. Judging by the surnames of the thirty-five newly appointed faculty for 2000, one could easily discern that only a few members of the group lacked German or Scandinavian ethnicity. The obvious bias in the selection process defied the existence of a large pool of refugees with excellent academic credentials and experiences and with a potential to add *uni* to Lund – *versity*.

There were also complaints about blatant racism at Lund. Charges involved actions by both faculty and students. During parades associated with LU's quadrennial carnevals, crude strains of racism not unlike what this university had experienced during the 1930s might lead to the conclusion that a restrictive social club atmosphere still thrives at the institution. Floats with whites in blackface meandered through Lund during both 1994 and 1998, and worse than the racism on display was the deafening silence from university officials. Rather than rebuke students for depicting cannibals, a Swede posing as "Shaka Zulu" won first-place honors and 10,000-kronor for impersonating an African male. Fitting a general pattern of segregated education, Södertörn College opened to 1,200 students on August 23, 1996. Located in a Stockholm ghetto, it reflected a general impression in Sweden that alien youths without an academic background should have their own college.[228]

In theory for immigrant adults, Sweden offered a complete educational program. Studying Swedish by far was the most popular introductory course. Without a mastery of the language, students could not continue their studies. In effect a failure to achieve competency excused discrimination and exclusion. This problem had not always prevailed. In 1973 when workers were scarce and jobs were plentiful, the government and employers launched a most effective work-study plan. Under it employees while at work received hourly wages as they learned Swedish. At 240 hours of language study spread over thirty weeks, the cooperative plan had one major fault. It could function only during a period of low unemployment. Whenever foremen could choose from a large pool of workers, hiring non-Swedish speakers did not make much sense. The result was an end to the program in 1986.

Thereafer, *Sfi* (*svenska för invandrare* or Swedish for immigrants) instruction entered a state of flux. With study stipends going to students, discussions occurred about whether or not it would be fair to penalize the immigrants who abandoned language programs. Uncertain about how to improve performance, pedagogs, in attempts at finding an effective approach, debated teaching methodology. The suggestion from Queen Silvia to fellow immigrants to speak better Swedish was one of the silliest bits of advice that emerged during debates over language. Her Swedish was not only imperfect grammatically, but it had a heavy Germanic tone. As much as she probably meant well, her advice directly served racists who had attributed their failures to hire immigrants to poor commands of Swedish.

In addition to trying to teach outsiders a Scandinavian language, the nation offered a full range of other educational programs. At the bottom was *grundvux* (basic adult education) for illiterate immigrants, and then there was *komvux* (literally high school for adults) for more advanced studies. Training people for specific jobs was *AMUs* (*arbetsmarknadsutbildnings* or job-market training's) responsibility. It was not unusual for foreigners—and Swedes—to become stuck literally in one of these programs. Yet after a threatened cutback of money for alien education in Göteborg, Somalians complained that funding still existed for native children's participations in "such things as horsemanship, *innebandy* [indoor bandy] and Tai Chi."

Extravagance and general inconsistency characterized several immigrant-education programs. Although a trip to America resulted in a fascinating experience for participants, sending eight residents from Rosengård to the United States on an alleged fact-finding mission in 1999 exemplified government wastefulness. The basic premise behind continuing education was challenged by Economist Dan-Olof Rooth. It was his finding that the addition of more terms of Swedish schooling "has [had] no statistically positive effects, and sometimes even a negative effect, on the probability of [aliens] being employed." His research led to a conclusion that Swedish work experiences counted for more than time invested in education or training.[229]

Moreover residential segregation was behind many alien problems. On the peripheries of every Swedish metropolis, large apartment blocks have been housing immigrants and *social* (down-and-out individuals living on welfare) Swedes for more than a generation. To anyone viewing these complexes from 500 meters, everything appears pleasant, modern, and liveable. After a closer examination, they reveal something entirely different, however. Being areas methodically avoided by Swedes with other options, these communities early in their histories assumed all the characteristics of a ghetto enclave. Residing in a project signified entrapment and stigmatization. In Sweden, despite boasts of a prevalence of such cherished ideals as *jämlighet*, a wrong address became an identity badge soon after the construction and settlement of large housing estates on municipal outskirts. To measure reaction after 1990, a stranger to Stockholm would only need to mention Rinkeby to a Swedish resident of this city or say Rosengård to a counterpart in Malmö. In both instances negative responses and grimness would likely result.[230]

The process of ghettoization occurred for different reasons, but always the consequences were similar. Both private realtors and communal housing authorities either forced or steered immigrants into residence parks at the edge of cities. By refusing to show, rent, or sell apartments to outsiders, agents often left immigrants choiceless. Many other aliens freely decided, without coercion and influence, to live in ghettos because of their proximities to both relatives and countrymen. Interestingly whatever the cause or motivation, surveys of Swedish opinion revealed less hostility to having immigrants for neighbors than what real-estate companies had perceived.

Sociologist Kirsti Kuusela discovered the circulation of two myths, and both would be shown as false. According to one communes had a practice of assigning only the best places to immigrants, but in point of fact "they get those places which Swedes do not want." The second myth claimed aliens were responsible for most problems in their outlying housing parks. More often than not, it was not they, but Swedish drug addicts and single mothers with social problems. "Older Swedes," noted Malmö property-management executive Per-Henrik Hartmann, "often react impetuously when a tenant with a foreign name moves in. It is evident that we are influenced by this."

Overgeneralizing could lead to irritation as *Malmö Kommunala Bostäder* or *MKB* (Malmö Communal Residences) discovered from an attempt to obtain tenants' reactions to alien neighbors. Asked to rate from one to five the truth or fallacy of the statement, "I think it should be nice to have an immigrant family as neighbors," *MKB* resident Magnus Nilsson considered the inquiry "a remarkable and disagreeable question" because for him "it does not play any role if the neighbor is an immigrant or a skinhead so long as the person is a good neighbor." With property one other matter tended to grate increasingly on Swedes. Foreigners purchasing *stugor* (summer cottages) was "a nightmare for many Swedes: the Germans are buying up Sweden."[231]

Whatever factors had accounted for ghettoizing, every measure of a life standard or of an amenity indicated just how important a location could be to personal well-being in Sweden. No matter if it were the number of aborted fetuses, access to nighttime public transportation, automobile ownership per 100 residents, convenient banking, health resources, personal income, welfare dependency, daycare, police protection, or the maintenance of public facilities, ghetto areas fared disproportionately poorer than other neighborhoods in those cities where demographers have collected data. With ample justifications and for good reasons, reporters Maciej Zaremba and David Lagercrantz were not exaggerating when they referred respectively to Gävle's Gimo as "racist hole number three in Sweden" and Stockholm's Alby as "Sweden's worst suburb, . . . our Bronx, our most precarious ghetto."

Yet, on the positive side, outlying areas were vibrant and cosmopolitan. Norrköping's Navestad and Marielund, Rosengård, Rinkeby, Norra Fäladen, and upwards of forty other similar residential entities across Sweden were not nearly as sterile as other communities. Everybody did not look like one of the *Svenssons*—mom, dad, or their blond-headed children—and nor was every other parked vehicle a car with a ski rack, a boat, or a caravan. The fact that Rinkeby was known as "the global village" swelled her residents with civic pride. Malmö boasted of 161 different nationalities, and considerably smaller Lund had 124. As much as each ethnic group's survival relied upon its own inner strength, a consensus was reached among Sweden's ghetto dwellers that potential benefits could result if they and Swedes developed opportunities for interaction and had less isolation from one another.

Both natives and outsiders agreed that general reporting on ghetto life and problems was one-sided and biased. The indigenous public was curious about occurrences in outlying housing estates, and the press used sensational headlines such as "weapon pause in Rinkeby center" to feed on this interest. Three of four Stockholm daily newspapers—*Dagens Nyheter*, *Aftonbladet*, and *Expressen*—each covered Rinkeby in a series of articles which dealt with the neighborhood as if it were an exotic city in a distant foreign country. Evidence notwithstanding, Justice Minister Freivalds could still mendaciously tell an interviewer that "we have no ghettos in Sweden" without receiving so much as a listener's murmur of challenge to an erroneous claim.[232]

At roughly 18 percent, immigrants represented seemingly a large enough constituency to coalesce into a powerful political force in democratic Sweden, one so strong that it should have had capacity to push through changes such as enactment of meaningful laws for curtailing most forms of discrimination and segregation in employment, education, and housing. With achievement of no notable accomplishments and much to do legislatively to protect minority rights, one might ask what occurred politically to render outsiders so powerless over their own futures. In theory at least Swedish democracy has provided more generous terms for citizenship and offered better opportunities for noncitizens' participation and inclusion in the political process than other nations. Voting in local elections became a privilege after 1975 for everyone over eighteen-years old and three years of residency in Sweden. For noncitizen members of the Church of Sweden, meeting basic voting requirements have also made them eligible to vote in church-board elections. Moreover any citizen of a European Union member state has voting privileges for Swedish delegates to the EU parliament. With generally liberal terms available for full citizenship and possibilities for residential aliens to influence elections at several levels, outsiders seemingly have had enough power at their disposal to alter disagreeable aspects of living in Sweden.

For minorities neither the securing nor the brokering of real political power has ever occurred, however. Successive elections from 1976 through 1998 have shown declining immigrant interest and participation in Swedish politics. As a group for this timeframe their voting percentage has gone from 60 percent to less than 40 percent. Chileans at over 62 percent were the minority most likely to have voted in 1991, and Finns at roughly 38 percent demonstrated the least desire for participation. "Get-out-the-vote" campaigns among aliens ironically appeared to have been counterproductive, producing fewer and not more voters on election days.[233]

Analysts gave many explanations for declining voter turnouts. Apathy, unfamiliarity with the political system, issues and platforms, and/or candidates, cynicism, language problems, weak solidarity with Swedes and society, doubts about influence, and homeland-focused interests—and not those of the adopted land—and problems were common reasons citied. Greek migrant to Sweden and ex-*riksdag* member Alexander Chrisopoulos—whose political departure in 1991 left the legislature temporarily without alien representation—interpreted matters alternatively. As a *vänster* party member, he naturally enough gave a Marxian twist to this gradual abandonment of traditional electoral politics by outsiders. Lost interest, concluded Chrisopoulos, had not come as a result of immigrant status; rather it had been due to the fact that aliens largely belonged to an increasingly marginalized working class. Rojas, in contrast, attributed a decline in voting to the fear major political parties had of offending racists and xenophobes, hence their unwillingness "to gamble on immigrants." The Chilean academician suspected in final analysis that "immigrants were having the same problems in politics as [they were] in society generally; they are not entering in."

Compositions of the national unicameral assembly confirmed adherence to "a Swedes-only" membership policy. From 1990 to 2001, fewer than five different non-Nordic delegates served. After the 1998 election, Nalin Baksi replaced Fonseca as the only representative without roots either in Sweden or in a neighboring country. She was a devoutly Muslim Kurdish emigrant from Turkey with a reputation for restraint. Caught in a candid mood, she refused to make her usual excuses for Sweden's failtures to deal fairly with immigrants. Given this rare moment in candor for a reporter was a bold utterance that the nation was a "white males' society; it is dreadful and is the explanation for low voter participation among immigrants." Gaining alien support and confidence in the political process would require more than placing three foreigners at the head of a May Day procession of leading Social Democratic marchers in 1998 as had been done in Stockholm on May 1. It would also demand more than using a happy-faced, little brown-and-white figure of a man as a symbol of a political party as the Social Democrats did at the same event in 2000.[234]

Immigrants' opportunities at communal and county levels of government or in political-party organizations were no better than they were for joining the *riksdag*. Combined for three levels of government—national, county, and township—as the following table notes, non-Europeans held five offices after the 1994 general election.

Total non-Swedes by Category & Party in National, County, Township Governments, 1994

PARTY	Other Nordic	Other European	Non-European	TOTAL
Environment	9	6	1	16
Left	9	4	2	15
Social Democrat	6	2	1	9
Moderate	4	3	0	7
New Democrat	7	0	0	7
Folk	4	2	0	6
Christian Demo.	4	2	0	6
Center	2	1	0	3
All Other	6	3	1	10

235

The 1998 general election did not improve matters. A check of fifty-three communes closest to Göteborg—in an area known as *Västsverige* (West Sweden)—reveals the extent of alien powerlessness. From a total of 2,413 township council members, forty-eight were born outside the Nordic region. With seven of seventy-three councilmen, Borås' record was best both in terms of numbers and percentages. At 9.6 percent of all seats, non-Nordic aliens had slightly more people in government than what their percentage of inhabitants might justify. Borås had 96,214 residents; 8,243 of these, or 8.6 percent of the township population, had non-Nordic roots. Going a step higher in the power structure of government to check into the fifty-three communal executive boards for non-Nordic members, one uncovers only four persons at this level: a Russian woman who came to Sweden in 1947, a Dutch woman who arrived in 1952, and two former West Germans who had spent twenty-eight and almost forty years in Scandinavia. According to Aurell Baldauf who had migrated to the Nordic kingdom in 1948 and who had obviously adapted well to Sweden's prejudices, "they [board members] must sit still and wait until it is their turn to talk. It is not for sure that this will work for all immigrants."[236]

Of outsiders who managed to overcome great odds to gain political offices, two types emerged. One was Sweden's equivalent of an "Uncle Tom," women and men who praised everything and criticized nothing. Ismail Kamil fit nicely into this classification. As a Kurd from Syria, he described his time in Sweden as follows: "I came to Sweden [in 1976], and I won everything: democracy, being met with respect, [knowledge] people can have worth, [and] even the climate." The Folk Party placed Kamil's name second on its listing of candidates for the county council in Uppsala. By Swedish standards the Kurd exemplified how every immigrant should feel about life in Sweden; he showed humility, gratitude, and praise.

At the other extreme were aliens like Fonseca who gained political posts because of their foreign backgrounds and who used their offices as forums to degrade Sweden and demand radical changes favorable to outsiders. Despite being a popular public figure among fellow aliens, the Colombian in no time became persona nongrata in the Social Democratic Party. Accustomed to his enemies' threats and harassment, he found them now even shocking him with how low they were willing to stoop to ruin him politically. Included among the actions was a foolish attempt before the 1998 election to link Fonseca to fraud. It backfired because the plotters had conceived it so poorly. From its start Rinkeby's spokesperson understood perfectly well what was happening to him. As he noted for supporters, "they [his enemies] will do whatever it takes to stop me." Opposition and torment only added to Fonseca's resolve to continue. "I do not intend to give up," he promised. "There are both foes inside the party and outside who disapprove of me, but now it has gone too far. This is criminal [a reference here to a hacker invading Fonseca's homepage to threaten him, his wife, and young son]."[237]

Frustration with established political parties led to periodic discussions among immigrants about the feasibility of them forming a coalition. Thus at different times in Uppsala, Stockholm, and Malmö, alien leaders threatened to offer their people an alternative slate of candidates. Each time efforts did not go beyond discussions or did not develop into substantial movements. Just the idea of immigrants bolting was frightening enough for the established political parties to result in their warnings of dire consequences for Sweden and aliens. Careful at first to empathize with "the frustration among the new Swedes," an editor of *Expressen* in 1998 then proceeded to connect every imaginable horror to the idea of starting party based upon "different skin color and ethnicity." For evidence the writer advised readers to look at Rwanda, the Balkans, Nazi Germany, and the United States—places where race and origins mattered so much as conditions for belonging to political parties—to determine if they wanted something similar to occur in Sweden. He promised the development of an equally strong or stronger reaction if aliens in Sweden were successful at uniting politically.

Although Fonseca's position would change after his misfortunes in the *Riksdag*, Social Democrats took a somewhat different stand toward the Latin American leader in 1993 when they imagined him with a bright future in their party. Fonseca then was viewing the idea of an immigrant party as something that "should be interpreted as a desperate move. It can be a cry in the desert against being outsiders." It was his advice then for fellow aliens to "go into the Swedish society . . . and demand influence . . . against the egotism that is increasingly spreading in Sweden."[238]

Although difficult to organize on account of the splintering of foreigners into groups, their receiving of grants that disallowed political involvement, and the lingering of discord between different ethnic and national peoples, protests by immigrant minorities in Sweden still represented the best hope for progress. Several public displays occurred for one cause or another, but demonstrations tended to unite a particular ethnic group for a stand on behalf of or against one action and to be local efforts like a gathering of Kurds and Iraqis in Malmö on

April 4, 1991. They had assembled to express opposition to Saddam Hussein's brutality in Iraq.

One exception to the rule of disunity did develop. As with the growth of kudzu vine, a massive movement spread among immigrants to stage a united work stoppage. The goal of organizers was to gain recognition of foreigners as important contributors to the Swedish economy. Declared a strike by its steering committee, an orchestrated event of doing no work began at ten on the morning of February 21, 1992—the United Nations' day against racism—, and it lasted officially for two minutes. Among other things, storekeepers closed their shops, cooks abandoned kitchens, and the conveyor belts stopped at the Saab automobile assembly plant in Trollhättan. Hailed a success in terms of its participation and support, the curtailment of activity was a failure insofar as its results. What had begun as a demonstration by aliens quickly evolved into a farce because almost every man, woman, and child participated. It also turned into a telegenic opportunity for politicians to discuss an interest in everybody's rights and to pose for photographs with immigrants.[239]

Integrating into and adjusting to a new society have never been easy for newcomers to any nation, but these tasks were even harder for non-Europeans coming to an insular nation like Sweden. With an established culture and a set structure operated for and administered by an indigenous people, a majority of the Nordic kingdom's residents implied by their words and deeds that if there were to be any adapting, it must not be they but outsiders who should accept new ways. This explains the nature of a populistic revolt that occurred across Sweden. Natives had determination to preserve a nation they knew and loved. On the other hand, politicians—especially Social Democrats—, by unplanned duplicity, voiced their old concerns for the downtrodden people who had come to Sweden but acted only on behalf of fellow Swedes' concerns.

Herein was the conflict with an official government position that would explain why programs from the outset were doomed to failure. Swedes acting through their elected officials expected and demanded that outsiders accept an inferior position in society and assimilate. Meanwhile politicians pretended to preach toleration and multiculturalism. Since it was the people who interfaced with immigrants and decided the terms of these relationships, the only effects of stated programs in the final analysis were mixed messages and confusion. Double-talking officeholders wanted to appear as generous as possible to the immigrant electorate, but they did not want to push Svensson into supporting outspoken xenophobes. As alien groups were being subsidized to hold onto and perpetuate traditions, Swedes in public office advised members of these organizations to incorporate themselves into Swedish life.

Successful immigrants—ones who had buried, hidden, or subordinated their old lives while they rejoiced publicly about everything acquired from a blissful existence in Sweden—unwittingly helped the charade. Such favorites as Ludmila Engqvist, Queen Silvia, and Cyndee Peters won over the hearts of natives by punctuating interviews with statements of endearment for "their" *Sverige* (Sweden). There was a bit of irony in this, too. While Swedes loved to hear praise, they were negative toward many aspects of their nation. It was perfectly normal for them to express pessimism, criticisms, and melancholy, but any comparable attitudes or statements from immigrants were considered a personal affront to Sweden and ingratitude for the opportunity to reside there in a Nordic paradise.

Other factors are also worthy of noting. It was acceptable for natives to borrow from foreigners, but impositions by aliens on Swedes were forbidden. Thus Swedish youths freely copied foreign youths' habits, speech, and dress, and aliens could entertain and educate by teaching Swedes how to tango, sing gospel, or belly dance. The key in these instances was in the instigation. The reality was that Swedes always chose what they wanted to take from the many different cultures present in Sweden. Finally deference and politeness proved very helpful to immigrants. The Chinese who came to Sweden from Vietnam blended quietly into Nordic society because they did not complain, impose, or demand. In most cases Swedes reacted positively to the deferring demeanors of most Southeast Asians.[240]

Sweden's poor were generally immigrants, and as such they developed complete subcultures. These either reflected an immitation of what they had brought from homelands or had become a hybrid of the past and of discoveries from living in Scandinavia. As different statistical measures indicate, outsiders had the lowest income levels. A parliamentary committee on immigration policy released a 1996 report entitled "Sweden, the future and diversity?." Among other things in its conclusion, non-European aliens tended, regardless of their education and previous work experiences, to consume less and to be at lower income levels than the other segments of Swedish society. Plain and simple, noted the study, these aliens were the most likely persons to become excluded and to be marginalized. Moreover for life's necessities, they and others from outside the Nordic region had the greatest dependency on welfare.

Evidence abounds for the correctness of these conclusions. A look at income figures per ethnic group reveals that Swedes averaged 201,900 kronor in 1994. At the bottom Turks and Somalians had respective incomes of only 118,700 and 120,900 kronor. Such figures caused reflections and comparisons, but worse for equalitarian-minded Swedes, scholars now were discussing an emergence of "a new underclass." This was an embarrassing reality for a nation that had prided itself in knowing that hopeless poverty only existed elsewhere. In 1992 *Göteborgs-Posten* published a revealing series entitled in English, "ONE CITY TWO WORLDS." Articles compared mostly Swede-inhabitated Näset to alien-dominated Lövgärdet. Income statistics for 1989 showed Swedish families in their enclave averaging 259,000 kronor while Lövgärdet households having less than half as much or 120,000 kronor. Money was only one factor separating two city neighborhoods. Neither side of town really was comprehending how the other lived. Ignorance led to myths and false generalizations. For example ten-year old Natalie from the immigrant area imagined that "Swedes were a little tricky." Moreover, the willingness to admit to domestic shortcomings meant that pictures of despair and hopelessness on television and in the press were suddenly originating from Jönköping, Sweden, and not—quite as much as earlier—from Appalachia or Harlem.[241]

To survive in a hostile environment, aliens in Sweden did what outsiders have done so many times elsewhere; they networked to form their own special institutions. With literally several thousand examples from which to illustrate the nature and diversity of their formations, a mention of just a few will suffice as verifications of the mixed developments within miniscule societal units that were emerging outside the mainstream of official or traditional activities. As a way of combating increased drug use among immigrants and their offspring, Dr. Riyadh Albaldawi knew he and other alien health providers could obtain better results than the Swedish medical community. After all, he concluded, a foreign doctor understood how aliens might expect a reprisal like deportation or imprisonment from going with a drug-related problem to someone at a state-run clinic. Knowing the reluctance of immigrant abusers to seek needed professional assistance to break an addiction was what led Albaldawi and some medical associates to form *SIMON* (*svenska invandrare mot narkotikamissbruk* or Swedish immigrants against drug use). Since it was an agency without any direct affiliation to regular public-health channels, it could reassure as it went about curing clients who had been afraid to become patients at Swedish clinics or hospitals.

To provide a mechanism to fight cultural oppression and attain respect, Arabian, Albanian, and Roma women joined forces in Malmö and forged an immigrant women's network. Their motto of "give us justice, not charity" characterized a common resolve for improvement. On another front, just as there was suspicion of Swedish medical practice, distrust also existed for the Swedish judicial system. Several immigrant groups subsequently established their own legal apparati to deal with a range of issues that covered everything from divorce to harassment. In cases of wives suspected of infidelity, Turkish immigrants ignored Swedish law to empathize with husbands who had beaten adulterous spouses. What was spousal abuse to Swedes was considered to be acceptable retaliation to Turks. It would be utterly pointless for such women to complain about domestic violence to Swedish police or seek civil divorces since the inner community neither recognized nor accepted official responses. Among this alien minority verdicts from extralegal proceedings carried more authority and impacted with greater effect. Peers who had judged a wife guilty of having betrayed her husband concluded with family and friends that ostracism and public humiliation were deserved consequences for adultery.[242]

Swedish prisons provide excellent evidence of societal inbalance and prejudice. The number of inmates with immigrant backgrounds surged disproportionately to the percentage of aliens in the total population. In Swedish criminology experts have long accepted the premises that criminals are made and not born, that responsibility for crimes rests with environmental factors, and that long sentences after convictions are based upon false societal determiners such as partiality and fear. Yet in the case of immigrant violators of law, harshness tended to push aside all theoretical reasoning. Swedes were more likely to report crimes committed by aliens, and again foreigners developed a feeling of marginalization.

Worthlessness and low personal esteem occurred early in the lives of many youths with non-Swedish backgrounds. As inferiority complexes and negative self-images grew, so did alienation. Even when these young people had been born in Sweden, they increasingly saw themselves as outsiders who needed to battle for respect and recognition. Already by adolescence because of a perceived low position in society and not many prospects for productive futures, anger and frustration often began to be exhibited in antisocial activity. Detrimental behavior included gang activities and a moral code based around toughness and fights with "svennar" (immigrant slang for Swedes). Among a large number, a nihilistic philosophy of life prevailed. As one hostile young man explained his reactions to living in Sweden, "I shit on the society that has shit on me." When asked to explain why smashing a new Porsche with a chain had resulted, another youth justified his rage by saying, "I become damned furious only from hearing the word Östermalm (Stockholm's most exclusive section)."

By 1990 immigrant youths between the ages of fifteen and eighteen accounted for twice as many solved crimes as their native counterparts. As much as grim reality might have already warned society then of the dire consequences from not acting constructively to address abuses which aliens had been enduring, corrective steps would not occur in the 1990s. Measure criminality by imprisonment, and you have an indication just how much the number of non-Swedish inmates had risen from 1990 to 1995 at the nation's seven major prisons. Proof that Swedish justice was not blind comes from judicial as well as penal records; both collaborate how much more likely immigrants were to receive jail terms for committing the same crimes as Swedes. Look at the second table; it breaks down crimes into categories and note the percentage of each type for which foreigners have been convicted. By any fair extrapolation from these statistics, one irrefutable conclusion emerges: for identical crimes immigrants without Swedish citizenship were much more likely to receive prison terms than natives. If it were not so, there is no way to explain why they represented more than fifty percent of the prison population, but their crime commission rate for any category of crime did not exceed 28 percent.

Alien and non-European Populations at Swedish Prisons

PRISON	Population %=Alien Citizens	% Foreigners=non-European
KUMLA	57	36
TIDAHOLM	53	25
HALL	47	20
NORRTÄLJE	39	26
MALMÖ	47	27
HÄLLBY	37	19
KALMAR	41	22

By Category, Percent of Total Crimes Committed by Foreign Citizens

CRIME	% Committed by Foreign Citizens
RAPE	27
CHILD ABUSE (7-14 YEARS)	27
CHILD ABUSE (0-6 YEARS)	25
ATTEMPTED MURDER	23
FEMALE ABUSE	22
MURDER	21
ILLEGAL THREATS	18
MISTREATMENT OF MEN	18
THREATENING AN OFFICIAL	17
VIOLENT RESISTANCE	17
PICK POCKETING	28
HEINOUS ROBBERY	23
GOODS SMUGGLING	23
SHOPLIFTING	21

243

Even one of the decade's most brazen and brutal crimes did not cause attitudes to change and remedial actions to begin. In the early hours of December 4, 1994, three young men with a military automatic carbine opened fire at the entrance to trendy Stockholm nightspot Sturecompagniet, killing three people and injuring nineteen others. Revenging a security guard who had denied the trio's passage into the establishment earlier in the evening, a shooting hours later resulted from many factors, including drug-induced hallucinations and the likely wretched backgrounds of the gunman and his accomplices. Breaking with the usual police and media practice of withholding identities of wanted persons and convicted criminals, law enforcement officials this time quickly submitted an all-points bulletin to Swedish media of the suspected persons' names and descriptions.

Although police warned that each member of the threesome—a Swede, an Iranian, and a Chilean—should be considered equally dangerous, newspaper and television reports quickly focused most attention on Guillermo Marques "Nano" Jara, an immigrant who had come with his refugee parents to Sweden from Chile as a five-year old. A subsequent divorce left Nano in his mother's custody and separated from a father who had gone to Paris. Although Nano's first signs of trouble occurred in a primary grade with a resultant placement in a special observation class, it would not be until after his sixteenth birthday that he had his first problem with police. After he had grown older and drugs had induced spurts of violent behavior, Nano explained for a Swedish judge why he and friends had begun to destroy property and fight. As he understood a proclivity for troublemaking, "The reason for the tumult apparently stems from youths who are without meaningful diversions and with aversion toward police; we chose to disturb law and order and thwart simultaneously police efforts to maintain law and order." Jara was sixteen-years old when he shared his motivations for a court. His testimony demonstrated profound insight, and he understood what factors were behind delinquent acts by alien juveniles in Sweden. Rather than trying to harness Jara's knowledge of hostilities into something productive and positive, Swedish society allowed a deterioration of a smart young man's keen insights into immigrant rage to reach a point where he would become a vicious killer. Seven months after the nightclub murders, a court sentenced Jara to life in prison.[244]

There was also a category of criminal activity that involved immigrants but rarely Swedes. Stemming from radically different gender roles, affronts to family honor for some ethnic minorities could result in murders of women who stepped outside their group for relationships. It was also common for charges of rape to be filed against foreign men who had misinterpreted Nordic women's reputation for sexual promiscuity. For non-Europeans just seeing a female bus driver for the first time or being supervised at work by a woman were shocking experiences that defied their customs and religious beliefs. These unfamiliar roles by Middle Eastern standards both intimidated and frightened many strict Muslim men. It was common for them to view Swedish women as enigmas and threats to their patriarchal positions. Feeling greater pressure to exert more control in an atmosphere permeated with female liberation, men used to dominating wives and daughters now asserted even more control in Muslim homes. They first met suspected liberal tendencies among their wives and daughters with warnings, and male heads of households could react violently if "misbehaving" persisted. Swedish social authorities were generally helpless at stopping arranged marriages, and attempts at denying families a right to prohibit their girls from dating whomever they wanted proved futile. In most cases interventions by society in family disputes involving female rights came too late to prevent physical abuse and murders.

At the other end men and male teenagers with non-European heritages easily misread and mistook signals from Swedish women and girls. Late on a January night in 2000, near a Stockholm subway station, as a case in point, a gang rape of a drunk fourteen-year old Swedish girl occurred. Perpetrators of the crime were seven young aliens who allegedly had misjudged incoherency and strange movements by their victim as her way of inviting them to initiate intercourse. At least these were their explanations for what had prompted a sexual attack. DNA evidence notwithstanding, a court in Solna agreed in part with the boys' judgment of her desires. The judge found only three of seven immigrant youths guilty, and he sentenced them to reform school.[245]

Drugs and gang warfare also became integral parts of immigrant crime. Smuggling and selling illegal substances appeared to have resulted as logical consequences of accepting refugees from warzones where drug trafficing had financed one side's fight with another in civil wars. Kurds, Iranians, Turks, and Kosovo Albanians had reputations for being conduits in the Afghanistan heroin trade, and African tribes had been using and selling drugs for centuries. Being jobless and having drug contacts, aliens quite naturally resumed what they had done prior to their departures for Sweden.[246]

As in Jara's case, drug use and gang warfare went together. Alien young people found excitement in fighting skinheads and neo-Nazis. Often between 1990 and 2001, police intervened to break up battles between immigrants and natives. Attacks could arise whenever a numerical advantage seemed to exist for one side, and identifying the enemy was easy. A gang of hateful Swedes often had shaven heads, and members liked to wear emblems from the Third Reich. Darker physical appearances were generally enough to mark the thugs from non-Nordic backgrounds. As Criminologist Leif G. W. Persson claimed, one could easily find more similarities than differences between these hostile factions. As he put it, "skinheads and immigrant gangs-[were as much]-alike as berries." No matter, the clashes were violent, and it was common for some victims to suffer skull fractures and internal injuries.

Alien-on-alien crimes also occurred. The worst example was arson at a Halloween party in Göteborg on October 29, 1998. Embittered by a request to pay a forty-kronor entrance fee, four young Iranian immigrants sought revenge by deliberately setting a fire in the stairwell that led to the second-floor hall where the event was underway. The act of sealing a lone exit in flames brought horrifying deaths to 63 young people.[247]

In terms of immigrant-on-native crime, the experience of John Sohlberg walking home after midnight on July 21, 1999, represented an all too common event in modern Sweden. Returning to Malmö after a long day in Denmark, the Swede found himself alone in the unwanted company of two young men. With a knife pressed against Solberg's throat, one assailant grabbed a victim's wallet as an accomplice demanded the code to an ATM card. What occurred during this night was an altogether familiar crime in Sweden. As with so many other robberies, the thieves were immigrant youths. As common as the mugging and its perpetuators had been, Solberg's reactions were refreshingly unique. Unlike many Swedes who would have exploded angrily at public officials for having allowed too many "blackheads" into the country, he refused to place the blame for a frightening experience only on aliens. As much as he demanded more police protection, Solberg did not find a full answer in increased patrols. A solution to the problem of street crime, in his judgment, would require much more; "I am afraid that all of Malmö will become like this [Rosengård] if segregation continues to develop." Sohlberg urged a complete overhaul of neighborhoods in Malmö to insure integration and an end to flight by Swedes to the "calmer surrounding townships." He also called for more dialogue between natives and immigrants.

Had Swedish politicians shown Solberg's wisdom, crime and a multitude of other social and economic problems which accounted for despair along with the frustration which Jara expressed to a Swedish court might have been less severe. Alien criminality in Sweden was simply a reflection of everything else wrong with native and outsider relationships. In pursuit of a viable solution to the enormous problems of prejudice and discrimination which nonindigenous folk experience in Sweden, it is a pity the twenty-four hours of sunshine that Norrland has during June cannot brighten and inspire minds and imaginations of Swedish politicians to do what is right and just instead of what is easy and popular.[248]

Chapter V

An Insidious Conundrum

Prior to a continuing refugee influx that the military coup in Chile had spurred in 1973, Sweden had prospered as few other nations. Measured by many different yardsticks of wealth, the Nordic nation either led or ranked among the top five countries in every major category. Industries were busy and diverse, humming along and producing everything from jet airplanes to hand-crafted blown glass. A tag or stamp of "Made in Sweden" on any item from the kingdom meant quality. Looking back on a halycon period, one can almost understand why so many geography-dazed Americans have confused Switzerland and Sweden. Both, after all, had long histories of neutrality, and the two nations had reputations for precision. Making matters more difficult, their English names begin with the letters Sw, and geographies and climates of the two are associated with snow, mountains, and skiing. More significantly in the early 1970s, statistical data for these Sw twins closely matched.

Ranking national wealth by almost any standard placed them in lockstep for almost every category. There was a major difference, however. For followers of current events during the Cold War, Swiss fame resulted from secrecy, aloofness, and insularity, whereas Swedish assertiveness of authority and righteousness marked an intrusion in world affairs. Perched almost atop the world, Swedes seemed to look condescendingly at much that was passing under her watchful observation, gaining in the process a world reputation as a nation of "busy bodies." Colonialism and apartheid in Africa, conservativism and military juntas in Latin America and Southeast Asia, racism and inequality in the United States, and the global arms race were a few of the issues which excited Swedes and caused their disapprobation and negative reactions. The memorable act when Prime Minister Palme pointed an accusatory finger and lectured President Richard M. Nixon and the United States on Vietnam was perhaps the most memorable and representative of Sweden's absorption with lesson-giving and moralizing. Between the removal of Alexander Dubcek in Czechoslovakia by Russian troops in 1968 and the crushing destruction of

President Salvador Allende Gossens' constitutionally elected government in Chile in 1973 by a military junta, opportunities existed several times for top Swedish officials to assert superiority and impartiality. Accepting the exiles from these two oppressed nations and condemning both the Soviet Union and the generals in the Latin American nation for cruelty and usurpation of basic human rights strengthened Sweden's claim to being neutral in the Cold War. In the first instance communist forces had intruded, and in the second case it had been the United States of America in support of Chilean anti-Marxists.

Sweden was wanting more than simple recognition from her objectivity. By giving refuge to Czechs, Chileans, and subsequently several leaders from South Africa's anti-apartheid movement, Swedish leaders like Palme were in an obvious search for praise. Not only did they want to be seen as important players in the drive for international peace, but they also wanted to project a positive image of Sweden as the bright beacon in a dark world.

In many respects, their drive was successful. Oppressed peoples began to show a belief in the Middle Way with their feet, choosing Sweden as their final destination. In the minds of Swedish planners this choice of the Nordic kingdom gave them and the nation an unprecedented opportunity to prove an important point. They would illustrate for every nation in the world to grasp how diverse peoples from different backgrounds should be treated and could be interwoven into a society without problems. Thus a whole program would successively unfold for not only integrating aliens into society smoothly but for demonstrating as well to skeptics why prejudice and racism were not the inevitable appendages of multiculturalism.

Sweden—once again would assume the role of unsolicited teacher to the United States and other countries who proclaimed equal opportunities but who in fact practiced something else—would give valuable lessons on how to mix peoples without producing animosity among historically antagonistic groups. Eliminating the usual pitfalls of blending peoples, races, religions, and rival ethnic groups was possible, thought the social scientists, because they would insure that the main sources of friction were missing. These people engineers in tandem with seemingly visionary Social Democratic politicians would plan programs which would eliminate the normal impasses for aliens to health care, education, decent housing, and other amenities. Sweden would in effect then become a social laboratory, and immigrants would be the mice in experiments. By leading newcomers to Sweden through an introductory maze of orientation, knowledge of Swedish, and awareness of the Swedish mindset that government is there to help with almost any problem, Swedes would make the diverse nationalities and races of the world into their clones. Upon conclusion of this great human experiment Sweden would be in a position to showcase results for doubters everywhere. Admirers would be in awe of Sweden, applauding once more an achievement from this creative, peace-loving people, the precursor of solutions to social problems, the exemplar of fairness, and among nations the only provider of universal humane treatment to all residents.

There was only one problem with the plan. A majority of Swedes did not subscribe to it. Simply put, they did not intend to cooperate by accepting foreigners on equal terms with themselves. With no expectations of failure, contingencies did not exist to deal with recalcitrance and obstruction. If the reaction in Sweden were analogous to anything in the United States, it would have been America's public housing debacle. American social engineers who had surveyed substandard residences and slums sincerely believed their vision of replacing delapidated eyesores with modern buildings would be beneficial to everyone. As planners they imagined themselves as not only progenitors of attractive, revitalized neighborhoods but as the endowers of hopefulness and progress. By the fiftieth birthday of federally funded public housing, liberals and conservatives were able to agree in general that this government effort at viable community development had failed miserably. Just as public-housing projects had not fulfilled their visionaries' expectations of improving the lives of thousands of poor Americans, the dreams and asperations of Swedes about being able to transform their nation into a harmonious land with multitudes of diverse peoples and cultures all working in unison and rapturous harmony were dashed as well. Watching in dismay, Swedish idealists observed failure as the indigenous population rejected newcomers. In Sweden with foreigners like in America with slum clearance, misjudging human nature occurred. Neither the so-called "brain trusters" behind public housing nor Sweden's sanguine social engineers who had opened their nation to population hetereogeneity were good at foreseeing the negative consequences of their plans.

Yet as much as there were similarities, a major difference separated two naive attempts at remaking two societies. Unlike failed building estates whose occupancies could end with a few strokes from a demolition ball or well placed dynamite, outsiders in Sweden evolved there into permanent fixtures. As such they and natives have had a mutual interest in insuring one another's positive adjustments to change. In the process Swedes have needed to assume an extra responsibility. Although they have not done so to large degree, they must begin to treasure aliens as national assets and not as problems. Although it might take a generation or two for an appreciation of diversity's full impact, it can result from a concerted effort and a redirected mindset. Already by the end of 2000 one positive lesson has resulted from the Swedish experience of living with diverse races and ethnicities. After some thirty years of increasing diversity there was at least a general willingness to concede that this task of nation building with a mixture of the world's peoples would never be as easy and effortless as optimistic Swedes had once considered it. As difficult as an admission might have been three decades earlier, a few Nordic heretics at the start of the new millennium were even suggesting Sweden could learn a few lessons in the art of blending and succeeding from the United States.

There were both positive and negative signs for a possible good ending to Swedish diversification. Optimism for a successful conclusion was coming from ordinary Svenssons who encouraged and supported immigrants with their many demonstrations and protests against hateful acts. These efforts showed a consistent, spontaneous willingness to work for better interethnic and interracial relations. After tragedies such as race-motivated murders, assaults, and arson, grassroots activities on behalf of victims occurred to involve many thousand Swedes. Aside from more continuous, semi-permanent activities like the Five to Twelve movement and the elaborate underground network that was operating in Sweden as a means of hiding and moving runaway refugees to safety allover the nation one step ahead of the police, several other positive actions developed. In all probability they reflected a mixture of disgust and embarrassment with what had occurred in a specific locale.

Marches against racism became both a community catharsis and an act of collective disassociation. One could also view benefits of organized reactions against racism in another context. They not only allowed participants to make public statements that communicated through their appearance an abhorrence for what had happened, but demonstrating might have had a purgative effect on marchers' consciences as well because the act of protesting relieved a personal responsibility for or an association with hate and prejudice. Whether in small communities or large cities, the benefits seemed to be the same for participants in demonstrations against racial violence. Events in Herrljunga after a beating of a local immigrant shopkeeper by racist thugs illustrated common lessons from so many of these emotional outpourings. An assembly of 2,000 residents gathered to rally in response to violence in this commune of 7,000 inhabitants. This action against racism and violence represented the community's way of announcing its absolution from the crime, and it provided individuals a forum from which to proclaim disgust with a wanton act and to declare no personal responsibility for this kind of distardly behavior.

Even such gigantic spectacles against prejudice and xenophobia as those that occurred in Stockholm and Göteborg were really not much different than the smaller gatherings against overt acts, but the big city equivalents occurred on a grander scale and were more likely to attract the participations of famous entertainers and national political leaders. Moreover anonymity prevailed at larger events, but being identified on the side of law and fairness by neighbors was important where people generally recognized each other. Whether rallies were large or small, there were only so many ways to express remorse for the ugliest manifestations of racism. With many thousands joining in parades against hatred and denouncing racism and xenophobia at rallies, a cynic could be excused for wondering whom was left with prejudice in Swedish society.[249]

Several communes with bad reputations for racial violence sponsored campaigns to improve their image. First Karlskrona and then Klippan tried to do this. In the first city, a navy port long associated with nazi sympathizers, civic groups and politicians on at least two occasions did what they could in order to erase negative associations with their community's residents. They drafted plans and formed umbrella bodies to deal with racism. In Klippan, a commune associated with Sweden's most publicized racist murder, there was groping to find a way to disconnect the place from a gruesome stabbing death. To this end, it created a network against racism, invited in guest speakers for lectures on multiculturalism, and involved young people in various antiracist projects. On the outskirts of town after neo-Nazis had established their base of operations there at a secluded cottage-turned-compound, local government leaders tried legal means in the beginning to flush out this unwanted fascist presence. Failing at this, they ridded the community of fascists by acquiring the headquarters through purchase. Thereafter a razor-wire enclosed, video-camera protected base became Klippan-owned property.

In a very different campaign Robertsfors in Norrland fought not only to retain a refugee camp but also its popular alien manager. Jabar Amin won over township residents' respect with openness and frugality. In the process he had not endeared himself to leaders of the Immigration Board in Norrköping. His criticisms of waste, bureaucratic delays, and the long waits for judgments were behind the dismissal, but the official reason was incompetency, a judgment that aroused unity and resolve in Robertsfors. United in a resolve to inform Board officials of the commune's displeasure with the decision, the people staged an impressive demonstration on June 16, 1993. Naturally for Amin who reported how much he had been "impressed by the will of Robertsfors," the effort gave expression to the citizenry's confidence in his ability, but it did not restore his authority at the shelter for asylum seekers.[250]

Beside communal actions against racism, individual acts of heroism and kindness abounded. Involvements against prejudice and statements on behalf of brotherly bonds with aliens took courage, and they were always potentially dangerous endeavors as Lisa Jansson and Rune Brustad would discover in two separate incidents in 1994. A fifteen-year old boy spotted a "Crush racism" button on Jansson, an acquaintance of the teenager's mother. Inflamed by it, he called her a "communist devil" and then, using a hand with brass knuckles, landed a hard blow on her upper arm with his fist. Seeing the attack, seven of the teenager's friends joined in the assault, slugging the overmatched woman repeatedly until she dropped unconsciously to the floor. There her assailants continued their punishment, kicking her prone body repeatedly. Although all the viciousness occurred in a Stockholm restaurant, nobody there did anything to rescue Jansson.

Several hundred kilometers away in Jönköping, Brustad did react and suffered the consequences. After watching a gang of skinheads pursue two immigrant boys, he calmly intervened to advise the tormentors to end their chase. His response provoked the bullies. Unappreciative of a bystander's interference, ten or eleven skinheads pounced on Brustad, kicking him in the face and body thirty to forty times. Although the rescuer sustained a broken nose, a swollen eye, and many lacerations and bruises, this hero would not have any regrets afterward about what he had done to provoke violence. Asked to comment on how he would react in the future to skinheads, Brustad responded definitively: "I would not hesitate to say the same thing again."

For outspokenness politicians faced dangers, too. Daring to share their positive convictions about foreigners could bring death threats. As the Justice Minister, Freivalds discovered such consequences in 1997. Nazi leader Niclas

Löfdal sent her a letter bomb that could have seriously injured the officeholder or even have killed this Social Democrat had it not been for an alert post office employee's suspicions about a package in transit to her.

Maria Leissner, a delegate to the *Riksdag* from the Folk Party, was also a trauma sufferer as a result of racists' threats. For claiming the refugee policies of Sweden were too harsh and assisting asylum seekers in their bids to obtain residence permits, she became a target of hate. Although Leissner admitted to being afraid, the terror campaign did not deter a resolve to continue. In a bold press release, the announcement read that she "was not thinking of giving up."

Altogether in Sweden examples of stubbornness, determination, bravery, benevolence, and activism occurred. Whether it was four newspaper editors daring to publicize the names and pictures of Sweden's top neo-Nazis, Social Democrat Wallström becoming "mom" to a Somalian civil war orphan, or Iris Berggren continuing her work among immigrant youths in Rinkeby, there was an abundance of courageous acts and desires to improve relationships and fight racism. Even to some extent when leftist counterdemonstrators broke through police barriers to battle skinheads and neo-Nazis over control of the streets, their actions deserved praise for bravery and xenophobic dissent.[251]

Although the tradition of Sunday-morning worship disappeared almost entirely as a weekly Swedish ritual, state and free church leaders commanded respect. As with natives churches generally were not successful at inducing foreigners to attend services, but the failures at attracting aliens as members did not discourage a ministering to or an advocating for minority needs. The Reverend Ingemar Simonsson, a regular contributor of articles to Malmö and national publications, represented the Swedish state church at its best. With the news media better at attracting readers than the churches were at drawing in worshipers, the vicar's pulpit for preaching sermons on love and tolerance became the daily press. Simonsson warned his special congregation—the one that read instead of listened to his words—of "the threat from brown terror." Readers were advised to "react against racism now" as well as to realize that "immigrants can teach us to live better."

Inasmuch as the newspaper pastor represented the best instincts and moral instruction of Swedish Lutheranism, other actions and decisions by church officials would contradict Simonsson's mission. After arsonists had destroyed Trollhättan's mosque, Achbishop Gunnar Weman discovered how church intransigence and bureaucracy could upset good intentions. He and others in the Church of Sweden had wanted to promote goodwill among the Muslims by donating a Sunday offering to the reconstruction of their house of worship, but the proposal ran into opposition on the grounds there could be no deviations about the central church office's designees as official recipients of collections. It would not be the last time recalcitrance would foil clerics who were interested in fostering harmony with Muslims. In early 1999 Bishop Lars-Göran Lönnermark ruled Yaghoob Mullazai could not work as a cleaner at Dammsvedjans Church in Borås. The custodian's Islamic faith disqualified him from job eligibility because the Lutheran Church demanded membership of all its employees.[252]

For a handful of sports which encouraged immigrants to participate, the opportunities to compete in athletic events and belong to teams proved to have greater impact on integration than so many other activities and programs that were intended to coalesce peoples. As Dahlin in Malmö and Larsson in Helsingborg showed early in sports careers, football—soccer in the United States—has a black-and-white ball that moves equally well into goals whether kickers are ethnic Swedes, persons of mixed heritage like the aforementioned stars, or players without any Swedish roots such as Yksel Osmanovski, a son of Macedonian immigrants. Progressing from school and football in Malmö to a professsional career on an Italian club, the first generation Macedonian-Swede offered advice from his own experiences to minority youths on how to fulfill potentials in Sweden. No proponent of multiculturalism, Osmanovski suggested assimilation and efforts at "try[ing] to melt into the Swedish style." It was his contention that the success or failure of foreigners in Sweden would often depend upon how well they "understand how the Swedes live and think."

By sponsoring athletic activities, Mölndal's police expected the effort to lead to "the establishment of good relations between peoples." Doubters questioned at the outset of the program what the officers were trying to accomplish. Despite much initial skepticism, sports bridged the cultural gap between native and alien participants, fostered more understanding, and undermined somewhat the myths each side had been believing about the other.[253]

Short of imposing tougher penalties for violations of personal rights and enacting meaningful laws against discrimination, various agencies along with parliament tried everything between 1990 and 2001 to combat violence. There were discussion groups, lectures, speeches, sermons, articles, posters, internet homepages, campaigns, condemnations, contests with prizes, festivals as well as celebrations, concerts, demonstrations, solidarity and unity movements, boycotts, subsidies to organizations, petitions and pledges, declarations of communal and national periods of grief, workshops to foster mutual respect and understanding, and school activities and lesson plans.[254] Yet bad things continued to happen. Obviously, solutions to the insidious conundrum in the monarchy were not going to come from affixing "Stop Racism Now" decals on Göteborg's fire trucks, casting a young black male actor opposite a youthful Swedish actress in key romantic roles in "Vinterviken," a Romeo-and-Juliet film, or selecting a "salt-and-pepper" pair for a hackneyed television program about alleged relationships of immigrants and natives.[255]

Partiallly at the root of Sweden's problem was an education system not prepared to focus its students on the realities ahead for the Nordic nation and many other industrialized countries. In Western Europe and Japan, good times were about to turn into nightmares of gigantic magnitude. Each year as the median age of First World populations grew older, a ticking timebomb came closer to exploding. Depending upon the nation, it would occur soon after the millennium if a significant number of immigrants were not introduced into national labor forces. Importing workers would be the only sensible way for developed countries to defuse their common problem of aging populations.

All deficiencies in American schools aside, their pupils had exposure to two important lessons about their nation, which were not being taught across Europe and Japan. Students in the United States learned that their ancestors—whether slave, indentured, or free—with invaluable assistance from indigenous natives built America. Also inculcated into their educations was appreciation for the symbolic significance of the Statue of Liberty. From her place in New York Harbor, Lady Liberty with a torch beckoning foreigners to continue the unfinished job of nation-building has attracted tourists and inspired American boys and girls for many generations. European and Japanese educators do not have comparable lessons to instill in their pupils. Their national histories are about dynasties, emperors, kings, wars, and conquests. Emphases are seldom about immigration and the achievements from diversity. Although not always true as chapter one hightlights, emigration until 1960 always seemed to be the more relevant force than immigration in European and Japanese development.

In Swedish higher education research has centered on extraneous issues about immigration and refugees, with charges of prejudice and bias often the centerpiece of intellectual debates. In particular two members of the Swedish academic community caused much of excitement. Ingrid Björkman and Kajsa Ekholm Friedman were main figures in a ceaseless debate over whether or not they were racists, contributed to racist thought, were handmaidens of racism, or were simply detached scholars who had reached independent, alternative conclusions about migration to and asylum in Sweden From her position at Göteborg University, Björkman became a most conversial researcher because of her twin hypotheses about what she had ascertained to be resultant negative effects from Sweden's practice of harboring exiles from the Third World. Simply and briefly she claimed these peoples were Swedish liabilities whose presence would only damage the kingdom. Their liability, she argued, was a totally incongruous cultural background for contributing anything positive to Sweden. With non-Europeans in residence in Scandinavia, the only outcome from her perspective would be inevitable clashes with the native population. Since in her mind extreme incompatibility existed between Swedes and aliens from poor lands, nothing positive could come to Sweden from mixing people who have nothing in common with the native population. Moreover Third World migrants, as a result of their absence from homelands, were retarding progress in impoverished nations where they belonged as contributors. In what would become an ongng tit-for-tat debate with other Swedish scholars, Björkman proposed, elaborated, and defended arguments for returning asylum seekers. Consequently her detractors and critics attacked on both a personal and professional level. As one vilifier supposed, either the woman was a racist who knowingly developed justifications for prejudicial policies by Sweden or she allowed herself to be used inadvertently as the able assistant to xenophobes and racists. Whichever it did not matter. Enemies of aliens, according to her critic, were gaining the same results and benefits from her published arguments and analyses.[256]

Ever sensitive to the era of fascist dictatorships and a legacy of Swedish universities as pro-Nazi bastions, many members of the academic community wanted to distance themselves after the war from an unflattering international reputation. To do this they carefully surveyed colleagues' work for evidence of extreme rightwing, nationalistic tendencies.[257] Ekholm Friedman would become a victim of such careful scrutiny after *Dagens Nyheter* published her views on multiculturalism. As a Lund University social anthropologist, she had done research that led her to conclude that Sweden's standard of living was being reduced by "new" residents who lacked sufficient "loyalty [to] and solidarity" with their adopted land. Within a week harsh reactions followed her prediction that Sweden would suffer negative consequences from immigrants and asylum seekers. Colleagues from Ekholm Friedman's discipline quickly disassociated themselves from her hypothesis. In the process they countered with opposing interpretations and accused their fellow social scientist of "demagoguery with mental blinkers." In the hysteria that followed disclosure of her conclusions, demands came for her dismissal, and one person even filed a formal complaint with police. It accused her of racial agitation. Eighteen days after the appearance of the controversial article, she again used *Dagens Nyheter* but this time to restate her position. Writing with less hostility toward alien influences, she did her best to extricate herself from any presumed associations with skinheads and fascists. About them and their beliefs, Ekholm Friedman was emphatic, asserting in no uncertain terms that "I am not xenophobic." Her efforts successfully ended an academic witch hunt, and there were no more challenges to her allegations about pending perils from opening up Sweden to diverse peoples.[258]

During the 1997-1998 schoolyear a case of what to do with a confessing neo-Nazi unfolded for the Swedish academic community to resolve. It reached a crisis stage after doctoral student Karolina Matti had invited a fellow fascist, Dan Berner, to lecture at Umeå University on December 5. Seen as stretching beyond the limits of academic freedom by school officials because she did not intend to offer opportunities for counterpoint to Berner's claims, several at the university considered the idea of a neo-Nazi's use of campus facilities for the sole purpose of glorifying racist beliefs as breaching all standards of acceptable conduct for an instructor. As a result the administration expelled Matti from the institution.

This was only the beginning of her problems. Indicted as an accomplice to Berner in racial agitation, she was facing prison if Prosecutor Björn Ericsson succeeded at pressing the state's charges against her. Aware of risks ahead the ex-graduate student, before a district court, denied any direct attachment to Nazis or their philosophy, but the trial ended in a guilty verdict. After success at appealing her conviction, Matti changed her story altogether, claiming now to be too "tired to continue sneaking. I do not have anything against telling my opinions." Thus at her second court hearing she freely admitted to thinking that "nazism is a very fascinating ideology." Then just a few days after the first anniversary of Berner's lecture, a Swedish appeal court found Matti and Berner guilty as charged, a verdict Sweden's high court upheld July 7, 2000.[259]

In view of alleged xenophobia and the fact that Björkman and Ekholm Friedman fostered debates, there was seldom criticisms for the many other social scientists who minutely examined immigrants and refugees as if a person with an alien background was bacteria on a petri dish and these scholars were microbiologists. Neither the wisdom of draining public revenue into an assortment of projects of dubious worth nor the ethics of probing intrusively received much public notice. Almost every phase of the immigrant experience became a research topic for scholars at three facilities dedicated to such inquiries, among faculties of several departments at Swedish universities, and with graduate students.

Worthless studies clog the shelves of Swedish libraries. For a sociology doctoral dissertation at Umeå University, Birgitta Löwander examined "racism and antiracism on the agenda: studies of television news reporting during the beginning of the 1990s." Britt Hultén's seminar paper in journalism dealt with "the picture of refugees, immigrants and racism in the Swedish press [for] week 46, 1991." After having found among post-1950 immigrants a return-to-homeland rate of 56 percent, Miguel Benito debunked Sweden's claim to being an immigrant nation. Elsie Söderlindh Franzén discovered that the newcomers with poor educations were "stuck in the rigid Swedish school system," a fact that would "stamp [them] as handicapped for work." Rojas interviewed first-generation immigrant youths for "Sweden's unloved children."

Bel Habib, an expert himself on ethnic relations, became a lone crusader against these kind of studies. Opposition came because "immigrant research has helped to create barriers from outside cultural and ethnic bases. We have got problems in Sweden with immigrants not so much because of the cultural differences, but because of our view of cultural diversity." Grasped in essence by Bel Habib from scholarly inquiries was the conclusion that an overemphasis on differences by investigators made their work somewhat responsible for a "we and they" attitude that prevailed among natives and aliens. As he put forth a claim, "In standard studies anthropologists and social scientists have tried to analyze the misunderstanding between immigrants and Swedish personnel in different societal sectors. A critical check shows that so-called immigrant investigations have done more harm than good. It is characterized in a majority of cases by picturing other cultures as exotic."

Not unexpectantly individuals with vested interests in doing immigrant research disagreed with Bel Habib. At countering his argument about harmful effects, neither two professors nor a researcher at Sweden's Immigrant Institute and Museum in Botkyrka could offer much more than self-serving defenses of their activities. At over 42 million kronor for fiscal years 1991 through 1993, the budget for research into international migration and ethnic relations was a dear price to pay, especially if Bel Habib was correct about the work's deteriorating effect on native-alien relationships.[260]

Schools, in the minds of many leaders, had important roles to play in the fight against racism and xenophobia. Efforts at promoting the development of healthy outlooks abounded from the earliest grades through gymnasium. The government pumped money into projects whose aims were inculcating respect and appreciation for different cultures. An example of this was 500,000 kronor earmarked at the end of 1995 to Karlstad to reshape opinions against prejudice and for democracy. Schools used these allocations for a variety of projects and purchases, including student exchanges, theme days on refugees, essay-writing contests, and domestic-science classes on the foods of different cultures. For assignments on racism at different age levels, the Immigrant Institute in Borås released three guides that recommended readings on prejudice and racial discrimination. For teachers, the Office of the Discrimination Ombudsman made available an elaborate kit on the latest pedagogic approach to teaching about racism and xenophobia. Moreover in order to remove offensive pictures, depictions, and stereotypes of world sections, nations, and peoples, several educationists at every Swedish school of education reviewed and analyzed textbooks and course materials. To keep teachers current on skinheads, Nazis, and racist organizations, several primers were printed for circulation.[261]

Despite many efforts to change attitudes, public-opinion surveys of students and teachers indicated a significant degree of prejudice among both groups. Stated in percentages and released in 1998, a poll of 5,540 teachers revealed they had these feelings about race and aliens:

1.8% opposed interracial couples having children
7.7% thought HIV and Aids were nature's punishments for perversity
3.7% believed segregated societies were best
27.2% judged as natural, children seeing and valuing racial differences
11.0% wanted non-Europeans to return to their homelands
3.9% believed Jews have exploited the Holocaust
2.6% believed the Holocaust lacked relevance
4.8% concluded Jews had too much world influence
6.0% wanted to hear less about Nazis and Jewish exterminations
15.8% surmised aliens had come in order to exploit the welfare system
45.4% believed culturally deviant norms explained the nonacceptance of gypsies
13.2% considered Muslims parents ignored their children's best interests
27.7% saw Islam as a threat to Western social and cultural advances
36.1% felt government and mass media withheld truth about alien costs
57.5% considered democracy as Sweden's best government alternative

Teachers working in schools with concentrations of immigrant children were 25 percent more negative than their peers with primarily native pupils. In 1997 CEIFO surveyed opinions of 8,000 young people between the ages of twelve and twenty and found their thoughts and suggestions filled with prejudice:

34.0% agree that returning non-Europeans "home" would be desirable
12.2% have listened to racist music
21.0% believe different cultures should be separated
27.0% oppose the construction of mosques in Sweden
12.7% have experienced bad treatment because of their origins
17.1% have had contact with materials from a racist organization
42.0% have had contact with a racist organization
 7.8% have read a racist magazine or newspaper
11.2% have read an antiracist magazine or newspaper
11.0% believe "race mixing" went against natural law
12.0% thought Jews had excessive influence in the world
29.0% believe there was too much talk about Nazis and the Holocaust
23.0% consider HIV to be nature's punishment of homosexuals

Supportive evidence indicating an abundance of engrained racism and prejudice among both pupils and educators revealed itself in different forms between 1990 and 2001. City school chief Persson won open support from eighty-two teachers for his asinine proposal that would have prevented additional aliens from moving to Malmö. It was not the first instance of absurd reasoning from an educator. In Eskilstuna, almost five years before Persson would make a foolish proposal, school rector Lars Palm had suggested problems in Sweden would disappear if there were suddenly no immigrants. The agenda of in-service teacher institutes seldom concerned Sweden's many minorities, and those that had did not provoke much interest among educators. A case in point was poor attendance at a Malmö workshop. If it indicates anything about teacher interest in gaining knowledge about and bettering skills with immigrant pupils, then this program was a fiasco because only thirty of the commune's thousand-member faculty showed enough enthusiasm to attend a one-day seminar and lecture session held on November 1, 1999.[262]

All was not glum, however; some positive signs did come to education. In Lund pupils at the College of Technology worked successfully to remove a Sweden Democrat from student government. Also at the collegiate level the national council for post-gymnasium studies supported a stand at Dalarna College for the dismissal of a prospective teacher on the grounds of his pro-Nazi sympathies. In clarifying its support the national board stated that "a student in training for a teaching career, who during his or her practical teaching period in a elementary school, expresses in words his feelings for antidemocratic opinions should be failed." Education Minister Thomas Östros commended the action, underscoring how "it is most splendid that the college is vigilant." Schools successively at all levels began tolerating less from neo-Nazis. One district after another banned outward displays of racist beliefs. Viewed as disruptive and racially agitative, the right of students to display and wear such hate symbols as swastikas on school property lost in a freedom-of-expression case decided in 1996 by Sweden's highest court.

Authorities were less successful at eliminating racist graffiti and slogans at schools. Work crews could not keep ahead of youths who were determined to leave painted, printed, and etched symbols on walls, doors, and furniture. In Älvsjö, one of Stockholm's southern suburbs, a rector who had just claimed to have attained racial harmony among pupils under his charge was then questioned by a television investigative reporter about the school's overall appearance. With a camera focused on swaszikas and slogans such as "Hitler was a good man," "White Power," and "Nazi Power" scrawled on and near the schoolhouse, the bewildered and embarrassed school official was left speechless, unable to explain all the hateful grafitti at an institution with very few foreigners.[263]

The police also maintained a mixed role in Swedish racism. Observers, especially ones from the extreme left, often questioned officers' objectivity during confrontations between antiracists and skinheads. Among various Marxists and syndicalists a general consensus emerged that law enforcement officers were shielding skinheads and neo-Nazis from their most militant foes whenever one side confronted the other. Several accusations to this effect surfaced after cops had checked leftist counterdemonstrators from attacking parades of fascists. Further evidence of partiality occurred in 1999 during a lockup in Nybro. A large group of neo-Nazis from allover southern Sweden had begun assembling there for a party when police arrived to prevent the gathering. A melee followed an attempt to intervene peacefully. It ended in several arrests, including the detainment of three fascists who were taken into custody and placed in a cell. Then later that night police jailed an antiracist agitator and locked him together with the Nazi trio. While alone for five minutes with a nemesis, the three rightwing youths beat their adversary unmercifully. According to sworn testimony, the on-duty attendant at the jail did not respond to screams for assistance because he claimed to have heard nothing. While apologizing for the attack, a police spokesperson defended the mixing of known enemies in the same cell, stating no other arrangements had been possible that night.

Police once again aroused suspicions almost two months later when on November 19, 1999, they did not halt Nazis from parading into a Trelleborg courtroom with swastikas and other fascist symbols. Their display came at the trial of the two fellow skinheads who had beaten a Jewish music director a few months earlier in Vellinge. Passivity toward allowing such defiant regalia at a Swedish judicial proceeding became the subject of much subsequent criticism. Ironically only weeks earlier, a top police official had been "accusing Säpo of shielding rightwing extremists."

Obviously not all law enforcement officers in Sweden were negative and unsympathetic toward aliens and their leftist supporters. On a positive note in Uppsala for example, police worked to overcome their prejudices by attending forums and having closer contacts with immigrants. A bit of humor resulted at times from their efforts at understanding. One officer told of showing a school group of mostly immigrant youths the municipal police station. Upon entering the basement the guide pointed to a door, stating it was "the torture chamber." Thereupon alien youngsters turned white with fear written across their faces. The policeman then opened the door to show the trembling visitors a weight-lifting room.[264]

Refugee and immigrant policies also affected Sweden's foreign policy. For a country adept at solving the problems of other nations, embarrassment came to Sweden because her aliens had been suffering so many unpleasantries. As a nation with more experience offering critical advice than receiving it, the monarchy found itself in a role reversal on several occasions during the 1990s. Greek diplomats became upset in 1998 with Pascalidou's mistreatment, and at the end of 1999, both French and German officials disapproved of the Scandinavians' apparent nonchalant attitude about Nazism.

Swedish positions underwent major changes in many other persons' minds as well. From the United States the Ku Klux Klan began seeing Swedes as prime candidates for recruitment. In hopes of chartering Swedish klaverns Klansmen aimed specially designed foreign-language internet homepages at a Swedish audience with the purposes of interesting Nordic people in KKK ideology and membership.

Officially there were also differences. After years of pride for having Europe's most generous asylum policy, Sweden began to conform to both the United Nations and the European Union. No longer a generous maverick, the northern monarchy adopted a program that was more or less similar to what existed elsewhere on the continent and around the world. Then as a means of disguising conformity, Sweden made little gestures that were reminiscent of a more liberal past. Examples came with France's request for the extradition of suspected Algerian terrorists who had been captured in Sweden. Rather than return them immediately as French police had requested, Swedish diplomats refused to act without a guarantee of a fair trial for these suspects after their release to France from Swedish custody.[265]

At forcing unplanned foreign-policy initiatives, several interesting cases developed from immigrants and citizens. In three separate but noteworthy incidents demonstrators protested at embassies. A protest at German diplomatic headquarters in 1992 proved a bit ironic because participants had come because of their convictions that authorities in Rostock were not doing enough to protect the city's refugees and immigrants. Although the ambassador chose to ignore the discontent at the gates to his country's diplomatic legation in Stockholm, he could have been indignant, demanding an official apology for Swedish hypocracy after citation of an equally dismal Swedish record of not shielding her minorities from racist thugs.

At both the Iraqi and Iranian embassies, demonstrations ended violently. On April 7, 1991, armed Kurds tried storming the Iraqi diplomatic compound, but automatic-weapon fire would thwart the invasion. Therewith to prevent bloodshed police used dogs to disperse the Kurds. In the process of restoring order officers detained thirty-four protesters. In the wake of this disturbance troublesome questions remained about the shots and the identity of the weapon's user. Nobody from the embassy assisted in the investigation. Swedish authorities subsequently sent a protest note to Iraq's ambassador, demanding a surrender of the automatic rifle and gunman's name. After four days and with no indications of cooperation, the Swedish ministry of foreign affairs toughened its position. It ordered an Iraqi attaché's immediate expulsion, and it issued a simple ultimatum: surrender the weapon within twenty-four hours or more diplomats must leave the mission for Baghdad. On the fifth day of the crisis compliance finally came with surrender of the gun.

This would not be an end to difficulties with Iraqis. During 1992 police discovered a spy who had been operating on instructions from the embassy. This planted agent had been sent to observe and report on Iraqi refugees who were living in Trollhättan. Only months earlier before the discovery of this operation, Säpo had expelled an Iraqi charge d'affairs for espionage.

Iran also experienced embassy problems. On April 5, 1992, dissidents carrying Molotov cocktails descended on her outpost in Lidingö. This action was coincidental to similar violence at various other diplomatic headquarters operated in European capitals by the theocracy. The arson outside Stockholm caused extensive damage. Swedish police arrested and held twenty-four persons suspected of involvement in the Lidingö firebombing. Prime Minister Bildt considered "it . . . intolerable that Sweden has become a violent scene of action for conflicts which have their roots in other parts of the world."[266]

Events such as those at the Iraqi and Iranian diplomatic missions helped to explain why diverse opinion existed among Swedes about outsiders. Many uncertainties arose about adjusting to, integrating, and assimilating aliens. A survey of articles in newspapers on the relationship of natives and newcomers reveal mixed views and considerable disagreement. The question of what to do caused confusion and discussion. Optimistic forecasters of Sweden's future imagined an integrated land with diversity bringing harmony and stability. Pessimists predicted a disintegrated country not unlike Rwanda or Yugoslavia. Margareta Grape, a woman who worked for Stockholm's integration, feared Sweden would become like the United States. As she put it, "the Swedish debate on the multicultural society has heretofore concerned mostly the struggle against prejudice and intolerance, but there are worrying signs that American multicultural concepts are gaining a foothold. American multiculturalism presupposes that people are different, that they will stay different, and that they maintain their primary affiliations within their own ethnic groups." She disliked what were perceived as trends from America. These, she thought, would lead to "a kind of tribalism or . . . ethnic federalism." In this system, according to Grape, "multiculturalism's winners are therefore the well situated white middle class who are not called upon to do anything more than to accept that some university places and some jobs are set aside for people who are black, Spanish American, Asian, women, homosexual, or who belong to some other quota groups."

Provocative but in fact generally incorrect, Grape's views of American multiculturalism were an oversimplification of what has been dynamic change in the United States. Examine, for example, marriage statistics from the USA. Ethnic and racial interrelationships have increased there at a fast pace. Jew-Gentile ties are almost as commonplace as bonds between Jewish brides and grooms, and interracial marriages between African Americans and Caucasians are no longer unusual or forbidden. Between 1990 and 2001 in the choice of life partners, Sweden stood in sharp contrast to the United States. For evidence survey a month of wedding announcements and photographs in any major Swedish newspaper. Tabulating attests to a lopsided tally that confirms Swedes overwhelmingly marrying other Swedes.

Unlike Grape others observers saw the real problem. Teacher Fredrik Eklöf was one person who comprehended what was wrong in Sweden. According to his summary of the problem, "we the Swedish Swedes are the biggest hurdle to integration here in the land." Two Swedes and an alien teacher reached about the same conclusion in an article they wrote together for *Göteborgs-Posten.* "In many lands diversity is seen as a resource, but in Sweden we are afraid of differences and conflicts. Homogeneity impedes development and leads to intellectual inbreeding." Molin, the ex-head of immigrant administration in Göteborg, did not find evidence of an integration policy. One was missing, he noted, because "a negative attitude by the population's majority does [what it has to do] to shut out the new Swedes." Riksdag member Sten Lindström did not believe his country had reached the first stage of agreeing about goals and definitions. As much as people of goodwill have agreed "benevolence should be replaced by genuine integration," a problem of understanding remained. It is a case, the politician claimed, when nobody "has yet decided what we mean by the words we are using."[267]

Lindström was correct; there was no agreement about definitions. For Swedes and aliens who attempted to give racism meaning (and many tried to do just that), it became—in the broadest sense—every action involved with opposing not only immigrants but also immigration and was—by its narrowest meaning—only acts of overt misbehavior against minorities. By employing the latter application, even some of the most recalcitrant individuals—such as the drummer for a popular white-power band—did not consider themselves racists. Thus for MUF chair and riksdag member Ulf Kristersson, "there is no racism in Sweden" except perhaps the "50-something repulsive persons who only the police can look after. We must be nuanced and call things by their right names." Looked at correctly many inhabitants, according to this youthful politician, were definitely suffering from "ignorance, uncertainty, and fear." Kristersson especially objected to the portraits "spread in the mass media" of young people and schools as "colonies of bacteria." According to his reading of young Swedes and institutions of learning, their descriptions in newspapers and on television "were genuinely untrue."

Others drew distinctions between racism and xenophobia, and it was not uncommon to look at how prejudice and discrimination were affecting society. In order to assess blame and make corrections, several people tried to find the sources of Sweden's fight with outsiders. Kjell Jonsson revealed an interesting explanation for why Swedes have had difficulties defining racism. He pointed out in *"Sverige, Europa och främlingen"*(Sweden, Europe and the Foreigner) that racism is a relatively new word. A translation from the German *rassismus*, it did not enter the Swedish language until 1939. No matter what, why, or who about racism and racist, a consensus was not being reached on how to define a manifestation that was occurring or on how to deal with its uglier effects.[268]

Like Kristersson, many Swedes mistakenly viewed racism as only acts by skinheads and hate groups. Since they personally had never assaulted an outsider and had not yelled "Sieg heil" at anyone, there was an assumption of innocence. Therefore beside the fright and injuries "overt" racist individuals committed, they were clearly responsible for mistaken associations Svenssons would be making about skinhead and neo-Nazi crimes and their own behavior. With a clean record compared to committers of atrocies, the average native felt that he or she was clear of prejudice and discriminatory behavior. Svensson's personal judgment of exemption from such awful charges represented the most important corollary damage that resulted from published reports about crimes of hatred. By being neither a perpetuator nor a supporter of such despicable acts as the ones seen on television and described in newspapers, Svensson did not sympathize or empathize with doers of horrible deeds. To show the world a negative reaction to these, a repulsed ethnic Swede tended to join others of similar persuasion in massive demonstrations against what were considered to be aberrations of Swedish attitudes. Satisfied with what had been protested, good citizen Svensson went home with a good feeling about having made an important statement against prejudice. Then on the following day as a human-resource manager or a shopkeeper, the same cleansed individual passed over a number of job applicants with strange names or monitored carefully shoppers with non-Nordic appearances. In the Swede's mind, no foreigner would ever be happy working at fictional *Bara Svenskarna Fabrik AB* (Only the Swedes Factory, Inc.) on account of cultural differences, and outsiders needed to be watched more carefully in stores than Swedes because of a greater proclivity toward criminality. At least these were Svensson's justifications. Of course none of these responses were considered racist or prejudicial; they were simply representative actions of Swedish reality and practicality in the 1990s. Often a tipoff to Svensson's prejudice would be his or her tendency to preface responses to matters concerning immigrants and refugees with: "Jag är inte rasist, men . . ." ("I am not a racist, but . . .").[269]

Overabundant hate crime was a constant reminder to Svensson of the need for personal efforts on behalf of brotherhood. Informed Swedes knew the red-hot embers of a Swedish fascist movement before the Third Reich's collapse did not cool completely after Hitler's suicide in 1945. Flickers remained ready to rekindle. Well known in Sweden was the story of Ingvar Kamprad, the founder and principal owner of the IKEA furniture empire, as a carrier of the link between wartime and peacetime Nazi activities. During the war when he was a sixteen-year old lad with nineteenth-century family roots in Sudetenland, this future international businessman joined *nordisk ungdom* (Nordic Youth), a group patterned after *Hitlerjugend*. Its agenda was to "chase away all Jews and other paracites who split and rob Gentiles and poison their blood." As late as the 1950s, Kamprad had affiliation with the pro-Nazi *Nysvenska Rörelsen* (the New Swedish Movement). Its leader, Per Engdahl, was a close friend of the do-it-yourself furniture master.

In postwar Sweden Nazis existed and worked on many fronts through several organizations. The World Union of National Socialists became the largest umbrella body. Begun in 1962 it had spread by 1989 to Sweden and twenty-six other nations. It functioned as both an assembly and propaganda organ, instilling in young Nazis a global mission of struggle on behalf of Caucasians everywhere. England was the skinhead-movement's fountainhead. Ian Stuart Donaldson is usually credited as its main politizer and link to neo-Nazism. The National Front, Great Britain's extremely nationalistic political party and a xenophobic organization, was the inspiration for Sweden's *Bevara Sverige svenskt*. Internationally English and Italian fascists began exchanging ideas about plans for an armed struggle. Around a common bond of hatred of Jews, Middle Eastern extremists and Europeans formed close links. A fidelity also occurred with American hate groups such as the Ku Klux Klan and White Aryan Resistance (WAR). The latter group was the model for Sweden's *Vitt Ariskt Motstånd* (or *VAM*). Swedish fascists like cohorts in other countries split over tactics. There were openly militant, revolutionary groups as well as parliamentary-type political parties. *Riksfronten* (the State Front), *Unga Nationalsocialister* or *UNS* (Young National Socialists), *VAM*, and *Nationella Alliansen* (the National Alliance) all believed armed struggle and intimidation would be keys to power, whereas *Sverigedemokraterna* and *Hembygdspartiet* (the Home District Party) were willing to use legal means to gain control of Sweden.

Two facts are interesting to note about Swedes' fascination with fascism. At the main branch of the Stockholm public library, *Mein Kampf* in Swedish has circulated more than any other book and also has tended to disappear the most as well. During February 1990, for example, forty-nine residents were waiting to borrow it. Moreover Swedish wartime citadels of nazism reemerged in the 1990s—as Karlskrona would—to become once again centers of neo-Nazism.[270]

Although a scholar needs to be careful when profiling and categorizing skinheads and neo-Nazis, hesitancy is not altogether necessary when one tries to comprehend and explain the draw of extremism. From interviews and an investigation of members' backgrounds, Norwegian researcher Töre Björgo found seven factors which accounted in large part for an attraction to white power groups:

*Ideology & Politics: lack of attention from the system. This includes individuals who do not feel their views are represented in traditional political parties and who sense they are strangers in these groups.

*Provocation & Rage: less interest in ideology. For these joiners, engagement is a protest act in itself. They see themselves frustrated by and denied the advantages which they have heard that refugees and aliens have allegedly been getting at the expense and to the exclusion of natives.

*Protection: fear of vulnerabilty. These are especially victims of lone immigrants or immigrant gangs and thus have become joiners of hate groups.

*Seekers: uncertain individuals. They manage to move across all the extreme sectors—left first, then right—looking all the time for "truth" and what might seem "correct" at the moment.

*Excitement/Thrill Seekers: dull persons. They become interested because of uniforms, weapons, violence, etc.

*Young Rebels: people who enjoy being on the outside. As with hippies from the 1960s and early 1970s, this group likes to engage in acts that provoke and rebel from societal norms and standards and from the older generation.

*Seekers after a Family and/or Father Figure: people with unhappy childhood experiences. These joiners have come from problem-filled families and have bad close relationships, especially with fathers. They see the older activists as father figures.

Björgo's list likely explains why many people joined, but he overlooked some reasons. Anders Högström who led and then left the *Nationalsocialistisk Front* (National Socialist Front) between 1994 and 2000 discovered a personal fascination with order and manipulation. Simply put he received a thrill when people had been influenced enough to follow his commands. As he explained this, "For me, it had to do with the feeling of being able to steer and create the mass individual, the character, something you yourself compose. It becomes drama, a hypocrisy. . . . It does not matter if it is the raising or lowering of emotions; the importance is the feeling of affinity." In looking for roots one should not overlook such factors as disappointments over an ended relationship and deep-seated psychological problems like depression and aggressive behavior. Love of weapons should be added as a factor, too. Per Ingvar Magnusson from the Sjöbo Party viewed his activity as his way of providing a necessary service to people without representation. Hence he viewed his work for a maverick group essentially as a duty because "popular criticism must have a voice." A final category included joiners whose heritage included relatives who had set a family tradition of fascist beliefs and xenophobia.[271]

Neo-Nazis used many different means to exploit these factors to interest and enlist young people in their diabolical activities. Racist flyers, pamphlets, magazines, and newspapers were frequently used to spread a message of hate. Preceding an "antiracist gala" set for December 3, 1999 in Lomma, a suburb of Malmö, members from "Behold Sweden Swedish" placed handbills under the windshield wipers of parked automobiles and in mailboxes, and they also were at two schools, handing them to students. There were two motives behind the distribution. One was to frighten away prospective attendees, and the other was to besmirch and intimidate sponsor Björn Egerstedt, a Moderate politician and township chair of the committee for recreational activities. This time, the scare tactics and the effort to ruin a reputation failed. The attempt at reducing attendance actually gave organizers an opportunity to do some publicizing of their own. They used the threats to reassure young people of the many safety precautions in place to insure a problem-free night. As for a reaction from the intended target, Egerstedt considered being cited by racists as an opening for him to demonstrate a brave front: "We shall not submit to them who have done this [prepared and distributed handbills]—that matter is clear. If we do that, they will get a feather in their caps."

To entice and interest people in the cause of racism, organizers utilized a wide range of products. During the 1990s, a literal onslaught of short-lived, Swedish-language magazines and newspapers appeared in Sweden. Among these were *Storm*, *Rahowa!*, *Streetfight*, and *Sveriges Framtid* (Sweden's Future). As they came and disappeared, Per Jönsson's efforts on behalf of hate remained noteworthy. He owned Warrior Publications, the leading distributor of racist literature, music, and paraphenalia. Through his company, one could buy a variety of English, American, and German-produced periodicals. From Warrior, racist recordings circulated to listeners across Europe. Song lyrics with an anti-Semitic, Nazi, or racist theme especially fascinated youths and drew their interest as did texts that attacked such allegedly immoral people as gays, drug addicts, pornographers, and rapists (by definition, a sexual act that was between a Nordic and someone else). Formats varied, but Country-and-Western, Arian Folk, Black Metal, and Viking Rock were the most popular music classifications with antisocial, prejudicial themes. Among many artists who performed for this audience, Ultima Thule and Dirlewanger were the most popular.

The internet also became an invaluable tool for recruiting new members. Colorful, action-filled homepages attracted many readers. Opening these sites might have resulted from curiosity, but the contents often struck chords with social misfits described in preceding paragraphs. An impressive variety of racist music was available from Warrior on the internet. In May 1999 lovers of hate lyrics could select from an internet listing of 322 different compact-disc titles.

For the most part the Sweden government did nothing to stop or discourage the spread of racist publications, inciteful lyrics, and offensive computer materials. There were some meager efforts at raiding, arresting, seizing, and blocking sellers as well as producers, productions, and internet sites, but legal technicalities in Swedish law effectively handicapped any control of these materials and aided in freeing individuals who had been charged in their connection.[272]

Spectacular defiances of authority constituted an important aspect of the neo-Nazi program and agenda. There were Swedish and German highpoints to celebrate on a massive scale. These featured demonstrations that gathered as many participants as possible to parade in tight formation, wear black pants, leather boots, and shirts, and display red and black swastikas on their sleeves. Great pleasures seemed to come to marchers when they raised their right arms at 180-degree angles to shouts of "Sieg heil" at antiracist protestors, spectators, and police as they waved Nazi banners and Swedish flags all along the route of their demonstration. Suitable Swedish occasions for such displays by neo-Nazis included the battle death of Charles XII on November 30th and the birth of Gustav II Adolf on November 6th, the two favorite kings of Swedish nationalists. Of course Rudolf Hess and Hitler—patron saints of neo-Nazis everywhere—were recipients of praise in Sweden at the same times as in other nations. Militant rightwingers also arranged concerts and parties to which the special guests were fellow believers from neighboring countries.

Provocation was an important part of demonstrations as their requests to counter Social Democrats and Left Party members on May 1—international labor's day of solidarity—would show. Nothing seemed to please large contingents of assembled fascists more than opportunities to confront and battle leftwingers. For demonstrators and counterdemonstrators alike, the goal was proving which side was toughest and bravest in a fight. To prepare for melees neo-Nazis studied martial arts and attended military-style training camps. Even if their confrontations involved police, neo-Nazis were confident of slim risks for long detentions. Anyhow an arrest record was something to be coveted as testimony to and evidence of dedication and loyalty.[273]

In the propagation of xenophobia and racism, neo-Nazis received help from many diverse groups and individuals. In politics, of course, there were several parties—local and national—which preached against Sweden's intake of more refugees and immigrants. In Skåne alone twenty-three of these had come into existence with various agendas and platforms. Astonishly after the general election of 1999 all had secured representation in at least one local township government. *Framstegspartiet* (the Progressive Party) won seats in Bjuv after it had plastered Helsingborg city buses with placards declaring tax revenues should be going to police, health care, and education and definitely not to immigrants. In Höör *Sverigedemokraterna* campaigned for a stop to all non-European migrations to Sweden, an organized retreat of immigrants from Sweden, and a prohibition against the adoption of non-European children.

Apparently free of all affiliations, John Ausonius, Sweden's so-called "laserman," aided the neo-Nazi cause by frightening aliens around Stockholm with gunfire directed at them. *VAM* leaders also prepared the way for fascists by stealing weapons, terrorizing, and preaching hatred. Criminal motorcycle clubs such as *Brödraskapet* (the Brotherhood) MC, the Bulldog MC, and the White Wearwolves MC allied with fascists. The latter gang's leader, Niclas Löfdahl, had a long history of racist involvement; his log of activities included posting a bomb to Justice Minister Freivalds and cofounding *Ariska Brödraskapet*.[274]

A small core of members working alone or together in small gangs did the neo-Nazis' "work." Modern equivalents of Hitler's storm troopers, these operatives had assignments to perform. Specific targets included Jews, blacks, non-Europeans, troublesome politicians, antiracists, leftists, and syndicalists. Acts were verbal or physical, and objects of their actions were injecting a victim with fear or beating someone. A threatening letter or a telephone call was often enough to intimidate a critic, but occasionally assignments demanded more overt acts such as spraying exterior surfaces in ghetto areas with racist slogans and Nazi symbols.   Then the idea was frightening residents into either withholding testimonies at race-related trials or not reporting racially motivated crimes to police.   Plans occasionally included murder, seizures of stockpiled weapons, or thefts of large sums of money.   For instance in 1991 Nazis boldly broke into the police station at Lidingö; they left with thirty-six pistols.   As a means of funding activities racist organizations robbed banks and post offices.

When fascists and skinhead allies participated in violent acts, their marked-for-murder casualties were victims like syndicalistic union leader Björn Söderberg.   Three neo-Nazis shot him dead in 1999.   Spontaneous acts could also occur.   Just being seen with a disliked emblem emblazoned on or pinned to a jacket such as Helena Håkansdotter had could set off reactions.   Her mistake was being seen wearing an SSU jacket by three neo-Nazis.   "Socialist bastard," they screamed at her, "we shall mark you."   True to their threat, two young men pinned down the woman as a third used a knife to carve a swastika into her cheek.   Altogether, seized records reveal that some 400 persons were on a Nazi list of designated foes.

After bombs had exploded to destroy an automobile owned by an antiracist journalist during the summer of 1999 and then a few months later in October a syndicalist office in Gävle, police began taking more seriously fascists' written and spoken boasts.   Officers finally started to follow leads more diligently and to give better protection to such warned individuals as the eighty-eight-year old veteran antiracist, Ingrid Segerstedt Wiberg.   Police placed the old woman under patrol after racists had sprayed prejudicial slogans and swastikas on her Göteborg house.   In large white letters on one of its windows appeared the words *Död åt Zog* (Death to the Zionist Occupation Government).

With limited resources and manpower, conditions in the Swedish police corps favored Nazis because law-enforcement officers were unable to provide the necessary protection threats warranted.   Musician Mikael Wiehl understood the problem very well.   On October 25, 1999, after a screamed out "Sieg heil" had followed an early-morning explosion at the entrance to his Malmö home, he notified police immediately with a description of what had just transpired at his residence.   Yet, so late as mid-afternoon October 26, 1999, no officer had come to investigate Wiehl's complaint.   Ignoring the call for police assistance caused him to reflect about a trend of worrying proportions and to empathize: "Slowly but certainly, they [Nazis] are growing stronger. . . . However, I do not want to blame individual policemen as it deals with how you divide up resources."

From the beginning of 1999 through Wiehl's complaint, tabulated crime statistics confirmed more Nazi-perpetuated violations in Malmö than during any previous year, and this trend was characteristic of Sweden.   As the figures verify for 2000 racist acts committed against persons and their property were accelerating upward at an alarming rate, this despite the general reluctance to classify all criminal commissions by skinheads and neo-Nazis against ethnic and racial minorities and leftists as race-inspired criminality.   If a lighter side could be found in grim news, it involved a swindling attempt by a man who had placed Nazi literature on the backseat of his automobile before using an explosive to blow apart the car's rearend. He had hoped to exploit the debate about fascist violence to collect on insurance, but police doubted his account and succeeded at wringing a confession from the schemer.[275]

Regardless of neo-Nazis' criminality, government officials did not act appropriately to an existing internal threat. Although German postal and bank authorities had denied fascists in the Federal Republic access to their services, counterparts in Sweden refused to do likewise. In a valid attempt to weaken neo-Nazis' financial activities and sales of merchandise, Karlskrona Township spokesperson Björn Fries and attorney Lennart Eriksson requested a similar response in their country, but Managing Director Lennart Grabe of the central post office refused because he missed the direct link between mail-box rentals and crimes. Foiled on Sepember 23, 2000, Fries and Eriksson wondered where they might turn next in their fight against fascism.

More than four years earlier Växjö opposition leader Bo Frank had more or less felt similar frustration after a township majority government of Social Democrats, Leftists, and Greens had rejected a ban on renting township-owned properties to known Nazis. "Scandalous," responded Commissioner Frank, the bill's sponsor and a Moderate. Their vote sanctioned, in effect, the continued availability of public-owned properties to racists. Nationally as long ago as January 18, 1990, seven Social Democrat members of the Riksdag had wanted legislation that would outlaw racist groups and would forbid discrimination. Moreover there had been advice to prioritize the fight against race-motivated crime. No actions were taken on these proposals.[276]

By December 31, 2000, all organizations—regardless of their goals or policies—operated without impediments because of Sweden's confused twist on the meaning of human rights. According to it, endowing such privileges as freedoms of assembly, expression, and organization to every individual and group—no matter their actions, motives, policies, or goals—garnered a greater importance in the minds of politicians than protecting a person's right to peace and tranquility or preserving such foundations and pillars of national integrity as law, order, justice, and fairness. Given nationhood's dependence upon self-preservation and self-protection, there were times when these entities must be weighed against freedom. By failing to proclaim totalitarianism's threat to the monarchy, officials showed not only blindness but an ignorance of potentially harmful effects from excessive freedom to groups bent on destroying freedom and democracy. Delegates to the *riksdag* ignored a fundamental UN resolution which urged nations to ban any organization whose intention was a denial of basic human rights. Sweden, having once supported this principle in the General Assembly and having failed to adopt it into domestic law, obviously showed hypocracy as well as contempt for a universal protection.

Lawmakers by not acting also endangered the lives of all who had quit a hate group or informed on one. Simply stated a former neo-Nazi could never completely depend on government protection. Consider Tobias Malvå's experiences after his departure from *nationalsocialistisk front*. He had faced so much anxiety that he and his girlfriend were forced into hiding. Exit, an organization headed by ex-Nazi Kent Lindahl and a recipient of funding to facilitate departures, could offer quitters moral support and provide useful tips on adjusting to new life styles, but it lacked the necessary authority and means to protect against vengence by resentful fascists determined to prevent any confessions from ex-members. During Exit's first two years of existence poor support explains in part why it could assist only eighty persons safely through a process of disassociation.

Moreover it is worth asking how a leaver could ever feel safe in Sweden after *Säpo* Commissioner Torbjörn Ekblom's announcement that racist crimes did not pose a threat to society and his accusation that members of the Swedish news media were largely to blame for many unfortunate racial incidents due to their tendency to exaggerate racism's effects on the nation. No wonder with a person in charge of national security having a cavalier attitude about dangers from the extreme right why one might not want to take seriously what Swedes were doing to outlaw different forms of discrimination.

Whether prejudicial practices continued because of the toothlessness of laws or were consequences from staff members' inabilities to cope with all the enforcement tasks before them, not much could alter a lack of results. Facts belie an intention of Swedes to heed the stated purposes of antidiscrimination legislation, and they generally did not fear consequences from their inactions. Herewith, Sweden had until July 19, 2003, to comply with a European Union directive of June 29, 2000, against discrimination. If an earlier UN resolution indicates how Sweden will comply, nothing will change. Regardless if past events are a guide to future actions or inactivities, two matters will remain in the forefront; arguments and results will not change, but Swedes will continue to debate unresolved issues and will forestall a meaningful enactment.[277]

From January 1, 1990 through December 31, 2001, racist crimes netted only light sentences from Swedish courts. Throughout the period they tended to have a boys-will-be-boys attitude toward Nazi and skinhead criminals. For convictions two different cases in separate courtrooms confronted prosecutors with similar obstacles to overcome, and they illustrate the peculiarities of the monarchy's system of justice. In the first one a Moroccan visitor to Lund in April 1990 became a murderer's victim. Police almost at once accused an eighteen-year old youth of killing the tourist, but the teenager never went to trial. By pinning blame on an unknown assailant, the young man gained a release after maintaining his innocence. Without enough evidence to obtain an indictment, a prosecutor's chances of convicting the suspect were none. By being set free, he demonstrated the absurdity of the judicial system. Had he committed the crime or been an accomplice, Sweden will likely never know the answer because police had not been given any option but to accept a story about a "mystery" figure's involvement.

Almost ten years later to the day three neo-Nazis each denied in court responsibility for firing the gun that had killed syndicalist Söderberg. Hence the prosecutor was left with only one option. He could only pursue convictions for the lessor crime of being accomplices to murder. Hampus Hellekant and Björn Lindberg, the two oldest defendants, each was sentenced to six years' imprisonment, and Jimmy Niklasson who was twenty at the time of the political assassination received four years, six months, a concession given him because he was three and two years younger than his friends. Here was another example of judicial imbecility. Without a determination as to which one had actually shot Söderberg, all three should have been equally guilty of planning and carrying out a calculated, cold-blooded murder.[278]

Short prison terms for the dastardly deed of deliberately killing a person because of his political views clearly show how this society has diminished the value of human life. Deciding whether or not capital punishment is a morally correct stance for a governments to take or if it is in fact a heinously cruel and unusual punishment are matters beyond the scope of this study, but it is fair to ask if neo-Nazis should not have received harsher penalties for murdering their foes. A careful check of the cases cited in endnote 278 reveals a disturbing pattern of sentences that must be judged as insults to the dignity and worth of victims of hatred and revenge. Each was selected because of either prejudice, racism, xenophobia, or political involvement. Here are a few sample acts and the judgments announced after guilty verdicts:

*Trollhättan, 1993, three codefendants in the destruction by arson of a mosque—3½ and 2½ years, and juvenile-home detention.

*Stockholm, 1999, freedom for five defendants in the Pascalidou case.

*Strängnäs, 1997, four skinheads freed after beating a nine-year old immigrant boy.

*Flen, 1990, three youths received six months after a conviction for having thrown a Molotov cocktail at a refugee-residence hall.

*Stockholm, 1999, a Nazi whose beating of two immigrants was caught on video film was sentenced to a three-month jail term.

*Malmö, 2000, two Nazi attackers of African mother and daughter were not charged with any crime.

*Trollhättan, 1993, thirty-four months in jail for so severely beating a Somalian that it caused irreversible brain damage.

*Göteborg, 1992, six and seven years for murdering an Iraqi drug dealer.[279]

Serious consideration must be given to another dimension of racist crime and of instances of discrimination. Whichever wrong had been committed, one aspect often ignored would still have future relevance. With the median age of natives edging upward and the birth rate for ethnic Swedish women spiraling downward, the cost of pensions and health care for the nation has begun to be carried by an ever-decreasing work force. In Skåne alone over 5,000 nurses, doctors, and teachers will reach the age of retirement by 2005. With so many anticipated turnovers from salary earners to pension recipients, or put another way, with a significantly massive-scale transition from a nation of taxpayers to one of welfare takers, all would be fine if two conditions were met. First of all the void left by the retiring of skilled and educated workers must be filled with equally able replacements. Forecasters unfortunately anticipate shortages for all three work classifications. Second of all at least one person and possibly as many as three must be working and paying taxes just to cover the pension and welfare benefits of each additional professional retiree. Regrettably Sweden's low birthrate and inadequate educational system are in capable of refilling so many slots created by this many professional departures from the workforce. Herein could be the unfolding of a potentially valuable role for immigrants in Swedish society. Given opportunities to practice their professions and utilize their educational training, outsiders theoretically could provide solutions to a major labor problem. On the other hand if Swedish society and institutions insist on a pluralistic setup that denies a valuable human resource from making valuable contributions, aliens will simply compound the problem of additional pensioners by remaining essentially tax burdens instead of productive workers.

Given the extreme urgency and seriousness of a near future employment emergency in certain fields and the largest portion of 18 percent of all national inhabitants being unable to contribute at their maximum level through no fault of their own, one could and possibly should conclude that committing both acts of physical violence and employment discrimination against aliens constitute in some respects treason or sedition against Sweden's future. The *Random House Unabridged Dictionary* defines treason as "the betrayal of a trust or confidence" and "a violation of allegiance to one's state," whereas its definitions of sedition are the "incitement of discontent or rebellion against a government" or "any act, writing, speech, etc., directed unlawfully against state authority, the government, or constitution, or calculated to bring it into contempt or to incite others to hostility, ill will or disaffection." In light of consequences to Sweden's development, acts against immigrants, be they violent or discriminatory, might easily be judged as treasonous and seditious because outsiders were assets and insurance against acute labor shortages.

Instead of wrangling over fine points about individual rights, *riksdag* members, township councils, and county officers need to sharpen laws and increase penalties as they apply to discrimination and hate crimes. Political parties and leaders must initiate a massive campaign to readjust Swedish attitudes and explain concretely why amelioration is so vital to the future of the nation. Swinging to a more pragmatic view of multiculturalism and to a tougher stand against violators of future national interests through their acts of hate or prejudicial treatment must be seen as essentials for the commonweal. Hope not hatred should be a constant message drummed into the populace. Heretofore nobody has spoken so bluntly nor so candidly to Swedes about the dire consequences of their incorrect actions. Some have hinted about the value of aliens to Swedish society, but unfortunately direct, straight-from-the-hip talk has been altogether missing. A manpower crisis is ahead if attitudes do not change immediately. With about 9-million people and one of the longest life spans in the world, Sweden will spin quickly downward if she does not adopt an American mindset toward newcomers and does not do something similar to the Affirmative Action program of the United States. The goal of integrating minorities more effectively into Sweden must be paramount among law and policy makers. Affirmative Action has shown that it does push people into jobs and education. As some of the world's most avid newspaper readers and followers of current affairs, Swedes surely can do better at treating minorities fairly and at punishing racist criminals more severely if only reasons are intelligently presented and emphasized until the message can alter behavior and improve legislation.[280]

There is no puzzle about what Sweden must do. The insidious aspect of the conundrum is the inability (or is it an unwillingness) of a well-read, world-traveled population to understand the complications awaiting the nation in the near future if no efforts are made immediately to promote genuine brotherhood and reverse welfare's intrusively destructive effect on outsiders' lives. If the enigma remains unresolved, Sweden's future is bleak. A simple warning from Abraham Lincoln about the dangers of a house divided should impregnate the Swedish consciousness as no others. In a nationally televised interview April 30, 2001, Hip-Hop Artist "Feven" was insistent about not viewing herself as the least bit Swedish despite having lived in Stockholm since early childhood. If only an Eritrean-born songstress were in denial about herself, no need for concern would exist. Unfortunately for Sweden's future, many immigrants who arrived after 1973 and many of their offspring agree with Feven. Since outsiders constitute nearly one-fifth of Sweden's inhabitants, the words of Lincoln demand close attention and positive responses from the indigenous population.[281]

Endnotes

[1]SVT (2 Fe 2000).

[2]Gunnar Myrdal. *An American Dilemma: The Negro Problem and Modern Democracy* (New York, 1962), I, li-lxii.

[3]*VK* (14 Mr 1996); Cait Murphy. "The New Europeans." *Fort* (21 De 1998), 87-97. In both sources Myrdal's study has come into focus, with authors of each maintaining an American dilemma "is increasingly a European one as well."

[4] "Black, blanc, beur," *Econ* (5 Je 1999), 16, 19; "Hear the soulbird sing," *Econ* (10 Je 2000), 117-121; *AB* (31 Oc 1997); *SDS* (1998-99); *CSM*, No 19 (1992).

[5]"Port in a storm," *Econ* (21 Au 1999), 29-30; "A tragedy and a shame," *Econ* (27 Fe 1999), 37-38; "Mixed messages," *Econ* (13 My 2000), 39-40; "Playing the race card," *Econ* (7 Oc 2000.

[6]*SvD* (11 Oc 1991); "Germany's neo-Nazis" and "Togetherness: a balance sheet," *Econ* (12 Au & 30 Se 2000), 16-17 & 32; *Metro* (9 No 2000).

[7]"Belgium's Dewinter of discontent." *Econ* (14 Oc 2000), 42.

[8] "Nasty, ubiquitous and unloved." *Econ* (20 Mr 1999), 36, 41.

[9] "Foreign Relief." *Econ* (30 Se 2000), 42, 45.

[10]*IHT* (9 My 2000); "Trouble." *Econ* (24 Jl 1999), 27; *SvD* (29 Jl 1991).

[11]*OD* (9 Fe, 24 Se 2000).

[12]*SDS* (28 Au, 1999).

[13]*Ibid.* (1 Oc 1999).

[14] "Testing Danish tolerance," *Econ,* (28 Au 1999), 24.

[15]*SDS* (9 No 1999, 27 Ja 2000).

[16]*Ibid.* (29 Se 2000).

[17]*AB* (2 Je 1990, 27 Ap 1998); *DN* (21 Je, 5 Jl, 8 De 1991); *GP* (22 Au 1991); *ÖK* (18 Oc 1994); *NT* (7 No 1994); *VK* (14 Mr 1996); *SP* (10 No 1997).

[18]"How Europe Stacks Up," *Fort* (21 De 1998), 51-56.

[19]Interestingly Peter Brimelow, an immigrant to the United States from the United Kingdom, has tried to warn his adopted country about a pending "immigration disaster" in a sensational study citing typical European xenophobic arguments against immigrants. Peter Brimelow. *Alien Nation: Common Sense About America's Immigration Disaster* (New York: 1996).

[20] Norman Macrae, "Will You Ever Be Able to Retire?," *Fort* (29 My 2000), 30; Murphy, "The New Europeans," 87-97; "Go for it" & "A continent on the move," *Econ* (6 My 2000), 15-16 & 21-25; "Europe flunks the graduate course," *Econ* (4 Fe 1995), 28; "Alien scientists take over USA!," *Econ* (21 Au 1999), 38; *SvD* (30 Ja 1990); *AB* (21 Au 1992); *GP* (20 Au 1994); *DN* (1 Mr 1999); *IHT* (3 Mr 1999); *Times* (29 Ja 2000); a trio

of new books, although only briefly examined, offer seemingly superb analyses of European xenophobia and racism; see: Nicholas Fraser. *The Voice of Modern Hatred: Encounters with Europe's New Right* (New York, 2000); Paul Hainsworth, ed. *Politics of the Extreme Right: From the Margins to the Mainstream* (New York, 2000); Jeffrey Kaplan and Tore Björgo, eds., *Nation and Race: The Developing Euro-American Racist Subculture*, Boston, 2000.

[21]*DN* (12-17 Ja, 19 Fe, 13 Mr 1990); *Arb* (16 Ja 1995); *SDS* (15 Fe 1992, 27Ja, 13 Mr, 6 My 2000); *HD* (25 Se 1996); *BT* (9 Fe 1998).

[22]*VLT* (8 De 1993); *BT* (27 De 1997); *NT* (5 De 1997); Ingvar Svanberg & Mattias Tydén. *I nationalismens bakvatten: om minoritet, etnicitet och rasism* (Lund, 1999), 7-32.

[23]Svanberg & Tydén. *I nationalismens bakvatten*, 7-22; Adam Heymowski. "Resande eller 'tattare' en gammal minoritet på väg att försvinna." in Ingvar Svanberg, ed. *I samhällets utkanter: om "tattare" i Sverige* (Uppsala, 1987), 13-21.

[24]Svanberg & Tydén. *Sverige och förintelsen: Debatt och dokument om Europas judar 1933-1945* (Stockholm, 1997), 181; Ingrid Lomfors. *Förlorad barndom återvunnet liv: de judiska flyktingbarnen från Nazityskland* (Göteborg, 1996), 79-82, 89, 304-305; Olle Häger. "Aningslöshet." in Jan Guillou, ed. *Antirasistiskt lexikon* (Stockholm, 1997), 10-16; *SvD* (11 Fe 1991, 13 Au 1993); *Exp* (24 Je 1990, 1 Au 1995); *AB* (30 Jl 1990); *DN* (28 Ja 1994); *HD* 18 My, 29 No 1996); *NT* (11 No 1997). In fairness to Sweden there were exceptional cases when individuals did receive exile, including grants to such celebrities as Willy Brandt, Bruno Kreisky, Nelly Sachs, Leise Meitner, and Georg Klein.

[25]Rochelle Wright. *The Visible Wall: Jews and Other Ethnic Outsiders in Swedish Film* (Carbondale, 1998), 5-9, 12-44, 48-59, 61-7, 70, 321, 389, 391; Lennart Lundmark. "Samerna och den svenska rasismen." *Populär historia*, No. 4 (1998), 40-44; Gregory Michael Dorr. "Assuring America's Place in the Sun: Ivey Foreman Lewis and the Teaching of Eugenics at the University of Virginia, 1915-1953." *The Journal of Southern History* 66 (2000), 266; Ingrid Segerstedt Wiberg & Ingrid Lomfors. *När Sverige teg: om nazisternas förföljelser* (Stockholm, 1991), 154-5; Svanberg & Tydén. *I nationalismens bakvatten*, 31-42; Aron Neuman. "Antisemitismen." in David Glück, Aron Neuman, & Jacqueline Stare. *Sveriges judar: deras historia tro och traditioner* (Stockholm, 1997), 117-125; Eric Wärenstam. *Fascismen och nazismen i Sverige 1920-1940: Studier i den svenska nationalsocialismens, fascismens och antisemitismens organisationer, ideologier och propaganda under mellankrigsåren* (Stockholm, 1972), 13-30; Helene Lööw. "Sveriges rasistiska förflutna." *Pockettidningen R* 21 (1991), 21; Lena Berggren. *Nationell upplysning: drag i den svenska antisemitismens idéhistoria* (Stockholm, 1999), 347; *HD* (10 Je 1996); *Kunskap som kraft* (Stockholm, 1997), 21; Alva & Gunnar Myrdal. *Kris i befolkningsfrågan* (Stockholm, 1934); *Dagen* (30 Mr 1996).

[26]Neuman. "Antisemitismen," 45-51; Wärenstam. *Fascismen och nazismen*, 13-30, 32-9, 179-84.

[27]Wärenstam, *Fascismen och nazismen*, 40-71, 179-184; Lena Berggren. *Från bondeaktivism till rasmystik: om Elof Eriksson antisemitiska skriftställarskap 1923-1941* (Umeå, 1997); Berggren. *Nationell upplysning*, 345-349.

[28]Bosse Schön. *Svenskarna som stred för Hitler: ett historiskt reportage* (Stockholm, 1999), 9-10; *SDS* (20 De 1999); *DN* (31 De 1990).

[29]Lars-Åke Skagegård & Tobias Hübinette. *Hatets återkomst: om fascism, nynazism och rasism i dagens Sverige* (Stockholm, 1998), 74-77; Inga Lundström & Marja-Leena Pilvesmaa. "Rastanken i folkhemmet." State Historical Museum *Annals* (1995), 24-26;

Siiri Matvejevna. *Välkommen till Sverige* (Copenhagen, 1996); Annu Liikkanen. *Med lapp om halsen* (Helsingborg, 1995), 7; Glück, Neuman, Stare. *Sveriges judar*, 43-51; *DN* (6 No 1997, 18 Se 1999); *SvD* (11 Oc 1991); *Arb* (16 Ja 1995); *UNT* (13 Ja 1998); Schön. *Svenskarna som stred för Hitler*; Lars Borgersrud. "Wollweber-organisajonen i Norge." 2 vols., unpublished Ph. D. dissertation, Oslo University, 1994, vol. I, 394-8, 403-7, 413, 420, 425-8, 493, 662.

[30]Christer Lundh & Rolf Ohlsson. *Från arbetskraftsimport till flyktinginvandring* (Stockholm, 1994), 12-3; *SDS* (29 Ap 2000); *VLT* (8 De 1993, 28 Jl, 11 Au 1997); *DN* (6 No 1998); *Dagen* 10 Se 1993); *GP* (7 Se 1999); *SvD* (16 Mr 1991).

[31]Carl-Ulrik Schierup. "Etnicitet och arbete." in Schierup & Sven Paulson, eds. *Arbetets etniska delning* (Stockholm, 1994), 10-1; Lundh & Ohlsson. *Från arbetskraftsimport till flyktinginvandring*, 12-3, 25-7.

[32]Schierup. "Etnicitet och arbete," 10-11; Walter Repo. "All världens bilbyggare." *Mig* (No. 2, 1998), 16-20.

[33]*VLT* (8 De 1993).

[34]Thomas Gür. *Staten och nykomlingarna: en studie av den svenska invandrarpolikens idéer* (Stockholm, 1996), 291, 298; *DN* (6 No 1998).

[35]Andreas Hadjourdes & Christian Kellberg. *Vi sålde våra liv* (Stockholm, 1978); Arne Redemo. *De nya svenskarna: en debattskrift om den svenska invandrarfrågan* (Stockholm, 1968); *SvD* (17 Se 1996); *SDS* (12 Ap 1997); *GD* (16 My 1990).

[36]*GP* (3, 5, 16, 18 Se 1997, 14 Oc 1998); *SvD* (27 Jl 1990, 1 Jl 1992); *GD* (17 No 1995); *DN* (17 Mr, 22 Au 1990, 22-3 Je 1997); *UNT* (2 De 1995).

[37]Lasse Winkler. "Siriusgatan—en segregerad stadsdel." *NiS* (No. 3, 1990), 40-8; *DN* (2-4Ja, 2 Je, 29 Au, 18-9 No 1990, 20 No, 17 De 1998); *Exp* (17 Mr 1997).

[38]Norrköping homepage.

[39]Short for *Statens Invandrarverk* or Immigration Board.

[40]*DN* (10 Fe, 27 Mr, 24 Au). When communal leaders were asked if they should have a right to veto the intake of refugees, a third responded affirmatively. This and notes through fourteen are from 1990.

[41]*Ibid.* (27 Mr, 9 Ap, 5, 8 Je); *NT* (28 Mr, 9 Ap). Immigration Minister Maj-Lis Lööw refused to believe most Swedes opposed refugees; she called supporters "the silent majority." *MVT* (28 My).

[42]*NT* (7 Ap); *DN* (12 Ap).

[43]*NT* & *DN* (18 My).

[44]*AB* (14 Ap); *UNT* (18 My).

[45]Further talks between Immigration Bureau, Building Board, and Wibarco negotiators resulted in a compromise settlement of 175 residents and fifteen barracks.

[46]*DN* & *NT*, 25 My.

[47]Sweden's police come under critical scrutiny in Chapter IV.

[48]*DN* (26-7 My, 5 Je); *NT* (26 My, 5 Je); *GP* (2 Je); *Exp* (30 My); *AB* (14 Je).

[49]*AB* (14-5 Je); *DN* & *NT* (15 Je).

[50]*SDS* (22 Ja); *ÖC* (24-3 Fe-Mr); *GP* (21 My); *NN* & *DN* (1 Je); *SvD* (16-7 Je); *Exp* (19 Je); *Bar* (9 Jl).

[51]*SvD* (16-17 Je).

[52]Chapter III is devoted to policy making and politicians.

[53]Although acts against refugees had preceded Kimstad, their significance is less important because they had not connected to widely publicized community protests; hence they were not models for future actions. As with the state of Mississippi's summer of 1964, Sweden's in 1990 has also been called "a long, hot summer." In addition

several incidents occurred in 1990 after the one-month rush, and refugees remained targets throughout the decade. Descriptions of and analytical reports on the worst of these will follow in Chapter IV. For 1990 see: *SDS* (22 Ja, 23-4 Jl); *GP* (6 My, 2 Je); *DN* (6, 26-8, 30 My, 2-3, 11, 19, 25 Je, 24 Jl, 7 Se, 24-5 Oc, 11 No); *VLT* (28-9 My); *MVT* (28-9 My); *NT* (28 My); *BB* (29 My); *LT* (28-30 My); *TSL* (28-9 My); *KK* (2 Je); *BLT* (5 Je); *NN* (11 Je, 3 Se); *Arb* (17 Au); *NS* 1 No); "Det Brinner." *Sr* (no. 2, 1990): 2. Although there will be a full discussion of skinhead and neo-Nazi crimes directed randomly at persons not "looking" or "sounding" Swedish or at defenders of targets in Chapter IV, examples of post-1990 hate crimes aimed at refugees are in: *SvD* (15 Mr, 6 Ap, 26 Oc, 13 No, 2 De 1991); *GP* (15 My, 2-3, 15 No 1992); *VK* (19 Fe, 14 Ap, 29 Je, 27 Jl, 16, 30 Se 1993); *Arb* (1 Mr, 30 Ap, 7 Oc 1995); *HD* (2 Ja 1996); *AB* (30 Jl, 22-3 Oc 1998); *Exp* (31 Au, 8 Se, 17 No 1998); Bertil Murray. "Åter på flykt mitt i Sverige." *Annals 1997/1998* (Uppsala: Allmänna förlag, 1998), 45-9. Statements against refu-gees and immigrants by individual Swedes were often followed by "but . . . .," ". . .Men jag är inte rasist!." *Sr* (no. 2 1993), 4.

[54]*LT* (28-31 My 1990); *DN* (27 My 1990).

[55]Several newspaper accounts of violence given in note 16 mention its effects and highlight the precautions taken to stop it; they also note how refugees in Sweden were continuing to experience torment rather than the expected blissful hiatuses from homeland horrors. Also see: Axel W. Karlsson. "Flyktingar och invandrare, rasister och vanliga svenskar." *Ny Social Debatt* 7 (1996), 114; Charles Westin. "Tortyr." *I & M* 18 (Oc 1991), 84-87; Pieter Bevelander, Benny Carlson, Mauricio Rojas. *I krusbärslandets storstäder: om invandrare i Stockholm, Göteborg och Malmö* (Stockholm, 1997), 7; Lena Häll Eriksson. "Ny flyktingpolitik." *Se mig, hör mig* (Stockholm: 1995), 7; *SDS* (18 Fe 2000).

[56]Daniele Joly. *Refugees: Asylum in Europe?* (London, 1992), 12-3; Sahlberg. "Slut på den generösa flyktingpolitiken?" *NiS* (no. 1, 1990), 28-32; Akbar Golrang. *I gränslandet mellan iransk och svensk kultur* (Borås, 1997), 67-8; Namdar Nasser. *På vägen till Sverige: sju sällsamma berättelser om sju iranska flyktingar* (Stockholm, 1999), 11, 42; Sahlberg. "Kvotflyktingar direkt till kommunerna." *NiS* (no. 1, 1990), 42-5; Maria Appelqvist. *Responsibility in transition: a study of refugee law and policy in Sweden* (Umeå, 1999), 192-3; Berith Andersson-Aravena. *Främling och vän: en handledning i hur man kan arbeta mot främlingsfientlighet och rasism* (Stockholm, 1989), 15. In 1991 Sweden increased its annual quota from 1,250 to 2,000, her first change in fifteen years. *SvD*, 27 Ap, 15 My 1991; *Arb*, 6 Ja 1991, 30 Se 1995.

[57]Christina Rogestam. "Ribban för asylsökande höjs oavsiktligt?" *NiS* (no. 6, 1990), 1; Mannerfelt. "'Nya lagen—en halvmesyr.'" *NiS* (no. 1, 1990), 19-21; Sahlberg. "Vi har nått taket." *NiS* (no. 1, 1990), 22-5; Mannerfelt. "Långa köer på utredningsslussen." *NiS* (no. 1, 1990), 14-8; *SvD* (30 Ja, 28 Mr, 15 Au 1990, 9 Jl 1991); Sahlberg. "22,000 väntar på besked om de får stanna." *NiS* (no. 1, 1991), 10-3; "S.O.S. Asyl." *Sr* (no. 1, 1990): 8-11; *YA* (7, 20-2, 24, 26-9, 31 Mr 1990); *DN* (15, 17, 19 Fe, 7, 15, 18-28 Mr, 5 Ap, 27 Jl 1990); Sahlberg. "Hårdnande klimat på flyktingförläggningarna." *NiS* (no. 1, 1991): 2-5; "S.O.S. Asyl.." *Sr* (no. 1, 1990), 8-11; *GP* (8 Ap 1999); *Arb* (5 Ap 1990). Regarding stopovers in a second country on the way to a third for asylum, rules were clear and inflexible. It was the second country that assumed responsibility for accepting the refugee. For an example, see: *SvD* (10 Se 1991).

[58]*AB* (27 Ap 1998); *DI* (3 Fe 1993). During Rogestam's five years as *Siv* General Director, 200,000 people sought Swedish asylum, whereas her predecessors' ten- and

eight-year tenures witnessed only 30,000 and 78,000 seekers; see Christina Rogestam. "Dags att sätta punkt." *NiS* (no. 1, 1993), 1.
[59]Reza Banakar. "Debatt på låtsas." *I & M* 18 (De 1991), 3-10; Ingrid Segerstedt Wiberg. *Min mot-bok* (Göteborg, 1999), 13; Sahlberg. "Bengt-Erik Ginsburg: Vänta med hiv-testen." *NiS* (no. 3, 1993), 31-3; *DN* (13 Mr, 3, 5 My 1990, 5 Ja 1997, 27 Mr 1998); Peter Nobel. *Polisen och invandrarna* (Stockholm: Discrimination Ombudsman, no, 2, 1988), 6; *HD* (14 No 1996); *SvD* (5 Fe, 18 De 1991, 15-6 Ap 1998); *GP* (24 Ja 1992); Marie Crole-Rees. "En vanlig dag på svenska flyktingslussen." *NiS* (no. 2, 1992), 10-3; Sahlberg. "Stöt inte bort dom som behöver hjälpen mest!" *NiS* (no. 2, 1992), 44-9; Christina Rogenstam. "Invandrarverket utreder människan bakom ärendet synligare." *NiS* (no. 2, 1992), 1; Sahlberg. "Migrationsverket—framtidens utlänningspoliser?" *Mig* (no. 1, 1997): 32-5; *ST* (10 Se 1994); *Från ansökan till beslut—ett asylärendes gång* (Norrköping, 1997), 4-11. The practice of finger-printing was controversial because copies of specimens went into a pan-European Union archive for use by member nations. *DN*, 21 De 1998.
[60]*VK* (27 Au, 9 Se, 1 Oc 1993); *DN* (18 Oc, 15 De 1990); *AB* (21 Ja 1994); *HD* (2 Au, 3 De 1996); *SDS* (7 Mr 2000); *SvD* (3 Je, 29-1 Jl-Au 1991); Vesna Maldaner. "'Vi kommer alltid kallas för jävla zigenare.'" *NiS* (no. 3 1991), 46-8; Bo Levin. "Zigenarna får skulden." *NiS* (no. 3, 1991), 13-6. Despite more attempts at Swedish sanctuaries, skepticism prevailed among *Siv* officials toward asylum seekers from the ex-Soviet Union at the turn of the century; see statistics in *SDS* (26 No 2000).
[61]*DN* (12, 14 Fe 1993); *NA* (29 Ja 1993, 17 Jl 1995); *Exp* (26 Ja 1993, 13 Se 1994); *GD* (5 Oc 1998); *VK* (16, 25 Ja, 20 Fe, 10 De 1993); *SvD* (20 Mr 1995); *Arb* (11 Ja, 1, 8 Fe 1993, 2, 27 Ap, 6 Je, 22 No 1995); *SDS* (27 Oc 1992, 4 Ja 1998, 21-3 My 2000); *AB* (20-1 Fe 1994); *GP* (30 Se, 27, 29 Oc, 15 De 1992); *HD* (17 Fe, 27 Au, 25 Se, 10 No 1996); *NT* (15-6 Oc 1997, 21 Jl 1999); Conny Hetting. "Sekunder från döden." *Mig* (no. 5 1995), 38-42.
[62]*VK* (3 No 1993).
[63]*SDS* (27 My 2000); STV 2. "Striptease" (7, 14 No 2000).
[64]*DN* (21 Fe, 3-4 Ap 1990); *UNT* (23, 27 Ja 1993, 18 De 1996); *SDS* (25 My 2000); *SvD* (25 My 1991); *VK* (13 Fe 1993); *GP* (31 De 1992).
[65]*IDAG* (12 Ja 1990); *DN* (16 Ja, 22 Mr, 11 Ap, 22, 25-6 My, 14 De 1990); *GP* (25 My 1990, 6, 8, 15, 30 My 1992); *SvD* (18 Ja 1990, 1 Jl 1992); *YA* (21-2 Mr 1990); Michael Melanson. "Från skjutfält till skjutfält." *NiS* (no. 1, 1994): 24-5; Sahlberg. "15.000 kom i juli—Situationen är bekymmersam." *NiS* (no. 4, 1992): 17.
[66]"Rädda Barnen kritisk till mottagandet av ensamma barn." *Sr* (no. 1, 1990), 14; Crole-Rees. "En vanlig dag på svenska flyktingslussen," 10-3; *SvD* (9, 16 Fe, 13-4 My, 3 Au 1991); *SDS* (25 Fe 1990, 1 Jl, 22 Au, 10 Se 2000); *GP* (14 De 1991, 15 Ja, 1 No 1992); *Exp* (12, 18, 27 Mr 1991); Michael Melanson. "Livet på flyktingslussen." *NiS* (no. 3, 1993): 2-5; Olson. "Alldeles för go' för sitt bästa." *Mig,* (no. 6, 1995), 18-21; *DN* (3 Ja 1990); *HD* (11 My 1996).
[67]Sahlberg. "Flyktingprojektet." *NiS* (no. 2, 1990): 12-30; *SDS* (13 Se 1994, 23 Se 2000); *YA* (28, 30 Mr 1990); *NT* (20 Fe 1990); *AB* (2 Je 1990); *SvD* (25 Ja, 2, 22 Se 1991, 30 Au, 16 Se 1998); *Arb* (18 Jl, 9 Au 1991); *GP* (16 Oc 1990, 9 Ap 1992, 3 Oc 1998); *DN* (20 Fe, 22, 29 No, 14, 16 De 1990, 3 Se 1991, 26 Au 1998); Björn Fryklund & Tomas Peterson. *"Vi mot dom": det dubbla främlingsskapet i Sjöbo* (Lund, 1989), 207.
[68]Skurup, Åstorp, and Vellinge, with less drama and publicity and without a colorful personality like Olsson leading them, also held out against participation. For details of other communal opposition, see: *SvD* (1 De 1991, 16 Oc 1993); *NT* (20 Fe 1990); *HD*

210 Endnotes

(28 Fe, 8 Oc, 31 De 1996); *GP* (8 Ja, 7 Fe, 1 Ap, 15, 22-3 Au 1992); *DN* (1 Mr, 13 Je 1990); *SDS* (13 Se 2000).

[69]*VK* (12 Ja, 10 Fe, 5, 13, 27-8 My, 10 Se, 1 Oc, 2 De 1993); *SvD* (15 Fe 1991, 18 Se 1993); *GP* (11 Jl, 16 Se 1992); *DN* (12 Oc 1992); Ingemar Gens. "Den mjuka slussen till Sverige." *NiS* (no. 5, 1990), 46-9; Åke Daun, Leif Stenberg, Leif Svanström, Stig Åhs. *Invandrarna i välfärdssamhället* (Stockholm, 1994), 54-9. With fluctuating refugee revenues, communal experiences were unique as the following newspaper reports attest: *DN* (4-5, 20 Ja, 22, 25 Mr, 28 Ap, 19 Je, 23 Au 1990, 12 Oc 1992); *SDS* (19, 27 Oc 1992, 7 Se, 22 No 2000); *GP* (5 Ja, 14 Au, 28 No 1992); *Exp* (10 Se 1993); *VK* (29 Ap, 16, 23, 25 Je, 27 Au, 14, 30 Oc, 1-2, 7, 21 De 1993); *SvD* (10 Ap, 25 Je, 9 Au 1991); *ST* (6, 12 Ap 1997); *NA* (29 Ja 1993); *HD* (1, 28 Mr, 4 Oc, 7 No 1996); *NT* (2, 11, 14, 16 Ja, 18 No 1997); Sahlberg. "På flyktingförläggningen i Oxelösund—'Vi ser inte mycket av krisen.'" *NiS* (no. 6, 1992), 33-6; Olson. "Nytt liv i byn." *Mig* (no. 2, 1995), 12-9. Norrland was not the only section that offered refugees cordiality and positive experiences. Despite what might easily be misinterpreted as Norrland's favorable attitude toward refugees, Immigration Bureau subsidies could not induce every commune in the region to take strangers. By refusing Moskogel Commune earned the epiteth, "the new Sjöbo." *PT* (25, 27-8 Ap 1990).

[70]Appelqvist. *Responsibility in transition*, 192-3; *SvD* (27 Fe, 25 Ap, 16 My, 1 Je, 10 Jl, 12 Se, 13 No, 17, 21 De 1991); *DN* (21 Mr, 25 Ap, 17 My, 8, 19 Jl, 30 Se, 19, 21 Oc, 17, 22 No 1990); Hans Göran Franck. "Beslutet måste upphävas." *Sr* (no. 2, 1990), 14-5; Cajsa Malmström. "Utlänningsnämnden—'Läkarna måste övertyga.'" *NiS* (no. 4, 1993), 12-3; Christina Rogestam. "En generös och human flyktingpolitik?" *NiS* (no. 6, 1992), 1; "Få invandrare på den andra nordiska flykting- och invandrarkonferensen." *Sr* (no. 2, 1990), 16; Reinhold Jonson. "Invandrarministern mötte uppvaktning med kyla." *Sr* (no. 1, 1991), 14. Unanticipated drops and missed increases occurred at other times in the decade, too. *AB* (12 Ap 1995); *SDS* (6 Jl, 6 No 2000).

[71]*HD* (16 My 1992); *GP* (11, 21, 23, 30 Ap, 18, 21 Je, 1, 8 Jl, 13, 23 De 1992); *AB* (30 No 1992); *Exp* (9 Se 1993); *VK* (17 No 1993); *Dagen* (10 Se 1993); Christina Rogestam. "Omöjligt att sia om framtiden." *NiS* (no. 1, 1991), 1; Malou Jergner Ekervik. "Skepp har kommit lastade med över 20000 asylsökande." *NiS* (no. 4, 1992), 13-6.

[72]*DN* (13 Fe 1993).

[73]*Ibid.* (3-4 Ja, 6 Fe 1990, 16 Ap 1994); *SvD* (13 Fe 1990, 5, 16, 27 Fe, 21 Mr, 8-9 Se 1991); *SDS* (2 Mr 1992, 3 Ja 1997, 22 Au 2000); *Exp* (23 Ja 1995; 29-1, 4, 10 Mr-Ap 1998); *Arbb* (22 Au 1994); *BT* (2 Ap 1998); *VK* (31 De 1997); "Rädda Barnen kritisk till mottagandet av ensamma barn." *Sr* (no. 1, 1990), 14; *HD* (29 Je 1996); Cajsa Malmström. "Nätverk flyktingbarn." *NiS* (no. 1, 1994), 16-9; Margareta Brandell-Forsberg. "Flyktingbarn Riskbarn." *I & M* 18 (Oc 1991), 62-4; *Flyktingbarn i Sverige: Huvudrapport 1990/91* (Stockholm, 1991), 8; *UNT* (6 Oc 1993); *AB* (1, 16 My 1998); *NT* (21 Oc 1997); *GP* (18 De 1991, 24 Jl 1996); *NA* (17 Au 1996).

[74]*UNT* (14, 21 My 1990); *DN* (4-5 Ja, 20 Se, 27 Oc 1990); *YA* (30 Mr 1990); *SvD* (6 Fe 1990, 31 Ja, 24 My, 7 De 1991); *GP* (27 My, 17 Je, 8 Au 1992); *SP* (15 Mr 1990).

[75]*SvD* (20-1 Mr, 6 Ap, 2 Je, 20 Oc 1991, 16 Oc 1993); *NN* (8 My 1990); *GP* (3 De 1992, 4 Fe 1993).

[76]*NT* (17 My 1997); *DN* (7 My, 21,31 Au, 27 No 1990, 7 Ja 1997); *SvD* (18 Mr, 14 Ap, 8 My, 12, 22 Jl 1991); *Arb* (21 Fe, 18 Je, 30 Oc 1995); *VK* (31 Mr, 19 My, 8 Je, 29 Se, 2 No 1993); *GP* (4, 21, 27 Au, 6, 23-4 Se, 8 Oc, 12 De 1992); *ST* (2 My 1996); Sahlberg. "Utvisning hot mot kriminella asylsökande." *NiS* (no. 6, 1992), 37-8.

4

[77]*NT* (11 Ap 1990); *DN* (2, 13 Mr, 9 Ap, 28 My, 6 Je, 13, 23 Jl, 15 Au, 17, 29 Se, 7 Oc 1990); *SvD* (10 Ja, 2 Mr, 13, 15 My, 5 Je, 13 No, 2 De 1991); *GP* (3 Jl 1990, 5 Mr, 15 Au, 30 Se 1992); Sahlberg. "Här får asylsökande chans att jobba." *NiS* (no. 1, 1991), 14-7; *UNT* (28 Mr 1992); *GD* (17 My 1990); *BB* (29 My 1990); *VK* (3 De 1993); *Bar* (27 No 1990); *Sr* (no. 2, 1994), 1.

[78]*Arb* (10 Oc 1995); *SvD* (26 Fe, 7 Au, 21 Se 1991, 25 Fe, 21 Ap 1992); "Vill invandrarverket spara pengar på barnen?" *Sr* (no. 2, 1991), 16; *DN* (3, 20, 28 Ja, 6 Ap 1990, 4, 6, 28 De 1991, 24 Mr 1992, 16 Ap, 24 Je 1994; 2 Jl 2, 1995; Oc 20, 26, No 2, 1997; Ap 6, 1998); *Exp* (Ja 27, 1995); *HD* (Mr 21, 1996); *SDS* (19 Oc 1991, 11 Je 1993, 10 My 1995, 2 Ja 1997, 5 De 1999, 10 My, 16 Je 2000); *NT* (4 Ap 1997); *GP* (11 Ap 1993, 22 Ja, 16 Ap, 16 Oc 1999); *VK* (17 Fe, 9 Se, 23 No 1993); *UNT* (21 Fe 1990); *AB* (25 My 1994, 18 My, 19 No 1998, 28 Oc 1999); Birgitta Öjersson & Bo Levin. "Teatern kom med kafé, butik och kultur." *NiS* (no. 1, 1992), 8-10; Olson. "Hemsnickrat från Aneby." *Mig* (no. 5, 1995), 13-7; Veronica Fareld. "Utvisad." *Sr* (no. 3, 1993): 8-9; Saleh Oweini. "I väntan på asyl." *I & M* 18 (Oc 1991), 22-3; Jonny Sågänger. "Flykting och blind." *NiS* (no. 1, 1991), 38-43; Cajsa Malmström. "Tortyroffer måste få hjälp." *NiS* (no. 5, 1991), 6-11; Ingela Björck. "Här lindras ångesten." *NiS* (no. 5, 1991): 12-5; Cajsa Malmström. "Daghem för flyktingbarn." *NiS* (no. 3, 1992), 19-22; Cajsa Malmström. "Läkare kritiska tortyroffer i kläm." *NiS* (no. 4, 1993): 10-2; Michael Melanson. "Buss och bagage." *NiS* (no. 5, 1993), 4-5; Svante Rosenberg. "Flyktingmotståndet blev en vändpunkt." *NiS* (no. 6, 1990), 46-7; Britta Lineback. "Vända hem i värdighet." *Mig* (no. 5, 1995), 24-8; Kaj Annebrant. "Fördjupade kontakter att vänta i Sandviken?" *Sr* (no. 2, 1990), 13; Daun. *Invandrarna i välfärdssamhället*, 22-7; *Dagen* (9 Ja 1991, 2 Jl 1998); *GD* (2 Ja 1992). Daily allowances were slightly less in 1997.

[79]*SvD* (20 Mr 1995); *SDS* (29 Jl 1998); *GP* (6 No 1992); *HD* (4 Jl, 23, 28 Au, 28 No 1996); *NT* (20 Se, 10 Oc 1997); Sahlberg. "Kommunernas flyktingmottagande: statens bidrag räcker inte." *Mig* (no. 4, 1998), 12-4.

[80]Roland Jacobsson. "Mot passivitet: En flykting berättar." *I & M* 18 (Oc 1991), 24-6. Most of these are discussed in Chapter IV.

[81]*SvD* (4, 7, 28 Fe 1992); *NA* (29 Ja 1993); *GP* (7 Jl 1992, 29 Au 1994, 16 My 1999); *HP* (28 Mr 1996); *SDS* (20 Se 1992, 20 Fe 1993, 11 Au 1999, 17 Fe, 16 Ap 2000); *Bar* (16 Ap 1991); *UNT* (6, 9, 11 Oc 1993); *GD* (16 My 1990, 24 Je 1991); *ST* (29 Au 1990); *DN* (27 My, 11 No, 18 De 1990, 7 De 1991, 21 Fe, 24 Mr, 9 Oc 1992, 6 Fe 1997); *NT* (28 No 1997).

[82]*SvD* (20 Ma, 3 Au 1991); *DN* (21, 24 Ja, 6 Ap, 3 Se, 23 No 1990); "Fest för stöd åt iranska flyktingar." *Sr* (no. 1, 1993), 4; *AB* (17 Fe 1994); *HD* (12 No 1996); *GP* (21 Ja 1990, 3, 5, 12, 18 Ja, 26 My 1992); *Bar* (28 No 1990); Christina Rogenstam. "Tolkfrågan viktig för Invandrarverket." *NiS* (no. 4, 1992), 39; Emma Feigenberg. "Tolkslarv." *NiS* (no. 4, 1992), 38; *Arb* (17 Ja 1995); *SDS* (5 My 1992).

[83]Sahlberg. "22.000 väntar på besked om de får stanna." *NiS* (no. 1, 1991), 10-3. Although in general living under a threat of deportation was the most horrific experience of being a refugee, fear of infiltrated agents in camps probably caused as much or more fright for some asylum seekers. See *SvD* (15 Fe, 8 Je, 14 No 1991).

[84]*Bar* (27 No 1990); *DN* (24 Ja 1990); *SDS* (24 Ja 1990).

[85]*HD* (16 Au 1996); *SDS* (23 Ja 1990); *NST* (18 Ja 1990); *DN* (13 Se 1990); *VK* (9 Mr, 15 Jl, 4 Oc, 16 De 1993); *SvD* (22 Oc, 19, 28 De 1991, 22 Jl 1992); *GP* (28 Ja 1992, 4 Je 1993); *SP* (11 Ap 1997); *Arb* (22 No 1995).

[86]*DN* (2-4, 7, 9, 12-4, 17, 19, 21-2, 26, 28 Ja, 1, 6-7, 9-10, 18, 21-2 Fe, 20-1 Mr, 4 Ap, 9 Je 1990); *SDS* (4, 10 Ja, 21 Fe 1990); *GP* (7, 16, 21 Ja 1990); *Exp* (29 Je 1990); Reinhold Jonson. "S.O.S. Asyl." *Sr* (no. 2, 1990), 9-11; *HP* (16 Ja 1991).

[87]*UNT* (2 De 1992); *GP* (1 Jl 1990); *AB* (3 Ja 1992, 23 Mr 1995); *SDS* (8 Au 1990, 17 Mr 1995); *SvD* (16 Ja, 15 Fe, 5 Ap, 29 Je, 10 Jl 1991, 27 Oc 1993, 3 Ap 1995, 22 De 1996); *VK* (30-3 No-De *1993*); *Arb* (21-2 Mr, 27 Ap 1995); *ST* (12 Se 1994); *HD* (30 No 1996).

[88]*UNT* (25-6 No, 2, 16 De 1993); *ÖC* (9 De 1993); *SP* (26 No 1993); *DN* (10 De 1993); *VK* 25-7 No, 4 De 1993); *SvD* (25 No 1993); *GP* (24 No 1994); *Arb* (1 Mr 1995); *AB* (21 Ja 1994); Linn Hjort. "Inte ens ärkebiskopen kan få oss följa Sveriges lagar!" *Sr* (no. 1, 1994), 10-1.

[89]*VK* (5 Mr, 20-2, 25, 28-30 Oc, 1, 3, 27-30 No, 1-4, 6-7, 8-10, 13, 27, 31 De 1993, 18 Ja 1995, 12-9 Ja, 10, 27 Fe, 3, 6, 10 Ap, 23 Au, 28 De 1996); *AB* (23 No 1994, 13, 16-7, 19-20, 23, 26 Ja 1996); *DN* (26 Fe 1994, 13, 19 Ja, 27 Fe 1996); *Arb* (12 Ja, 11 Mr, 30 Je 30, 5-6 Jl, 10-1, 14 Au, 16 No 1995); *GP* (10 Jl 1995, 24 Ja 1996); *SvD* (16, 19 Ja 1996); *SDS* (26 Fe 1996); *NWT* (18 Ja 1996); *HD* (12-7, 25 Ja, 2, 9, 14, 17, 28-9 Fe, 2 Mr, 13 Ap, 14 My, 1, 16-7 Au, 21 Oc, 1 No 1996); *Exp* (18-9 Ja, 3 Je 1996); Editorial "Vad håller 'Blomman' på med?" *Sr* (no. 3, 1994), 2; Olson. "Lärdomar från Åsele." *Mig* (no. 1, 1996), 1; Olson. "Tillbaka till skrivbordet." *Mig* (no. 1, 1996), 2-3; *NT* (13 Oc 1997). There were three interesting postscripts to the Sincari saga: Son Siyar who had gone into hiding won his case, receiving asylum October 31, 1996; the two fathers have remained underground; and Rojda—after having been allowed to return to Åsele from a miserable existence in Diyarbakir, Turkey, to finish her high-school education—concluded her stay in Sweden as a guest at a party honoring King Carl Gustaf's twenty-fifth anniversary on the throne. Åsele Township Council Chair Bert-Rune Dahlberg chose her to accompany him to the festivities.

[90]*ÖC*, 21 No 1991; *SvD*, 17 Je 1990, 25 No 1993, 19 Je 1994; *GP*, 4 My, 6 Jl, 25 Se, 15 De 1992; *SDS*,

13 Jl 2000; *AB*, 21 Je 1994, 8 Au 1996; *DN*, 5 Jl 1992, 20 Ap 1993, 7 No 1999; *VK*, 23 Mr, 21 Ap, 7

Se, 21 Oc 1993; *Exp*, 7-8 Se 1993.

[91]Björn Rydström, Sören Edgar, & Åke Jungdalen, "Stor spännvidd i statsrådens utbildning: Politiska eliten dåligt utbildad," *Sunt Förnuft*, no. 7 (1997): 28-31. Blomberg's mangling the Sincari case exemplified how oversimplifying complex questions had serious effects; he like predecessors and successors holding the cabinet post of immigration minister had no background whatsoever for handling a sensitive job.

[92]*Arb* (17, 23-4, 30 Mr, 25 Ap, 5 My, 28 Je, 13, 23 No 1995); *SvD* (17 Ja, 24, 26 Ap, 24 My, 3 Se 1991, 25 Jl 1992, 17 Au 1994, 27 Ap 1997); *AB* (9 Jl 1993, 10 Oc 1994, 15 Au 1998, 27 Oc 1999); *NT* (20 Ja 1997); *BT* (11 Fe 1998); *NWT* (7 Se 1995, 2 De 1998); *ST* (10 Se 1994, 4 My 1996); *SDS* (9 Fe 1990, 16 Je 1991, 26 Jl 26, 29 No 1996, 17 Se 1997, 5 Ja 2001); *HD* (13 Oc 1992, 3, 12, 24 Ja, 18 Jl, 1 Au, 12, 16 Oc, 29 No 1996); *DN* (14, 20, 23, 26 Ja, 9 Fe, 30 De 1990, 29 Oc 1992, 11 Fe, 4 No 1993, 5 Ja 1995, 29 No 1996, 14 Ja, 12 No 1997, 16, 19 Je 1998, 30 My 1999); *VK* (8 My, 26 Jl, 9, 21 Se 1993, 21 De 1994); *GP* (15 Fe, 9, 17, 31 Jl, 6 Au, 28 Se, 6, 9-10 Oc 1992, 23 Mr 1994, 6 Mr 1995, 12 Je 1997, 15 Ja 1998); Sahlberg. "Utan pass kan de inte avvisas." *NiS* (no. 6, 1993), 34-6; Mannerfelt. "Tillbaka i Kosovo." *NiS* (no. 5, 1993), 1-3; Sahlberg. "Asyl i Sverige." *Mig* (no. 2, 1995), 20-1; Veronica Fareld. "Utvisad." *Sr* (no. 3, 1993), 8-9; Editorial "Försvara asylrätten!" *Sr* (no. 1, 1993), 2; Matz Nilsson. "Svensk

flyktingpolitik?!—deportation verkställs." *Sr* (no. 1, 1990), 4-5; Mohammed Alasaad. "Solidaritet i handling och inte bara i ord." *Sr* (no. 1, 1990), 5; Birgitta Öjersson & Bo Levin. "Häktespersonalen tog med sig avvisad tillbaka." *NiS* (no. 1, 1992): 12-5; "Låt mig få stanna!" Sr (no. 4, 1992), 7; *Exp* (8 Oc 1998).

[93]*HD* (21Fe 1992, 12, 26 Ja, 1 Fe, 21 Mr, 11 Ap, 5 Jl, 25, 31 Au, 25 Se, 20, 31Oc 1996); *NT* (14 Mr, 2, 19 Jl, 14 No 1997); *VK* (22 Mr, 1 Ap, 21 Au, 22, 25, 30 Oc 1993); *GP* (28 Ap, 4 My, 14 No 1992, 16 De 1995, 31 Mr 1998); *Arb* (11 Fe, 16 Au, 11, 19 Oc, 20 No 1995, 27 Ja 1996); *FK* (13 Se 1990); *ÖK* (20 Je 1990); *KK* (5 Je 1990); *HP* (2 My 1998); *AB* (19, 26 No 1993, 15 Ap, 18 My, 30 Au, 1, 3, 24 Se, 24-5 No, 2 De 1994, 19, 26 Ja, 25 Jl 1996, 23, 26 Ap, 29 My 1998); *ÖC* (1-2 Mr 1990, 9 Au 1994); *SDS* (26 Ap 1991, 2 Ap 1998, 8, 23 Je, 13 Jl, 10 Au, 13 Se 2000); *Exp* (8-9, 11-2, 14-5 Se 1993, 29 Je 1994, 19 Mr, 9 My, 31 Jl, 1 Au, 9 Oc 1998); *SvD* (8 Fe, 18 Mr, 19, 27 My, 14, 24, 30 Je, 4, 19 Jl, 13 Se 1991, 28 Mr 1992, 20 No, 7 De 1996, 19 De 1997); *DN* (4 Ja, 2 Mr, 15 Jl, 26 Oc 1990, 29 Se 1991, 3 Je 1995, 1 Fe 1996, 6 Ap, 3 Je 1998); "Afrikanska asylsökande diskrimineras." *Sr* (no. 2, 1996), 9; Sahlberg. "Asyl i Sverige." *Mig* (no. 1, 1995), 32-3; Eva Aldstedt. "Asylhanteringen rättssäker." *NiS* (no. 3, 1994), 108-9; Sahlberg. "Viss kritik mot Utlänningsnämnden." *NiS* (no. 3, 1994), 110; Sahlberg. "Ny flyktingpolitik." *NiS* (no. 1, 1992), 17-21; *AB* (26 Ap 1998). Assuming duties from the police, ARB became the agency that decided refugee cases in 1992.

[94]*AB* (21-3 Au, 16 No 1994); *NT* (30-3 Je-Jl 1997); *SvD* (10 Jl 1991, 3 Jl 1997); *Exp* (27 Mr 1991). People accused and/or convicted of crimes have their identities protected by anonymity laws, and *Siv* records are not open, hence the author's failure to bring closure to either case. Various complications involving families scheduled for deportation were regular challenges for *Siv* and ARB; for cases: *SvD* (19 Ap 1991); *AB* (22 Au 1994); *Arb* (23 Fe 1995); *GP* (10 Oc 1999). Detected lies brought about automatic deportation, see *AB* (11 Mr 1994).

[95]*SvD*, 2 Ja, 8 Fe 1991, 1 Au 1992, 15 My 1994; *DN*, 5 Mr 1994, 3 Fe 1996; *VK*, 16 Se 1993, 21 De 1994;

Arb, 24 Fe, 12 Ap 1995; *GP*, 5 Mr 1993; *SDS*, 17 No 1994.

[96]*SvD* (12-3 Fe, 23 Ap, 4 My, 8 Je, 10, 20 Jl, 3 Au 1991, 25-6, 29 Oc 1993, 14 Ap 1994, 15 My 1999); *DN* (3-5, 11-2 Ap 1991, 5 My 1992, 20 De 1997, 31-1 Mr-Ap 1998); *SDS* (15 Se 1992, 26 Ap, 25 Je, 17 Jl 2000); *GP* (29 Ja, 6 Mr, 17 My 1992, 25 Ja 1997, 7-8 Ap, 9 Je, 11 Oc 1999); *Arb* (25 Fe, 13 No 1995, 5 No 1999); *SP* (18, 20 Ap 1991); *UNT* (18 Mr 1993); *ST* (10 Se 1994); *GD* (16 No 1996); *NWT* (18 Ja 1996); *Arbb* (12 Fe 1994); *VK* (13 Oc 1993, 18 Ja 1995); *HD* (16-9 Se, 13 No 1996); *Exp* (24 My 1998); Eva Aldstedt. "De gömmer flyktingar." *NiS* (no. 3, 1994), 102-7; Mannerfelt. "Hadije gömmer sig för att slippa avvisas." *NiS* (no. 1, 1991), 6-7; Mannerfelt. "Att leva 'under jorden': 'Mardrömmarna tar över mitt liv.'" *NiS* (no. 1, 1991), 8-9; Olson. "Få gömställen kvar till kära barn." *Mig* (no. 6, 1995), 4-7.

[97]*NST* (18 Ja 1990); *DN* (20 Ja, 1 Au 1990, 4 Ja 1994, 6 Se 1996); *GP* (16 Mr 1992); *SvD* (12 Ap, 13, 19 Je, 18 Au, 27 De 1991); *Exp* (20 Ja 1996); *ST* (27 Ap 1996); *NST* (20 Ja 1990).

[98]*DN* (9-10, 13, 16 No 1996); *SvD* (20, 26 No 1996); *Bar* (14 De 1996); *AB* (20 Ap 1998).

[99]*Exp* (23 No 1999); *SDS* (16 Je 2000); *GD* (29 Au 1999); *DN* (22-3 No 1996, 28 Jl, 4, 10 Au 1999); *GP* (14 Oc 1999).

[100]*VK* (26-7 Oc 1990, 11, 13-4 Au, 15, 26 Oc 1993); *Arb* (31 Oc 1995); *NT* (1 Jl 1995); *SDS* (4 Ja 1997); Marianne Hjort. "Han gömde flyktingar." *Sr* (no. 1, 1994), 12;

214 Endnotes

AB (20 Mr 1998); Christina Rogestam. "Förbud mot barnförvar?" *NiS* (no. 1, 1992), 1; Sahlberg. "Kvar på förläggning trots avvisningsbeslut." *NiS* (no. 3, 1993), 12.

[101]*DN* (11 Mr 1990, 17 Ap 1991); *SvD* (11 Au 1990, 5 Fe 1991); *NS* (17 Oc 1990); *GP* (2 De 1993); *AB* (20-6 Ap 1998); *NT* (20 Je 1997).

[102]*NT* (29 My, 5, 19 Jl, 9 Oc 1997); *VK* (22 De 1993, 28 My, 18 Je 1998); *HD* (21 Se 1996); *SDS* (9 Jl 1999, 25 Mr, 2, 12 Ap, 3 Je 2000); *Arb* (21 De 1995); *SvD* (22 Mr 1995); *GP* (14, 22 Oc 1992, 12, 31 Mr 1996, 29 Mr 1997, 20 Fe, 17 Au 1999); *AB* (2 My 1998); Olson. "Ingen kan åka hem på en dröm." *Mig* (no. 5, 1995), 18-21; *Dagen* (13 Jl 1990); Lodenius & Wikström. *Vit makt och blågula drömmar*, 17. To coax Somalians to their homeland, Sweden budgeted 5,000,000 kronor.

[103]*VK* (25 No, 4, 6 De 1993); *DN* (17, 20 Mr, 10 Ap 1990, 28 Ja 1994, 11 Se 1998); *AB* (16 Ja 1992, 28 No 1994); *HD* (25 Ja, 21 Au, 25 Se 1996); *TSL* (31 My 1990); *HT* (7 Ap 1990); *Bar* (11 Fe 1993); *LT* (30 My 1990); *Exp* (1 Au 1995, 22 Ja 1996, 27 Au 1998); *Arb* (4 Ap, 5 My, 4 Jl 1995, 24 Ap 1997); *Dagen* (25 My 1991); *SvD* (8 Jl 1990, 24 Mr 1991, 27 Oc 1996, 17 Ap 1998); *SDS* (19 Oc 1993, 21 No 1996, 7 Je 2000); *GP* (3 Jl, 20 Au, 11 Se 1992); Hans Lindquist. "Ingen Glistrup i sikte—ännu?" *NiS* (no. 1, 1991), 18-21; Sahlberg. "Ny flyktingpolitik." *NiS* (no. 1, 1992), 17-21; Lena Ringqvist. "Misstro och hat mot de asylsökande." *NyS* (no. 5, 1992), 30-2; Irka Cederberg. "Ny lag skapar kaos." *NiS* (no. 5, 1994), 12-5; Sahlberg. "Tomas Hammar: 'Politikerna har missuppfattat opinionen.'" *NiS* (no. 6, 1993), 16-21; Sahlberg. "'Vi måste få en mer genomtänkt asylpolitik.'" *NiS* (no. 1, 1990), 38-42; Olson. "Nya paragrafer." *Mig* (no. 3, 1995), 2-5; Olson. "Snabba besked om ny flyktingpolitik." *Mig* (no. 4, 1995), 4-5; Titti Hasselrot. *Sverige blandat: svar på vanliga frågor om invandrare och flyktingar* (Stockholm, 1994), 31, 35-6; Anna-Lena Lodenius & Per Wikström. *Vit makt och blågula drömmar: rasism och nazism i dagens Sverige* (Stockholm, 1997), 17; Sahlberg. "Human Rights Watch' kritik av svensk asylpolitik." *Mig* (no. 6, 1996), 33-6; *ÖC* (4 De 1993); *VLT* (31 My 1990).

[104]Based upon the author's own observations, informal conversations with numerous visitors and alien residents, and tourist guide books.

[105]Rydström *et al.* "Politiska eliten dåligt utbildad," 28-31.

[106]*AB* (Mr 15, 1992).

[107]Petter Johansson & Lasse Winkler. "Kalabaliken i Biskopsgården." *NiS* (no. 4, 1990), 10-4; *DN* (Se 7, 1990); *SvD* (Se 10, 12, 1991); "'Sätt tak på invandringen.'" *Sr* (no. 3, 1990), 2-3; Reinhold Jonson. "Ny utlänningslag på gång." *Sr* (no. 1, 1991), 14. For more on the Palme legacy, see Anders Lange. *Flyktingskap, boende och agens* (Stockholm, 1991), 5.

[108]*DN* (19, 24 Ja, 19 Fe, 1, 5, 8, 19, 29 Je, 25 Au, 11 Se 1990); *SvD* (1 Je 1990, 29 My, 16 Je, 2 Au 1991); GP (2 Je 1990); *SDS* (7 De 7 1990); *Arb* (29 Ja 1990); *AB* (24 Oc 1991). *Arbetet* and *Aftonbladet* are Social Democratic organs.

[109]Linnéa Gardeström. *Att främja goda etniska relationer: en utvärdering av projekt som fått bidrag genom Kommissionen mot rasism och främlingsfientlighet* (Stockholm, 1991), 54; *Mångfald mot enfald* (Stockholm, 1989), I: 11, 17, 37, 39, 43, II: 13-9; *Working Documents* (Borås, 1986); *DN* (21 Fe, 2 Ap, 28 My, 2-3 Je 1990); *SvD* (26 Ap, 2 Je 1990, 24 Ap, 22 My 1991); *SDS* (7 Fe 1990); *Arb* (31 Ja, 15 Fe, 14 Mr, 10, 31 My 1990); *AB* (14 Je, 11 Au, 20 Oc 1990); *VK* (31 Mr 1990); *VLT* (8 Ja 1991); *Exp* (9 Ap 1990); *GP* (31 Mr 1991).

[110]*DN* (24, 27 Mr, 23 Au, 9 No 1990); *YA* (29 Mr 1990); *SvD* (2-3, 23 Ja, 2 De 1991); *Förslag till åtgärder vid särskilda händelser med rasistiska inslag* (Stockholm: 1998), 9; RPS. "Rasism och främlingsfientlighet: en undersökning av brottslighet med rasistiska

eller främlingsfientliga inslag m . m." (Stockholm, 1988), 9; Jesus Alcalá. . . . *icke tillräckliga skäl* . . . (Stockholm, 1988), 24-34, 111; Erland Bergman & Bo Swedin. *Solidaritet och konflikt: etniska relationer i Sverige* (Stockholm, 1989), 45; *Arb* (11 Jl 1995); *GP* (17 Ja 1992).

[111]*DN* (28 Je, 14 Jl 1990); *Exp* (26 Se 1990).

[112]*AB* (27-30 My, 14 Je, 4 Jl 1991).

[113]*DN* (25 Fe, 11, 13 Mr, 2, 9 Je, 26 Jl 1990, 15, 31 May 1991); *SvD* (14 Je, 26 Jl 1990, 6, 12, 27 Fe, 4, 19-20 Mr, 25, 27, 29 Ap, 4, 8, 24 Je, 14 Au, 2, 16 Se 1991); *Arb* (22 Mr 1990, 8, 25 Je, 18 Jl, 9 Au 1991); *SkD* (7 Au 1991); *UNT* (18 My 1990); *HP* (16 Ja 1991); *NT* (28 Mr 1990); *HD* (12 Se 1991); *GP* (8 Ja, 14 Fe, 20 Je, 12 Oc 1990, 16 Je 1991); *AB* (6 Je 1990); *SDS* (29 Je 1990); *Bar* (9 Jl 1990); "Vi kan vända trenden!" *Sr* (no. 3, 1991), 2; Sahlberg. "Helene Lööw: Sverigedemokraterna, rasister i nya kostymer." *NiS* (no. 2, 1991), 28-30.

[114]*AB* (1, 8, 11 Je, 3 Jl, 4 Au, 1, 15 Se 1992, 7, 11 Je 1993); *GP* (18 Je 1991, 23 Fe, 22, 27, 30 Jl, 1, 14 Au, 3, 30 De 1992); *DN* (3 Ap, 1, 5 De 1992, 4 Se, 6 Oc 1993); *SvD* (2 Se, 7 De 1991, 13 Au, 27 Se 1993); *SDS* (31 Ja 1992, 28 My, 6 Je 1993); *GD* (28 Au 1993); *Arb* (22 Au 1993); *iDAG* (12 Au 1992); *VK* (14, 21 Au 1993); *ÖC* (3 Se 1993); *NT* (14 Jl 1992); "SR ställer riksdagspartierna mot väggen." *Sr* (no. 3, 1993), 6-7.

[115]*DN* (16 Ap, 3 My, 11 Jl 1992, 14 Je, 5 Se, 9, 19 No 1993, 18 Mr, 17 My, 6 Jl 1994); *SvD* (3 No, 20 De 1991, 10 Fe, 12 Mr, 29 Je, 3 De 1993, 3 Je, 15 Se 15 1994); *SDS* (15 My, 24 No, 4, 16 De 1991); *GP* (29 Oc, 6 No 1992, 19 Se, 30 De 1993, 17 Fe 1994); *Exp* (9, 11, 13 Se 1994); *AB* (15 Mr 1992, 19 Oc 1993); *ÖC* (27 De 1991); *HD* (7 Au 1992); *NT* (17 Au 1994); *VK* (22 Je 1993); *Dagen* (11 Jl 1991); Appelqvist. *Responsibility in transition*, 192-3; Sahlberg. "'Sverige är fortfarande bäst.'" *NiS* (no. 5, 1992), 44-7; Sahlberg. "Parlamentarisk kommitté ser över invandrar- och flyktingpolitiken." *NiS* (no. 3, 1994), 98-9.

[116]*GP* (19 Ja, 22 Ap, 27 Je, 22 Jl, 11, 20-1, 29 Au, 16 Se, 9, 11 Oc, 11 No 1992, 7 Ja 1994); *SDS* (6 Fe, 27 Mr, 29 Oc, 4 No, 5 De 1992, 10 Ap, 5 Oc 1993, 23 Mr 1994); *DN* (16 De 1991, 21 Fe, 14, 18, 24 Jl, 21 Au, 20 Se 1992, 21 Je, 13 Au, 22 Oc 1993, 12, 18 Mr, 5, 18, 27 Ap, 2, 20 My, 11 Jl 1994); *AB* (28 Oc 1991, 6 Jl, 11 De 1992, 17 Mr 1994); *ÖC* (25 Au 1992, 22 Oc 1993); *Arb* (15 My 1992, 8 Fe, 28 Se 1993, 5 My, 17 Je, 5 Jl 1994); SvD (17 Mr, 12 Ap, 27 Au 1994); *HD* (29 My, 13 Oc 1992, 3 Fe 1994); *GD* (4 My 1993); *SkD* (27 Je 1994); *Dagen* (22 Fe 22 1994); *VK* (23 Je 1993); *NA* (11 Ja 1992).

[117]*SvD* (20 No 1991, 3, 15 Je, 14 Oc, 26 No 1993, 6 Se 1994); *ÖC* (10 No 1993); *Exp* (8 Se 1994); *AB* (23 My, 25 No 1993); *Arb* (22 Fe 1993, 7 Ap 1994); *SP* (23 Jl 1992); *DN* (16 Oc 1993).

[118]*DN* (19, 27 Se 1990, 6 Ap 1992, 8, 16 Je, 13, 25 Au, 18 Se 1993, 30 Mr 1994); *SvD* (6 Fe, 18 Oc, 12, 28 De 1991, 20 Fe 1993); *AB* (17 My 1994); *ST* (12 Se 1994); *Dagen* (22 Fe 1991).

[119]*GP* (7 Oc, 14 No 1993, 17 Mr 1994); *DN* (No 9, 1993).

[120]*GP* (3 Ja, 5, 9, 11, 21, 26 Fe, 5 My, 3 Jl 1992); *SvD* (31 Oc, 14 No, 3, 17 De 1991, 20 Jl 1992); Kenneth Lewis. "Förbud mot rasistiska organisationer." *Sr* (no. 3, 1992), 17; *VK* (19 Oc 1993).

[121]*GP* (1, 5-6, 10 Fe 1992, 3 Fe 1993); *AB* (15 Mr 1992); *Exp* (7 Se 1993); *SvD* (12 De 1991, 30 Ja 1992).

[122]*UNT* (27 Mr 1993); *SvD* (5 Fe, 25 Au 1992, 8 Oc 1993, 12 Fe 1994); *GP* (28 Jl 1992); *DN* (8 Jl 1992); *HD* (12 De 1991); *AB* (11, 15 Au 1994).

[123]*DN* (24 Se 1993); *GP* (21 Ap 1994); *SvD* (16 Fe 1992); *SDS* (22 Au 1993); *VK* (20 Ap 1993); *BT* (15 Fe 1993); *Arb* (8 Ap 1994); *Exp* (3 Oc 1994); Christina Råbergh.

"Social ingenjörskonst eller frivilliga krafter." *I & M* 19 (Ap, 1992), 7-13. Rojas' cause almost won approval in 1990; see: *DN* (15 Ju 1990).

[124]*AB* (24 Au, 20 No 1992, 7 Oc 1993). See also: *Arb* (7 De 1995); *SvD* (19 Oc 1994); *DN* (18 Ap 1996); Hans Nestius. *"Och vi som ville så väl-"*: *19 röster om det mångkulturella Sverige* (Stockholm, 1996), 172; Per-Olof Mattsson. "Rasismen i Sverige dag för dag." *Sr* (no. 1, 1994), 4-5.

[125]*AB* (24 Oc 1994); *DN* (31 Au 1994).

[126]From 1994: *SvD* (26 Oc, 24 No, 1 De); *Arb* (6 De); *Exp* (28 De); *NA* (18 No); *GP* (8 No); *DN* (17 De).

[127]*Exp* (4, 13 Ja 1995).

[128]From 1995: *DN* (23-4, 29 Mr, 1, 28 Ap, 3 My); *Arb* (26 Ja, 29 Mr, 6, 25 Ap); *AB* (14 Mr, 4, 10 Ap); *GP* (26 Fe); *Exp* (6 Fe); *BT* (24 Ap); *SDS* (24 Mr). For background, see: *VK* (19 My 1993).

[129]*Arb*, Fe 25, Jl 1, 3, Au 2, 1995; *DN*, Oc 4, De 16, 21, 29, 1995; *ÖK*, Oc 16, 1995; *AB*, Ja 1, 6, 1996; *Exp*, Oc 2, 1995.

[130]From 1996: *VK* (13, 15-6, 20 Ja, 4 Ap); *HD* (18, 23-4, 27 Ja, 9 Fe); *SvD* (24 Ja, 3 Fe, 18 Ap); *NA* (4 Mr); *DN* (25 Fe); *GD* (19 Fe); *GP* (15 Fe); *Exp* (15-6, 20 Ja); *DI* (19 Ja); *AB* (15 Ja, 3 Je). Åsele caused Moderates to undergo a self-examination that would leave a resultant split between liberalizers and hardliners.

[131]Olson. "Invandrarpolitik endast för nyanlända." *Mig* (no. 2, 1996), 2-5; Ryström *et al.* "Politiska eliten dåligt utbildad," 28-31.

[132]*DN* (4 Je 1996).

[133]By Schori and SD backers: *SvD* (12 Se, 26 No 1996, 12 My, 15 De 1997, 3 Ap, 25 Je 1998, 12 My 1999); *DN* (4, 11 Je, 28 Se, 9 Oc 1996, 24 Ja, 23 Fe, 15 No, 30 De 1997, 27 Fe 1998, 16 Ap 1999); *AB* (12 De 1996, 19 My 1997, 29 Ap, 4 Au 1998); *NT* (11 Ja 1996, 27 Je 1998); *SDS* (25 My 1998); *Arb* (30 Oc 1998); *GP* (17 Au 1996); *VK* (1 Oc 1996); *ÖK* (21 No 1996); *Exp* (18 Se 1996). Critics of Schori: *DN* (6 Je, 26, 29 Se, 4, 26 Oc, 16 No, 4 De 1996, 12 Fe, 14 Jl 1997, 17 Fe, 3, 31 Mr, 9 Je, 16 Au, 15 De 1998, 14, 17 Ap 1999); *AB* (13 Ap, 7 Je, 3 De 1996, 1, 24, 30 Ap, 4 My, 30 Jl 1998, 7 Ap, 18 My, 8 Je 1999); *SvD* (19 Se, 11, 26 Oc, 4, 27 No 1996, 19 Mr, 18 My, 23 Je 1998); *NT* (15 Oc 1996, 3 Ja, 5, 17 Fe, 19 Mr, 21 My, 27 No 1997); *Exp* (10, 25 Se, 2 Oc 1996); *GP* (22 Au 1996, 23 Au 1997, 10 Oc 1999); *Arb* (13 Je, 19 Oc 1996, 22, 26 My, 15 Jl 1998, 25 Oc 1999); *HD* (15 Se, 6 No 1996); *VK* (11 Se 1996, 3 My, 29 Jl 1997, 17, 19, 21 My 1999); *ÖK* (20 No 1996); *NWT* (4 De 1996); *SP* (5 Ap 1997); *NA* (3 My 1997); *Dagen* (31 Mr 1999); *SDS* (10 My 1998, 13 Fe, 27 No 2000).

[134]*SDS* (4, 15, 18, 21, 25 My 1997, 3 Je 2000); *SkD* (10, 24 Ja 1999); *SDS* (2 My 1997, 27 Mr 1998); *AB* (15 Au 1997); *BT* (26 Je, 3 Jl 1997).

[135]*DN* (5 De 1996).

[136]From 1997: *Ibid.* (3, 5, 12, 15 Ap, 9 My, 8 Je 8); *SvD* (7, 12, 17 Ap, 19 Je); *SDS* (8, 26 Ap); *AB* (9, 17, 22, 24 Ap, 25 My, 25 Jl); *SP* (29 Ap); *NT* (14 Mr, 7 Au); *GP* (16 Ap); *Arb* (27 Mr).

[137]*DN* (17 Fe 1995); *HD* (26 Ja 1996).

[138]From 1996: *SDS* (29 No); *HD* (5 Je, 19 No, 6, 11De); and *GP* (31 My 1997).

[139]*NT*, Oc 4, De 31, 1997; *SvD*, Oc 10, 1997; *GP*, Oc 10, 1999; *Exp*, Je 27, 1999.

[140]*SDS* (7 Fe, 27 Ap, 13 Jl 2000).

[141]*Ibid.* (6 De 1995, 28 Oc, 16 De 1999); *Arb* (27 Oc, 27 No 1995); *HD* (17 Se 1996); *NT* (13 Je 1997).

[142]Reinhold Jonson. "Succé för folkfest mot rasism." *Sr* (no. 3, 1991), 10; STV "Dokument inifrån," 19 Ja 2000; *Förbud mot rasistiska symboler m.m.* (Stockholm,

1996), 7; *Arb* (1 Ap, 3, 12, 18 De 1995); *GD* (17 No 1995); *HD* (17 Ja, 28 Mr, 10 Ap, 21 My, 10 Se 1996); *SDS* (4 Jl 2000).
[143]*AB* (1 Ja 1996); *Exp* (31 Mr 1998); *SDS* (4-5 No 1999, 23 Mr 2000).
[144]*Migrationsverkets* homepage.
[145]*GD* (14 My 1990); *VK* (25 Oc 1990, 26 Ja, 27 Ap, 10 My 1993); *SvD* (5 Fe, 6 Ap, 28 My, 20 Je 1991); *DN* (30 Oc, 1, 11 No, 14 De 1990, 24 Mr 1992, 8 Je, 5 Au 1993, 20 Ja 1996); *GP* (21 Ja 1992); *NT* (2 Mr 1993, 8 Fe, 21 My, 3 Au, 23 Oc 1996, 7, 24 Je, 6 Au, 2 Oc 1997); *HD* (22 Fe, 25, 27-8 Je, 3 Oc 1996); *SDS* (1 Je 1993); *ÖC* (11 No 1993); *UNT* (28 Oc 1994); *Arb* (4 My 1995).
[146]Sahlberg. "Flyktingprojektet." *NiS*, 16; Birgitta Öjersson. "Äntligen en plats i svensk bostadskö." *NiS* (no. 2, 1990), 2-5; Anneli Axelsson. "Chilenare i Simrishamn." *NiS* (no. 2, 1990), 6-11; *DN* (27 Ja, 1 Fe, 4 De 1990, 19 Ap 1991); *SvD* (11 Ja, 14 My 1991, 9 Mr 1992); *SkD* (26 Oc 1991); *GP* (25 Ja, 16 Se 1992); *VK* (13, 15 Ap, 7 My, 8 Jl 1993); *Arb* (23 Je, 15 Jl, 22 De 1995); *HD* (5 Au 1996); *NT* (4, 30 Oc 1997). Social Democrats liked to claim Sweden had not abandoned generosity, citing expenditures as evidence. Critics found this explanation irrelevant to the question. *SvD* (10 My 1999).
[147]*NT* (18 Mr 1997).
[148]*DN* (12 De 1992); *GP* (2 De 1992); *BT* (1 Je 1990); *KK* (31 My 1990); *GD* (3 De 1991, 30 De 1992).
[149]*VK* (26 Ja 1993); *UNT* (2 Mr 1993, 28 Oc 1994); *DN* (16 Je 1993); *ÖC* (11 No 1993); *AB* (11 Mr 1994).
[150]*SvD* (13 De 1995, 25 Ap 1996); *NT* (14 Ja 1996); *AB* (23 Ja 1996); *HD* (25 Je 1996).
[151]*HD*, Je 27-28, 1996; *NT*, Oc 14, 1996; Ja 20, 1997; *DN*, Ap 12, 1998; Fe 23, 1999; *SvD*, Ap 23, 1998.
[152]Karlsson. "Flyktingar och invandrare, rasister och vanliga svenskar," 115; *VK* (18 Ja, 20 Mr 1995); *DN* (14-5, 19 Fe 1995, 21, 28 Ja, 21, 24 Au, 25 Se, 19 No, 30 De 1996, 14 Je 1998, 25 Fe, 17 Au 1999); *GP* (18 Je 1992, 11Oc 1996, 1, 3 Ap 1998); *Exp* (26 Ja 1994, 28 My, 4, 14 Je, 12 Jl 1999); *SDS* (10 Ap 1995, 12 Se 1996); *SvD* (25 Se 1994, 18 Se, 3 Oc 1996); *NT* (5 Au 1998); *AB* (10 Jl 1999).
[153]*GP* (21 Mr 1994, 19 My 1998, 4 Je, 24 Au, 8 Oc 1999); *SkD* (28 Jl 1999); *SDS* (22 Oc 2000); *DN* (1 Mr 1999); Aje Carlbom. "Gemenskap eller utanförskap." *I & M* 37 (Fe 2000), 14-5; SVT (1 Fe 2000).
[154]Ylva Bydén. *Kulturarv för alla: Arbetet mot främlingsfientlighet och rasism vid landets kulturarvsinstitutioner* (Stockholm, 1998), 7-8; José Alberto Diaz. *Unga tankar om rasism: uppsatsantologi från Europaåret mot rasism* (Stockholm, 1998), 4-5; Cecilie Östby. *Lika och olika tjejer* (Stockholm, 1996), 3, 7-43 and *Mångfald och fnitter: kan tjejer vara rasister?* (Stockholm, 1996).
[155]*NT* (16 Ja, 4, 21 Oc, 3 No, 3 De 1997, 2 My 1998, 7 Je, 9, 25 Oc 1999); *Arb* (16 Fe, 1 Ap 1995, 17 Au 1999); *HD* (18 Fe 1996); *VK* (5 Se 1996); *ÖC* (20 My 1998); *UNT* (22 Je 1999); *DN* (19 Oc, 27, 29 No, 13 De 1998, 1 Mr 1999); *GP* (22 Se 1997, 29 Au, 11 Se 1999); *AB* (28 Jl, 9 Au 1999); *Exp* (25 Mr, 27 No 1998, 6 Mr 1999); *SvD* (16 Se 1996, 24 My, 3 Je 1997, 30 Mr 1998); *SDS* (2 Je 1998, 17 De 1999).
[156]*GP* (28 Se 1996, 8 Je 1998, 25 Oc 1999); *SvD* (16 Se 1996, 27, 31 Jl, 6 Au 1998, 17 Se, 5 No 1999); *NT* (19 Mr, 21 Oc 1997); *HD* (18 Fe 1996).
[157]Thomas Gür. *Positiv särbehandling är också diskriminering* (Stockholm, 1998), 13-6, 106; Reza Banakar. "Kvotering skapar inga nya jobb." *I & M* 22 (Se, 1995), 7-11; *UNT* (31 Oc 1997); *GD* (14 Oc 1998); *ÖC* (17 Ja 17 1998); *SvD* (4 Au 4 1998, 1 No 1999).

218 Endnotes

[158]Hans Nestius. *"Och vi som ville så väl-,"* 99; Vesna Maldaner. "'Lika bra som en svensk blir man aldrig.'" *NiS* (no. 3, 1991), 15-7; Staffan Wolters. "I Sverige räknas tid och resultat." *NiS* (no. 5, 1992), 48-9; *DN* (30 De 1996).
[159]*DN* (11 Se 1999).
[160]*HD* (28 Au 1996); *NT* (9 Oc 1996, 29 Se 1997); *Arb* (29 Se 1997); *AB* (29 My 1996); *SvD* 11 Je 1996).
[161]*SvD* (26, 29 Jl 1998).
[162]*SDS*, Se 7, 1998; Se 1, No 18, 1999; Au 21, Se 7, Oc 22, 2000; *SvD*, No 25, 1998; Se 15, Oc 25, 1999; *AB*, Au 9, 29, Se 17, 1999; *NT*, My 8, 12, Se 9, 1998; *GP*, Se 26, Oc 10, 1998; Au 23, Oc 8, 1999; *NA*, Se 8, 1998; *Bar*, Se 15, 1999; *BT*, Se 13, 1999; *SP*, Fe 24, 1999; *Exp*, Mr 4, 1999; *DN*, De 17, 1998; Fe 14, 1999; *GD*, Oc 17, 1998; *ÖC*, Je 15, 1999; *Lundian*, Ja, 2001.
[163]*GP* (12 Ap, 19 No 1992); *UNT* (30 Je, 3 Au 1992).
[164]Interview with Madubuko Arthur Diakité, 21 De 2000; *Invandrarföreningar i Lund*, n. d.. A diverse sample of newspaper accounts of immigrant organizations' problems and activities: *SDS* (20 Au 1997, 13, 19 No, 3, 7, 19 De 1999, 1, 12 Ap, 24 My, 29 Je, 25 Jl 2000); *HP* (6 Oc 1995); *GP* (20 Fe 1990, 7 My 1997); *GP* (11 Au, 20 De 1992, 25 My 1998); *SvD* (10 Jl, 11 De 1991, 7 No 1993); *VK* (1 Oc, 4 De 1993); *HD* (20, 22 Mr, 27 Ap, 21, 30 Oc 1996). See also: Lasse Lidén. "Teater kan stoppa våldet." *Sr* (no. 4, 1994), 6-7; "'Afrikanska asylsökande diskrimineras,'" 9; Olson. "Invandrarförbund: mera svenska än någonsin." *Mig* (no. 2, 1996), 8-11; Gür. *Staten och nykomlingarna*, 300.
[165]Reprint of Council Directive 43EC of 29 June 2000, *Lundian*, 2000. There were attempts at turning xenophobia into a key issue, but Social Democrats and the other main parties avoided the topic of aliens almost completely. See: *Exp* (24 Ap 1998); *HP* (9, 13 Je 1998); *AB* (12 Au 1998); *NT* (24 Ap 1997).
[166]Following the application used in Sweden, native equates here to individuals of "pure" ethnic Swedish backgrounds, and immigrant refers loosely to everyone else.
[167]Variances on leisure are based upon conversations and interviews with literally hundreds of Swedes and immigrants and upon descriptions given in numerous man-looking-for-woman, woman-looking-for-man searches published weekly in most Swedish newspapers. When in a search for a compatible companion, Swedish men and women tend to list nature activities as a favorite leisure activity. For a personal experience with the aloofness of Swedes, see: "A (good) morning in Stockholm." The Office Professional. DS och A & O (no. 2, 2004), communications@colinmoon.com.
[168]Leaders Anna-Greta Bergman and Jack Nilsson, *Lunds Arbetsförmedlingens akademiskta projekt*, 27 Fe 2001.
[169]Tirfe Mammo. *Två sidor av samma mynt* (Järfälla: Self-Help Promotion, 1996), 11-4, 17; STV. "Aktuellt" (16 Fe 1999); Britt-Marie Ericson. "Bortsorterad." *Säljaren* (no. 6, 1998), 8-9; *DN* (30 Ja, 2 Mr, 22 My, 1 Je, 14 No 1990, 18 De 1993, 18 Mr 1994, 20 Se, 1 Oc 1995, 18 Au 1996, 7 Jl 1998, 6 Oc 1999); *UNT* (21 My 1990); *SvD* (12 Fe 1990, 26 Fe, 28 Oc 1991, 5 Au 1993, 12 Fe 1995, 16 Se 1996, 17 Oc 1998); *NT* (10 Fe 1990, 31 Oc 1996, 17 Jl, 30 Se, 14-5, 20, 28 Oc 1997); *HD* (8, 11 Ja, 15 Fe, 21 Mr, 24 My, 10 Oc 1996); *GP* (31 Mr, 29 Se 1992, 6 Fe 1995, 19 My, 4 Je 1998, 4 Mr, 3 Ja, 16 Au, 10 Se, 7 Oc 1999); *AB* (1 Ap, 22 Jl 1992, 8 Ja, 9 Fe, 19 Mr 1994, 1 Je 1996; *Dl*, 10 Fe 1999); *Arb* (4 Jl 1995); *VK* (19 Jl 1993); *Exp* (26 Ja 1998); *BT* (4 Ap 1999); *SDS* (4 Mr, 16 Au, 21 Se, 25 No 1997, 1 Au, 28 Oc 1999, 6 Fe, 15 Mr, 1, 13, 28 Ap, 14 Au, 13 Se, 7 Oc 2000); Sahlberg. "Mycket skrik för lite ull." *Mig* (no. 5, 1997), 40-5; Sahlberg. "Trelleborgsmodellen: Dela på jobben—chans för arbetslösa." *Mig* (no. 4, 1998), 10;

Stefan Danielsson. "1000 platser lediga i pågående projekt . . . men arbetsförmedlingen skickar inga deltagare." *Mig* (no. 5, 1998), 19-26; Edward Sevume. "Kan särbehandling av arbetssökande invandrare försvaras?" *Mig* (no. 6, 1998), 14-5; Britta Linebäck. "Larmsignal om invandrarjobben." *Mig* (no. 4, 1995), 2-3; "Maria Leissner (fp) intervjuas av David Schwarz." *I & M* 22 (Je 1995), 15-7; Elsie C. Franzén. "Formandet av en underklass eller hur man söker jobb i Sverige." *I & M* 23 (Oc 1996), 14-6; Eva Löfgren. "Hitta jobben innan de finns till." *I & M* 23 (Oc 1996), 17-9; Jasim Mohamed. "Utan chans?" *Mig* (no. 3, 1996), 7-10. Regarding language, one person even suggested parenting improved with Swedish competency.

[170]Lise Blomqvist. "Somalia." *Mig* (no. 3, 1997), 12-24; Stefan Danielsson. "Kurser, praktik och projekt efter projekt men inget JOBB." *Mig* (no. 3, 1998), 22-7; Britta Linnebäck. "Sökes: Nya öppningar för invandrare." *Mig* (no. 1, 1996), 4-14; Joy Mahlasela. "En sydafrikansk betraktelse på nåd och onåd." *I & M* 19 (Ap 1992), 3-6; Halina Vigerson. "Polacker i Sverige." *I & M* 21 (De 1994), 104-9; Per Broome, *et al. Varför sitter "brassen" på bänken? eller Varför har invandrarna så svårt att få jobb?* (Stockholm: SNS förlag, 1996), 33; Lena Liljeroth & Mauricio Rojas. *Svenska främlingar: Att älska Sverige med dess fel och brister* (Stockholm: Gedins förlag, 1997), 57, 136; Kerstin Ekström. *Kvinna i Sverige: Porträtt av åtta flyktingkvinnor* (Stockholm: Carlsson bokförlag, 1995), 8-15; Sahlberg. "Flyktingprojektet," 12-30; STV (1 Fe 2000); Annika Ortmark Lind. "Släpp in oss!" *Amelia* (1999), 170-7; Mauricio Rojas. *Sveriges oälskade barn: att vara svensk med ändå inte* (Stockholm: Brombergs bokförlag, 1995), 13, 18; Binnie Kristal-Andersson. *Psychology of the refugee, the immigrant and their children: development of conceptual framework and application to psychotherapeutic and related support work* (Lund: Lund Univ. Press, 2000), 18; Cajsa Malmström. "Oroande självmordstal tryggare i invandrartäta områden." *Mig* (no. 2, 1998), 8-14; *SDS* (22 Se 1997, 30 Ja 1999, 18 Fe, 8 Jl, 29 Au 2000); *AB* (19 No 1994); *GP* (5 Ja, 25 Mr, 2 Ap 1992, 12 Se 1999); *DN* (5 Mr, 18 My, 1, 9 Je, 8 Oc 1990, 8 No 1993, 11 My 1999); *Exp* 28 De 1998); *SvD* (24 Oc 1994, 24 Mr 1998); *VK* (18 My 1990); *NT* (12 Fe, 27 Au 1997); *Arb* 29 Ap, 4 Jl 1995); *HD* (15 Ja 1996); *UNT* (12 Fe 1992). Without doubt, the most startling and revealing study was one that involved eighty-five Chilean and sixty-seven Iranian children; they were examined for twenty-six identifiable symptoms or indicators of disturbance that ranged from irritation to bed wetting. For the Chileans, 8.6% of the girls and 36.4% of the boys were at levels of psychic risk; for Iranians, it was 6.5% of the girls and 22% of the boys. Full details of the breakdowns by symptoms and ethnic group, see: Orlando Mella, "Hemlandstrauma och mottagningsstress," *I & M*, 17 (Oc 1991), 68-72.

[171]Solvig Ekblad. "Ohälsa försvårar integrationen." *M & I* 23 (Se 1996), 15-7; *SDS* (1, 27 Ap 2000); *Arb* (27 Ja 1992, 21 Mr 1995); *DN* (22 Se 1990, 21 Fe 1992, 11 Se, 1 Oc 1995); *GP* (25 My 1998, 4 Fe 1999); *LC* (2 Mr 1990, 10 Au 1991); *SvD* (11 Fe 1992); *DI* (12 No 1996); *AB* (1 Ja 1996); *UNT* (21 My 1990).

[172]Olson. "Gillar lågutbildade invandrare städjobb?" *Mig* (no. 1, 1996), 15; Charlotta Sjöstedt. "Giftstädare." *NiS* (no. 5, 1990), 39-41; "Invandrare fast i skitjobben." *NiS* (no. 1, 1993), 25-7; Dan-Olof Rooth. *Refugee immigrants in Sweden: educational investments and labour market integration* (Lund: Lund Univ. Econ. Studies 84, 1999), 12-3; Hasselrot. *Sverige blandat*, 50-4; Ylva Brune. *Invandrare i svenskt arbetsliv* (Norrköping: Siv, 1993), 6, 107-19; *SvD* (1 Fe 1991, 28 Fe 1992); *DN* (14 Jl 1990, 19 Ja 1996); *SDS* (4 Se 1998, 14 Jl, 24 No 1999, 11 Mr, 5 De 2000); *AB* (25 Ap 1998); *HD* (8 Oc 1996); *Exp* (10 Se 1993, 8 My 1998).

[173]*SDS* (2 Oc, 2-4, 17, 30 De 1999, 12-3, 22 Mr, 20 Au 2000); *SäT* (28, 30 Jl 1999); *DN* (30 Jl 1999); *NT* (28 Oc 1997); *Arb* (18 De 1995, 26 Oc 1999); *Exp* (18 Se 1998); *HD* (11 Oc 1996); *UNT* (22 No 1993); *SvD* (20 Fe, 20 No 1991); *AB* (3 Ja 1992); *GP* (15 Au 1992, 8 Ja 1999); *VK* (19, 23 Oc 1990); Woukko Knocke. "Facket och invandrarna." *I & M* 23 (Oc 1996), 5-9; Johanna Johnsson. "'Facket gör inte tillräckligt.'" *SIFtidningen* 79 (no. 12, 1999), 18; Johanna Johnsson. "Regionchef i SIF beredd betala antinazists böter." *SIFtidningen* 79 (no. 11, 1999), 18; Tommy Zetterwall. "'Vardagsrasism finns i alla samhällsklasser.'" *SIFtidningen* 80 (no. 11, 2000), 6; Margareta Wadstein. "Även facket måste förebygga etnisk diskriminering." *SIFtidningen* 80 (no. 13, 2000), 13; Graeme Atkinson. "Kämpa mot rasism och fascism i facket!" *Sr* (no. 4, 1991), 22-3.

[174]*SDS* (11 Fe, 4 My, 16 Je, 8 Jl, 10 Au, 8 Oc 2000); *Exp* (4 Ap 1998); *GP* (11 Oc 1992); Mannerfelt "Flora jobbar för vår 'gemensamma framtid.'" *NiS* (no. 2, 1994), 14-5; Mats Adolfsson. "Chipsfabriken—kvinnornas FN." *Mig* (no. 2, 1995), 14-7; Britta Linebäck. "Muslim hemma svensk på kontoret." *Mig* (no. 2, 1996), 12-6; Manne Fridell. "Olika bakgrund ger dynamik." *Mig* (no. 3, 1998), 37-9; Gunilla Ernflo. "Invandrare, kvinna, teknisk chef: Zeljka säger inte nej till mer makt." *Mig* (no. 6, 1998); author to *Mormors* staff (2 Mr 2001).

[175]*SDS* (22 Se 1997, 22 Oc 1999, 28 Ap, 9 Se, 8 Oc 2000); Ali Najih. "Invandrarföretag: Inte bara pizzerior och kiosker." *I & M* 22 (Je 1995), 2-6; Lise Blomqvist. "Lönen och äventyret lockade." *Mig* (no. 3, 1996), 12-5; Börge Nilsson. "1000-tals Polskor." *NiS* (no. 4, 1990), 40-5; Rolf Hertzman. "Svenska språket—nyckeln till eget företag." *Du & Co* (no. 4, 2000), 25-7; *Exp* (26 Ja 1998); *HD* (16 Oc 1996); *NT* (5 Fe, 10 Mr 1997); *SvD* (9 Mr 1992); *NA* (4 Mr 1996); *DN* (24 De 1990, 12 Oc 1998); *Arb* (8 Au 1995); Regnell Tobias. "Wilson Santana startade eget." *NiS* (no. 1, 1993), 22-4; "Eget företag: Enda vägen till framgång?" *Internationella Affärer* (4 Se 1992) in *NiS* (no. 1, 1993), 28-34; Lena Udd. "Allamanda kvinnokooperation med egen design." *NiS* (no. 1, 1993), 35-8; Ludvig Rasmusson. "På grekiska Poseidon lever musiken och dansen." *NiS* (no. 2, 1992); Stefan Danielsson. "Rosa Sanches har en idé." *Mig* (no. 4, 1998), 2-6.

[176]*Arbb* (12 Fe 1994). For sample attacks that include details of murder, arson, bombings, telephone threats, and assaults of alien owners and their businesses, see: *TSL* (28 My 1990); *GP* (31 Ja, 2-3, 6 Fe, 3 Jl 1992); *NT* (29 My, 14 Je 1990); *VK* (2 Mr, 14 Au 1993); *AB* (16 Ja 1994); *Arb* (6 Mr, 15 Jl, 6 Au, 2 Oc 1995); *SDS* (3 Se 1993, 13 My 2000); Ander I. Nilsson. "Sin egen lyckas smed." *NiS* (no. 5, 1994), 24-8; Hasselrot. *Sverige blandat*, 7-14.

[177]*AB* (7 Au 1994); *Exp* (6 De 1998); *NT* (8 Au, 17 Se, 9 Oc 1997); *HD* (11 Ap 1996).

[178]*NT* (30 Oc 1997); *SDS* (6 Jl 2000).

[179]*Exp* (4 Ap 1998); *NT* (7 My, 3 De 1997); *SDS* (20 Jl 2000); STV news coverage (week 10, 2001.)

[180]Anna von Melen. *Samtal med vuxna adopterade* (Stockholm: Rabén Prisma, 1998), 54-60, 65-75, 79-80, 94-5, 110, 113, 115, 135-9, 151-61, 184-91; Anders Jonsson. *Några anteckningar om kulturmöten, etnocentrism och rasism* (Örebro: Örebro College, 1993), 4-7; Rebecka Brick. *Upptakt!: 22 ungdomar säger sitt!* (Smygehamn: Save the Children, 1998), 31-3; Ingrid Lundberg. *50 år i Sverige: vägen till det mångkulturella samhället* (Stockholm: Stiftelsen Sverige, 1993), 36; "Readers' letters." "Adoptionens dramatiska konsekvenser." *I & M* 20 (Ap 1993), 1; AB (18 Oc 1991); Marianne Cederblad. "Sverige, adoptionsland." *I & M* 18 (Oc 1991), 76-9; Eva Norlander & Marianne Cederblad. "Ifrågasatt identitet." *I & M* 20 (Se 1993), 14-7; *HD* (7 De 1996); *SvD* (7 Se 1996); Arb (8 Ja 1995).

[181]*GP* (29 No 1992).

[182]Svenska Kommittén mot Antisemitism. *Det eviga hatet: om nynazism, antisemitism och Radio Islam* (Stockholm: Albert Bonnier förlag, 1993), 11, 161-205; Peter Nobel. *Tankar i tigertid* (Stockholm: Brombergs, 1992), 19-20; Lööw. "Sveriges rasistiska förflutna, 20-9; Stéphane Bruchfeld. *Förnekandet av förintelsen: nynazistisk historieförfalskning efter Auschwitz* (Stockholm: Swedish Committee against Anti-Semitism, 1996), 27-9; *GP* (21 Mr, 5 Ap, 5 My, 25 Se, 2, 22 Oc, 26-7 No 1992, 28 Ap 1994, 3 Fe 1995); *Dagen* (10 Ap 1996); *DN* (30 Je, 20 Au, 25 Oc 1990, 7 De 1991, 4 Jl 1999); *SvD* (29 Au 1990, 10 Jl, 22 Au 1991); *Arb* (2 Mr 1993, 27 Ja 1996); *AB* (30 Jl 1990, 26 Ap 1995); *HD* (11 Ap 1996); *Exp* (24 Je, 19 Se 1990, 21 Ap, 28 De 1998); *SDS* (28 No 1999, 29 Ap 2000).

[183]Irka Cederberg. "Svårt leva rättroget." *NiS* (no. 5, 1994), 20-3; Skadestånd för rasism." *Sr* (no. 3, 1991), 3; *DN* (15 My 1990, 30 Mr, 18 Ap 1994, 11 My 1999); Anna-Lena Lodenius & Per Wikström. *Nazist, rasist eller bara patriot?: en bok om den rasistiska ungdomskulturen och främlingsfientligt orienterad brottslighet* (Stockholm: Atlas, 1999), 81-6; *GP* (8 My, 26-7, 30 No 1992, 7 Se 1999); *HD* (29 Mr, 26 Oc 1996); *Arb* (4 Jl 1995); *NT* (9 Jl 1997); *BT* (9 Fe 1998); *SDS* (31 Jl, 18 Au, 9-10 No 1999, 10-1 Ap, 7 Oc 2000); *Metro* (10 No 1999).

[184]Based upon conversations with many Swedish men, including one who admitted to having paid for sexual favors from an African American prostitute during a short visit to New York in 1977 because of his curiosity. Zemya Hamilton, with a Swedish mother and a Jamaican father, suspected as a teenager that Swedish boys "wanted to try [sex] with a Negro," and Camilla Henemark, the daughter of Swedish-Nigerian parents, also felt Swedish males assumed black women would make more exotic bed partners; other dark-skinned starlets included: Kayode "Kayo" Shekoni, Fransesca Quartey, Titiyo, Jeanette Söderholm, Ardis, Leila K, Astrid Assefa, and Neneh Cherry. Alban Nwapa & Tom Hjelte, *Svartskallarnas sammansvärjning* (Stockholm: Norstedts förlag, 1992), 10-19, 28-31, 54-59, 104-110; Erland Bergman & Bo Swedin, *Vittnesmål: invandrares syn på diskriminering i Sverige, en rapport från* Diskrimineringsutredningen (Stockholm: Liber förlag, 1982), 94-97; *AB*, 26 Fe, 6 Mr, 11 Se 1994; *Exp*, 11 Se 1993; *DN*, 26 My 1991, 4 De 1996; "Rasrisk," *Sr*, no. 1 (1993), 10; *VK*, 2De 1993; *NA*, 13 No 1998.

[185]Carina Ågren, "Nu slåss han med ord istället för nävar," *Sr*, no. 1 (1992), 12-13; Nestius, *"Och vi som ville så väl-,"* 79, 82-87; Nwapa & Hjelte, *Svartskallarnas sammansvärjning*, 32-36; *AB*, 21 Se 1993, 8 Ap, 3 Jl, 21 Au, 3 Se 1994; *GP*, 4 My 1994; *DN*, 19 No 1990, 25 Je 1997; *Exp*, 11 Se 1993, 14 Fe 1998; *HD*, 23 Se 1996; *VK*, 30 Oc 1993; *SDS*, 11 Mr, 10 Ap, 24 My 2000. Ex-national basketball coach Charles Barton, an African American, almost left Sweden in 1993 because of doubts about wanting to raise his children in a racist nation; Mattsson, "Rasismen i Sverige dag för dag," 5.

[186]Mai Palmberg. *Afrika i skolböckerna* (Stockholm: SIDA, 1987); Anna Sjöwall. *Kulturmöten i barnomsorg och skola: antirasistiskt arbete med barn* (Lund: Studentlitteratur, 1994), 41; *Stora svensk-engelska ordboken* (Stockholm: Läromedelsförlagen språkförlaget, 1989), 587, 888-9; *SDS* (25 Ap 2000).

[187]*Aftonbladet* in 1994 published an unscientific poll of Swedish male opinions about blacks; it clearly did not reflect honesty about Swedish attitudes and actions toward the minority. Had 85 percent really thought blacks were enriching Swedish life, more demands for greater opportunity and stronger legal curbs against discrimination would have resulted. *AB* (8 Ap 1994). Reactions to Swedish women with mulatto children supplies strong evidence of a double gender standard. Caroline Tovatt freely told of her bad experiences with strangers: "A white woman who has a black child is clearly very

provocative in Swedish men's eyes. Insinuations and direct taunts are often very sex-fixated. Prejudices about 'black men with bestial desire' have subjected one to being called nigger whore or being subjected to comments such as 'I know whom you have lain with.' It is as if these persons feel threatened and unable to accept a Swedish woman actually falling in love with an African man." *Arb* (20 Fe 1995). Also see: Hasselrot. *Sverige blandat*, 71; Lars Malvin Karlsson. "Att tvingas möta fördomar & rasism." in Eva Amundsdotter, ed. *Modet att mötas* (Stockholm: Bokförlaget Prisma, 1996), 7-12; *SvD* (14 No 1991).

[188]Sahlberg. "Somalier icke önskvärda i Sverige?" *Mig* (no. 2, 1998), 31-3; "Förste svart byråkrat i Stockholms stadshus." *Sr* (no. 1, 1996), 6; Bergman & Swedin. *Vittnesmål*, 94-7.

[189]Karlsson. "Att tvingas möta fördomar & rasism," 7-12; Nora Weintraub. "Var tredje Afrikan hotad på gatan." *I & M* 23 (Oc 1996), 10; "Rikskonferensen kritisk till flyktingpolitiken." *Sr* (no. 1, 1997), 3; "Stopp vid krogen om du har svart hår!" *Sr* (no. 3, 1994), 11; Lodenius & Wikström. *Nazist, rasist eller bara patriot?*" 81-6; *AB* (27-8 No 1992, 5 De 1994); *DN* (8 De 1994); *Arb* (25 Ja, 8 Fe 1995); *HD* (31 Ja, 25 My, 26 Je 1996); *NT* (29 Ja 1997); *SvD* (29-30 Jl 1991, 30 Au 1996); *SDS* (7, 11 Jl, 19 Au, 21, 26 Oc 1999, 15, 18 Je 2000. Discrimination at pubs and night clubs most often affected blacks, but other minorities were victims; "Krogar diskriminerar svarta." *Sr* (no. 4, 1992), 5.

[190]Bergman & Swedin. *Vittnesmål*, 25-33, 62, 64; 94-7; Gellert Tamas. "Hiphop—invandrarungdoms musik, 'Man ska vara cool.'" *NiS* (no. 1, 1992), 22-6; *DN* (18 My, 4 De 1996, 15 De 1998); *AB* (2 Mr 1992); *SDS* (30 Ap 2000).

[191]During literally many hundred trips between Sweden and Denmark, the author experienced passport control only once, and it occurred when his son's friend from Ghana was a passenger. *SDS* (27 Oc 2000).

[192]*HD* (12 Ja 1996); *SvD* (23 Jl, 25 Au 1991); *AB* (29 Au, 15 Se 1994); *SDS* (27 No 1999).

[193]*GP* (4 Au 1992); *VK* (29 Jl, 30 Au 1993); *DN* (5 Ja 1995); *Arb* (5 Ja, 1 Fe 1995); *HD* (1, 3 Ap 1996); Mattsson. "Rasismen i Sverige dag för dag," 4-5.

[194]For first reports of the murder, see: *SDS* (10-2 Se 1995); for trial-related details and a look at Klippan, see: *HD* (26, 30 Ja, 28 Fe, 3, 15-6, 23 Mr, 18, 21 My, 1, 4, 18-9, 21, 25-6, 30 Je, 12 Jl, 1, 15 Au, 1-4, 10-1, 15 Se, 3 Oc 1996); for other views, see: *Exp* (21 Ja 1996); *SvD* (3 Oc 1996); Irka Cederberg. "Blodstänkt småstadsidyll." *Mig* (no. 1, 1996), 26-31; Per Svensson. "Bara en neger." *Anno* (1996), 36-44; for other verdicts, see: *HD* (10 Oc, 14 No, 19 De 1996); "Vår närvaro hade stor symbolisk betydelse." *Sr* (no. 2, 1996), 5.

[195]*SDS* (21 Oc 1999, 9, 30 Ap, 2 My 2000); *HD* (30 Au 1996); *AB* (2 De 1992, 1 Ja 1996); *Exp* (27 Se 1998); *GP* (30 Ja, 13 Oc 1992); Per-Åke Westerlund. *Vänd dom aldrig ryggen: lärdomar av antirasistiska kampen* (Farsta: Rättviseböcker, 1996), 9-15; "A nation of criminals." *The Economist* (24 Fe 2001), 40; Cederberg. "Blodstänkt småstadsidyll," 26-31; Per Kahnberg. *Varför kommer de hit?* (Örebro: Bokförlaget Libris, 1989), 23.

[196]*HD* (30 Au 1996); *Arb* (18-20 Ap, 11 My, 27 Se, 5, 28 No, 13 De 1995, 28 Jl 1997); *Exp* (7 Se 1993, 7, 24 Fe, 22 Mr, 8, 21 My, 3, 18, 25 Je, 27 Jl, 7 Se, 2 Oc, 17, 24, 27 No 1998); *DN* (8 Se, 11 No 1990, 20 No 1994, 22 My, 16 Je, 16 De 1998; *NT*, 1, 12, 27 Fe, 2, 14 Oc 1997); *SvD* (11 Au 1992); *HD* (21 No 1996); *AB* (4 Je 1994, 1 Ja 1996); *SDS* (15 Se 1992, 5, 24 No 1999, 4-5, 15 Je, 13 Se 2000); *GP* (6 Jl 1992); Bergman & Swedin. *Solidariet och konflikt*, 52; Ylva Brune. *Vålberg i nyheterna: en kamp mellan*

tolkningsmönster (Göteborg: Göteborg univ., 1996), 4, 6, 8, 18-22, 31; Anna-Lena Lodenius. "De nya, unga rasisterna." in Guillou. *Antirasistiskt lexikon*, 95-103; Anika Agebjörn. "Ingen rasism i Vålberg?" *Mig* (no. 4, 1996), 36-41.

[197]*SvD* (9, 13 No 1991); *GP* (30 Ja, 1 Fe 1992); *SDS* (1 Fe 1992, 1 Se 1993).

[198]*SvD* (14 No 1991); *Arb* (28 Au, 27 Se 1995); *SDS* (24 No 1992, 4-5 Au, 26 Se 2000); *GP* (12 Ap, 15 No, 8 De 1992, 22 Se 1996); *AB* (2 Ja 1992, 19 Ap 1995); *Exp* (30 Se 1995, 18 My, 29 Je, 17 Se 1998).

[199]*GP* (29 Oc, 7, 30 No, 1 De 1992); *SDS* (1 De 1990); *AB* (2 De 1994); *Arb* (30 No 1991).

[200]*HD* (18-9 Ja 1996); *GP* (12 Fe 1992); *SvD* (22 Au 1991).

[201]*GP* (25, 29 Ja, 9 Fe, 6 De 1992); *HD* (21 My 1992); *Exp* (29 No 1998); *Arb* (5 No 1999).

[202]*AB* (14 Je 1990); *NT* (30 Oc 1997); *SDS* (19 Ap 2000).

[203]*GP* (18 Ja 1992); *HP* (6 Oc 1995); *Exp* (13 Ja 1995, 27 Au 1998).

[204]*GP* (31 My 1992).

[205]*StT* (26 Je 1990); *SDS* (4 Ap, 26 Se 2000); *HD* (20 Mr 1996); *SvD* (22 De 1991).

[206]*DN* (28 My 1990); *AB* (18 Ap 1994); *VK* (27 Jl 1993); *Arb* (10 Ap, 27 Se, 17 Oc 1995); *NT* (2 Oc 1997).

[207]*GP* (7 Je 1992).

[208]*AB* (17 Ap 1996).

[209]*GP* (10 Fe 1992).

[210]*SDS* (21 Oc 1999); *GP* (27 De 1992); *DN* (29 Au 1996); *AB* (29 No 1999).

[211]*UNT* (28 Mr 1992, 18 Fe 1997); *Exp* (8 Se 1993); *SDS* (27 Ja, 6, 27 Mr, 25 Jl 2000); *NBK* (25-6 Ap 1990); *DN* (1-2 Mr, 29 Ap, 10 Se 1990); *NT* (25 Je, 25 Se 1997); *Arb* (25 My 1995); Ylva Brune. "Var plåga har sitt skri för sig." *NiS* (no. 3, 1994), 90-7; Ylva Brune. *Svenskar, invandrare och flyktingar i rubrikerna* (Göteborg: Göteborgs univ., 1996), 14-5; *Uppväxtvillkor [19]93:3: Svartskallar och vitlökar* (Stockholm: National Youth Advisory, 1993), 20-1; Ylva Brune, ed. *Mörk magi i vita medier: svensk nyhetsjournalistik om invandrare, flyktingar och rasism* (Stockholm: Carlsson bokförlag, 1998), 9-11; Ylva Brune. "Vi och Dom." *I & M* 20 (Je 1993), 16-21; Birgitta Löwander. "Massmediernas konstruerade värld." *I & M* 20 (Je 1993), 22-7; Johanna Parikka. "Stackars invandrare?" *I & M* 17 (Je 1990), 10-3; Britt Hultén. "Mediernas bild av flyktingarna." *I & M* 17 (De 1990), 86-90.

[212]*Exp* (5, 8 My, 23, 27-8 No, 11 De 1998).

[213]*Exp* (30-1 Mr 1998); *HD* (30 Au, 18 Oc 1996); *SDS* (17 Je 2000); Eva F. Dahlgren. "Vården sviker invandrare med värk." *Mig* (no. 5, 1995), 8-12; Monica Löfvander. "Sjukvård över språkgränser." *I & M* 18 (Oc 1991), 36-8; Hartmut Apitzch & Luis Ramos-Ruggiero. "Dialog med förhinder." *I & M* 18 (Oc 1991), 39-41.

[214]Sahlberg. "Här gråter vi ibland men skrattar för det mesta." *NiS* (no. 5, 1991), 2-9; Ragnhild Larsson. "Allt fler äldre invandrare: Svårt med svenskan på gamla dar." *Mig* (no. 3, 1998), 44-8; *HD* (15 No 1992, 8 Je 1996); *GP* (16 My, 1, 7, 29 Se 1999); *ÖC* (15 My 1999); *DN* (23 My 1990); *SDS* (10 Mr 2000).

[215]Bergman & Swedin. *Solidaritet och konflikt*, 52.

[216]*SDS* (20 Oc 1990, 4, 10, 24 No 1999, 12 Ap, 10 Je, 7 Se, 25 Oc 2000); *HD* (12 Ja, 28 Fe, 25 Mr, 28 Ap, 3-4 Je, 17 Se 1996); *DN* (11 Ap, 13 My, 20 Oc 1990); *NS* (19 Oc 1990); *SvD* (30 Au, 4 No 1996); *GP* (8 Ja, 4 Fe 1999); *AB* (29 Jl 1993); *Exp* (16 Ja 1996, 25 My, 26 No 1998); *UNT* (31 My 1990); *Metro* (10 No 1999); Paolo Silva & Maria Wetterstrand. "Integration—på vems villkor?" in Joe Franz, ed. *Tankar inför drakens tid* (Stockholm: National Coordinating Committee for the European Year against Racism,

1997), 20-8; Gerald Charette. "Readers' letters." *I & M* 19 (Se 1992), 1; Refik Senir. "Om fördomar och varuhusexpediter." *NiS* (no. 2, 1992), 20-1.
²¹⁷Patrick Moreau & Elisabeth Carelli, eds. *Muslimer i Sverige* (Norrköping: Siv, 1988), 97-9; Sahlberg. "Muslimer pluggar svensk demokrati." *NiS* (no. 2, 1992), 47-8; "Vi försöker skapa förståelse och trygghet." *Sr* (no. 3, 1993), 7; Richard Grügiel-Adolfsson. "De kommer från syd och öst: invandrar- och flyktingarbete i Växjö stift" (Växjö: Växjö bishopric, 1998), 38, 44-6.
²¹⁸*GP* (12 My 1990, 16 Ja, 15, 25 Au, 14 Oc, 20 No, 22 De 1992); *DN* (7 Ap, 12, 22, 29 My 1990, 7 Ap 1994); *ÖC* (5 No 1993); *NST* (20 Ja 1990); *HD* (4 Ja 1996); *SvD* (31 Ja, 12, 25 Fe, 8 Au, 22 Oc, 12 De 1991); *Exp* (4 Au, 10 Se 1993, 17 Ja 1997); *SDS* (2 De 1997, 28 Fe 1998, 29 No, 28 De 1999, 7 Ap, 7, 17 Jl, 11 No 2000); *Arb* (22 Au 1995); *NT* (1 Ap 1997); Åsa Brattlund & Jan Samuelsson. *Islam—en folkrörelse: Muslimer i svenskt samhällsliv* (Skellefteå: Artemis bokförlag, 1991), 17; Berggren. *Från bondeaktivism till rasmystik*, 132-4; Håkan Hvitfelt. "Den muslimska faran: om mediabilden av islam." in Brune, ed. *Mörk magi i vita medier*, 72-82; Marcus Johansson & Tomas Uddin. "Jämställdhet för alla?" *I & M* 22 (Mr 1995), 16-21; Åke Sander. "Muslimerna i Sverige. *I & M* 20 (Ap 1993), 3-12; Jonas Alwall. "Religionsfrihet [crossed through] endast för svenskar?" *I & M* 20 (Ap 1993), 13-20; Marianne Hjort. "Fundamentalismen måste bekämpas." *Sr* (no. 4, 1994), 3.
²¹⁹*DN* (29 No 1990); *SvD* (8, 10, 13, 24 Mr 1991); *AB* (11 My 1994); *SP* (17 Fe 1997); *NT* (3 Ap 1997); *Exp* (24 Je 1998); *SDS* (8-9 De 1999, 6 Mr, 11 No 2000); Åsa Hammar. *I främmande land: om lojalitet, heder, arbetslöshet och självrespekt* (Stockholm: Federativ, 1998), 41-106; Carita Forslund. "Musik och religion för själens skull." *Mig* (no. 6, 1997), 2-7; Bitti Ingemansson. "Halalslakt hos Scan i Skara." *Mig* (no. 6, 1997), 44-8.
²²⁰*GP* (15 Mr 1992); *VK* (16 Au, 3 Se 1993); *Arb* (25 Mr 1995); *SDS* (23 Mr 2000); *HD* (9 Fe 1996).
²²¹Anneli Gustafsson. "'Håll kyrkporten öppen för Allah.'" *Mig* (no. 1, 1996), 33-7; *Alla olika, alla lika* (no. 3, Jl-Au 1995), 5; Hasselrot. *Sverige blandat*, 67, 72-4; *VK* (20 Au 1993); *GP* (29 Au 1994); *Arb* (26 Mr 1995).
²²²*SDS* (11 My, 6 Oc, 7 No 1999, 31 Mr, 1, 29 Ap, 2, 8, 27 My, 21-2 Je 2000); *DN* (8 Se, 15, 24, 30 Oc, 8-9 No, 15 De 1990, 8 Je 1993, 22 My 1998); *SvD* (8 Ja, 7 Fe, 22 Ap, 17 My, 17 Au, 9 Se, 11 No 1991, 29 No 1999); *GP* (15 De 1990, 12 Ja, 17 Mr, 12, 16 Ap, 4 Se, 28 Oc 1992, 28 Mr 1999); *AB* (14 My 1994, 21 Ap 1997); *Arb* (9, 22 Je 1995); *HD* (15 No 1992, 20, 29 Ja, 23 Fe, 17 Mr, 17, 27, 30 Je, 16 Au 1996); *NT* (18 My 1990, 14 Mr, 14 Oc, 21 No, 10 De 1997); *NWT* (14 Je 1997); *VK* (21, 30 Ap 1993); Mannerfelt. "Språkklasser lösningen på dåliga svenskkunskaper?" *NiS* (no. 5, 1994), 16-9; Ann-Margarethe Livh. "Leder till utslagning." *Sr* (no. 4, 1991), 9; Kenneth Hyltenstam. "Illa genomtänkt hemspråksförslag." *I & M* 19 (Ap 1992), 3-7; Hariton Tomboulides. "En reform på villovägar." *I & M* 19 (Ap 1992), 8-9; Katrin Goldstein-Kyaga. "Värdet av kunskap." *I & M* 18 (Fe 1991), 33-5; Gunnar Edrén. "Missriktad reform." *I & M* 17 (Je 1990), 14-6; Ingela Palmér. "Läkande kraft." *I & M* 18 (Oc 1991), 80-2; Aila Aune. "Minoritetsbeteendets fördelar." *I & M* 18 (De 1991), 11-3; Sune Hultqvist, "Viktigast: Förståelse för invandrarna." *I & M* 18 (Ap 1991), 10-1; Ingvar Rönnbäck. "Skolan som samhällets problemlösare. *I & M* 22 (Oc 1995), 8-11; Karsten Douglas. "svenskundervisningen ger en förskönad Sverigebild." *I & M* 23 (Ap 1996), 32-5; Britt-Ingrid Stockfelt-Hoatson. "Invandrarelever en resurs att ta vara på!" *NiS* (no. 1, 1992), 35-6; Britta Weiler. "Bor man i Sverige ska man lära sig svenska—men hur?" *Sr* (no. 1,

Mahmut Baksi. *Små slavar* (Stockholm: np, 1976), 4-5; Gür. *Staten och nykomlingarna,* 291; Christina Rodell. "Rätten till hemspråk i fara." *Sr* (no. 3, 1991), 3.

[223] *HD* (17 Mr 1996); *DN* (15 My 1991, 19-20 No, 16 De 1998); *GP* (19 My 1998); *Exp* (26 Au 1998); *SDS* (27 No 1999, 12, 26 Ap 2000); *AB* (19 Je 1994); Mannerfelt. "Mot alla odds—'Invandrarskola' utsedd till Stockholms bäste skola." *Mig* (no. 3, 1997), 28-32; Lars-Erik Borgegård, Johan Håkansson, & Dieter K. Müller. "Hur förändras bosättningsmönstret när invandrarna blir fler?" *I & M* 22 (Oc 1995), 29-33.

[224] *SvD* (7 Au 1991); *HD* (31 Ja 1996); *NT* (24 Ap, 25 Se, 20 No, 6, 19 De 1997); *Exp* (17 Au 1998); *GP* (12 Ja, 8 Ap 1999); *SDS* (13 De 1999, 7, 16 Ap, 15 Au 2000); Anika Agebjörn. "Lika barn leka bäst?" *Mig* (no. 6, 1995), 10-6; Gunilla Ernflo. "Skolor & integration." *Mig* (no. 5, 1997), 2-10; Ingela Björck. "Multikulturalism: Ett tecken på nedgång." *Mig* (no. 6, 1995), 31-3; Lise Blomqvist. "Kulturkrock i duschen." *Mig* (no. 1, 1996), 46-8; Anna Jacobsson. "På majoritetens villkor." *I & M* 22 (Oc 1995), 12-5.

[225] *DN* (3 De 1991, 8 Ja 1992); *GD* (15 My 1990); *VK* (19-20 Ja 1993); *AB* (24 De 1996); *NT* (11 Fe, 23 My 1997); *SDS* (11 My, 28 Oc 1999); Annika Holm & Siv Widerberg. *Då bestämde jag mig för att leva* (Stockholm: Rubén & Sjögren, 1990), 13-4, 43-6; Inger Raune. *Välkommen eller-: att arbeta i skolan mot främlingsfientlighet* (Stockholm: Public Orphanage, 1993), 24-7; Andreas Konstantinides. *Undervisning för internationell och interkulturell förståelse: en studie på högstadiet i Malmö* (Malmö: Teachers College, 1994), 18, 23; Staffan Selander. *Rasism och främlingsfientlighet i svenska läroböcker?* (Härnösand: Institute for Pedagogical Textbook Research, 1990) 3, 50-1.

[226] *SDS,* 2, 6 Oc 1999, 1 Ap 2000; *iDAG,* 14, 24 Oc 1999.

[227] *SDS,* 5 No 1999, 8, 22 Mr 2000. After a Bunkeflostrand school had rejected a plan to bus in Rosengård children, Berga tentatively accepted thirteen out-of-district pupils for the fall term.

[228] *SDS* (25 My 1998, 19 My, 5 Au, 28 No 1999, 15 Je 2000, 24 Mr 2001); *AB* (8, 19 No, 3 De 1993); *SvD* (7 Je 1991); *NT* (2 Ap, 28 My 1997); iDAG (24 Oc 1999); Ann Eriksson. "Hjälper ungdomarna med läxorna." *NiS* (no. 6, 1991), 2-5; Mannerfelt. "Emilia och Rohan—invandrare men också svenskar." *NiS* (no. 6, 1990), 4-7; *DN* (23 Ap 1990); *HD* (24 Au 1996).

[229] *DN* (24 Ja, 19 Mr, 21 Je, 21 Au 1990); *SvD* (20 Se 1991, 4, 29 Oc 1993); *GP* (10 De 1992, 8 Ap 1998, 22 Ja 1999); *AB* (16 Se 1993); *VK* (19 Oc 1990, 13 Ja 1993); *HD* (4 Ja, 23 Ap, 15 No, 7, 18 De 1996); *NT* (25 Ja, 29 Au, 27 Oc 1997); *SDS* (28 No 1996, 28 Jl, 11, 29 No, 20 De 1999, 28-9 Ap 2000); Elsie Söderlindh. *Invandringens psykologi* (Stockholm: Natur & Kultur, 1984), 66-8; Gür. *Staten och nykomlingarna,* 298; Rooth. *Refugee immigrants in Sweden,* 11; Lise Blomqvist.. "Alfabetisering i Sverige." *Mig* (no. 2, 1995), 8-11; Sahlberg. "Skolverkets utvärdering SFI bättre än sitt rykte." *Mig* (no. 3, 1997), 8-11; Sahlberg. "För Sis finns inga hopplösa fall." *Mig* (no. 2, 1998), 22-5; Karl-Olov Arnstberg. "Tala bättre svenska säger drottningen." *Mig* (no. 4, 1995), 48-9; Sahlberg. "SFI—vad är det?" *NiS* (no. 2, 1994), 16-7, 22-3; Lena Pierredal. "SFI på nytt sätt—Bach, Mozart, viskningar och rop." *Mig* (no. 3, 1997), 2-6; Sahlberg. "Svårt lära språket när man aldrig träffar svenskar." *Mig* (no. 1, 1997), 18-25; attending an *Arbetsförmedlingen* meeting 27 Fe 2001, put the author in contact with an Iraqi and a Russian Ph.D. who have taken many *AMS* classes ever since their arrivals in Sweden in the 1980s.

[230] The author's attempt at selling an apartment in 1993 on Skarpskyttevägen in Lund's Norra Fäladen, a city neighborhood recognized by Lundians as alien inhabited, clearly disputed the polls and verified a prejudice by Swedes against living among

immigrants. Since a newspaper for-sale listing had given only a general description, price, and telephone number, respondents often asked first for a location. Upon hearing an address, Swedish callers replied, *"Tack så mycket"* (thanks so much), thus ending their search for more details. Turning to the only real-estate agent in the city who was interested in the task of selling the unit, the author and family were able to move because the agent found buyers, a Chinese couple, for what sons Peter and Patrik at ages twelve and fourteen had recognized after a few weeks of living there as their "ghetto" residence. For details on the area, see: Daisy Flemister & Birgitta Kjöllerström Käck. *Norra Fäladen: ett mångkulturellt samhälle i praktiken* (Borås: Library School, 1997).

[231]*DN* (3, 7-8 Ja, 17 Mr, 10 Ap, 12, 18 Oc 1990, 3 Oc 1994, 19-20 No, 16 De 1998, 12 Ap 1999); *SvD* (14 Je, 17 Oc, 24 De 1991, 28 Oc 1998); *GP* (17, 23 Se 1992, 21 Mr, 8 Ap, 3-6 My 1994, 16 Oc 1997, 7 Ja 1999); *AB* (1 Au 1994); *Arb* (27 Ja, 13 Ap 1995, 21 Jl 1998); *HD* (29 Fe, 11 Mr, 18 Ap, 9 Au, 10 Oc 1996); *NT* (20 Je, 23 De 1997); *Exp* (25-6 Ja 1998); *UNT* (23 Ap 1999); *GD* (20 Au 1999); *SDS* (19 Oc 1990, 13-5 No 1996, 6 Au, 14, 19 Se, 21 Oc 1999, 19 Ja, 7 Fe, 7 Mr, 4 Se, 22 Oc 2000); Stefan Andersson. *Assyrierna* (Stockholm: Tidens förlag, 1983), 66-8, 70; Bengt Turner, ed. *Bostadssegregation* (Lund: Liber läromedel, 1980), 7; Schwarz. "Missriktad flyktningmottagning," 2; Kirsti Kuusela. "Etnisk bostadssegregation." *I & M* 17 (May 1990), 15-9; "Assyrier—integration eller minoritetsliv?" *NiS* (no. 5, 1993), 38-41; Olson. "Saknar egen nation." *Mig* (no. 4, 1995), 18-23; Dieter K. Müller. "Svenska fritidshus under tysk flagg." *I & M* 22 (Se 1995), 3-6.

[232]*DN* (17 Ja, 21 Mr, 18 Ap, 2 Je, 29 Au, 18-21 No 1990, 26 Jl 1994, 2 Oc 1995, 19 Au 1999); *SvD* (20 Fe, 10, 18 No 1991, 27 Je, 18 Jl 1994, 21 Ap 1995, 16 Se 1998); *GP* (1 Je 1990, 5 Ja 1999); *AB* (2-4 Ja 1990, 18 Se, 26 Ap, 16 Je 1994, 1 Ja, 9 Ap 1996); *Exp* (9 Se 1993, 9 Je 1995, 11 Mr, 8 Ap 1998, 11 Mr 1999); *UNT* (7 Fe 1990, 22 No 1993); *NT* (12 Fe, 29 My, 30 Oc, 7 No, 10 De 1997); *Arb* (31 Jl 1999); *Arbb* (12 Fe 1994); *VK* (8 My 1993); *GD* (20 Au 1999); *IHT* (7 Oc 1998); *SDS* (24 Jl 1990, 5 Oc 1996, 13, 23 No, 10 De 1999, 27 Mr, 2, 5, 19, 29 My, 11, 20-1 Je, 24, 26 Se, 22, 30 No 2000); Cecilia Modig, ed. *Möten i Rinkeby* (Stockholm: bokförlaget Prisma, 1983), 77; Elisabeth Magnusson. "'Invandraröppet i Lövgärdet.'" *NiS* (no. 6, 1992), 6-9; Irka Cederberg. "Segregation och elände eller bo internationellt." *NiS* (no. 2, 1994), 8-13; Mannerfelt. "Förortens invandrade svenskar." *Mig* (no. 3, 1997), 45-9; Tobias Regnell. "Folk flyr jobben." *NiS* (no. 1, 1994), 1-4; Reza Eyrumlu. "Segregationens många bottnar." *I & M* 22 (Ap 1996), 36-8; Lars-Erik Borgegård. "Rinkeby—en global by i Stockholm." *I & M* 22 (Oc 1995), 12-5; Schwarz. "'Vi måste angripa våldets orsaker.'" *I & M* 22 (De 1995), 3-7; Enrique Pérez-Arias. "Chilenarna i Sverige: Självförvållade segregation." *I & M* 23 (Ap 1996), 8-11; Ulf Tjader. "Sju av tio utländskharkomst." *I & M* 22 (Je 1995), 12-4.

[233]Wiwi Samuelsson. *Det finns gränser* (Stockholm: Sveriges utbildningsradio, 1993), 159-61; Schwarz. "Det låga valdeltagandet." *I & M* 18 (Au 1991), 2; Sahlberg. "Fler invandrarväljare i år?" *NiS* (no. 4, 1994), 17-9; Sahlberg. "Medborgare innanför eller utanför murarna?" *Mig* (no. 2, 1997), 12-7; *SDS* (27 Oc 1992); *AB* (15 Mr, 12 Oc 1994); *Arb* (8 Au 1995); *DN* (11 Se 1998); *GP* (29 Ja 1992, 3 Oc 1998); *NT* (10 Se 1998).

[234]*SvD* (30 Mr, 19 My, 16-7 Au, 16 Se 1991, 9 Mr 1992, 9 Ap 1999); *Arb* (26 No 1993, 13 My 1994, 21 Mr 1998); *AB* (20 Au 1994); *DN* (11 No 1990, 12 Se 1994, 17 Ap, 9 No 1996, 14, 25 My, 16 Se 1998, 3 Oc 1999); *HD* (11 No 1996); *UNT* (14 Fe 1998); *SDS* (25 Se 1998, 4 Oc 1999, 7 Mr 2000); *Exp* (8 Mr, 1 My, 18 Oc, 16 De 1998); Lise Blomqvist. "Det handlar inte bara om invandrare." *Mig* (no. 1, 1997), 28-31; Sahlberg. "Varför röster inte invandrarna?" *NiS* (no. 3, 1991), 18-9; Ann Eriksson. "På systugan i

Fittja. 'Vi röstar på dom som hjälper oss.'" *NiS* (no. 3, 1991), 20-3; SVT. "Drottningen, Ludmila och alla de andra" (1 Fe 2000); Woukko Knocke. "Segregationens pris." *I & M* 23 (Se 1996), 18-20. Ghetto residents' likelihood to vote increased if "their" candidates were featured. Overall immigrant voting in 1998 was at 38 percent, but in Tensta—Baksi's home area—it ranged from 73 to 83 percent. Rinkeby had 49 percent, Rosengård 55, and Navestad 58. Gunilla Ernflo. "Nalin och Maria—Kanaler till makten." *Mig* (no. 5, 1998), 2-7.

[235]*Alla olika, alla lika* (Jl-Au, 1995), 6-7.

[236]*GP* (3 Ja 1999). For a 1994 election breakdown, see: *Vit makt?: en studie av invandrares och deras barns representation inom politik, förvaltning, näringsliv, organisationer och media* (Stockholm: Youth against racism, 1995), 20-55.

[237]*DN* (11 Se 1990, 31 Au 1994, 17 Fe 1998); *AB* (28 Ja, 17 Fe 1994); *HD* (12 Se 1996); *NT* (13, 24 Je, 22 De 1997); *Exp* (13 Ja, 25 Jl, 12 Au 1998); *UNT* (14, 17-8 Fe 1998); *VK* (24-6 Fe, 2, 16 Mr, 16 No 1998); *SDS* (26 Jl 1998).

[238]*UNT* (23 Fe 1993, 18 Fe 1998); *SvD* (22 Se 1993); *SDS* (14 Se 1997, 31 Ja 1998); *Exp* (21 Ja, 18 Fe 1998); Marianne Hjort. "Behövs ett invandrarparti?" *Sr* (no. 1, 1993), 4; Lars Taxén. "Botkyrkapartiet: Från moské kampanj till invandrarexport." *Sr* (no. 4, 1991), 9.

[239]*SvD* (5, 7 Ap, 27 My 1991); *DN* (19 Ja, 11 De 1990, 21 Fe 1992); *GP* (15 De 1990, 2, 22 Fe 1992); *SDS* (1 Fe 1992); Schwarz. "Etniska strejker." *I & M* 19 (Ap 1992), 2.

[240]The author primarily gleaned information for this paragraph from literally hundreds of frank discussions with natives and aliens—the employed and jobless, educated and semi-illiterate, professional and blue-collared, skilled and unskilled, and entrepreneurial and proletarian. In addition, research into the following sources provided impressions and conclusions in support of somewhat unavoidable subjectivity of interpreting remarks and intonations from so many individuals; each source notes either conflict with or adjustment to living as a newcomer to a nation: Soleyman Ghasemiani. *Mångkulturella getton: den demokratiska apartheiden* (Angered: Hanaförlaget, 1997), 13-4, 107-9; Lena Olsson. "Om du gör så blir jag ledsen." *NiS* (no. 3, 1993), 34-5; Nils-Erik Nilsson & Kjell Lund. *Förälder i nytt land* (Solna: Naturia förlag, 1992), 17; Nadia Banno Gomes. *Tjejer kan!: En bok om Exit, en mångkulturell tjejgrupp i Botkyrka* (Tumba: Center for Cultural Diversity, 1996), 12-5; *DN* (24, 28 No, 6, 10 De 1990, 3-4, 8, 10-1 Se 1991, 15 Mr, 2 Jl, 22 Au, 28 No 1993, 3 Je 1994, 22 Je 1995, 10-2, 14 Je, 12 Oc 1996, 27 Fe, 22-9 Je, 10, 15 Au, 4 No 1997, 19 My 1998); *SvD* (8 Mr, 18 My, 6 Au 1991, 3 Mr 1992, 22 Se, 27 Oc 1993, 12 Je 1994, 22 Ap 1995, 27, 30 Au, 3-4 Se, 7 De 1996, 12 Mr, 15, 31 Jl, 2 Se 1997); *GP* (21, 28 Ap, 5 My 1991, 30 Ap, 1 No 1992, 14 My, 20 De 1995, 14 My 1998, 12 Ja, 3, 24 De 1999); *AB* (28-9 Fe, 1-2 Mr 1992, 21 Se, 7 No 1993, 5, 10, 12 Je 1994, 13 Ap 1995); *VK* (23 Ja, 14 Se 1993, 19 Se 1995); *UNT* (15 No, 29 De 1993, 2 My 1994, 14, 23 Oc, 11, 14 No, 23 De 1997, 17 Fe, 6 Jl 1998); *Arb* (26 Se 1993, 22 Mr 1994, 12 Ja, 10, 20-1 Mr, 1 Je, 8 Oc 1995, 20 De 1997); *HD* (15 No 1992, 18 Fe, 4, 15 Mr, 20 Oc, 8 De 1996); *NT* (24 My 1997); *Exp* (14 Se 1993, 30 Se 1995, 19 Je 1998, 19 Fe 1999); *BB* (25 My 1990); *Bar* (7 Mr, 21 Je 1990, 23 My 1991, 12 Oc 1994); *GD* (30 De 1992, 16 Mr 1997); *ÖK* (29 Jl 1992); *VLT* (15 De 1993); *KK* (31 My 1990); *ÖC* (24 Mr 1990, 28 No 1991); *SP* (5 Fe 1994); *NA* (28-30 De 1995); *Dagen* (1 No 1994); *SDS* (21 Se 1990, 27 My 1991, 3 Fe 1992, 3, 30 Mr, 15 Au 1993, 22 Je, 25 Oc 1995, 4 Au 1997, 2 Oc, 21 No, 27 De 1999, 1 Fe, 25 Mr, 10 Ap, 17 Je, 21 Jl, 13, 26 Se 2000); Britta Linebäck. "Den osynliga minoriteten." *Mig* (no. 4, 1995), 14-7; Liv Hellmers. "Tonårsröster om kulturkrockarna." *NiS* (no. 6, 1990), 14-7; Ragnhild Larsson. "Föda barn, fest eller plåga?" *Mig* (no. 4, 1996), 28-32; Eva Molin. "Ramesh från Iran: Tar de

bästa bitarna ur varje kultur." *NiS* (no. 2, 1993), 31-2; Eva Molin. "Katherine från Chile: Svenska tjejer har nog mer frihet." *NiS* (no. 2, 1993), 33-4; Karin S. Sharma. "Kulturkrockar." *I & M* 18 (Oc 1991), 6-8; Wuokko Knocke. "Kulturens mångfald." *I & M* 21 (Fe 1994), 16-8.

[241]*GP* (4, 8, 11-2, Oc, 17 No 1992); *DN* (22 My, 27 Je, 12 De 1990, 9 No 1996); *SvD* (30 Oc 1993, 18 Se 1996, 10 Ja 1998); *SDS* (24 Au 1993); *AB* (18 My 1994); *Arb* (27 Mr 1995); *BT* (16 Oc 1996); *NT* (30 My 1997); *Bota eller skrota invandrarpolitiken?* (Norrköping: *Siv*, 1996), 76; Sahlberg. "Sverige, framtiden & mångfalden?" *Mig* (no. 3, 1996), 16-21; Daun, *et al. Invandrarna i välfärdssamhället*, 142-3, 155-6.

[242]*DN* (20 Mr 1990); *GP* (29 Je 1992); *VK* (8 Ja 1993); *SvD* (23 Au 1994); *SDS* (16 Au 1997, 30 No 1999, 25 Mr, 16-7 Ap 2000); Riyadh Albaldawi. "Invandrarnas narkotikamissbruk." *I & M* 18 (Ap 1991), 21-5.

[243]Jan Ahlberg. *Invandrares och invandraresbarns brottlighet: En statistik analys* (Stockholm: Crime Prevention Advisory, 1996), 119-23; Sahlberg. "Är invandrarungdomar mer kriminella än svenskar?" *NiS* (no. 6, 1990), 24-33; Gellert Tamas. *Sverige, Sverige, fosterland: om ungdom, identitet och främlingskap* (Stockholm: Liber, 1995), 6-7, 30; Eva Grahn & Ingela Kåhl. *Det heliga brödraskapet: massmedia, rasism och sexism* (Malmö: Cat Art, 1994), 12-3; Daun, *et al. Invandrarna i välfärdssamhället*, 164-6; *ÖC* (10 No 1990); *DN* (22 De 1990, 15-6 My 1991, 20 My 1994, 23 Fe, 3, 5 Mr 1997); *SvD* (21, 25 Ja, 19 Mr, 11 Je 1991, 7 No 1993); *AB* (3-5 Mr 1992, 21 Au 1994, 1 Ja 1996); *GP* (17 Au, 30 Se 1992, 19-20 De 1995, 27 Ap 1997, 25 My 1998); *Arb* (30 Je, 26 Se, 29 No 1995); *HD* (18 Oc 1996); *NT* (2 Ap, 2 Au 1997); *SDS* (18 Se 1997, 10 Au 1999); Ingert Nilsson. "Invandrare och kriminalitet." *Mig* (no. 1, 1997), 36-41.

[244]*AB* (4-8, 21-2 De 1994); *Arb* (21 Ja, 30 Je 1995); Mannerfelt. "Micke, en i gänget—Man får inte banga ur." *Mig* (no. 1, 1995), 2-6.

[245]*SDS* (2 Ap, 29 No, 14 De 1998, 25 Mr, 11 Ap, 6 My 2000); *DN* (19 Ja 1990, 2 Fe 1997); *Exp* (5 Fe, 11 Mr, 13 Je, 28 No 1998); *VK* (22 Fe 1993); *AB* (16 Oc, 9 No 1994, 4-6, 19 Au, 18 De 1998); *HD* (14 Au, 13 De 1996); *NT* (11, 19 Fe, 26 Mr 1997); *UNT* (6 Fe 1997); *GP* (25 My 1998); Jasim Mohamed. "Ungdomarna går inte i fädrens spår." *NiS* (no. 5, 1994), 40-1.

[246]*DN* (7 Au, 13 Se 1990); *PT* (27-8 Ap 1990); *SvD* (26 Oc 1993); *HD* (23 Fe 1996); *SDS* (22 Jl 2000).

[247]*SvD* (20 Ja, 3 Mr 1991); *VK* (8 Oc 1993); *Arb* (19 Je 1995); *HD* (4, 15 Mr, 21 Oc 1996); *NT* (2 Ap 1997); *SDS* (27 Ap, 9 Je 2000); Bitti Ingemansson. "Sorgen bröt barriärerna." *Mig* (no. 6, 1998), 2-6.

[248]*SDS* (9 Au 1999); Charles Westin. "Migration och kriminalitet." *I & M* 23 (De 1996), 5-8.

[249]*GP* (31 Ja, 4, 9, 11, 21 Fe, 30 No 1992, 12 Je 1997); *SDS* (1 Fe 1992, 28 Au, 10 No, 1, 4, 9, 12 De 1999, 27 Ja 27, 2 My 2000); *Exp* (7 Se 1993); *Arb* (26 No 1995); *HD* (26 Je, 10 No 1996); *NT* (3 Mr, 25 Ap, 2-3 Jl, 15 Oc, 10, 18, 20, 28 No, 1, 8 De 1997); *VK* (4 De 1991.

[250]*BLT* (6 Je 1990); *DN* (27 Fe 1998); *VK* (12, 14-5, 17, 24-5 Je 1993); *HD* (29, 31 Ja, 17, 29 Fe, 5, 13-4, 19, 26-7 Mr, 24 Ap, 29 No 1996); *SDS* (16 Ja, 24 My, 23 Je, 20 Jl, 6, 13, 29 Au , 27 Se 2000).

[251]*GP* (1 Fe, 1 Je, 30 No 1992); *DN* (8 My, 1 De 1990); *SvD* (31 Ja 1991); *Exp* (26 Se 1990, 12 Se 1993, 18 Se 1998); *AB* (23 Ja, 28 Je, 7 Au 1994); *BT* (5 No 1993); *SDS* (1 De 1999). Ronny Landin died in 1986 as a result of placing himself in the middle of a skinhead assault on immigrants at a Nynäshamn camping place. As literally thousands

did nothing but watch as horror unfolded before them, skinheads kicked and slugged Landin to death. In memory of his courage, an annual prize is awarded in his name every year to other fighters against racism in Sweden. "Ronny Landins minnesfond tio år." *Sr* (no. 1, 1996), 2.

[252]Positive acts: *AB* (22 Se 1990); *SDS* (14 Oc 1991, 7, 18 No 1999); *Arb* (4 No 1991, 23 De 1995); *Dagen* (4 Ja 1991, 20 Jl 1996); *GP* (2, 21 Fe 1992); *SvD* (19 No 1991, 1 Au 1993, 4 Au 1996); *VK* (20 Se 1993); *BT* (3 Mr 1996); *HD* (17 Jl 1996). Negative acts: *SvD* (13 Au 1996); *VK* (13 Se 1993); *Exp* (11 Se 1993); *GP* (12 Ja 1999). The free churches' record of welcoming outsiders into their fellowships was better than that of the state church.

[253]*SDS*, My 11, No 13, 1999; *GP*, Se 4, 1992; *HD*, Oc 6, 1996; Walter Rep and Pernilla Lorentzson, "Världslaget från Hjällbo," *Mig*, No. 1, 1995, 8-11.

[254]*DN* (7, 19 Je 1990, 3 De1991, 22 Au 1993); *SvD* (2 Au 1990, 14, 29 No, 11, 20 De 1991); *ÖC* (10 Au, 2 De 1991); *GP* (24 No 1991, 9-10, 31 Ja, 3, 5 Fe, 5 Mr 1992, 7 Je 1993, 13 No1996); *VK* (20 Se, 1 De 1993); *AB* (21 No 1990); *Arb* (27 Ja 1990, 30 Mr 1994); *BT* (5 No 1993); *SkD* (11 Se 1996); *Dagen* (13 Fe 1996); *HD* (17 Ja, 19 Mr, 25-6 My, 7 Je, 6 No 1996); *NT* (28 Oc, 6 De 1997); *Exp* (2 No 1998); *SDS* (22 My 1997, 9 Jl, 10, 17, 30 No 1999; *Acceptera!* (Stockholm: Fritze, 1998), 15, 17-8, 20, 22; Maria Hansson. *Pow-Wow: en handbok för rådslag mot rasism* (Stockholm: Youth against Racism, 1998), 8-19; Per-Erik Wentus, Seyitxan Anter, & Karl-Gustav Vinsa, *Den sociala frågan och rasismen* (Göteborg: Socialist Party, 1994), 5-8, 10-1, 15; Abby Peterson. *Neo-sectarianism and rainbow coalitions: youth and the drama of immigration in contemporary Sweden* (Aldershot, UK: Ashgate, 1997), 56-75; "Antirasistiska aktiviteter i Storstockholm." *Sr* (no. 1, 1993), 3; Karl-Olov Arnstberg. "Omöjligt bekämpa slummen med pilbåge och golfklubba." *Mig* (no. 1, 1996), 30-1; José Alberto Diaz. "Rasism utan ras?" *I & M* 19 (Je 1992), 3-8.

[255]*GP* (9 Ja 1992); *HD* (18Ja, 17 Se 1996).

[256]*SvD* (19, 29 My, 5, 11, 16, 22 Je, 2, 9, 14, 20, 28 Jl 1993, 2 Ap, 7 My, 19 Je, 3 De 1994, 17, 27 Jl, 10 Au 1995, 29 Ja, 4 Mr, 16 No, 6 De 1996, 12 No 1997, 16, 23, 25 Fe, 24 Mr 1998); *DN* (2 Oc 1993); *iDAG* (7 Oc 1993); *Arb* (2 No 1993, 16 Fe, 1 Jl, 15 Au 1994); *AB* (6, 10, 21 Mr, 4 Ap 1994, 14, 21 Mr, 20, 26 Ap 1995, 4, 13, 20 Jl 1999); *GP* (18 Mr 1996); *UNT* (13, 25 No 1997); *Bar* (23 Ap 1999); Ingrid Björkman, Jan Elferson, & Åke Wedin, *Flyktingpolitikens andra steg: återvandring som utvecklingsstöd* (Stockholm: SNS, 1996), 95.

[257]*HD* (13, 24 Oc 1992); *VK* (3 Mr 1993); *Exp* (16 Ja 1996); *NT* (12 Ap 1997); *SDS* (8, 12 Ap 2000); Kjell Magnusson. "Kosovoalbaner—mellan minoritet och nation." *NiS* (no. 4, 1992), 17-20; "Högerextremist lärare på socialhögskolan." *Sr* (no. 2, 1992), 10; Westerlund. *Vänd dom aldrig ryggen*, 26.

[258]From May, 1997: *DN* (6, 12, 15, 24); *SvD* (16, 25); *SDS* (17); *UNT* (20); *Arb* (22).

[259]*SvD* (15 De 1997); *NT* (15, 23 De 1997); *Exp* (20 Mr, 24 Ap, 2-3 Je, 3, 8 De 1998); *AB* (4 Jl 1999); *SDS* (8 Jl 2000). In contrast to Matti's encounters with legal problems and an end to her studies for a neo-Nazi lecturing under her auspices, an immigrant instructor at Mälardalen College in Eskilstuna suffered no consequences from a similar invitation. There were two differences to note, though; he had requested permission, and he had countered false claims. *Exp* (4 Mr, 27 Oc 1998).

[260]Birgitta Ländin. "Forskning i invandrarnas tjänst." *I & M* 20 (Fe 1993), 22-5; Anders Lange. "Bel Habibs korståg." *I & M* 19 (Je 1992), 19-23; Harald Runblom. "Debatt om invandrarforskning: viktiga uppgifter." *I & M* 19 (Ap 1992), 26-9; Britt Hultén. *Det onda och det goda Sverige: bilden av flyktingar, invandrare och rasism i*

230 Endnotes

svensk press vecka 46 1991 (Stockholm: Univ., 1993); Birgitta Löwander. *Rasism och antirasism på dagordningen: studier av televisionens nyhetsrapportering i början av 1990-talet* (Umeå: Univ., 1997); *SvD* (4, 13, 15 Ja 1992); *GP* (31 Ja 1992); *NT* (17 Mr 1990); *Arb* (20 Fe, 26 Mr, 13 Jl 1995); *SDS* (24 Ap, 28 No 1992, 17 Se 1997); *DN* (30 Ja 1990). With literally hundreds of studies—many of whom are listed in bibliography—to cite, only the most relevant ones to the paragraph are included.

[261]*SP* (12 Mr 1990); *DN* (12 Mr, 6 Je 1990, 6 Ap 1996); *SvD* (14 No 1991, 8 Jl 1997); *GP* (29 Ja 29, 6, 20 Fe 1992); *VK* (6, 17 Fe, 22 Oc 1993); *AB* (30 No, 12 De 1994); *Arb* (12 De 1995); *SDS* (17 No, 12 De 1999, 30 Au 2000); Kristina Lindegren. *Åtgärder mot främlingsfientlighet och rasism i skolan* (Stockholm: Parliamentary Inquiry, 1996), 1, 5, 9, 11; Sabina Almgren, Ulla Rantakeisu, & Bengt Starrin, "Vi måste visa att vi inte är rasister" (Karlstad: Centre for Public Health Research), 1996), 2; Lena Liljeroth. *Skinnskallar: rasister, nationalister eller hyggliga unga män?* (Stockholm: Gedins, 1995); Ann Lodenius & Per Wikström. *Vit makt och blågula drömmar* (Stockholm: National Police Board, 1999), 18; *Lärutbildning med ett interkulturellt perspecktiv* (Stockholm: European Year Against Racism,1998); Magne Raundalen & Gustav Lorentzen. *Barn och rasism* (Lund: Studentlitteratur, 1995), 8; Lodenius & Wingborg. *Svenskarna först?*; Elsa Bender & Brita Dahlgren. *Rasfördomar* (Borås: Immigrant Institute, 1976); Susanne Gille, Margareta Rydberg, & Gerd Åkerlund. *Rasfördomar och invandrarproblem: ett kommenterat urval barn- och tonårsböcker om rasdiskriminering och om fördomar mot invandrare* (Borås: Immigrant Institute, 1981); Anne Alenbro Lindström & Lena Hansen. *Om invandrare och rasmotsättningar: ett urval barn- och ungdomsböcker 1980-1986* (Borås: Library School, 1988), 30.

[262]Marianne Håkansson, *et al. Rasistiskt och främlingsfientligt våld* (Stockholm: Fritzes, 1998), 14-5; *SvD* (13 Jl, 18 Oc 1991); *AB* (29 No 1994); *NT* (12 Je 1997); *SDS* (20 Oc, 2, 23 No 1999); Anders Lange *et al.Utsatthet för etniskt och politiskt relaterat våld m m, spridning av rasistisk och antirasistisk propaganda samt attityder till demokratin m m bland skolelever* (Stockholm: Center for Immigrant Research, 1997), 1, 68-72.

[263]*Arb*, Oc 13-14, No 24, De 10, 1995; *HD*, Fe 10, Mr 15, 17, 26, Ap 10, Oc 18, No 22, 1996; *SDS*, Se 7, De 14, 22, 1999; STV, Fe 24, 2000.

[264]*SvD* (2 De 1991); *VK* (13 Ja 1996); *NT* (11, 13 No 1997); *Exp* (2 Jl 1999); *SDS* (28 Se, 16 Oc, 20 No 1999); Karolina Hemlin. "'Vi styrs av fördomar.'" *Sr* (no. 1, 1997), 9; STV (Spring 2000).

[265]*DN* (19 Je 1990, 5 Jl 1992); *SvD* (10 Jl, 13 Se 1991, 24 Fe 1992); *GP* (28 Jl, 6 Oc 1992, 6 Se 1996); *Arb* (9 Se, 1, 22 No 1995); *HD* (21 Fe 1996); *AB* (5 Ap 1996); *Exp* (7 Fe 1998); *SDS* (15 Fe 1992, 19 No, 2 De 1999, 25 Mr 2000); *NT* (15 My 1990); STV (1 Fe 2000).

[266]*SvD*, Ap 8-13, 20, No 1, 1991; *GP*, Ap 6-7, My 23, Au 29, 1992.

[267]*DN* (9 Ja 1990, 10 Oc 1992, 31 Au 1994, 17 Oc 1996); *GP* (13, 29 Oc 1992, 23 Fe, 9 Ap 1994, 19 My 1995, 17 Oc 1997, 24 Au, 28 No 1999); *SvD* (18-9 Ap 1995, 23 Je, 6, 24 Jl, 17-8, 20 Se 1996, 13 Ap, 30 Au, 6, 16, 18-9, 24 Se 1997); *VK* (15 Se, 22Oc 1993); *Exp* (17 My, 7, 13 Se 1993, 2 De 1998); *Arb* (1 Oc 1993, 28 De 1995, 15 Fe 1999); *UNT* (18 My 1990, 4 Oc 1991, 17 Oc, 19 No, 10, 16, 24 De 1997); *NT* (10 My, 23 De 1997, 19 De 1998); *SkD* (25 Fe 1992); *Dagen* (3 My 1996); *ÖK* (2 Je 1998); *SP* (6 Au 1997); *SDS* (24 Se 1997, 6 My 2000); *Metro* (24 No 2000); Schwarz. "Svenska attityder." *I & M* 19 (Se 1992), 2; Sahlberg. "Ökad främlingsfientlighet i en otryggare värld?" *NiS* (no. 2, 1992), 35-7. Wedding photos and stories in *DN, SvD, SDS,* and *GP* were surveyed

during either May or June to see whom was marrying whom in Sweden. Typical was the May tally from *DN*; it showed 184 all-Swede weddings and 6 multi-ethnic partnerships.

[268]*DN* (23-5 Fe, 19, 22 Je 1990, 20 No, 3 De 1991, 7 Ja, 5 De 1992, 8 Au, 4-5 Se, 30 No, 5, 13 De 1993, 22 Se 1996); *SvD* (21, 30 Se, 29 No 1991, 13 Mr 1994, 8 Ja 1995, 1 Se 1998); *GP* (10, 12, 16 Mr, 2 Ap, 29 Oc 1992); *VK* (28 No, 17 De 1991, 29-30 Se 1993); *Exp* (10 Jl 1992, 10 Se 1993, 13 Se 1994); *AB* (1 Je 1990, 23 Oc, 8 No 1991, 3 Ja, 18, 20 Mr 1992, 21 Se 1993, 6 Je 1994, 1 Ja 1996); *Arb* (30 No 1991, 27-8 Fe 1992, 18 Oc 1993, 9 Jl 1994, 12 De 1995); *HD* (19 Ja, 30 No 1996); *NT* (25 Ap, 21 Jl 1997); *SDS* (22 Ja, 4 Fe 1992, 7 Fe, 17 Mr, 20 Je 2000); *HT* (7 Ap 1990); *ÖC* (28 No 1991, 7 Fe, 16 Oc 1992, 20 Se, 5 Oc 1993); *SkD* (13 De 1991); *Arbb* (26 No 1991); *SP* (7 Fe 1992, 5 Mr 1999); *NA* (5 Je 1991); *HP* (6 Oc 1995); *LT* (29 My 1990); Kjell Jonsson."Sverige, Europa och främlingen." in Kerstin Thorsén, ed. *Rasism och etniska konflikter: vad kan skolan göra?* (Stockholm: Board of Education, 1991), 21; Birgitta Löwander. "Rasism i verkligheten och i nyheterna." in Brune, ed. *Mörk magi i vita medier*, 88-92; Per Wirtén. "Det svenska rasförtrycket." in Håkan A. Bengtsson & Wirtén, eds. *Epokskifte* (Stockholm: Atlas, 1997), 159-65.

[269]*SDS* (23 No 1991, 13 Se 1999); *NN* (16 Je 1990); Lodenius & Wikström. *Nazist, rasist eller bara patriot?* 53-6.

[270]Thomas Sjöberg. *Ingvar Kamprad och hans IKEA: En svensk saga* (Stockholm: Gedin, 1998, 85-129, 134-41; *Exp* (16, 18 My 1998); *SvD* (8 Se 1991); *DN* (22 Fe 1990); *AB* (8-9 No 1994); *SDS* (19 No 1999); Heléne Lööw. *Nazismen i Sverige 1980-1999: den rasistiska undergroundrörelsen: musiken, myterna, riterna* (Stockholm: Ordfront, 2000), 28-9, 88, 92-3, 95-103, 105-6; Pia Kristmansson. *Möten och mångfald* (Stockholm: Youth Board, 1995), 14; STV (16 No 1999); Lodenius & Wikström. *Nazist, rasist eller bara patriot?*, 9-14, 17-39; Skagegård & Hübinette. *Hatets återkomst*, 74-92. In fairness to Kamprad, he amended a Nazi past by aiding Polish and Czech Jews.

[271]Lööw. *Nazismen i Sverige 1980-1999*, 216-7, 244-6, 254; *SDS* (24 Se 1997, 24 No 1999); *Dagen* (31 My 1996); *AB* (28 Oc 1991, 23 Mr 1994, 13 My 2000); *SvD* (2 Je 1990); *HD* (31 My, 26 Jl 1996); *NT* (13 No 1997).

[272]*SvD* (6 Je 1991, 21 Ap 1995); *AB* (22 Oc 1991, 10 Fe, 7 Mr, 2 De 1994); *DN* (22 Au 1993); *VK* (26 No 1993); *Arb* (5 Oc, 5 No 1995); *HD* (9 Ja, 11 My, 10 Je, 7 Se, 16 No, 5 De 1996); *NT* (13 No 1997); *SDS* (16 Au, 1 Oc, 1, 8 De 1999, 16-7, 27 Ja, 9, 25 Mr, 28 Je 2000); Heléne Lööw. *Vit maktmusik* (Stockholm: Fritze, 1999), 7.

[273]*DN* (1 De 1990); *SvD* (14 No, 1 De 1991); *GP* (9 Mr, 25, 29 Ap, 2-3 My, 21-2 Oc 1992); *Exp* (6 Se 1993, 8 Ja 1998); *AB* (14 Jl 1994); *VK* (11 Oc, 1 De 1993); *Arb* (5-6, 12 No, 1 De1995); *HD* (4, 8 Fe, 18 Mr, 19 My, 15, 18-9, 22, 27 Au, 26 No, 5 De 1996); *NT* (26 Fe, 26 No 1997); *SDS* (9, 23 No, 2 De 1999, 10 Ap 2000).

[274]*DN* (26 Jl 1990); *SvD* (18 Se, 28 No 1991); *GP* (4 My, 3 Jl, 17 Au 1992); *AB* (16 Ja 1994, 1 Ja 1996); *HD* (5, 28 Je 1996); *NT* (24 No 1997); *SDS* (1, 3 De 1999).

[275]*SvD* (24 My 1991); *AB* (7 Mr 7, 3-4 My 1994); *VK* (2 Oc 1993); *Arb* (27 Mr 1995); *HD* (8, 25 Je, 8 De 1996); *NT* (16 Au 1997); *SDS* (25 Ap, 25-9 Jl, 12, 16, 20, 27-8 Oc, 4, 20, 22, 24, 27 No 1999, 23, 25 Mr, 11, 15, 29 Ap, 17 Je, 6, 20 Jl, 10 Au, 24 Se 2000); Westerlund. *Vänd dom aldrig ryggen*, 113-99.

[276]*DN* (18 Ja 1990); *Arb* (2 No 1995, 15 Fe 1996); *HD* (6, 8 Je, 17 Au 1996); *NT* (12 Fe 1996); *Dagen* (10 Ap 1996); *SvD* (30 Jl, 22 Au 1996); *GP* (30 No 1996); *SDS* (7 De 1990, 9 Au 1999, 12, 14 Se 2000).

[277]*SvD* (19 No 1990, 12 De 1991, 21 Ap 1996, 8 Jl 1997); *DN* (20 Je 1990, 10 Au, 16 No, 5, 10, 17 De 1991, 21 Fe 1992, 4 Se 1993, 20 Ja 1995, 21 Au 1996, 15 Je 1998); *VK* (19 Oc 1993); *Exp* (20 Oc 1993); *AB* (4 Fe 1994); *UNT* (17 My 1994); *Arb* (16 Ja 1995);

GP (20 Au 1996); *NT* (24 My, 12 De 1997); *FK* (13 Se 1999); SDS (25 Ja 1994, 23 Se, 28 Oc, 1, 11-2, 14, 31 De 1999, 20 Fe, 21 Je, 14 Au 2000); Margareta Wadstein. *DO och lagen* (Stockholm: Discrimination Ombudsman, 2001).

[278]*SDS* (28 Ap 1990, 1, 15, 18 De 1999, 9 Mr, 1, 15 Ap, 6 My 2000).

[279]*DN* (17 Jl 1990); *GP* (21 Jl 1992); *VK* (9 Se, 16 Oc 1993); *NT* (14 Oc 1997); *AB,*(20 My 1999); *SDS* (5 No 1999, 23 Ja 2000).   Check these citations for legal results from a variety of racist acts: *DN* (23 Fe, 19 Je 1990, 10 De 1991, 18 Mr 1993, 22 My 1998); *NN* (12-3 Je 1990); *NS* (28 No 1990); *SvD* (12, 24 Oc, 8, 16, 21, 30 No, 21-2 De 1991); *GP* (8, 10, 22 My, 24, 27 Oc 1992); *VK* (16 Ja, 14, 17, 25 Au, 30 Se 1993); *Arb* (11 Ap, 20 My, 1, 29 Jl, 23 De 1995); *HD* (12, 19, 23, 25 Ja, 21 Fe, 8 Mr, 14 Je 1996); *NT* (22 My, 23 Se 1997); *Exp* (5, 8, 16 Ja, 16, 18 Se 1998); *AB* (20 My, 3, 7 Jl 1999); *SDS* (11 Au, 29 Se, 12 Oc, 17, 29 No, 1-4, 6, 8-9, 15-7 De 1999, 9, 23 Mr, 26 Ap 2000). Unrelated to the lunacy of lenient judicial sentencings, one Stockholm attorney conditionally advised less punishments for alien-committed crimes if what was done represented legal behavior in the perpetuator's homeland.   In other words, a person's cultural background should, he thought, affect penalties for crime. *DN* (2 Mr 1990).

[280]*SvD* (13 Au 1990); *SkD* (2 Se 1993); *Exp* (9 Se 1993); *Arb* (3 Oc 1995); *NA* (10 My 1996); *BT* (13 Oc 1996); "Let the huddled masses in." *Econ* (31 Mr 2001), 11-2; "Bridging Europe's skills gap." *Econ* (31 Mr 2001), 67-8. Illustrative of the general thinking of Swedes on racism and immigration can be seen in: *BT* (7 Oc 1996); *SDS* (26 No 1999).

[281]TV4 (30 Ap 2001).

BIBLIOGRAPHY with Abbreviations

Newspapers:	Abbreviations:
Stockholm *Aftonbladet*	*AB*
Gävle *Arbetarbladet*	*Arbb*
Malmö *Arbetet*	*Arb*
Kalmar *Barometern*	*Bar*
Karlskrona *Blekinge Läns Tidning*	*BLT*
Borås Tidning	*BT*
Köping *Bärgslagsbladet* & Arboga *Tidning*	*BB*
Boston *Christian Science Monitor*	*CSM*
Oslo *Dagbladet*	*OD*
Stockholm *Dagen*	*Dagen*
Falun *Dala-Demokraten*	*DD*
Stockholm *Expressen*	*Exp*
Falun *Falu-Kuriren*	*FK*
Gävle *Gefle Dagblad*	*GD*
Göteborg/Malmö *GT Kvällsposten Idag*	*iDAG*
Göteborgs-Posten	*GP*
Halmstad *Hallandsposten*	*HP*
Helsingborgs Dagblad	*HD*
Hudiksvalls Tidning	*HT*
Paris *International Herald Tribune*	*IHT*
Jönköpings-Posten	*JP*
Katrineholms Kuriren	*KK*
Laholms Tidning	*LT*
Malmö and Stockholm *Metro*	*Metro*
Motala & Vadstena Tidning	*MVT*
Örebro *Nerikes Allehanda*	*NA*
New York *Times*	*Times*
Ängelholm *Nordvästra Skånes Tidningar*	*NST*
Luleå *Norrbottenskuriren*	*NBK*
Hässleholm *Norra Skåne*	*NS*
Norrköpings Tidningar-Östergötlands Dagblad	*NT*
Boden *Norrländska Socialdemokraten*	*NSD*
Härnösand *Nya Norrland*	*NN*
Karlstad *Nya Wermlands-Tidningen*	*NWT*
Piteå-Tidningen	*PT*
Malmö *Skånska Dagbladet*	*SkD*
Växjö *Smålandsposten*	*SP*
Strömstad Tidning	*StT*

Sundsvalls Tidning	*ST*
Stockholm *Svenska Dagbladet*	*SvD*
Malmö *Sydsvenska Dagbladet Snällposten*	*SDS*
Säffles Tidning	*SäT*
Mariestad *Tidning för Skaraborgs Län*	*TSL*
Uppsala *Upsala Nya Tidning*	*UNT*
Västerås *Vestmanlands Läns Tidning*	*VLT*
Umeå *Västerbottens-Kuriren*	*VK*
Ystads Allehanda	*YA*
Örebro-Kuriren	*ÖK*
Linköping *Östgöta Correspondenten*	*ÖC*

Magazine	Abbreviations:
The Economist	*Econ*
Ny i Sverige	*NiS*
Migranter	*Mig*
Stoppa rasismen!	*Sr*
Invandrare &Minoriteter	*I & M*
Fortune	*Fort*

Name	Abbreviations:
Karine Mannerfelt	Mannerfelt
Mark Olson	Olson
Lillemor Sahlberg	Sahlberg
David Schwarz	Schwarz

Periodicals:
"A continent on the move." *Econ*, 6 May 2000, 21-2, 25.
Adolfsson, Mats. "Chipsfabriken—kvinnornas FN." *Mig*, no. 2 (1995), 14-7.
"'Afrikanska asylsökande diskrimineras.'" *Sr*, no. 2 (1996), 9.
Agebjörn, Anika. "Ingen rasism i Vålberg?" *Mig*, no. 4 (1996), 36-41.
_____. "Lika barn leka bäst?" *Mig*, no. 6 (1995), 10-6.
Ahmadi, Fereshteh and Nader. "Iranier i Sverige: annorlunda individbegrepp." *I & M* 22 (De 1995), 16-21.
Alasaad, Mohammed. "Solidaritet i handling och inte bara i ord." *Sr*, no. 1 (1990), 5.
Albaldawi, Riyadh. "Invandrarnas narkotikamissbruk." *I & M* 18 (Ap 1991), 21-5.
Aldstedt, Eva. "'Asylhandteringen rättssäker.'" *NiS*, no. 3 (1994), 108-9.
_____. "De gömmer flyktingar." *NiS*, no. 3 (1994), 102-7.
"Alien scientists take over USA." *Econ*, 21 Au 1999, 38.
Alla olika, alla lika: tidning mot rasism & främlingsfientlighet. 1995-7.
Alwall, Jonas. "Religionsfrihet [crossed through] endast för svenskar?" *I & M* 20 (Ap 1993), 13-20.
"A nation of criminals." *Econ*, 24 Fe 2001, 40.
Andersson, Hans. "Nydemokrati och höger extremisterna . . . ." *Sr*, no. 1 (1992), 4-5.
Annebrant, Kaj. "Fördupade kontakter att vänta i Sandviken?" *Sr*, no. 2 (1990), 13.
"Antirasism är mångfald." *Sr*, no. 1 (1992), 2.
"Antirasist demonstration." *Sr*, no. 2 (1990), 12.
"Antirasistiska aktiviteter i Storstockholm." *Sr*, no. 1 (1993), 3.

Apitzsch, Hartmut and Luis Ramos-Ruggiero. "Dialog med förhinder." *I & M* 18 (Oc 1991), 39-41.

Appelblad, Håkan. "Kriminalitet och bostadbyten." *I & M* 22 (Oc 1995), 24-8.

"Arbetsgruppen för antirasistisk artistgala." *Sr*, no. 3 (1990), 5.

Arnstberg, Karl-Olov. "Omöjligt bekämpa slummen med pilbåge och golfklubba." *Mig*, no. 1 (1996), 30-1.

_____. "Respekt viktigare än välfärd!" *Mig*, no. 1 (1995), 7.

_____. "Tala bättre svenska säger drottningen." *Mig*, no. 4 (1995), 48-9.

"Assyrier—integration eller minoritetsliv?" *NiS*, no. 5 (1993), 38-41.

Atkinson, Graeme. "Kämpa mot rasism och fascism i facket!" *Sr*, no. 4 (1991), 22-3.

"A tragedy and a shame." *Econ*, 27 Fe 1999, 37-8.

Aune, Aila. "Minoritetsbeteendets fördelar." *I & M* 18 (De 1991), 11-3.

Axelsson, Anneli. "Chilenare i Simrishamn." *NiS*, no. 2 (1990), 6-11.

Banakar, Reza. "Debatt på låtsas." *I & M* 18 (De 1991), 3-10.

_____. "Kvotering skapar inga nya jobb." *I & M* 22 (Se 1995), 7-11.

_____. "Lagens dilemma," *I & M* 17 (Je 1990), 2-9.

Beerman-Zeligson, Judith and Chava Savosnick. "Intill sjunde släktled?" *I & M* 18 (Oc 1991), 73-5.

"Belgium's Dewinter of discontent." *Econ*, 14 Oc 2000, 42.

Berglund, Solveig. "Allt färre barn får hemspråksstöd." *NiS*, no. 2 (1990), 46-9.

Björck, Ingela. "Bijans verkstad." *NiS*, no. 5 (1994), 30-1.

_____. "Här lindras ångesten." *NiS*, no. 6 (1991), 12-5.

_____. "Multiculturalism: ett tecken på nedgång." *NiS*, no. 6 (1995), 31-3.

"Black, blanc, beur." *Econ*, 5 Je 1999, 16, 19.

Blideman, Ingrid. "Främmande kultur—en ursäkt?, Vem ska anpassa sig?" *NiS*, no. 2 (1991), 38-41.

Blomqvist, Lise. "Alfabetisering i Sverige." *Mig*, no. 2 (1995), 8-11.

_____. "Det handlar inte bara om invandrare." *Mig*, no. 1 (1997), 28-31.

_____. "Lönen och äventyret lockade." *Mig*, no. 3 (1996), 12-5.

_____. "Kulturkrock i duschen." *Mig*, no. 1 (1996), 46-8.

_____. "Sahra, ingen vanlig kvinna." *Mig*, no. 1 (1995), 14-5.

_____. "Somalia." *Mig*, no. 3 (1997), 12-24.

_____. "Svenska vänner." *Mig*, no. 1 (1995), 16-7.

Borgegård, Lars-Erik, Johan Håkansson, and Dieter K. Müller. "Hur förändras bosättingsmönstret när invan-drarna blir fler." *I & M* 22 (Oc 1995), 29-33.

Borgegård, Lars-Erik. "Rinkeby—en global by i Stockholm." *I & M* 22 (Oc 1995), 20-3.

Boukas, Andreas. "Den dolda diskrimineringen." *I & M* 17 (My 1990), 10-4.

Brandell-Forsberg, Margareta. "Flyktingbarn Riskbarn." *I & M* 18 (Oc 1991), 62-4.

"Bridging Europe's skills gap." *Econ*, 31 Mr 2000, 67-8.

Brodin, Jane and Marianne Lindberg. "Adoptivbarn med handicap." *I & M* 17 (Fe 1990), 21-2.

Brune, Ylva. "Taheera läser Koranen med barnen varje dag." *NiS*, no. 4 (1990), 5-9.

_____. "Varplåga har sitt skri för sig." *NiS*, no. 3 (1994), 90-7.

_____. "Vi och Dom." *I & M* 20 (Je 1993), 16-21.

Carlbom, Aje. "Gemenskap eller utanförskap." *I & M* 27 (Fe 2000), 14-5.

Carlson-Jacobsson, Marie. "Språket—ett maktmedel." *I & M* 23 (De 1996), 21-3.

Carlsson, Annica. "Skuggorna talar." *Mig*, no. 2 (1996), 34-9.

Cederberg, Irka. "Blodstänkt småstadsidyll." *Mig*, no. 2 (1996), 26-31.

_____. "Ny lag skapar kaos." *NiS*, no. 5 (1994), 12-5.

_____. "Segregation och elände eller bo internationellt." *NiS*, no. 2 (1994), 8-13.

_____. "Svårt leva rättroget." *NiS*, no. 5 (1994), 20-3.

Cederblad, Marianne. "Sverige adoptionsland." *I & M* 18 (Oc 1991), 76-9.

Charette, Gerald. "Readers' letters." *I & M* 19 (Se 1992), 1.

Crole-Rees, Marie. "En vanlig dag på svenska flyktingslussen." *NiS*, no. 2 (1992), 10-3.

Dahlgren, Eva F. "Vården sviker invandrare med värk." *Mig*, no. 5 (1995), 8-12.

Danielsson, Stefan. "Kaféet i Rosengård." *Mig*, no. 2 (1998), 2-7.

_____. "Kurser, praktik och projekt efter projekt men inget JOBB." *Mig*, no. 3 (1998), 22-7.

_____. "Rosa Sanches har en idé." *Mig*, no. 4 (1998), 2-6.

_____. "1000 platser lediga i pågående projekt . . . men arbetsförmedlingen skickar inga deltagare." *Mig*, no. 5 (1998), 19-26.

Darvishpour, Mehrdad. "Förbjuda rasistiska organisationer?" *I & M* 20 (Se 1993), 30-3.

"Demonstration mot de nya asylreglerna." *Sr*, no. 1 (1990), 12-3.

"Det brinner." *Sr*, no. 2 (1990), 2.

Diaz, José Alberto. "Invandrarna och pigjobben." *I & M* 23 (Ap 1996), 3-7.

_____. "Kulturell olikhet istället för rasåtskillnad." *I & M* 19 (Se 1992), 30-1.

Dorazio, Anita. "Svartfången 7:4 på kronobergshäktet." *Sr*, no. 3 (1990), 6-8.

Dorr, Gregory M. "Assuring America's Place in the Sun: Ivey Foreman Lewis and the Teaching of Eugenics at the University of Virginia, 1915-1953" *Journal of Southern History* 66 (My 2000), 257-96.

Douglas, Karsten. "svensk undervisningen ger en förskönad Sverige bild." *I & M* 23 (Ap 1996), 32-5.

Edrén, Gunnar. "Missriktad reform." *I & M* 17 (Je 1990), 14-6.

"Eget företag: enda vägen till framgång?" *NiS*, no. 1 (1993). First in *Internationella Affärer* (4 Se 1992).

Ekblad, Solvig. "Migration och valbefinnande." *I & M* 19 (Ap 1992), 14-8.

_____. "Ohälsa försvårar integrationen." *I & M* 23 (Se 1996), 15-7.

Ekervik, Malou Jergner. "Skepp har kommit lastade med över 20.000 asylsökande." *NiS*, no. 4 (1992), 13-6.

Elsbacher, Hansi. "Politikerna saknar ofta kunskap om Islam." *Sr*, no. 1 (1997), 6-7.

Englund, Göran. "Vad är en kulturrasist?" *I & M* 19 (Se 1992), 28.

Erikson, Britt-Marie. "Bortsorterad." *Säljaren*, no. 6, (1998), 8-9.

Eriksson, Ann. "Hjälper ungdomarna med läxorna." *NiS*, no. 6 (1991), 2-5.

_____. "På systugan i Fittja, 'Vi röstar på dom som hjälper oss.'" *NiS*, no. 3 (1991), 20-3.

_____. "Rinkeby kids: busarna—stämmor i samma kör." *NiS*, No. 2 (1992), 22-5.

Eriksson, Lena Häll. "Ny flyktingpolitik." *Se mig, hör mig* (1995).

Ernflo, Gunilla. "Invandrare, kvinna, teknisk chef: Zeljka säger inte nej till mer makt." *Mig*, no. 6 (1998), 22-6.

_____. "Nalin och Maria—kanaler makten." *Mig*, no. 5 (1998), 2-7.

_____. "Skolor & integration." *Mig*, no. 5 (1997), 2-10.

"Europe by the Numbers." *Fort*, 21 De 1998, 51-6.

"Europe flunks the graduate course." *Econ*, 4 Fe 1995, 27.

Eyrumlu, Reza. "Segregationens många bottnar." *I & M* 23 (Ap 1996), 36-8.

Fareld, Veronica. "Utvisad." *Sr*, no. 3 (1993), 8-9.

Feigenberg, Emma. "Tolkslarv." *NiS*, no. 4 (1992), 38.

"Fest för stöd åt iranska flyktingar." *Sr*, no. 1 (1993), 4.

"Foreign relief." *Econ*, 30 Se 2000, 42, 45.

Forslund, Carita. "Musik och religion för själens skull." *Mig*, no. 6 (1997), 2-7.

Franck, Hans Göran. "Beslutet måste upphävas i Sandviken?" *Sr*, no. 2 (1990), 14-5.

Franzén, Elsie C. "Formandet av en underklass eller hur man söker jobb i Sverige." *I & M* 23 (Oc 1996), 14-6.

Fridell, Manne. "Olika bakgrund ger dynamik." *Mig*, no. 3 (1998), 37-9.

Fruitman, Stephen. "Hatets kultur." *I & M* 27 (Fe 2000), 29-32.

"Främlingsfientlighet då och nu." *Sr*, no. 2 (1991), 3-4.

"Få invandrare på den andra nordiska flykting- och invandrarkonferensen." *Sr*, no. 2 (1990), 16.

"Förste svarte byråkrat i Stockholms stadshus." *Sr*, no. 1 (1996), 6.

"Försvara asylrätten!" *Sr*, no. 1 (1993), 2.

Gabrielsson, Gundi. "Kulturkrockar och kreativitet." *I & M* 18 (Ap 1991), 12-6.

"Gatorna tillhör alla!" *Sr*, no. 4 (1991), 2.

Gens, Ingemar. "Den mjuka slussen till Sverige." *NiS*, no. 5 (1990), 46-9.

"Germany's neo-Nazis." *Econ*, 19 No 1992, 16-7.

"Go for it." *Econ*, 6 My 2000, 15-6.

Goldstein-Kyaga, Katrin. "Värdet av kunskap." *I & M* 18 (Fe 1991), 33-5.

"Granater och knivar mot antiracisterna." *Sr*, no. 1 (1991), 12.

Gustafsson, Anneli. "Håll kyrkporten öppen för Allah." *Mig*, no. 1 (1996), 33-7.

Görski, Mieczyslaw. "Invandrarpolitikens inrikning och resultat." *I & M* 19 (Se 1992), 8-13.

_____. "Kvinnors ställning." *I & M* 19 (De 1992), 28-43.

Hallin, Ulrika. "Shoof! Kulturmöten på scenen i Tensta." *Mig*, no. 2 (1998), 42-8.

Hammar, Tomas. "Slå vakt om asylrätten." *I & M* 18 (Ap 1991), 17-20.

_____. "Varför behövs forskning?" *I & M* 19 (Fe 1992), 18-21.

Hansson, Håkan. "Edina från Sarajevo—ett i Europa." *NiS*, no. 3 (1994), 84-9.

"Hear the soulbird sing." *Econ*, 10 Je 2000, 117-8, 121.

Heikka, Gustaw. "Är Sverige ett rasistiskt samhälle?" *Samefolket*, no. 1 (1991), 18-20.

Hellmers, Liv. "Svensklärare bland invandrarungdomar: 'Man måste hugga tag i konflikterna.'" *NiS*, no. 6 (1990), 8-13.

_____. "Tonårsröster om kulturkrockarna." *NiS*, no. 6 (1990), 14-7.

Hemlin, Karolina. "'Vi styrs av fördomar.'" *Sr*, no. 1 (1997), 9.

Hertzman, Rolf. "Svenska språket—nyckeln till eget företag." *Du & Co*, no. 4 (2000), 25, 27.

Hetting, Conny. "Sekunder från döden." *Mig*, no. 5 (1995), 38-42.

Hjort, Linn. "Inte ens ärkebiskopen kan få oss följa Sveriges lagar!." *Sr*, no. 1 (1994), 10-1.

_____. "Någon måste visa att rasisterna har fel." *Sr*, no. 4 (1991), 3.

Hjort, Marianne. "Behövs ett invandrarparti?" *Sr*, no. 1 (1993), 4.

_____. "'Fundamentalismen måste bekämpas.'" *Sr*, no. 4 (1994), 3.

_____. "Han gömde flyktingar." *Sr*, no. 1 (1994), 12.

_____ and Per-Olof Mattsson. "*Aftonbladet* trycker rasistisk reklam." *Sr*, no. 2 (1993), 3.

Holmberg, Katrin. "S.O.S. Asyl." *Sr*, no. 3 (1990), 4.

"How Europé Stacks Up." *Fort*, 21 De 1998, 51-6.

Hultén, Britt. "Mediernas bild av flyktingarna." *I & M* 17 (De 1990), 86-90.

Hultqvist, Sune. "Viktigast: förståelse för invandrarna." *I & M* 18 (Ap 1991), 10-1.

Hyltenstam, Kenneth. "Illa genomtänkt hemspråksförslag." *I & M* 19 (Ap 1992), 3-7.

Håkansson, Bertil G. "Eduardo, 18 år, dömd för knivöverfall." *NiS*, no. 6 (1990), 21-3.

"Höger extremist lärare på socialhögskolan." *Sr*, no. 2 (1992), 10.

"Infinite Mass: The first revolutionary group in Sweden." *Sr*, no. 3 (1992), 12-3.

Ingemansson, Bitti. "Halalslakt hos Scan i Skara." *Mig*, no. 6 (1997), 44-8.

_____. "Sorgen bröt barriärerna." *Mig*, no. 6 (1998), 2-6.

_____. "Tonåringarna och deras hemlängtan." *NiS*, no. 6 (1990), 18-20.
"Invandrarna fast i skitjobben." *NiS*, No. 1 (1993), 25-7.
Jacobsson, Anna. "På majoritetens villkor." *I & M* 22 (Oc 1995), 12-5.
Jacobsson, Ingrid. "Livstycket stöder och värmer kvinnorna." *Mig*, no. 2 (1995), 2-5.
Jacobsson, Roland. "Mot passivitet: en flykting berättar." *I & M* 18 (Oc 1991), 24-6.
Johansson, Marcus and Tomas Uddin. "Jämställdhet för alla?" *I & M* 22 (Mr 1995), 16-21.
Johansson, Petter and Lasse Winkler. "Kalabaliken i Biskopsgården." *NiS*, no. 4 (1990), 10-4.
Johnsson, Johanna. "'Facket gör inte tillräcket.'" *SIFtidningen* 79, nos. 11/12 (1999), 18.
_____. "Regionalchef i SIF beredd betala antinazists böter." *SIFtidningen* 79, no. 9 (1999), 18.
Jonson, Reinhold. "Företagsledare vill öka invandringen!" *Sr*, no. 2 (1991), 15.
_____. "Invandrarministern mötte uppvakting med kyla." *Sr*, no. 1 (1991), 14.
_____. "Ny utlänningslag på gång." *Sr*, no. 1 (1991), 14.
_____. "S.O.S. Asyl." *Sr*, no. 2 (1990), 9-11.
_____. "Succé för folkfest mot rasism." *Sr*, no. 3 (1991), 10.
Karlsson, Axel W. "Flyktingar och invandrare, rasister och vanliga svenskar." *Ny social debatt* 7 (1996), 114-24.
Knocke, Woukko. "Facket och invandrarna." *I & M* 23 (Oc 1996), 5-9.
_____. "Kulturens mångfald." *I & M* 21 (Fe 1994), 16-8.
_____. "Segregationens pris." *I & M* 23 (Oc 1996), 5-9.
Kostoulas-Makrakis, Nelly. "Språklig assimilering bara en tidsfråga?" *I & M* 22 (Oc 1995), 16-9.
"Krogar diskriminerar svarta." *Sr*, no. 4 (1992), 5.
Kuusela, Kirsti. "Etnisk bostadssegregation." *I & M* 17 (My 1990), 15-9.
Lange, Anders. "Bel Habibs korståg." *I & M* 19 (Je 1992), 19-23.
Larsson, Ragnhild. "Allt fler äldre invandrare: svårt med svenskan på gamla dar." *Mig*, no. 3 (1998), 44-8.
_____. "Födde barn, fest eller plåga?" *Mig*, no. 4 (1996), 28-32.
Larsson, Stieg. "Extremhögern i Sverige: satsar inför valet." *Sr*, no. 2 (1991), 4-5.
Larsson, Svante. "Arbetsrehabilitering." *I & M* 18 (Oc 1991), 92-5.
Laszlo, Carlo. "Rastlös, nyfiken, slö-." *Svensk bokhandel* 42, no. 18 (1993), 25.
"Let the huddled masses in." *The Economist*, 31 Mr 2000, 11-2.
Levin, Bo. "Zigenarna får skulden." *NiS*, no. 4 (1991), 13-6.
Lewis, Kenneth. "Förbud mot rasistiska organisationer." *Sr*, no. 3 (1992), 17.
Lidén, Lasse. "Teater kan stoppa våldet." *Sr*, no. 4 (1994), 6-7.
Lind, Annika Ortmark. "Släpp in oss!" *Amelia*, no. 11 (1999), 170-7.
Lindholm, Ingrid Iverstam. "Det oönskade folket." *I & M* 22 (Mr 1995), 22-7.
Lindquist, Hans. "Ingen Glistrup i sikte—ännu?" *NiS*, no. 1 (1991), 18-21.
Linebäck, Britta. "Den osynliga minoriteten" *Mig*, no. 4 (1995), 14-7.
_____. "Larmsignal om invandrarjobben." *Mig*, no. 4 (1995), 2-3.
_____. "Med kameran som extra öga." *Mig*, no. 6 (1995), 28-30.
_____. "Muslim hemma, svensk på kontoret." *Mig*, no. 2 (1996), 12-6.
_____. "Svenska attityder." *Mig*, no. 5 (1995), 2-5.
_____. "Sökes: nya öppningar för invandrare." *Mig*, no. 1 (1996), 4-14.
_____. "Vända hem i värdighet." *Mig*, no. 5 (1995), 24-8.
Livh, Ann-Margarethe. "Leder till utslagning." *Sr*, no. 4 (1991), 9.
Lundian, 1990-2000.

Lundmark, Lennart. "Samerna och den svenska rasismen." *Populär historia*, no. 4 (1998), 40-4.

Lång, Ulrika. "Tre bosniska systrar i Småland." *Nis*, no. 3 (1994), 112-7.

_____. "Utan språk—svårt att förstå." *NiS*, no. 2 (1994), 32-7.

"Låt mig få stanna!." *Sr*, no. 4 (1992), 7.

Ländin, Birgitta. "Forskning i invandrarnas tjänst." *I & M* 20 (Fe 1993), 22-5.

Löfgren, Eva. "Hitta jobben innan de finns till." *I & M* 23 (Oc 1996), 17-9.

Löfvander, Monica. "Sjukvård över språkgränser." *I & M* 18 (Oc 1991), 36-8.

Löwander, Birgitta. "Massmediernas konstruerade värld." *I & M* 20 (Je 1993), 22-7.

_____. "Massmedierapportering om etniska relationer." *I & M* 20 (Fe 1993), 7-11.

Lööw, Heléne. "Sveriges rasistiska förflutna." *Pockettidningen R* 21, no. 2/3 (1991), 20-9.

Macrae, Norman. "Will You Ever Be Able to Retire?" *Fort*, 29 My 2000, 30.

Magnusson, Elisabeth. "'Invandraröppet i Lövgärdet.'" *NiS*, no. 6 (1992), 6-9.

Magnusson, Kjell. "Kosovoalbaner—mellan minoritet och nation." *NiS*, no. 4 (1992), 17-20.

Mahlasela, Joy. "En sydafrikansk betraktelse på nåd och onåd." *I & M* 19 (Ap 1992), 3-6.

Maldaner, Vesna. "Knarket dödar mitt folk." *NiS*, no. 5 (1994), 36-9.

_____. "'Lika bra som en svensk blir man aldrig.'" *NiS*, no. 3 (1991), 15-7.

_____. "Titta en utlänning!" *Mig*, no. 5 (1995), 34-5.

_____. "'Vi kommer alltid kallas för jävla zigenare.'" *NiS*, no. 3 (1991), 46-8.

Malmström, Cajsa. "Daghem för flyktingbarn." *NiS*, no. 3 (1992), 19-22.

_____. "Läkare kritiska tortyroffer i kläm." *NiS*, no. 4 (1993), 10-2.

_____. "Nätverk flyktingbarn." *NiS*, no. 1 (1994), 16-9.

_____. "Oroande självmordstal tryggare i invandrartäta områden." *Mig*, no. 2 (1998), 8-14.

_____. "Titta en utlänning!" *Mig*, no. 5 (1995), 34-5.

_____. "Tortyoffer måste få hjälp." *NiS*, no. 6 (1991), 6-11.

_____. "Utlänningsnämnden—'Läkarna måste övertyga.'" *NiS*, no. 4 (1993), 12-3.

Mannerfelt, Karine. "Att leva 'under jorden': 'Mardrömmarna tar över mitt liv.'" *NiS*, no. 1 (1991), 8-9.

_____. "Emilia och Rohan—invandrare men också svenskar." *NiS*, no. 6 (1990), 4-7.

_____. "Flora jobbar för vår 'gemmensamma framtid.'" *NiS*, no. 2 (1994), 14-5.

_____. "Förortens invandrade svenskar." *Mig*, no. 3 (1997), 45-9.

_____. "Hadije gömmer sig för att slippa avvisas." *NiS*, no. 1 (1991), 6-7.

_____. "Jag blir kär i nästan varje bok." *NiS*, no. 5 (1990), 22-5.

_____. "'Jag vill ha en generös flyktingpolitik.'" *NiS*, no. 3 (1994), 101-2.

_____. "Långa köer på utrednings slussen." *NiS*, no. 1 (1990), 14-8.

_____. "Micke, en i gänget—man får inte banga ur." *Mig*, no. 1 (1995), 2-6.

_____. "Mot alla odds—'invandrarskola' utsedd till Stockholms bäste skola." *Mig*, no. 3 (1997), 28-32.

_____. "'Nya lagen—en halvmesyr.'" *NiS*, no. 1 (1990), 19-21.

_____. "Språkklasser lösningen på dåliga svenskkunskaper?" *NiS*, no. 5 (1994), 16-9.

_____. "Tillbaka i Kosovo." *NiS*, no. 5 (1993), 1-3.

"Maria Leissner (fp) intervjuas av David Schwarz." *I & M* 22 (Je 1995), 15-7.

Mattsson, Katarina. "Invandrares företag: både exotiskt och alldagligt." *I & M* 23 (De 1996), 32-4.

Mattsson, Per-Olof. "Rasismen i Sverige dag för dag." *Sr*, no. 1 (1994), 4-5.

Melanson, Michael. "'Buss och bagage.'" *NiS*, no. 5 (1993), 4-5.

_____. "Från skjutfält till skjutfält." *NiS*, no. 1 (1994), 24-5.

_____. "Livet på flyktingslussen." *NiS*, no. 4 (1993), 2-5.

Mella, Orlando. "Hemlandstrauma och mottagningsstress." *I & M* 17 (Oc 1991), 68-72.

". . . Men jag är inte rasist!" *Sr*, no. 2 (1993), 4.

"Mixed Messages." *The Economist*, 13May 2000, 39.

Mohamed, Jasim. "Ungdomarna går inte fädrens spår." *NiS*, no. 5 (1994), 40-1.

_____. "Utan chans?" *Mig*, no. 3 (1996), 7-10.

Molin, Eva. "Katherine från Chile: svenska tjejer har nog mer frihet." *NiS*, no. 2 (1993), 33-4.

_____. "Ramesh från Iran: tar de bäste bitarna ur varje kultur." *NiS*, no. 2 (1995) 31-2.

Moreau-Raquin, Patrick. "Glåpord rasisttjat och växande dialog." *Mig*, no. 2 (1997), 38-41.

Müller, Dieter K. "Svenska fritidshus under tysk flagg." *I & M* 22 (Se 1995), 3-6.

Murkes, Jakob. "Readers' letters." *I & M* 19 (Ap 1992), 1.

Murphy, Cait. "The New Europeans." *Fort* 21 De 1998, 86-97.

Najib, Ali. "Invandrarföretag: inte bara pizzerior och kiosker." *I & M* 22 (Je 1995), 2-6.

Narti, Ann Maria. "Segregationens debatter—den segregerade debatten." *I & M* 23 (Oc 1996), 11-3.

"Nasty, ubiquitous and unloved." *Econ*, 20 Mr 1999, 36, 41.

Nilsson, Anders I. "Sin egen lyckas smed." *NiS*, no. 5 (1994), 24-8.

_____. "Vikingarock." *Mig*, no. 1 (1995), 24-9.

Nilsson, Börge. "1000-tals polskor." *NiS*, no. 4 (1990), 40-5.

Nilsson, Ingert. "Invandrare och kriminalitet." *Mig*, no. 1 (1997), 36-41.

Nilsson, Matz. "svensk flyktingpolitik?!—deportation verkställs." *Sr*, no. 1 (1990), 4-5.

Norlander, Eva and Marianne Cederblad. "I frågasatt identitet." *I & M* 20 (Se 1993), 14-7.

"När ingen annan reagerar . . ." *Sr*, no. 1 (1992), 3.

Odenyo, Carina. "Aids och rasism." *Sr*, no. 3, (1990), 11-4.

Olson, Mark. "Alldeles för go' för sitt eget bästa." *Mig*, no. 6 (1995), 18-21.

_____. "Få gömställen kvar till kära barn." *Mig*, no. 6 (1995), 4-7.

_____. "Gillar lågutbildade invandrare städjobb?" *Mig*, no. 1 (1996), 15.

_____. "Hemsnickrat från Aneby." *Mig*, no. 5 (1995), 13-7.

_____. "Ingen kan åka hem på en dröm." *Mig*, no. 5 (1995), 18-21.

_____. "Invandrarförbund: mera svenska än någonsin." *Mig*, no. 2 (1996), 8-11.

_____. "Invandrarpolitik endast för nyanlända." *Mig*, no. 2 (1996), 2-5.

_____. "Lärdomar från Åsele." *Mig*, no. 1 (1996), 1.

_____. "Magiskt möte i Helsingborg." *Mig*, no. 1 (1996), 16-21.

_____. "Nya paragrafer." *Mig*, no. 3 (1995), 2-5.

_____. "Nytt liv i byn." *Mig*, no. 3 (1995), 12-9.

_____. "Saknar egen nation." *Mig*, no. 4 (1995), 18-23.

_____. "Snabba besked om ny flyktingpolitik." *Mig*, no. 4 (1995), 4-5.

_____. "Tillbaka till skrivbordet." *Mig*, no. 1 (1996), 2-3.

Olsson, Lena. "Om du gör så blir jag ledsen." *NiS*, no. 3 (1993), 34-5.

Omsäter, Margareta. "Mauricio Rojas: 'Svenskarna måste se oss som vi verkligen är.'" *NiS*, no. 1 (1991), 48-9.

Oscarsson, Martin. "Flyktingar höjde sina röster." *Sr*, no. 2 (1991), 15.

Oweini, Saleh. "I väntan på asyl." *I & M* 18 (Oc 1991), 22-3.

Palmér, Ingela. "Läkande kraft." *I & M* 18 (Oc 1991), 80-2.

Parikka, Johanna. "Stackars invandrare?" *I & M* 17 (Je 1990), 10-3.

Peréz-Arias, Enrique. "Chilenarna i Sverige: självförvållade segregation." *I & M* 23 (Ap 1996), 8-11.
Pierredal, Lena. "SFI på nytt sätt—Bach, Mozart, viskningar och rop." *Mig*, no. 3 (1997), 2-6.
Persson, Henrik. "Är de tjuvaktiga kosovoalbanerna ekonomiska flyktingar? Och är de tjuvaktiga?" *Sr*, no. 3 (1992), 19.
Persson, Sören. "Skräddarsydd komplettering gav invandrare lärarjobb, brobyggare & förebild." *Mig*, no. 3 (1998), 30-6.
"Playing the race card." *Econ*, 7 Oc 2000, 56.
"Port in a storm." *Econ*, 21 Au 1999, 29-30.
Rasmusson, Ludvig. "Dessa fantastiska turkiska musiker . . ." *Mig*, no. 2 (1995), 40-4.
_____. "Från Sankt Göran och drakten Titiyo." *NiS*, no. 5 (1990), 2-7.
_____. "Han spelar Bellman på indianharpa." *NiS*, no. 5 (1990), 17-9.
_____. "På grekiska Poseidon lever musiken och dansen." *NiS*, no. 2 (1992), 44-6.
"Rasrisk." *Sr*, no. 1 (1993), 10.
Readers' letters. "Adoptionens dramatiska konsekvenser." *I & M* 20 (Ap 1993), 1.
Regnell, Tobias. "Folk flyr jobben." *NiS*, no. 1 (1994), 1-4.
_____. "Wilson Santana startade eget." *NiS*, no. 1 (1993), 22-4.
Repo, Walter. "All världens bilbyggare." *Mig*, no. 2 (1998), 16-20.
_____ and Pernilla Lorentzson. "Världslaget från Hjällbo." *Mig*, no. 1 (1995), 8-11.
"Rikskonferensen kritisk till flyktingpolitiken." *Sr*, no. 1 (1997), 3.
Ringqvist, Lena. "Misstro och hat mot de asylsökande." *NiS*, no. 6 (1992), 30-2.
Ritzén, Kenneth. "Islam i vardagen." *I & M* 17 (My 1990), 20-6.
Rodell, Christina. "Iranska flyktingrådet manar till självorganisering och kamp." *Sr*, no. 1 (1990), 6-7.
_____. "Rätten till hemspråk i fara." *Sr*, no. 3 (1991), 3.
Rogestam, Christina. "Dags att sätta punkt." *NiS*, no. 1 (1993), 1.
_____. "En generös och human flyktingpolitik?" *NiS*, no. 6 (1992), 1.
_____. "Folkfrågan viktig för Invandrarverket." *Nis*, no. 4 (1992), 39.
_____. "Förbud mot barnförvar." *NiS*, no. 1, (1992), 1.
_____. "Invandrarverket utreder människan bakom ärendet synligare." *NiS*, no. 2 (1992), 1.
_____. "Omöjligt att sia om framtiden." *NiS*, no. 1 (1991), 1.
_____. "Ribban för asylsökande höjs oavsiktigt?" *NiS*, no. 6 (1990), 1.
_____. "Samspel mellan forskning och praktiskt arbete." *I & M* 19 (Se 1992), 24-7.
"Ronny Landins minnesfond tio år." *Sr*, no. 1 (1996), 2.
Rosenberg, Svante "Flyktingmotståndet blev en vändpunkt," *NiS*, No. 6, 1990, 46-47.
Runblom, Harald. "Debatt om invandrarforskning: viktiga uppgifter," *I & M*, XIX, Ap, 1992, 26-29.
Rydström, Björn, Sören Edgar, Åke Jungdalen. "Storspännvidd i statrådens utbildning: politiska eliten dåligt utbildad." *Sunt Förnuft*, no. 7 (1997), 28-31.
Råbergh, Christian. "Social ingenjörskonst eller frivilliga krafter." *I & M* 19 (Ap 1992), 7-13.
"Rädda Barnen kritisk till mottagandet av ensamma barn." *Sr*, no. 1 (1990), 14.
Rönnbäck, Ingvar. "Skolan som samhällets problemlösare." *I & M* 22 (Oc 1995), 8-11.
Sahlberg, Lillemor. "Anpassa sej eller nej." *Mig*, no. 6 (1997), 34-5.
_____. "Asyl i Sverige." *Mig*, no. 1 (1995), 32-3.
_____. "Asyl i Sverige." *Mig*, no. 2 (1995), 20-1.
_____. "Bengt-Erik Ginsburg: vänta med hiv-testen." *NiS*, no. 3 (1993), 31-3.
_____. "'Det är bättre i Sverige än på många andra håll.'" *Mig*, no. 3 (1998), 40-3.

_____. "15.000 kom i juli—situationen är bekymmersam." *NiS*, no. 4 (1992), 17.

_____. "Fler invandrarväljare i år?" *NiS*, no. 4 (1994), 17-9.

_____. "'Flyktingarna orkar inte gå från provisorium till provisorium.'" *NiS*, no. 2 (1990), 31-6.

_____. "Flyktingmottagningen 1991-1996." *Mig*, no. 2 (1997), 34-7.

_____. "Flyktingmottagningen 1992." *NiS*, no. 3 (1994), 80-2.

_____. "Flyktingprojektet." *NiS*, no. 2 (1990), 12-30.

_____. "För en gemensam framtid." *NiS*, no. 4 (1994), 20-3.

_____. "För Sis finns inga hopplösa fall." *Mig*, No. 2 (1998), 22-5.

_____. "Heléne Lööw: 'Rasistiskt nätverk också i Sverige.'" *Nis*, no. 5 (1993), 28-31.

_____. "Heléne Lööw: Sverigedemokraterna rasister i nya kostymer." *NiS*, no. 2 (1991), 28-30.

_____. "Human Rights Watch' kritik av svensk asylpolitik." *Mig*, no. 6 (1996), 33-6.

_____. "Hårdnande klimat på flyktingförläggningarna." *NiS*, no. 1 (1991), 2-5.

_____. "Här får asylsökande chans att jobba." *NiS*, no. 1 (1991), 14-7.

_____. "Här gråter vi ibland men skrattar för det mesta." *NiS*, no. 5 (1991), 2-9.

_____. "Invandrarungdomar alls inga 'värstingar.'" *NiS*, no. 6 (1990), 2-3.

_____. "Invandrarverket 25 år." *NiS*, no. 3 (1994), 2-3.

_____. "Kommunernas flyktingmottagande: statens bidrag räcker inte." *Mig*, no. 4 (1998), 12-4.

_____. "Kosovoalbaner inte tillräckligt förföljda." *NiS*, no. 2 (1994), 26-30.

_____. "Kvar på förläggning trots avvisningsbeslut." *NiS*, no. 3 (1993), 12.

_____. "Kvotflyktingar direkt till kommunerna." *NiS*, no. 5 (1990), 42-5.

_____. "Läget, invandrarministern?" *Mig*, no. 1 (1995), 36-41.

_____. "Medborgare innanför eller utanför murarna?" *Mig*, no. 2 (1997), 8-11.

_____. "Med ritstift mot förtrycket." *NiS*, No. 5 (1990), 26-9.

_____. "Migrationsverket—framtidens utlänningspoliser?" *Mig*, no. 1 (1997), 32-5.

_____. "Muslimer pluggar svensk demokrati." *NiS*, no. 2 (1992), 47-8.

_____. "Mycket skrik för lite ull." *Mig*, no. 5 (1997), 40-5.

_____. "Norrköping—12.000 invandrare men bara fyra i fullmäktige." *NiS*, no. 3 (1991), 6-11.

_____. "Ny flyktingpolitik." *NiS*, no. 1 (1992), 17-21.

_____. "Nytt kaos?" *NiS*, No. 2 (1992), 15-9.

_____. "Parlamentarisk kommitté ser över invandrar- och flyktingpolitiken." *NiS*, no. 3 (1994), 98-9.

_____. "På flyktingförläggningen i Oxelösund—'Vi ser inte mycket av krisen.'" *NiS*, no. 6 (1992), 33-6.

_____. "Rösträtt och järnvägar." *Mig*, no. 3 (1996), 1.

_____. "SFI—vad är det?" *NiS*, no. 2 (1994), 16-7, 22-3.

_____. "Ska invandrare också vara med i leken?" *Mig*, no. 3 (1995), 6-10.

_____. "Skolverkets utvärdering SFI bättre än sitt rykte." *Mig*, no. 3 (1997), 8-11.

_____. "Slut på den generösa flyktingpolitiken?" *NiS*, no. 1 (1990), 28-32.

_____. "Somalier icke önskvärda i Sverige?." *Mig*, no. 2 (1998), 31-3.

_____. "Stor misstro mot Islam." *NiS*, no. 4 (1990), 18-21.

_____. "Stöt inte bort dom som behöver hjälpen mest!" *NiS*, no. 2 (1992), 44-9.

_____. "Sverige, framtiden & mångfalden?" *Mig*, no. 3 (1996), 16-21.

_____. "'Sverige är fortfarande bäst.'" *NiS*, no. 5 (1992), 44-7.

_____. "Svårt lära språket när man aldrig träffar svenskar." *Mig*, no. 1 (1997), 18-25.

_____. "Tai Chi." *NiS*, no. 5 (1990), 12-6.

_____. "Tomas Hammar: 'Politikerna har missuppfattat opinionen.'" *NiS*, no. 6 (1993), 16-21.

_____. "Trelleborgsmodellen: dela på jobben—chans för arbetslösa." *Mig*, no. 4 (1998), 10.

_____. "22.000 väntar på besked om de får stanna." *NiS*, no. 1 (1991), 10-3.

_____. "Utan pass kan de inte avvisas." *NiS*, no. 6 (1993), 34-6.

_____. "Utvisning hot mot kriminella asylsökande." *NiS*, no. 6 (1992), 37-8.

_____. "Varför röstar inte invandrarna?" *NiS*, no. 3 (1991), 18-9.

_____. "Vi har nått taket." *NiS*, no. 1 (1990), 22-5.

_____. "'Vi måste få en mer genomtänkt asylpolitik.'" *NiS*, no. 1 (1990), 38-42.

_____. "Viss kritik mot Utlänningsnämnden." *NiS*, no. 3 (1994), 110.

_____. "Äldre flyktingar." *Mig*, no. 1 (1997), 12-3.

_____. "Är invandrarungdomar mer kriminella än svenskar?" *NiS*, no. 6 (1990), 24-33.

_____. "Ökad främlingsfientlighet i en otryggare värld?" *NiS*, no. 2 (1992), 35-7.

Samuelsson, Wiwi. "Tak prövas för invandringen?" *NiS*, no. 1 (1991), 26-30.

Sander, Åke. "Muslimerna i Sverige." *I & M* 20 (Ap 1993), 3-12.

Santiago, Pancho Pérez. "Vänsterns lögner om exilen." *I & M* 19 (Fe 1992), 6-9.

Schwarz, David. "Allt är inte rasism." *I & M* 18 (De 1991), 2.

_____. "Det låga valdeltagandet." *I & M* 18 (Au 1991), 2.

_____. "Etnicitet som stigma." *I & M* 18 (Oc 1991), 3-4.

_____. "Etniska strejker." *I & M* 19 (Ap 1992), 2.

_____. "Jag (Ingvar Carlsson) vill ha en generös invandrarpolitik." *I & M* 20 (Fe 1993), 12-3.

_____. "Missriktad flyktingmottagning." *I & M* 18 (Ap 1991), 2.

_____. "Svenska attityder." *I & M* 19 (Se 1992), 2.

_____. "Svårt att bryta gamla tabun." *I & M* 19 (Fe 1992), 2-3.

_____. "'Vi måste angripa våldets orsaker.'" *I & M* 22 (De 1995), 3-7.

Senir, Refik. "Om fördomar och varuhusexpediter." *NiS*, no. 2 (1992), 20-1.

Sevume, Edward. "Kan särbehandling av arbetssökande invandrare försvaras?" *Mig*, no. 6 (1998), 14-5.

Sharma, Karin S. "Kulturkrockar." *I & M* 18 (Oc 1991), 6-8.

Similä, Matti "Kan Sverige bli mångkulturellt?" *I & M* 22 (De 1995), 12-5.

Sjögren, Annika. "Mångfaldens Sverige i tiden." *I & M* 23 (De 1996), 14-9.

Sjöstedt, Charlotta. "Giftstädare." *NiS*, no. 5 (1990), 39-41.

"Skadestånd för rasism." *Sr*, no. 3 (1991), 3.

"S.O.S. Asyl." *Sr*, no. 1 (1990), 8-11.

"SR ställer riksdagspartierna mot väggen." *Sr*, no. 3 (1993), 6-7.

Stockfelt-Hoatson, Britt-Ingrid. "Invandrarelever en resurs att vara på!" *NiS*, no. 1 (1992), 35-6.

"Stopp vid krogen om du har svart hår!" *Sr*, no. 3 (1994), 11.

Storesletten, Kjetil. "Invandraren är lönsam—bara han får ett riktigt jobb." *I & M* 23 (Oc 1996), 20-2.

"Svenska nynazister satsar på terrorism." *Sr*, no. 4 (1991), 6-7.

Svensson, Per. "Bara en neger." *Anno* (1996), 36-44.

Sverker, Jonathan. "En helt vanlig kyrka." *Mig*, no. 6 (1996), 26-31.

Swedin, Bo. "Sverige behöver en ny invandrarpolitik!" *NiS*, no. 1 (1992), 33-4.

Sågänger, Jonny. "Flykting och blind." *NiS*, no. 1 (1991), 38-43.

"'Sätt tak på invandringen.'" *Sr*, no. 3 (1990), 2-3.

Söder, Ulla-Stina and Eva Entrena. "Personlighet och utbrändhet." *I & M* 18 (Oc 1991), 27-30.

244 Bibliography

Tamas, Gellert. "Hiphop—invandrarungdoms musik, 'Man ska vara cool.'" *NiS*, no. 1 (1992), 22-6.

Taxén, Lars. "Botkyrkapartiet: från moské kampanj till invandrarexport." *Sr*, no. 4 (1991), 9.

"Testing Danish tolerance." *Econ*, 28 Au 1999, 24.

Thorgren, Gunilla, ed. "Rasism och politik." *Pockettidningen R* 21, no. 1 (1991).

Tjader, Ulf. "Sju av tio av utländsk härkomst." *I & M* 22 (Je 1995), 12-4.

"Togetherness: a balance sheet." *Econ*, 30 Se 2000, 27-8, 32.

Tomboulides, Hariton. "En reform på villovägar." *I & M* 19 (Ap 1992), 8-9.

"Trouble." *Econ*, 24 Jl 1999, 27.

"21 februari: mycket strul . . . men mäktigt till slut!" *Sr*, no. 1 (1992), 4-5.

Udd, Lena. "Allamanda kvinnokooperation med egen design." *NiS*, no. 1 (1993), 35-8.

"Vad hållar 'Blomman' på med?" *Sr*, no. 3 (1994), 2.

"Vi försöker skapa förståelse och trygghet." *Sr*, no. 3 (1993), 7.

"Vi kan vända trenden!" *Sr*, no. 3 (1991), 2.

"Vi måste vara många fler än rasister." *Sr*, no. 1 (1991), 12.

Vigerson, Halina. "Polacker i Sverige." *I & M* 21 (De 1994), 104-9.

"Vill Invandrarverket spara pengar på barnen?" *Sr*, no. 2 (1991), 16.

"Vågar vi hoppas?" *Sr*, no. 2 (1991), 2.

"Vår närvaro hade stor symbolisk betydelse." *Sr*, no. 2 (1996), 5.

Wadstein, Margareta. "Även facket måste förebygga etnisk diskriminering." *SIFtidningen*, no. 13 (2000), 13.

Weiler, Britta. "Bor man i Sverige ska man lära sig svenska—men hur?" *Sr*, no. 1 (1990), 16-7.

Weintraub, Nora. "Var tredje afrikan hotad på gatan." *I & M* 23 (Oc 1996), 10.

Westin, Charles. "Migration och kriminalitet." *I & M* 23 (De 1996), 5-8.

_____. "Tortyr." *I & M* 18 (Oc 1991), 84-7.

Westlander, Magnus. "Assyriska FF—etnisk mosaik fotbollen förenar." *Mig*, no. 3 (1997), 40-3.

Williams, Michael. "Vad händer med asylrätten." *Sr*, no. 3 (1990), 9-10.

Wilthorn, John. "Sanningen om händelserna i Sjöbo." *I & M* 19 (Se 1992), 29.

Winkler, Lasse. "Siriusgatan—en segregerad stadsdel." *NiS*, no. 3 (1990), 40-8.

Wolters, Staffan. "I Sverige räknas tid och resultat." *NiS*, no. 5 (1992), 48-9.

Wäremark, Lars. "Sverige bilden i sfi-undervisningen." *I & M* 21 (Je 1994), 16-21.

Yamasaki, Yukiyo. "Japaner i Stockholm." *I & M* 23 (Se 1996), 21-3.

Zetterwall, Tommy. "Vardagsrasismism finns i alla samhällsklasser." *Sifltidningen*, 79, no. 11 (2000), 6.

"Togetherness: a balance sheet." *Econ*, 30 Se 2000, 27-8, 32.

"Zigenares situation drastiskt församrad." *Sr*, no. 3 (1991), 3.

Ågren, Carina. "Nu slåss han med ord istället för med nävar." *Sr*, no. 1 (1992), 12-3.

Öjersson, Birgitta. "'Det hjälper ju inte om vi röstar!" *NiS*, no. 3 (1991), 2-5.

_____. "Erkki, Poet." *NiS*, No. 5 (1990), 8-11.

_____. "Äntligen en plats i svensk bostadskö." *NiS*, no. 2 (1990), 2-5.

_____ and Bo Levin. "Helena från Hagfors: 'Jag var rasist nu är jag gift med en "svartskalle.'"" *NiS*, no. 1 (1992), 11-2.

_____. "Häktespersonalen tog med sig avvisad tillbaka." *NiS*, no. 1 (1992), 12-5.

_____. "Teatern kom med kafé, butik och kultur." *NiS*, no. 1 (1992), 8-10.

Östlund, Helena. "Maryann lurades till Sverige." *Mig*, no. 5 (1998), 8-12.

Television and Internet:

STV (Swedish Television), 1999-2001.
Migrationsverkets homepage.
TV4 (Swedish Commercial Channel 4), 1999-2001.
Norrköpings homepage
Institutional, Organizational, and Governmental Releases:
Acceptera!. Stockholm: Fritze, National Coordinating Committee for the European Year against Racism,1998.
Adressbok: antifascistiska och antirasistiska grupper 1996. *Hasan's Friends against Violence and Racism,* Hägersten: 1996.
Ahlberg, Jan. Invandrares och invandrarebarns brottslighet: En statistik analys. *Stockholm: Crime Prevention Advisory, 1996.*
Almgren, Sabina, Ulla Rantakeisu, and Bengt Starrin. "Vi måste visa att vi inte är rasister." Karlstad: Värmland County Council Centre for Public Health Research, 1996:3, 1996.
Andersson-Aravena, Berith. Främling och vän: en handledning i hur man kan arbeta mot främlingsfientlighet och rasism. *Stockholm: Labor Movement Peace Forum, 1989.*
Arnstberg, Karl-Olov. Invandrare och fritid, Stockholm: Swedish Communal Organization, State Immigrant Commission, and Labor Dept., 1991.
Backström, Eva, et al, eds. Konsten att motverka främlingsfientlighet och rasism. Stockholm: State's Cultural Advisory, 1995.
Bender, Elsa and Brita Dahlgren. Rasfördomar. Borås: Immigrant Institute, 1976.
Bildt, Lars. Om Chilenare. Norrköping: State Immigrant Commission, 1988.
Bota eller skrota invandrarpolitiken? Norrköping: State Immigrant Commission, 1996.
Brick, Rebecka. Upptakt!: 22 ungdomar säger sitt! Smygehamn: Youth against Racism, Save the Children, 1998.
Bruchfeld, Stéphane. Förnekandet av förintelsen: nynazistisk historieförfalskning efter Auschwitz. Stockholm: Swedish Committee against Anti-Semitism, 1996.
Brune, Ylva. *Invandrare i svensk arbetsliv.* Norrköping: State Immigrant Commission, 1993.
_____. *Svenskar, invandrare och flyktingar i rubrikerna.* Göteborg: Göteborg Univ. Inst. for Journalism and Mass Communication, Work Report 63, 1996.
_____. *Vålberg i nyheterna: en kamp mellan tolkningsmönster.* Göteborg: Göteborg Univ. Inst. for Journalism and Mass Communication, Work Report 60, 1996.
Bustos, Enrique and Luis Abascal. *En psykologisk referens i arbetet med flyktingar och invandrare: att möta, bekämpa och övervinna fördomar, främlingsfientlighet och rasism.* Stockholm: Stockholm County Council, Immigrant Secretariat, Institute for Psychotherapy and Intercultural Communication, 1993.
Bydén, Ylva. *Kulturarv för alla: Arbetet mot främlingsfientlighet och rasism vid landets kulturarvsinstitutioner.* Stockholm: State Historical Museum, 1998.
Bäck, Henry. *Jugoslaviska invandrarföreningar i Sverige.* Stockholm: Center for Immigrant Research, 1989.
Diaz, José Alberto. *Unga tankar om rasism: uppsatsantologi från Europaåret mot rasism.* Stockholm: European Year against Racism, 1998.
Fakta mot rasism och invandrarfientlighet. Sundsvall: Göteborg and Medelpad Scout Districts, and the Swedish Scout Association, 1995.
Flemister, Daisy and Birgitta Kjöllerström Käck. *Norra Fäladen: ett mångkulturellt samhälle i praktiken.* Borås: Library School, 1997:52, 1997.
Flyktingbarn i Sverige: Huvudrapport 1990/91. Stockholm: National Board of Health and Welfare, 1991.

Frans, Joe. Rasism är ett hot mot världsfreden!: projektrapport med förslag till motåtgärder och uppföljningsprogram sammanställd av Joe Frans, Borås: Assoc. SOS Racism—Do not Mess with My Buddy, 1986.

_____. Tankar inför drakens tid. Stockholm: National Coordinating Committee for the European Year against Racism, 1997.

_____, ed. "Välkommen i princip." Borås: Periskopet Report on Seminar on Immigrant and Refugee Questions, Xenophobia, and Racism, 1988.

Från ansökan till beslut—ett asylärendes gång. Norrköping: State Immigrant Commission, 1997.

Främlingsfientlighet och rasism. Stockholm: Labor Dept. Report on Journalist Seminar 9-10 Je 1986, 1987.

Förbud mot rasistiska symboler m.m. Stockholm: Fritze, Dept. Series 1996:33, 1996.

Förslag till åtgärder vid särskilda händelser med rasistiska inslag. Stockholm: Nat. Police Board Report 1998:1, 1998.

Gardeström, Linnéa. Att främja goda etniska relationer: en utvärdering av projekt som fått bidrag genom Kommissionen mot rasism och främlingsfientlighet. Stockholm: Labor Dept., Commission against Racism and Xenophobia, and State Immigrant Commission, 1991.

Gille, Susanne, Margareta Rydberg, Gerd Åkerlund. Rasfördomar och invandrarproblem: ett kommenterat urval barn- och tonårsböcker om rasdiskriminering och om fördomar mot invandrare. Borås: Immigrant Institute, 1981.

Ginsburg, Råland, ed. Bekänna färg. Norrköping: State Immigrant Commission, Commission against Racism and Xenophobia, and Sweden's Educational Radio, 1988.

Glück, David, Aron Neuman, Jacqueline Stare, eds. Det judiska Stockholm. Stockholm: State's Cultural Advisory, 1988.

Gomes, Nadia Banno. Tjejer kan!: En bok om Exit, en mångkulturell tjejgrupp i Botkyrka. Tumba: Center for Cultural Diversity, 1996.

Grügiel-Adolfsson, Richard. "De kommer från syd och öst: invandrar- och flyktingarbete i Växjö stift." Växjö: Bishopric District Calendar 88, 1997/98, 37-52, 1998.

Gür, Thomas. När siffrorna ljuger: en granskning av studien "Vit makt?" från regeringskampanjen "Ungdom mot rasism." Stockholm: Timbro, 1995.

Hansson, Maria. Pow-Wow: en handbok för rådslag mot rasism. Stockholm: Youth against Racism, 1998.

Hultén, Britt. Det onda och det goda Sverige: bilden av flyktingar, invandrare och rasism i svensk press vecka 46 1991. Stockholm: Stockholm Univ. Journalism, Media, and Communication Series, 1993:6, 1993.

Individuell mångfald: Invandrarverkets utvärdering och analys av det samordnade svenska flyktingmottagandet åren 1991-1996. Norrköping: State Immigrant Commission, 1997.

Invandrings- och flyktingpolitik i den europeiska unionen. Stockholm: Foreign Office, 1994.

Jervas, Gunnar. Flyktingexplosionen—vår tids ödeskris. Stockholm: Foreign Policy Institute, 1994.

Jonsson, Anders. Några anteckningar om kulturmöten, etnocentrism och rasism. Örebro: Örebro College Sociology Section, Institute for Social Sciences, 1993.

Järtelius, Arne. Moderna pionjärer: Äldre invandrare i Sverige. Stockholm: Swedish Communal Organization, 1991.

Konstantinides, Andreas. Undervisning för internationell och interkulturell förståelse: en studie på högstadiet i Malmö. Malmö: Teachers College, 1994.

Knutsson, Bengt. *Assur eller Aram: Språklig, religiös och nationell identifikation hos Sveriges assyrier och syrianer*. Norrköping: State Immigrant Commission, 1982.

Kristmansson, Pia. *Möten och mångfald*. Stockholm: Youth Board, 1995.

Kunskap som kraft. Stockholm: Fritze Dept. Series 1996:74, 1997.

Landerberg, Björn. *Mångfald & möjligheter: ett magasin om mångfald från Europaåret mot rasism*. Stockholm: National Coordinating Committee for the European Year against Racism, 1998.

Lange, Anders. *Lärare och den mångkulturella skolan: utsatthet för hot och våld samt attityder till "mångkulturalitet" bland grundskole- och gymnasielärare*. Stockholm: Center for Immigrant Research, 1998.

_____, et al. *Utsatthet för etniskt och politiskt relaterat våld m m, spridning av rasistisk och antirasistisk propaganda samt attityder till demokratin m m bland skolelever*. Stockholm: Center for Immigrant Research, 1997.

Lindegren, Kristina. *Åtgärder mot främlingsfientlighet och rasism i skolan*. Stockholm: Parliamentary Inquiry, 1995-96: URD 3, 1996.

Lindström, Anders. *Insatser mot främlingsfientlighet och rasism: en utvärdering av projekt inom Invandrarverkets och Ungdomsstyrelsens ansvarsområde*. Umeå: Umeå Univ. Pedagogical Inst. Report 110, 1995.

Lindström, Anne Alenbro and Lena Hansen. *Om invandrare och rasmotsättningar: ett urval barn- och ungdoms-böcker 1980-1986*. Borås: Library School, 1988:7, 1988.

Ljunggren, Lena and Mario Marx. *Dina rötter och mina rötter—att möta barn från andra kulturer*. Stockholm: Save the Children, 1994.

Lodenius, Anna-Lena and Per Wikström. *Nazist, rasist eller bara patriot?: en bok om den rasistiska ungdomskulturen och främlingsfientligt orienterad brottslighet*. Stockholm: National Police Board, 1999.

Lundström, Inga and Marja-Leena Pilvesmaa. "Rastanken i folkhemmet," Stockholm: State Historical Museum *Annals* 1995, 24-26, 1995.

Lundvik, Anders. *Rapport beträffande interkulturellt synsätt*. Falun: Kopparberg County Board of Education, 1991:26, 1991.

Lärarutbildning med ett interkulturellt perspektiv. Stockholm: National Coordinating Committee for the European Year against Racism Conference Report, 15-7 December 1997, Kungälv, 1998.

Löwander, Birgitta. *Den försåtliga kulturrasismen: en studie av närradiosändningar i Stockholm, Malmö och Karlstad*. Haninge: Inspection Board for Radio and TV Report 2, 1998.

Lööw, Heléne. *Vit maktmusik*. Crime Prevention Advisory Report 1999:10. Stockholm: Fritze, 1999.

Mattera, Don. *Sverige och rasismens cancer*. Borgholm: Labor Education Organization Booklet Series, 1992.

Melldén, Eva. *Välkommen främling!?: en studie rörande flyktingpolitikens och flyktingmottagandets- påverkan på främlingsrädsla, främlingsfientlighet och rasism*. Sköndal: Foundation Greater Sköndal, 1992.

Millegård, Hans. *Rasism: handbok*. Surte: Göteborg's Immigrant Administration, 1995.

Moreau, Patrick and Elisabeth Carelli, eds. *Muslimer i Sverige*. Norrköping: State Immigrant Commission, 1988.

Murray, Bertil. "Åter på flykt mitt i Sverige." Uppsala: Bishopric *Annals* 1997/1998: 83, 45-49, 1998.

Mångfald mot enfald. Stockholm: Allmänna förlag for Commission against Racism and Xenophobia, Final Report of the National Public Inquiry 1989:13 & 14, 1989.

Nagy, Géza and Bertil Nelhans. *"Invandringen ger mig ångest":* om *invandrarfientlighet, opinionsyttringar och behovet av syndabockar.* Borås: Immigrant Institute, 1984.

Nobel, Peter. *Etnisk diskriminering: vad det är, vilka former det förekommer i, vad man gör åt det; en kort handledning från Ombudsmannen mot etnisk diskriminering.* Stockholm: Discrimination Ombudsman 87:1, 1989.

_____. *Polisen och invandrarna.* Stockholm: Discrimination Ombudsman 88:2, 1988.

Nordmark, Christer. *Strategier mot rasism och främlingsfientlighet.* Norrköping: State Immigrant Commission, 1995.

Nordström, Sonja, ed. *Rasismens varp och trasor: en antologi om främlingsfientlighet och racism.* Norrköping: State Immigrant Commission, 1995.

Norström, Ingrid, reviewer of Mai Palmberg. *Afrika i skolböckerna.* Stockholm: SIDA, 1987. Stockholm: His-tory Teachers' Assoc. *Annals* 1987/1988, 101-102, 1988.

När ord blir handling: om arbete mot främlingsfientlighet och rasism i några svenska skolor. Stockholm: School Dept., 1995.

Olika men ändå lika: om invandrarungdomar i det mångkulturella Sverige; betänkande. Stockholm: Allmänna förlag for National Public Inquiry's Youth Committee 1991:60, 1991.

Olson, Mark, Füsun Göfmen, and Ann Eriksson. *Inte lika svensk som du . . . .* Norrköping: State Immigrant Commission, 1986.

Om hets mot folkgrupp: delbetänkande. Stockholm: Liber förlag for National Public Inquiry on Discrimination 1981:38, 1981.

Palmberg, Mai. *Afrika i skolböckerna.* Stockholm: SIDA, 1987.

Peura, Markku and Tove Skutnabb-Kangas, eds. *Man kan vara tvåländare också: sverigefinnarnas väg från tystnad till kamp.* Stockholm: Sweden-Finland Archives, 1994.

Rasism och främlingsfientlighet: en undersökning av brottslighet med rasistiska eller främlingsfientliga inslag m m. Stockholm: National Police Board Report 1988:4, 1988.

Redemo, Arne. *De nya svenskarna: en debattskrift om den svenska invandrarfrågan.* Stockholm: Rabén & Sjögren for Institute for Labor Market Questions and Labor's Group for Immigrant Questions, 1968.

Rantakeisu, Ulla, Sabina Almgren, and Bengt Starrin. *Rasistiska trakasserier: en studie med utgångspunkt från händelser i Vålberg.* Karlstad: Center for Public Health Research Report 1997:1, 1997.

Rasismens varp och trasor: en antologi om främlingsfientlighet och rasism. Norrköping: State Immigrant Commission, 1995.

Rasistiskt och främlingsfientlighet våld: rapport från Arbetsgruppen med uppgift att motverka och förebygga rasistiskt och annat etniskt relaterat våld. Stockholm: Fritzes Department Series 1998:35, 1998.

Raune, Inger. *Välkommen eller-: att arbeta i skolan mot främlingsfientlighet.* Stockholm: Public Orphanage, 1993.

Rikspolisstyrelsen. "Rasism och främlingsfientlighet: en undersökning av brottslighet med rasistiska eller främlingsfiendliga inslag m.m. Stockholm: RPS rapport 1988:4, 1988.

Román, Henrik. *En invandrarpolitisk oppositionell: Debattören David Schwarz syn på svensk invandrarpolitik åren 1964-1993.* Uppsala: Center for Multiethnic Research, 1994.

Se mig, Hör mig. Stockholm: Children's Ombudsman and Public Orphanage Documentation from a Conference on Refugee Children's Needs and Rights, 1995.

Selander, Staffan. *Rasism och främlingsfientlighet i svenska läroböcker?* Härnösand: Sundsvall-Härnösand College Institute for Pedagogical Textbook Research Study 9, 1990.

Slå tillbaka! Mot ungdomsarbetslöshet, droger, rasism. Stockholm: National Organization for Aid to Perscription-Drug Addicts pamphlet 15, 1979.

Svanberg, Ingvar, ed. *I samhällets utkanter: om "tattare" i Sverige.* Uppsala: Center for Multiethnic Research Study 11, 1987.

Svart och vitt i grönt: värnpliktsinformation till ungdomar med invandrarbakgrund. Stockholm: Youth against Racism, 1996.

Tamas, Gellert. *Sverige, Sverige, fosterland: om ungdom, identitet och främlingskap.* Stockholm: Liber for Red Cross Youth Section, 1995.

Thorsén, Kerstin, ed. *Rasism och etniska konflikter: vad kan skolan göra?* Stockholm: Swedish Board of Education publication 91:2, 1991.

Ungdom mot rasism. Stockholm: Interior Dept. Committee for a Youth Campaign against Xenophobia and Racism Final Report, 1996.

Uppväxtvillkor [19]*93:3: Svartskallar och vitlökar.* Stockholm: National Youth Advisory, 1993.

Vad vore Sverige utan pizza?: tio uppsatser mot rasism och främlingsfientlighet. Stockholm: Discrimination Ombudsman, 1995..

Viscovi, Dino. *Med Loket mot framtiden: om unga arbetarklassmän, invandrare, EU och massmedier.* Göteborg: Göteborg Univ. Inst. for Journalism and Mass Communication Work Report 54, 1995.

Vit makt?: en studie av invandrares och deras barns representation inom politik, förvaltning, näringsliv, organisationer och media. Stockholm: Youth against Racism, 1995.

En värdegrundad skola: idéer om samverkan och möjligheter. Stockholm: Fritze Department Series 1997:57, 1997.

Wadstein, Margareta. *DO och lagen.* Stockholm: Discrimination Ombudsman, 2001.

Welin, Ritva. *Att arbeta med etniska attityder och mobbning i skolan: utvärdering av skolpersonalens arbete med en arbetsmetod i grundskolan.* Stockholm: Communal School Administration project group Preparedness against Ethnic Discrimination and Bullying final report, 1984.

Wentus, Per-Erik, Anter Seyitxan, Karl-Gustav Vinsa. *Den sociala frågan och rasismen.* Göteborg: Socialist Party, 1994.

Westin, Charles and Titti Hasselrot, eds. *Invandring och ungdomsopinion: bakgrund och belysning.* Stockholm: Youth against Racism and Civil Department Youth Delegation, 1995.

Westin, Charles. *Skolan, hjärtat, världen: invandring och ungdomsopinion—bakgrund och belysning.* Stock-holm: Civil Dept. Youth Delegation, 1992.

Working documents. Borås: Assoc. SOS Racism—Do not Mess with My Buddy, International Antiracist Summer Camp and Conference, 1986.

Yazgan, Ayla. *Turkiska flickor—andra generationen invandrare.* Norrköping: State Immigrant Commission, 1983.

Åtgärder mot rasistisk brottslighet och etnisk diskriminering i arbetslivet. Stockholm: Govt. Proposition 1993/94: 101, 1993.

Östby, Cecilie. *Lika och olika tjejer.* Stockholm: Youth against Racism, 1996.

_____. *Mångfald och fnitter: kan tjejer vara rasister?* Stockholm: Youth against Racism Girls Conference Re-port, 1996.

Books:
Adamson, Monica. *Återvändandet.* Stockholm: Bokförlaget Prisma, 1980.

250   Bibliography

Alcalá, Jesús. . . . *icke tillräckliga skäl* . . . Stockholm: Akademeja, 1988.

Amundsdotter, Eva, ed. *Modet att mötas*. Stockholm: Bokförlaget Prisma, 1996.

Andersson, Stefan. *Assyrierna*. Stockholm: Tidens Förlag, 1983.

Angel, Birgitta and Anders Hjern. *Att möta flyktingbarn och deras familjer*. Lund: Studentlitteratur, 1992.

Appelqvist, Maria. *Responsibility in transition: a study of refugee law and policy in Sweden*. Umeå: Umeå Univ. Press, 1999.

Arnstberg, Karl-Olov, ed. *Medaljens baksida*. Stockholm: Carlsson bokförlag, 1997.

Bajazidi, Ahmad. *I skuggan av fördomar*. Angered: Hanaförlaget, 1997.

Baksi, Mahmut. *Små slavar*. Stockholm: self-published, 1976.

Bengtsson, Håkan A. and Per Wirtén, eds. *Epokskifte*. Stockholm: Atlas, 1997.

Berggren, Lena. *Från bondeaktivism till rasmystik: om Elof Erikssons antisemitiska skriftställskap 1923-1941*. Umeå: Umeå Univ. Press, 1997.

_____. *Nationell upplysning: drag i den svenska antisemtismens idéhistoria*. Stockholm: Carlsson bokförlag, 1999.

Bergman, Erland and Bo Swedin. *Solidaritet och konflikt: Etniska relationer i Sverige*. Stockholm: Carlsson bokförlag, 1989.

_____. *Vittnesmål: invandrares syn på diskriminering i Sverige, en rapport från Diskrimineringsutredningen*. Stockholm. Liber förlag, 1982.

Bevelander, Pieter, Benny Carlson, and Mauricio Rojas. *I Krusbärslandets storstäder: Om invandrare i Stockholm, Göteborg och Malmö*. Stockholm: SNS förlag, 1997.

Björkman, Ingrid, Jan Elfverson, and Åke Wedin. *Flyktingpolitikens andra steg: återvandring som utvecklingsstöd*. Stockholm: SNS förlag, 1996.

Borgersrud, Lars. "Wollweber-organisajonen i Norge." Ph.D. diss., Oslo University, 1994.

Brattlund, Åsa and Jan Samuelsson. *Islam—en folkrörelse: Muslimer i svenskt samhällsliv*. Skellefteå: Artemis bokförlag, 1991.

Brimelow, Peter. *Alien Nation: Common Sense about America's Immigration Disaster*. New York: Harper Perennial, 1996.

Broome, Per, *et al. Varför sitter "brassen" på bänken? eller Varför har invandrarna så svårt att få jobb?* Stockholm: SNS förlag, 1996.

Bronsberg, Barbro. *Att komma till Sverige: fyra invandrarkvinnor berättar*. Stockholm. Esselte Stadium, 1983.

Brune, Ylva, ed. *Mörk magi i vita medier: svensk nyhetsjournalistik om invandrare, flyktingar och rasism*. Stockholm: Carlsson bokförlag, 1998.

Brändefors, Jan-Ove, Ulf Lundberg, and Vilgot Oscarsson. *Nya moment: socialkunskap*. Lund: Studentlitteratur, 1990.

Börjesson, Sven. *Återvandra eller . . .?* Stockholm: LTs förlag, 1989.

Daun, Åke and Billy Ehn, eds. *Blandsverige: om kulturskillnader och kulturmöten*. Stockholm: Carlsson bokförlag, 1988.

Daun, Åke, *et al. Invandrarna i välfärdssamhället*. Stockholm: Tidens förlag/Folksam, 1994.

deStoop, Chris. *Utan papper: människohantering i dagens Europa*. Stockholm: Ordfront förlag, 1997.

Diskrimineringsutredningen, *Att leva med mångfalden*. Stockholm: Liber förlag, 1981.

Dogan, Abdullah. *Massmedia och invandrare*. Stockholm: Stockholm Univ. Press, 1997.

Eftring, Annika, ed. *Hat och hot: en bok om främlingsfientlighet och rasism*. Stockholm: Fjärde Världen, 1996.

Ehn, Billy. *Sötebrödet: En etnologisk skildring av jugoslaver i ett dalsländskt pappersbrukssamhälle*. Stockholm: Tidens förlag, 1975.

Ekström, Kerstin. *Kvinna i Sverige: porträtt av åtta flyktingkvinnor.* Stockholm: Carlsson bokförlag, 1995.

Ericsson, Leif. *BSS—ett försök att väcka debatt: en sammanställning.* Stockholm: self-published, 1990.

Esping, Hans. *Dags för en ny migrationspolitik.* Stockholm: SNS förlag, 1995.

Fraser, Nicholas. *The Voice of Modern Hatred: Encounters with Europe's New Right.* New York: Overlook, 2000.

Fryklund, Björn and Thomas Peterson. *"Vi mot dom": det dubbla främlingsskapet i Sjöbo.* Lund: Lund Univ. Press, 1989.

Ghasemiana, Soleyman. *Mångkulturella getton: den demokratiska apartheiden.* Angered: Hanaförlaget, 1997.

Glück, David, Aron Neuman, and Jacqueline Stare. *Sveriges judar: deras historia, tro och traditioner.* Stockholm: Judiska Museet, 1997

Golrang, Akbar. *I gränslandet mellan Iransk och svensk kultur.* Borås: Berättar förlag, 1997.

Graham, Mark. *Classifications, persons and policies: refugees and Swedish welfare bureaucracy.* Stockholm: Stockholm Univ. Press, 1999.

Grahn, Eva and Ingela Kåhl. *Det heliga brödraskapet: massmedia, rasism och sexism.* Malmö: Cat Art, 1994.

Guillou, Jan. *Antirasistiskt lexikon.* Stockholm: Brevskolan, 1997.

_____. *Svenskarna, invandrarna och svartskallarna.* Stockholm: Norstedts förlag, 1996.

Gür, Thomas. *Positiv särbehandling är också diskriminering.* Stockholm: Timbro, 1998.

_____. *Staten och nykomlingarna: en studie av den svenska invandrarpolitikens idéer.* Stockholm: City Univ. Press, 1996.

Hadjourdes, Andreas and Christina Kellberg. *Vi sålde våra liv.* Stockholm: Askild & Kärnekull förlag, 1978.

Hainsworth, Paul, ed. *Politics of the Extreme Right: From the Margins to the Mainstream.* New York: Continuum, 2000.

Hammar, Åsa. *I främmande land: om lojalitet, heder, arbetslöshet och självrespekt.* Stockholm: Federativ, 1998.

Harrie, Anita, ed. *Invandrare och massmedia: en annan verklighet.* Stockholm: Norstedts förlag, 1999.

Hasselrot, Titti, ed. *Ottar 1983 och 1984.* Stockholm: Bokförlaget Prisma, 1984.

_____. *Sverige blandat: svar på vanliga frågor om invandrare och flyktingar.* Stockholm: Bonnier Carlsen, 1994.

Hazekamp, Jan Laurens and Keith Popple, eds. *Racism in Europe: A challenge for youth policy and youth work.* London: UCL Press, 1997.

Heyman, Anna-Greta. *Invanda Kulturer och invandrarkulturer.* Stockholm: Almqvist & Wiksell läromedel, 1990.

_____. *Invandrarbarn.* Stockholm: Carlsson bokförlag, 1988.

Holm, Annika and Siv Widerberg. *Då bestämde jag mig för att leva.* Stockholm: Rabén & Sjögren, 1990.

Horgby, Björn. *Dom där: främlingsfientligheten och arbetarkulturen i Norrköping 1890-1960.* Stockholm: Carlsson bokförlag, 1996.

Håkansson, Marianne, et al. *Rasistiskt och främlingsfientligt våld.* Stockholm: Fritzes, 1998.

Jaakkola, Magdalena. *Den etniska mobiliseringen av sverigefinnarna.* Stockholm: Centrum för invandringsforskning, 1989.

Jacobsson, Ingrid. *Kan man vara svart och svensk?: texter om rasism, antisemitism och nazism.* Järfälla: Bokförlaget Natur och Kultur, 1999.

252   Bibliography

Jervas, Gunnar, ed. *Migrations explosionen: bakgrund och alternativ till den felslagna flyktingpolitiken.* Stockholm: SNS Förlag, 1995.

Johansson, Kjell E., ed. *Brottsliga nätverk: orsaker, konsekvenser och motkrafter.* Stockholm: Carlsson bokförlag, 1998.

Joly, Daniele. *Refugees: Asylum in Europé?* London: Minority Rights Publications, 1992.

Jonsson, Stefan. *De andra: amerikanska kultur krig och europeisk rasism.* Stockholm: Norstedts förlag, 1995.

Järtelius, Arne. *Frihet, jämlikhet, främlingskap?: om invandrare i Sverige.* Stockholm: LT, 1982.

_____. *Mångkulturens Sverige.* Stockholm: Almqvist & Wiksell förlag, 1995.

_____. *Mångkulturur Sverige: Mångkulturens rötter, gränser och möjligheter.* Uppsala: Konsultförlaget, 1993.

Kahnberg, Per. *Varför kommer de hit?* Örebro: Bokförlaget Libris, 1989.

Kallifatides, Theodor. *I främmande land.* Stockholm: Svenska Dagbladet, 1985.

Kaplan, Jeffrey and Tore Björgo, eds. *Nation and Race: The Developing Euro-American Racist Subculture.* Boston: Northeastern Univ. Press, 2000.

Kristal-Andersson, Binnie. *Psychology of the refugee, the immigrant and their children: development of con-ceptual framework and application to psychotherapeutic and related support work.* Lund: Lund Univ., 2000.

Kullbom, Pierre and Per Landin, eds. *Politisk korrekthet på svenska.* Eslöv: B. Östlings bokförlag, 1998.

Kära främling: om svenskars och invandrares möten. Stockholm: Utbildningsförlaget brevskolan, 1992.

Lange, Anders. *Flyktingskap, boende och agens.* Stockholm: Centrum för invandringsforsking, 1991.

_____. *Invandrare om diskriminering II.* Stockholm: Centrum för invandringsforsking, 1996.

Layard, Richard, et al. *East-West Migration: The Alternatives.* Cambridge: MIT Press, 1992.

Lidén, Karin and Anne Nilsson Brügge. *Fem i tolv: några måste fly, några måste ta emot.* Stockholm: Carlsson bokförlag, 1992.

Liikkanen, Annu. *Med lapp om halsen.* Helsingborg: Inter Terras, 1995.

Liljeroth, Lena. *Skinnskallar: rasister, nationalister eller hyggliga unga män?* Stockholm: Gedins förlag, 1995.

_____ and Mauricio Rojas. *Svenska främlingar: att älska Sverige med dess fel och brister.* Stockholm: Gedins förlag, 1997.

Lindquist, Bosse, Susanne Berglind, and Kurdo Baksi. *Hakkors och skinnskallar: rasism från Auschwitz till Vålberg.* Stockholm: LL-förlag, 2000.

Lithman, Yngve, ed. *Nybyggarna i Sverige: Invandring och andra generation.* Stockholm: Carlsson bokförlag, 1987.

Lodenius, Ann and Mats Wingborg. *Svenskarna först?: handbok mot rasism och främlingsfientlighet.* Stockholm: Atlas, 1999.

Lodenius, Ann and Per Wikström. *Vit makt och blågula drömmar: rasism och nazism i dagens Sverige.* Stockholm: Natur och Kultur, 1997.

Lomfors, Ingrid. *Förlorad barndom återvunnet liv: de judiska flyktingbarnen från Nazityskland.* Göteborg: Göteborg univ., 1996.

Lundberg, Ingrid. *50 år i Sverige: vägen till det mångkulturella samhället.* Stockholm: Stiftelsen Sverige, 1993.

Lundberg, Svante. *Flyktingskap: latinamerikansk exil i Sverige och västeuropa.* Lund: Lund univ., 1989.

Lundh, Christer and Rolf Ohlsson. *Från arbetskraftsimport till flyktinginvandring.* Stockholm: SNS förlag, 1994.

Lundström, Stig, ed. *Vår gemensamma framtid.* Lund: Universitetsförlaget Dialogos, 1991.

Löwander, Birgitta. *Rasism och antirasism på dagordningen: studier av televisionens nyhetsrapportering i början av 1990-talet.* Umeå: Umeå univ., 1997.

Lööw, Heléne. *Nazismen i Sverige 1980-1999: den rasistiska undergroundrörelsen, musiken, myterna, riterna.* Stockholm: Ordfront, 2000.

Mammo, Tirfe. *Två sidor av samma mynt.* Järfälla: Self-Help Promotion, 1996.

Matvejevna, Siiri. *Välkommen till Sverige.* Copenhagen: Akaki Books, 1996.

Melen, Anna von. *Samtal med vuxna adopterade.* Stockholm: Rabén Prisma, 1998.

Mella, Orlando. *Chilenska flyktingar i Sverige.* Stockholm: Centrum för invandringsforskning, 1990.

Mosskin, Peter. *Glöm inte bort att jag finns.* Stockholm: Bonniers, 1997.

Månsson, Sven-Axel. *Kärlek och kulturkonflikt: Invandrarmäns möte med svensk sex- och samlevnadskultur.* Stockholm: Bokförlaget Prisma, 1984.

Modig, Cecilia, ed. *Möten i Rinkeby.* Stockholm: Bokförlaget Prisma, 1983.

Myrdal, Alva and Gunnar. *Kris i befolkningsfrågan.* Stockholm: Bonniers förlag, 1934.

Myrdal, Gunnar. *An American Dilemma: The Negro Problem and Modern Democracy.* 2 vols. New York: Harper & Row, 1962.

Nasser, Namdar. *På vägen till Sverige: sju sällsamma berättelse om sju iränska flyktingar.* Stockholm: Baran förlag, 1999.

Nestius, Hans. *"Och vi som ville så väl-": 19 röster om det mångkulturella Sverige.* Stockholm: Carlsson bokförlag, 1996.

Nilsson, Nils-Erik and Kjell Lund. *Förälder i nytt land.* Solna: Naturia förlag, 1992.

Nilsson, Peter. *Från främling till kompis.* Stockholm: LT, 1986.

Nobel, Peter. *Tankar i tigertid.* Stockholm: Brombergs, 1992.

Nwapa, Alban and Tom Hjelte. *Svartskallarnas sammansvärjning.* Stockholm: Norstedts förlag, 1992.

Nyström, Kenneth, ed. Encounter with Strangers: The Nordic Experience. Lund: Lund Univ. Press, 1994.

Ofstad, Harald. *Ta ställning.* Botkyrka: Sveriges Invandrarinstitut och Museum, 1989.

Peterson, Abby. *Neo-sectarianism and Rainbow Coalitions: Youth and the Drama of Immigration in Contemporary Sweden.* Aldershot, UK: Ashgate, 1997.

Raundalen, Magne and Gustav Lorentzen. *Barn och rasism.* Lund: Studentlitteratur, 1995.

Rojas, Mauricio. *Sveriges oälskade barn: att vara svensk men ändå inte.* Stockholm: Brombergs bokförlag, 1995.

Rooth, Dan-Olof. *Refugee immigrants in Sweden: educational investments and labour market integration.* Lund: Lund Univ. Econ. Studies 84, 1999.

Rosén, Anders. *Svar på tal—frågor och svar om rasism och invandrarfientlighet.* Stockholm: Fritidsforum, 1994.

Rystad, Göran, ed. *Encounter with strangers: refugees and cultural confrontation in Sweden.* Lund: Lund Univ. Press, 1992.

Salimi, Khalid. *Mångfald och jämställdhet om rasism, fördomar, kultur och identitet.* Stockholm: P M Bäckström förlag, 1997.

Samuelsson, Wiwi. *Det finns gränser.* Stockholm: Sveriges Utbildningsradio, 1993.

Schierup, Carl-Ulrik and Sven Paulson, eds. *Arbetets etniska delning*. Stockholm: Carlsson bokförlag, 1994.

Schwarz, David. *Svensk invandrar- och minoritetspolitik 1945-68*. Stockholm: Bokförlaget Prisma, 1971.

Schön, Bosse. *Svenskarna som stred för Hitler: ett historiskt reportage*. Stockholm: Bokförlaget DN, 1999.

Segerstedt-Wiberg, Ingrid. *Den sega livsviljan: Flykting öden under förvirringens och förintelsens tid*. Stockholm: Liber förlag, 1979.

_____. *Gömmare och andra*. Göteborg: Lindelöws bokförlag, 1997.

_____ and Berit Härd. *Jesus var inte svensk: humanitet flyktingar fördomar*. Stockholm: Carlsson bokförlag, 1986.

_____. *Min mot-bok*. Göteborg: Tre Böcker förlag, 1999.

_____. *När Sverige teg: om nazisternas förföljelser*. Stockholm: Norstedts juridikförlag, 1991.

_____, Anette Carlsson, and Ingemar Strandberg. *Sex år kvar . . . av barnets århundrade: FN's barnkonvention, Sverige och flyktingbarnen*. Stockholm: Carlsson bokförlag, 1994.

Sjöberg, Thomas. *Ingvar Kamprad och hans IKEA: En svensk saga*. Stockholm: Gedin, 1998.

Sjöwall, Anna. *Kulturmöten i barnomsorg och skola: antirasistiskt arbete med barn*. Lund: Studentlitteratur, 1994.

Skagegård, Lars-Åke and Tobias Hübinette. *Hatets återkomst: om fascism, nynazism och rasism i dagens Sverige*. Stockholm: Carlsson bokförlag, 1998.

Skarin, Sylvia. *Röster i Återförening*. Borås: Invandrarförlaget, 1997.

Skovdahl, Bernt. *Skeletten i garderoben: om rasismens idé historiska rötter*. Tumba: Mångkulturellt Centrum, 1996.

Stockfelt-Hoatson, Britt-Ingrid. *Bikulturell eller utanför?: undervisning av invandrare och minoriteter i Sverige och andra länder*. Stockholm: Författares bokmaskin, 1984.

Svanberg, Ingvar and Harald Runblom, eds. *Det mångkulturella Sverige: en handbok om etniska grupper och minoriteter*. Stockholm: Gidlunds bokförlag, 1988.

Svanberg, Ingvar and Mattias Tydén. *I nationalismens bakvatten: om minoritet och rasism*. Lund: Studentlitteratur, 1999.

_____. *Sverige och förintelsen: debatt och dokument om Europas judar 1933-1945*. Stockholm: Bokförlaget Arena, 1997.

Svenska Kommittén mot Antisemitism. *Det eviga hatet: om nynazism, antisemitism och Radio Islam*. Stockholm: Albert Bonniers förlag, 1993.

Söderlindh, Elsie. *Invandringens psykologi*. Stockholm: Natur och Kultur, 1984.

Tesfahuney, Mekonnen. *Imag(in)ing the other(s): migration, racism, and the discursive constructions of migrants*. Uppsala: Uppsala univ. geografiska regionstudier 34, 1998.

Turner, Bengt, ed. *Bostadssegregation*. Lund: Liber läromedel, 1980.

Tägil, Sven, ed. *Den problematiska etniciteten—nationalism, migration och samhällsomvandling*. Lund: Lund Univ. Press, 1993.

Wahl, Mats. *Sjöbo*. Stockholm: Carlsson bokförlag, 1988.

Wallin, Karin. *Att vara invandrarbarn i Sverige*. Stockholm: Wahlström & Widstrand, 1983.

Waltzer, Michael. *Om tolerans*. Stockholm: Atlas, 1998.

Westerlund, Per-Åke. *Vänd dom aldrig ryggen: lärdomar av antirasistiska kampen*. Farsta: Rättviseböcker, 1996.

Wright, Rochelle. *The Visible Wall: Jews and Other Ethnic Outsiders in Swedish Film*. Carbondale: Southern Illinois Univ. Press, 1998.

Wärenstam, Eric. *Fascismen och nazismen i Sverige 1920-1940: studier i den svenska nationalsocialismens, fascismens och antisemitismens organisationer, ideologier och propaganda under mellan krigsåren.* Stockholm: Almqvist & Wiksell, 1970.

Zilliacus, Margherita. *Flyktingboken.* Helsinki: Folkets bildningsförbund, 1988.

Ålund, Aleksandra. *Multikultiungdom: kön, etnicitet, identitet.* Lund: Studentlitteratur, 1997.

_____. *Skyddsmurar: etnicitet och klass i invandrarsammanhang.* Stockholm: Liber förlag, 1985.

Åstedt, Inga-Britta, ed. *Bakom bergen lämnade vi allt: antologi om flyktingbarn och deras föräldrar.* Stockholm: Utbildningsförlaget, 1990.

Index